# INDIANS FROM NEW YORK IN ONTARIO AND QUEBEC CANADA:

## A GENEALOGY REFERENCE VOLUME TWO

TONI JOLLAY PREVOST

HERITAGE BOOKS
2006

# HERITAGE BOOKS
*AN IMPRINT OF HERITAGE BOOKS, INC.*

### Books, CDs, and more—Worldwide

For our listing of thousands of titles see our website
at
www.HeritageBooks.com

Published 2006 by
HERITAGE BOOKS, INC.
Publishing Division
65 East Main Street
Westminster, Maryland 21157-5026

Copyright © 1995 Toni Jollay Prevost

Other books by the author:
*Indians from New York in Wisconsin and Elsewhere: A Genealogy Reference, Volume One*
*Indians from New York: A Genealogy Reference, Volume Three*
*The Delaware and Shawnee Admitted to Cherokee Citizenship and the Related Wyandotte and Moravian Delaware*

All rights reserved. No part of this book may be reproduced or transmitted in any form or by any means, electronic or mechanical, including photocopying, recording or by any information storage and retrieval system without written permission from the author, except for the inclusion of brief quotations in a review.

International Standard Book Number: 978-0-7884-0257-9

## Table of Contents

Dedication . . . . . . . . . . . . . . . . . . . . . . . . . . . . 1

Introduction . . . . . . . . . . . . . . . . . . . . . . . . . . . 3

Reference & Research Sources . . . . . . . . . . . . . . . . . . . 5
    Read Before You Begin
    Historical Notes
    Early Settlement of Canada
    Loyalist
    Reference Bibliography Sources
    Historical Bibliography Sources
    Treaties and Indian Policy Bibliography
    Maps and Locality Bibliography
    Miscellaneous Bibliography Sources
    Researching in Ontario
    Ontario Land Records
    Records of the Moravian Mission Among Indians of North America
    French Canadian Research
    French Jesuit Missionary Records
    The Lyman Copeland Draper Papers
    The Haldimand Papers
    The New England Society & The Church of England
    Fort Hunter & Queen Anne's Chapel
    Missionary & Church Records
    Church & Bibliography Sources
    Archives, Colleges, Libraries & Museums
    Canadian Census Records
    Military Sources
    Language
    Other Reserves in Ontario and Quebec
    New York Reserves
    The Nanticoke From Delaware And Maryland
    The Oneida in Wisconsin & the Seneca/Cayuga in Oklahoma
    Emigration/Immigration

Biographical References . . . . . . . . . . . . . . . . . . . . . 27

Brant County, Ontario Historical References . . . . . . . . . . . 45

Brant County, Ontario 1851 Census Abstract . . . . . . . . . . . 47

Brant County, Ontario Mohawk Institute 1851 Census Abstract . 103

Brant County Ontario 1881 Census Abstract (Section One) . . . . 105

Brant County, Ontario 1881 Census Abstract (Section Two) . . . 123

Haldimand County, Ontario Historical Notes . . . . . . . . . . 149

Cayuga & Mohawk 1851 Haldimand County, Ontario Census Abstract 151

Haldimand County Ontario 1881 Census Abstract . . . . . . . . 155

Hasting County Ontario 1881 Census Abstract . . . . . . . . . . 165

Middlesex County Ontario Historical Notes . . . . . . . . . . . 185

Middlesex County, Ontario 1851 Census Abstract . . . . . . . . . 187

Mount Elgin Industrial Institution 1851 Census Abstract . . . . 201

Prince Edward County 1881 Census Abstract . . . . . . . . . . 203

Deux Montagnes (Two Mountains) Quebec, 1851 Census Abstract . 205

La Prarie County, Quebec, Historical Notes Caughnawaga Reserve 213

La Prarie County, Quebec 1881 Census Abstract . . . . . . . . . 215

Huntington County, Quebec Historical Notes (St. Regis Mohawk) 247

Huntington County, Quebec 1881 Census Abstract . . . . . . . . 249

## DEDICATION

The author dedicates this book to my husband Ronald Prevost and Christopher and Nicholas Innis. They are direct descendants of Martin Prevost. Martin Prevost, who came from France, and Marie Silvestre-Olivier Manitobewich an Algonquin or Huron native, married on the 3rd of November 1644 in Quebec, Canada. This marriage is reported to have been the first sanctioned union between a Frenchman and a Native Canadian. Source: "The Jesuit Missionaries Among the Indians of Canada and the Northern and Northwestern States of the United States," By Reuben Gold Thwaites, 1610-1791, Ed., 73 Volumes in French, Latin and Italian, with a Page by Page Complete English Translation, Published 1895, Reprint Published 1959, New York, Published 1960 by Microcord Foundations, Washington, D.C., Volume V (5), Page 288.

## INTRODUCTION

This book is the second of three volumes intended to be genealogical reference guides for those seeking to identify a name or family relationship among the Indians who once lived in the state of New York and removed to Canada. This volume contains information about the Cayuga, Chippewa (Ojibway), Delaware, Mohawk, Munsee (Muncey), Oneida, Onondaga, Seneca and Tuscarora who either migrated to or were natives of Ontario and Quebec, Canada. Secondary surname information is included for the Abenaki, Montauk, Nanticoke, Ottawa, Penobscot/Passamaquoddy and Potawatomi. Information topics in this volume include: 1. A Historical Bibliography 2. A Military Bibliography 3. A Treaty & Locality Bibliography 4. Research Sources 5. A Biographical Bibliography. 6. A listing of the surnames found among the Indians who resided on other reserves in Ontario and Quebec in Canada and New York, Oklahoma and Wisconsin in the United States. 7. The 1851 & 1881 Canadian Census abstract of the surnames of the Indians who resided on reserves in Brant County, Ontario. 8. The 1851 & 1881 Canadian Census abstract of the surnames of the Indians who resided in Haldimand County, Ontario. 9. The 1881 Canadian Census abstract of the surnames of the Indians who resided in Hastings County, Ontario. 10. The 1851 Canadian Census abstract of the surnames of the Indians who resided on reserves in Middlesex County, Ontario. 11. The 1881 Canadian Census abstract of the surnames of the Indians who attended Mount Elgin Industrial Institution in Ontario. 12. The 1881 Canadian Census abstract of the surnames of the Indians who resided in Prince Edward County, Ontario. 13. The 1881 Canadian Census abstract of the surnames of the Indians who resided at the Oka Reserve in Deux Montagnes (Two Mountains) County, Quebec. 14. The 1881 Canadian Census abstract of the surnames of the Indians who resided in La Prarie County, Quebec, on the Caughnawaga Reserve. The 1881 Canadian Census abstract of the surnames of the Indians who resided on the Mohawk Reserve in Huntington or Huntingdon County, Quebec.

## DISCLAIMER

The term "Indian," is used in this book only to represent how it was used in original records and references. Accordingly a researcher should be aware that this term was created by a white colonial society. It may not be in favor with some native groups. The majority of the original records mentioned in this book is in the custody of the Canadian Archives. Material abstracted from the Canadian Census for this book should be used with caution. Some errors may exist. The original records that were used to compile this book often contained poor handwriting, faded ink and faded pages. This book is intended to be only a name reference source. It should not replace the research of any government or tribal records. For more information write the tribal offices. No attempt was made to alter the original name spellings for this book. All of the names were abstracted exactly as they appeared in the original records. Almost every county in Ontario in 1881 had Indian residents. In an attempt to list all of the Mohawks in Ontario some may have been missed. An apology must be given to the Mohawks that reside in Quebec, especially those on the Oka Reserve. The letters in the names of the Indians who resided on this reserve were difficult to read. Every effort was made to correctly abstract the surnames.

## REFERENCE & RESEARCH SOURCES

### READ BEFORE YOU START

"Read before you begin," was the best research advice I ever received. The foremost problem that will confront a novice researcher is the question, "where do I begin?" Unless you know your Indian ancestor's name and can identify him or her on government or tribal records, you face a common problem shared by many. Start with the understanding that no matter how much you know about your family the benefits of reading a good basic genealogy research guide can be invaluable. It is also true that any serious attempt to search for a Native American or Canadian ancestor should always be precluded by a study of their history.

Where can you find written material about Indians? 1. At your local library. 2. Through your public library's interlibrary loan system. 3. At local book stores. 4. At tribal museums. 5. At local Urban Indian Associations. 6. At Indian Pow Wows. 7. At municipal museums. 8. At college and university bookstores. 9. The Church of Jesus Christ of Latter-Day Saints (Mormon) Family History Library Center in Salt Lake City, Utah offers many rare out of print books about Indians on interlibrary loan to branch Family History Centers in the United States and Canada. These books have been made available on microfilm and microfiche. 10. The American Genealogy Lending Library offers microfilmed books on interlibrary loan. This company loans microfilms to public libraries, genealogy groups and individual members.

Basic American and Canadian research guides include: "The Researchers Guide to American Genealogy," by Val D. Greenwood, Genealogical Publishing Company, Inc., Baltimore, Maryland 1988 (See the Canadian Section). "The Source," by Arlene Eakle and Johni Cerny, Salt Lake City, Ancestry Publishing, 1984. This book contains basic American genealogy procedures. "Genealogical Research," Methods and Sources, Volume I & II, American Society of Genealogists, Copyright 1980 (It also includes a Canadian section). "In Search of Your Canadian Roots," Tracing Your Family Tree in Canada, by Angus Baxter, Genealogy Publishing Company, Baltimore, Maryland. "French and French-Canadian Family Research," by J. Konrad, 1985, Summit Publications, Monroe Falls, Ohio.

For a list of Canadian historical sources see the historical bibliography section in this book. A good history book about Indians in the United States is "A History of the Indians of the United States," by Angie Debo, University of Oklahoma Press, Norman and London, copyright 1989, eleventh Printing.

Tribal Locality Sources include: "Atlas of the North American Indian," by Carl Waldman, Facts on File Publications, Copyright 1985. "The Native American Directory," Alaska, Canada, United States, published by the National Native American Cooperative, San Carlos, Arizona, 1994. This comprehensive directory provides the addresses of Indian associations, colleges, museums, reservations and much more. "Indian America," A Traveler's Companion, by Eagle/Walking Turtle, John Muir Publications, Santa Fe, New Mexico 1989. This book provides addresses of reservations in the United States. "Atlas of American Indian

Affairs," by Francis Paul Prucha, University of Nebraska Press: Lincoln & London, 1990. This book provides old and new maps showing the locality of Indian reserves, forts, schools, and tribal land sales.

## HISTORICAL NOTES

The League of Five Nations, was created about 1560-70 to end conflict among tribes who lived in an area now known as the state of New York. The five nations included the Cayuga, Mohawk Oneida, Onondaga, and Seneca. The Tuscarora became the sixth nation to join the League about 1722. Today people from the Six Nations live in New York, Oklahoma and Wisconsin in the United States and Ontario and Quebec in Canada. The Six Nations Mohawk Reserve is located in Brant County, Canada in southern Ontario. Following the American Revolution this reserve became a refuge for Mohawk's and other native groups from the United States who had sided with the English. About 1780 Mohawk Chief Joseph Brant was given land on the Grand River in Canada by the British Government. Some Mohawks settled near Lewiston (Niagara County, New York) until 1783 before removing to Canada. Other native groups who lived at or near the Six Nations Reserve included the Cayuga, Delaware, Mississauga Chippewa (Ojibwa), Munsie, Oneida, Ottawa, Seneca and Tuscarora. Some Cayuga moved to Canada at the start of the Revolutionary War. Others joined the Seneca in Ohio or lived among tribes in New York. A mix of Delaware, Mahican and Munsie lived among the Cayuga on the Grand River in Ontario, Canada. Another group of Moravian Delaware settled on the Thames River in Ontario. The Oneida originally lived near Oneida Lake in New York. By the 1830's, some Oneida had removed to Canada while others settled in the Green Bay, Wisconsin area near the Brotherton and Stockbridge. The Ottawa who once had lived in the Northeast, today live in Kansas, Michigan, Oklahoma and Ontario, Canada. Some Seneca from western New York, settled on the Six Nations Reserve in Canada shortly after the Revolutionary War. Another Seneca group settled in the Sandusky area of Ohio. This group eventually removed to Indian Territory (Oklahoma). Some Tuscarora settled on the Six Nations Reserve. While others lived on a reserve in Niagara County, New York.

## THE EARLY SETTLEMENT OF CANADA AND ONTARIO

The year 1608 was the earliest attempt to settle Canada. In 1760 New France (Canada) came under British rule. In 1783 the area became known as the Province of Quebec. In 1788 the area that became known as Upper Canada (Ontario) was divided into four districts Lunenburgh, Mecklenburgh, Nassau and Hesse. In 1791 Quebec was divided into Upper and Lower Canada. The Ottawa River was the dividing line. Lower Canada (Quebec) was known as French Canada. Upper Canada (Ontario) was often called English Canada. In 1792 the district names were changed to Eastern, Midland, Home and Western. The Western District comprised the present area of Brant and Haldimand County, Ontario. A researcher will often see the terms "Fr. Can.," or "Eng. Can.," in use in United States Census Records. These terms indicate a place of birth in the Provinces of Quebec or Ontario. Upper and Lower Canada joined in 1841 and became Canada West (Ontario) and Canada East (Quebec). Canada West and Canada East is sometimes abbreviated in the census with the initials C. W., or C. E.

## LOYALIST

Land grants in Upper Canada (Ontario) were given to Loyalists who served the British cause during the American Revolution. Other groups such as Indians, British and German mercenary soldiers were also granted land in Ontario. Sources: "Public Archives of Canada," (Ottawa) Record Group 874 contains "Oaths of Allegiance," of Americans who wished to obtain a Crown Land Grants in Canada. The "Old United Empire Loyalist List," was prepared for the Crown Land Department. This list was published in 1885 and reprinted in 1976 by the Genealogical Publishing Co., Baltimore, Maryland. Loyalist's claims were published in the 1,436 page "Second Report of the Bureau of Archives for the Province of Ontario" in two volumes in 1904. Source: "Genealogical Research Methods and Sources," Volume 11, American Society of Genealogists, Part 2, Special Studies, Chapter 1, Ontario, "The Loyalists," pages 286-288. The Loyalist Gazette is published by the United Empire Loyalists of Canada, 23 Prince Arthur Ave., Toronto 189, Ontario.

## REFERENCE BIBLIOGRAPHY SOURCES

**ABRAMS, GEORGE H. J.**, "The Seneca People," Published by Indian Tribal Series, Phoenix, Arizona, Copyright 1976, page 32.

**ALL, STEVE AND HARVEY ARDEN**, "Meetings with Native American Spiritual Elders," Hillsboro, Oregon, Published by Beyond Words Publishing, 1990, 128 pages.

**BAXTER, ANGUS**, "In Search of Your Canadian Roots," Tracing Your Family Tree in Canada, Genealogical Publishing Co., Baltimore, Maryland, 1989, pages. 32-36.

**CANNIFF, WM.**, "The Settlement of Upper Canada," 1830-1910, Belleville, Ontario, 1971, Number 1, 27 pages, (A reprint) published at Toronto by Dudley and Burns in 1869, under the title of "History of the Settlement of the Bay of Quinte."

**CHICAGO TIMES NEWSPAPERS**: "The Tuscaroras," an article that appeared in the Chicago Times, August 13, 1885.

**CUMMING, WILLIAM P.**, "The Southeast in Early Maps," The University of North Carolina Press, Chapel Hill, North Carolina, Copyright 1962, Plate Number 51, 53 & 54 (The Tuscarora).

**DOTY, LOCKWOOD L.**, "History of Livingston County, New York," 1876, Chapter XI (11) page 21.

**FRENCH, J. H.**, "Historical and Statistical, Gazetteer of New York States," Copyright 1860, pages 307-313.

**GOODSPEED, W.A., AND C. L.**, "History of the County of Middlesex Canada," Belleville, Ontario, 1972, Number 36, Canadian Reprint, Series, originally published in 1889, at Toronto and London.

**JOSEPHY JR., ALVIN M.,** "Cornplanter Can You Swim?" American Heritage Magazine & Books, Volume XXX, Number 1, December 1968 Issue, Berne and Pan-American Copyright Conventions, page 4.

**PLAYTER, GEORGE FREDERICK,** "The History of Methodism in Canada," Published by A. Green, 1862, page 19.

**PRUCHA, FRANCIS PAUL,** "Documents of United States Indian Policy," Second Edition, University of Nebraska Press, 1990, page 5, "Treaty with the Six Nations" October 22, 1784.

**SANDERSON, M.A.,** "The First Century of Methodism in Canada," Volume 1, 1775-1836, Chapter 1, 1762-1792, pages 27, 28, Copyright by William Briggs, 1908.

**SENECA CENTENNIAL HISTORICAL COMMITTEE,** "The Township of Seneca," Centennial Year 1867-1967 (A pamphlet published in Haldimand County, Ontario, Canada).

**SMITHSONIAN INSTITUTE,** "Handbook of North American Indians," Washington D.C., Copyright 1988, page 487.

**VIOLA, HERMAN J.,** "After Columbus," The Smithsonian Chronicle of the North American Indians, Smithsonian Books, Washington D. C., Orion Books, New York, 1990, pages 105-119.

**WALLACE, PAUL A. W.,** "Indians in Pennsylvania," Pennsylvania Historical and Museum Commission, Harrisburg, Copyright 1989, page 171.

## HISTORICAL BIBLIOGRAPHY SOURCES

**BEAUCHAMP, WILLIAM M.,** "A History of the New York Iroquois," Now Commonly Called the Six Nations, New York State Museum, Bulletin No. 78, Albany, 1905.

**BEAUVAIS, J.,** "Kahnawake, A Mohawk Look at Canada," Available through the Cultural Centre, Kahnawake, Quebec, Canada.

**BOILEAU, GILES,** "Almanac Historique des Deux-Montagnes," St. Eustache, Quebec, Societe d' Edition et de Presse Messier et Perron 1981, 235 pages.

**COLDEN, CADWALLADER,** "The History of the Five Indian Nations of Canada," Which are dependent of the Province of New York in America, and are the Barrier between the English and the French in that part of the world, London, 1747.

**CREIGHTON, DONALD,** "A History of Canada," Haughton Mifflin Co., Boston Riverside Press, Cambridge, Boston, Mass., 1941.

**DEVINE, E. J.,** "Historical Caughnawaga," Montreal Messenger Press, 1922, 443 pages.

**FRASER, ALEXANDER,** "A History of Ontario," Its Resources and Development, The Canada History Company, Montreal, 1907.

**JENNINGS, FRANCIS,** "The History and Culture of Iroquois Diplomacy," A Guide to the Treaties of the Six Nations and their League, Francis Jennings et al. editors of the D'Arcy Mc Nickle Center for the History of the American Indian, The Newberry Library, Syracuse, New York, University Press, 1985, 278 pages.

**MAC LEAN, JOHN,** "Canadian Savage Folk," The Native Tribes of Canada, Published by W. Briggs, Toronto, Canada, 1896, 641 pages.

**O' CALLAGHAN, EDWARD BAILLEY,** Ed., "Documents Relative to the Colonial History of the States of New York Procured in Holland, England and France," by John Romeyn Broadhead, 15 Vols. Albany, 1853-1887.

### TREATIES AND INDIAN POLICY BIBLIOGRAPHY

**PARKER, A. C.,** "The Constitution of the Five Nations," or the Great Law of Peace, available through the Cultural Centre, Kahnawake, Quebec, Canada.

**PRUCHA, FRANCIS PAUL,** "Documents of United States Indian Policy," Second Edition, University of Nebraska Press, 1990, page 5, "Treaty with the Six Nations," October 22, 1784 (Mention's Johnston's Landing-Place upon Lake Ontario).

**UNIVERSITY OF TORONTO PRESS:** "Land Policies of Upper Canada," 1968, 378 pages. Studies in History and Government Number 9.

### MAPS AND LOCALITY BIBLIOGRAPHY

**BELDEN, H.,** "Illustrated Historical Atlas of Hastings and Prince Edward Counties, Ontario," Belleville, Ontario, Canada, Mika Silk Screening 1972, 82 pages.

**CUMMING, ROSS** "Historical County Atlases of Ontario," OGS Fam, Vol. 19, No. 1, Winter 1979, pages 31-34.

**CUMMING, WILLIAM P.,** "The Southeast in Early Maps," The University of North Carolina Press, Chapel Hill, North Carolina, Copyright 1962, Plate Numbers 51, 53 & 54. This book shows the location of the Tuscarora in North Carolina.

**EVANS, LEWIS,** "1755 Map of the Middle Colonies in America," showing Virginia, Maryland, Delaware, Pennsylvania, New Jersey, New York, Connecticut and Rhode Island, Lakes Erie, Ontario and Champlain area and part of New France, wherein lies ancient and present seats of the Indian Nations. A microfilm copy is available through the Church of Jesus Christ of Latter-Day Saints (Mormon) Family History Library Centers.

**FRENCH, J. H.,** "Historical and Statistical Gazetteer of New York State," Copyright 1860, pages. 307-313.

**ILLUSTRATED ATLAS OF THE COUNTIES OF HALDIMAND AND NORFOLK,"** H.R. Page & Co., Toronto, 1877-1879.

**LOVELL'S GAZETTEER OF BRITISH NORTH AMERICAN,** Montreal 1881, Published at Quebec, by John Lovell and Son.

**NATIONAL MAP COLLECTION NUMBER 5541,** National Archives of Canada, (A map of Gore District).

**NATIONAL NATIVE AMERICAN CO-OPERATIVE,** "Native American Directory," Alaska, Canada and United States." San Carlos, Arizona.

**ONTARIO LAND INDEX,** Ontario, Archives, Ottawa, Canada.

**SAUTHIER, CLAUDE JOSEPH,** "1777, Map of the provinces of New York and New-Jersey, with a part of Pennsylvania and the Province of Quebec," (Pennsylvania Archives, Third Series: Volume 1-10, app. 21). This map includes the boundaries of old Tryon County and Caroline County, New York, the country of the Six Nations, Indian towns, forts and the St. Regis Mohawk village.

**THE ILLUSTRATED HISTORICAL ATLAS OF THE COUNTY OF BRANT, ONTARIO,** Page & Smith, Toronto, 1875.

**UNITED STATES DEPARTMENT OF COMMERCE,** "Federal and State Indian Reservation Handbook," Printed in 1971.

**WALDMAN, CARL,** "Atlas of North American Indian," Facts on File Publications, Copyright 1985.

**WALKING TURTLE, EAGLE,** "Indian America," A Traveler's Companion, John Muir Publications, Santa Fe, New Mexico, Copyright 1989.

**YALE UNIVERSITY LIBRARY,** "A New and Correct Map of the Province of North Carolina, 1733," drawn by Edward Mosely, Map List 217. This map includes the locations of the Tuscarora in North Carolina.

## MISCELLANEOUS BIBLIOGRAPHY SOURCES

**HAMILTON COLLEGE.,** Clinton, New York., "A Compiled Census of the Six Nations in 1789," living in the general area of Buffalo Creek, Cazenovia and Cayuga Creeks (New York).

**LITTLEFIELD, DANIEL F. JR. & JAMES W. PARINS,** "Biobibliography of Native American Writers," 1772-1924, 1981, No. 2, Native American Bibliography Series.

## RESEARCHING IN ONTARIO

Research guides for Canada include: "In Search of Your Canadian Roots," Tracing Your Family Tree in Canada, by Angus Baxter, Genealogy Publishing Co., Baltimore, Maryland, 1989, "The Canadian Genealogy Handbook," A Comprehensive Guide to tracing your Ancestors in Canada, by Eric Jonasson, Winnipeg, Wheatland Press, 1978. "The Researcher's Guide to American Genealogy," by Val D. Greenwood, Chapter 24, Canadian Research, pages. 479-505, The Genealogy Publishing Co., Inc., Copyright 1988, Baltimore Maryland, "Genealogical Research Methods and Sources," Volume 11, American Society of Genealogists, Washington D. C. 1983, Part 2, Special Studies, Chapter 1, (Ontario) by Milton

Rubincam, pages. 285-307. "Ontario People," 1796-1803, Transcribed and Annotated by E. Keith Fitzgerald, with an Introduction and Index by Norman K. Crowder, Copyright 1993.

## ONTARIO LAND RECORDS

"The Ontario Land Index," includes the land sales that took place in the Province of Ontario from the late 1780's. The index is arranged in two ways. 1. In alphabetical order by the land owner's surname. 2. In alphabetical order by the Township. The Index is available at the Canadian Archives. It has been copied under the title "Ontario Archives Land Records Index," by Ontario, Computrex, Ltd. 1979. It is a great finding tool for locating an ancestor who may have settled in Ontario. It can also be used to find United Empire Loyalists who received land grants in Ontario. A microfiche copy is available through interlibrary loan at the Church of Jesus Christ of Latter-Day Saints (Mormon) Family History Library Centers. The Ontario land grant codes for the Ontario Land Index is described in "The Library," A Guide to the LDS Family History Library, edited by Johni Cerny & Wendy Elliott, Salt Lake City, Utah, 1988, Ancestry Publishing, Salt Lake City, Utah, 1988, pages 376-378. The Ontario Crown Lands Department Records 1792-1876 have been microfilmed on 289 reels. These records are in the possession of the Provincial Archivist, Ontario Archives, Toronto. They include Indian Land (Series C-111-7) Certificates of Sales, Volume 1, 1835 & Volume 2-7 1832-1867.

## RECORDS OF THE MORAVIAN MISSION AMONG THE INDIANS OF NORTH AMERICA

The original records of the Moravian Missions to the Indians in North American are in the Archives of the Moravian Church in Bethlehem, Pennsylvania. These records include information about Indians from the Fairfield, Ontario, Canada Mission and missions in New York, Connecticut, Pennsylvania, Indiana, Kansas, Ohio, Michigan and Georgia in the United States. These records begin with the Shekomeko Mission in New York in 1739. The text is in English and German. An index to the records of the Moravian Missions has been compiled by Carl John Fliegel, entitled "Index to the Records of the Moravian Mission Among the Indians of North America," New Haven Research Publications, 1978, Four (4) Volumes, 1,408 pages. Many Indian language dictionaries are included in these records. The original records have been microfilmed at New Haven, Connecticut by Research Publications, in 1969 on 40 reels of film. Also, see: "The Moravian Journals Relating to Central New York," 1745-1766, by Wm. M. Beauchamp, for the Onondaga Historical Association, 1916, Syracuse, New York, Dehler Press.

## FRENCH CANADIAN RESEARCH

Much of the genealogy of French Canadians has been compiled and published. Most French Canadians, but not all, were Catholic. The Catholic Church Records from the earliest settlement of Quebec have been indexed and published. They contain birth, marriage and death records. The four major sources used to compile French Canadian genealogies are: 1. The "Dictionaire Genealogique and Allied Documents," by Rene Jette, University of Montreal Press, 1983 Quebec, Canada, Two (2) Volumes, 1,133 pages. 2. The "Dictionnairie General des Familles Canadians," by L'Abbe Cyprian Tanguay, Seven Volumes, Montreal. 3. The Loiselle Marriage Index. 4. The Revest (Rivest) Marriage Index. To find these sources: 1. consult your public library interlibrary loan system. 2. Consult the Canadian Archives or the Archives of the Province of Quebec. 3. Consult your local book store. Copies of Rene Jette's volumes have been published. Microfiche copies are available on interlibrary loan for Rene Jette and Cyprian Tanguay's volumes through the Church of Jesus Christ of Latter-Day Saints (Mormon) Family History Centers. Microfilm copies of the Loiselle and Rivest Index's have been made available for research by the Canadian Archives. Copies of these indexes are available through interlibrary from the Church of Jesus Christ of Latter-Day Saints (Mormon) Family History Library Centers. Jette and Tanguay's books contain Indian entries for those who married French Canadian's. "The Loiselle Marriage Index," was compiled by Pere Antonin Loiselle, of the Couvent des Domincains, Montreal. It is an index too many of the Catholic marriages that took place from about the 1670's in the Province of Quebec and some adjacent areas. The Church of Jesus Christ of Latter-Day Saints (Mormon) Family History Center has published guides on how to use the Loiselle Index, the Revest (Rivest) Marriage Index and the "Dictionnarie General des Familles Canadians," by L'Abbe Cyprien Tanguay. A genealogy guide for French Canadian research is "French and French-Canadian Family Research," by J. Konrad, 1985, Summit Publications, Munroe Falls, Ohio. This book also contains addresses for Genealogy Societies for French-Canadians in Quebec and the United States. For more information, write to the Public Archives of Canada in Ottawa or the Archives Nationales du Quebec, P.O. Box 10450, St. Foy, Quebec, GIV 4N1. Historical Sources inclue: "The French Canadians," 1760-1967, by Mason Wade, St. Martin's Press, University of Toronto, Toronto, Ontario, Canada, 1968. "The Story of Chicoutimi, Quebec," By Paul D. Scott, Copyright 1991 by Paul D. Scott, First Edition printed by SCI Printers & Publishers, Orlando, Florida, Chapter 1, "The Influence of the French to the American Savage," "Daily Life in Early Canada from Champlain to Montcalm," by Raymond Deauville, Macmillan Publishing Company, 1968.

### FRENCH JESUIT MISSIONARY RECORDS

The French Jesuit missionaries were among the Indians of Canada and the Northern and Western states of the United States from about 1610 to the 1790's. The Jesuit mission records include information about the Abenaki, Huron and Iroquois from Acadia, Cape Breton and Quebec to Louisiana. These records are in French, Latin and Spanish. They have been published with a page by page English translation with the title "The Jesuit Relations and Allied Documents: Travels and Explorations of the French Jesuit Missionaries Among the Indians of Canada and the Northern and North-Western States of the United States 1610-1791," Under the Editorial Direction of Reuben Gold Thwaites, Published in Washington, D.C., by the Microcard Foundation, 1960, Original Copyright 1895. These records have been printed on 502 microfiche. A copy of the microfiche collection is available at the Church of Jesus Christ of Latter-Day Saints (Mormon) Family History Library Centers on interlibrary loan. The collection is arranged in chronological order. An index is included.

### THE LYMAN COPELAND DRAPER PAPERS

The Lyman Copeland Draper Papers (Manuscripts), 1815-1891 has been microfilmed on 147 reels. The original Draper Manuscripts are in the State Historical Society of Wisconsin. The manuscripts of particular interest to the Six Nations in Canada, New York and Wisconsin are included in the following volumes: "The Joseph Brant Papers," 1740-1807, Series F, Volume 1-3. "The Brant Manuscript Collection," 1778, Series F, (New York) Volumes 4-5, 1778, Series F, Volume 12, Brant's later years and death, (New York) Series F, Volume 13-15 Brant's relatives and descendants, Volume 15 F/36/36/2, Series F, Volume 16-18 Brant Manuscripts, (New York), Volume 19, Brant's Notes and letters, "The Sir William Johnson Papers." The "Guide to the Draper Manuscripts," has been prepared by Josephine Harper of the State Historical Society of Wisconsin. You can find microfilm copies of the Draper Manuscripts at: 1. Some college and universities 2. Through your local public library on interlibrary loan. 3. The Church of Jesus Christ of Latter-Day Saints (Mormon) Family History Centers has copies on interlibrary loan. 4. Consult the American Genealogy Lending Library.

### THE HALDIMAND PAPERS

The "Haldimand Grant," covered over 300,000 acres. In 1784 Sir Frederick Haldimand, Governor Chief of Canada granted to the Six Nations Iroquois parts of what is now Haldimand and Brant Counties in Ontario, Canada. "The Haldimand Papers," were donated to the British

Museum. The originals were microfilmed. A copy was deposited with the Archives of Canada, and the National Archives in Washington, D.C. "The Haldimand Papers," chronicle the events of the Revolutionary War from the Canadian & British viewpoint.

## THE NEW ENGLAND SOCIETY & THE CHURCH OF ENGLAND

The New England Society was established in 1649 as a trading company. It was established by members of the Church of England and Protestant Dissenters. After 1700 the society sent missionaries from England to New England and adjacent colonies. Many of these missionaries worked among the Indians. After the American Revolution was over the New England Society still maintained a relationship with the Mohawk in Upper Canada (Ontario). The original New England Society Records are housed at the Guildhall Library in London, England. The New England Company Records 1660-1906 have been microfilmed on 11 reels. Included in the New England Society Records is the following: Minute books, Commissioners of Indian Affairs at Boston, Massachusetts 1699-1784, Minute Books, Commissioners of Indian Affairs in New Brunswick 1787-1818, Correspondence, from Boston to London, Indian Affairs 1677-1761. Papers Relating to Indians 1669-1727. Microfilm copies of the New England Society Records have been made available in England. Copies of these films are available on interlibrary loan through the Church of Jesus Christ of Latter-Day Saints (Mormon) Family History Library Centers.

## FORT HUNTER & QUEEN ANNE'S CHAPEL

In 1708 several Iroquois were taken to England and were given an audience by the Queen of England and Governor Hunter. A few years after this meeting Governor Hunter built a chapel for the Mohawks in New York. This chapel was called the Queen's Chapel. It was enclosed by a stockade and named Fort Hunter. The Reverend Dr. Henry Barlcay and Reverend John Ogilvie of Trinity Church became the custodians of funds arising from the sale of the lands belonging to the Queen's Chapel Parish. The original records have been microfilmed under the title "County of Montgomery," Register of Queen Anne Chapel, Fort Hunter, New York State Library, Albany, Register of Baptisms, Marriages & Communicates & Funerals begun by Henry Barclay, Fort Hunter in 1734. Just a few of the surnames mentioned in the records of Queen Anne Chapel in the 1730's and 1740's includes Brant, Johnson, Montour and Wysenbergh. These records have been made available on microfilm. Consult: 1. Your local public library interlibrary loan system. 2. The New York State Library and the New York State Archives. 3. A copy is available on interlibrary loan through the Church of Jesus Christ of Latter-Day Saints (Mormon) Family History Library Centers.

## MISSIONARY & CHURCH RECORDS

The Methodists Missionaries had early missions among the Indians in Ontario, Canada. The Methodists worked among the Delaware, Huron (Wyandot) Mississauga Ojibwa (Chippewa), Munci, and some Shawnee, Seneca and Mohawk. The Moravian's had missions among the Delaware in Ohio and Michigan. A group of Moravian Delaware settled in Middlesex County, Ontario. In 1830 Phineas Young, the brother of Brigham Young, visited Upper Canada near Ernestown. In 1833 Brigham Young made missionary visits to the area of Addington in Frontenac County and Joseph Smith visited Mt. Pleasant. Other religious groups in Upper Canada at this time were the Baptists, Campbellites, Lutherans, Mennonites, Presbyterians and Quakers. The Baptists employed missionaries who worked among the Six Nations in, Brant County, Ontario, Canada.

## CHURCH BIBLIOGRAPHY SOURCES

**BARCLAY, HENRY,** "Register of Baptisms, Marriages, Communions & Funerals," of Queen Anne Chapel, Fort Hunter New York, (Church of England) beginning in 1735, New York Historical Society Library.

**BEAUCHAMP, WM. M.,** "Moravian Journals Relating to Central New York," 1745-66, For the Onondaga Historical Association 1916, Syracuse, New York, Dexler Press, 1916.

**BECHARD, HENRI S.J.,** "The Original Caughnawaga Indians," International Publishers, Canada, Montreal, 1976, 232 pages.

**BURTIN, NICOLAS-VICTOR,** "Histoire des Iroquois du Saut Saint-Louis avec Documents et pieces justifications." (Two Volumes) Completed in 1881.

**BENNETT, RICHARD E.,** "A Study of the Church of Jesus Christ of Latter-Day Saints in Upper Canada," 1830-850, (A Thesis) Department of History, Brigham Young University, August 1875, page 70.

**ECCLES, W.J.,** "Denonville et les Galeriens Iroquois," in Revue d'histories de L'Amerique Francaise, No. 14, pages 408-429, Montreal, Decembre 1960.

**FENTON, WILLIAM N., AND ELIZABETH L. MORE,** Father Joseph Francois Lafitau, 1712-1717, "Customs of the American Indians," Compared with the Customs of Primitive Times, (Two Volumes) Champlain Society, Toronto, 1974. (Mohawks at the Jesuit Mission at Caughnawaga.)

**FLIEGIL, CARL JOHN,** "Index to the Records of the Moravian Mission among the Indians of North America," New Heaven Research Publications, 1970, 1,403 pages, four (4) Volumes.

**HENRY, THOMAS R.,** "Wilderness Messiah," the Story of Hiawatha and The Iroquois, Bonanza Press, Copyright MCMLV, pages 219-222, 234, 236.

**HERRINGTON, WALTER S.** "The History of the County of Lennox and Addington," Toronto, Macmillan Company of Canada Ltd., 1931, pages 187-188.

**ILLUSTRATED HISTORICAL ATLAS OF THE COUNTY OF BRANT, ONTARIO** Page & Smith, Toronto, Canada, 1875, "The New England Society," page 61.

**JURY, WILFRID,** "Kanatakwenke, Fourth Site of the Mission," In Kateri Quarterly, Volume Eight, Number 1, Pages 6-9, Caughnawaga, P. Q., December 1955.

**KENNEDY, J.H.,** "The Jesuit and the Savage in New France," Yale University Press, 1950.

**MAGAZINES:** United States Catholic Inteligencer, United States Catholic Historical Magazine, American Catholic Quarterly, Canadian Indian and Catholic World.

**MORAVIAN CHURCH,** "Records of the Moravian Mission among the Indians of North America," New Haven, Connecticut, Research Publications: 1969 consist of forty microfilm reels of the original records in the Archives of the Moravian Church, Bethlehem, Pennsylvania. The text is in England and German. The "Guide to the Records of the Moravian Mission Among the Indians of North America from the Archives of the Moravian Church," Bethlehem, Pennsylvania. A "Index to the Records of the Moravian Mission Among the Indians of North American," compiled by Carl John Fliegel. These volumes Include many Indian Language dictionaries. The records begin with the Shekomeko, New York Mission 1739-1746.

**MORTENSEN, MR. AND MRS. HYRUM K.,** The Church of Jesus Christ of Latter-Day Saints, "Original Records Collected in New York at the Cumorah Mission," These records contain transcriptions of part of the Seneca Rolls. Included is census records from the Cattaraugus and Allegany Indian reservations, genealogical records and pedigree charts from members of the Cattaraugus Branch, Cumorah Mission, Versailles, New York. Some pedigree charts show relationships between Indians who resided at the Cattaraugus and Allegany reservation in New York and those living in Ontario, Canada.

**NELLES, REV. ROBERT BERTRAM, M.A.** "County of Haldimand," In the Days of Auld Lang Syne, Port Hope, Ontario, The Hamly Press Book Printers, 1905, Chapter IV, pages 25-28. The book includes information about the formation of Queen Anne's Mohawk Chapel, Fort Hunter and Mohawk Anglican Churches at the Bay of Quinte and Grand River area.

**PARKMAN,** "Jesuits in North American," Little Brown and Company, Boston, Toronto, 1963.

**PLAYTER, GEORGE FREDERICK,** "The History of Methodism in Canada," Published in Toronto, Canada, by A. Green, 1862, 414 pages.

**RECORDS OF THE NEW ENGLAND COMPANY,** 1660-1906. The New England Company was a trading company founded in 1660 as "The Company for Propagation of the Gospel in New England and Parts Adjacent in American." The original records are at the Guildhall Library, London (Call Numbers 7911-1912; 7920-7924; 7928-7930; 7932-7933; 7936, 7942, 7953-7957; 8010). The Church of Jesus Christ of Latter Day Saints has microfilm copies of these records which were filmed by the Genealogical Society of Utah in 1991. Among the records is the papers relating to Indians 1669-1727: Commissioners of Indian Affairs Boston, Massachusetts 1699-1859; from Boston to London, Indian Affairs 1677-1713.

**ROCHEMONTEIX, CAMILLE DE.,** "Les Jesuites et la Nouvelle-France au XVLLe siecle. 3 vols., Paris, 1896.

**SANDERSON, J.E.**, "The First Century of Methodism in Canada," 1775-1839, (Five Volumes) Copyright by William Briggs, Toronto, Canada, 1908.

**SHEA, JOHN GILMARY**, "History of the Catholic Missions Among the Indian Tribes of the United States," 1529-1854, 2nd ed. New York, 1870.

**THE CANADIAN MISSION, BRAMPTON, ONTARIO**, "The Great Canadian Mission," A Jubilee History, The Church of Jesus Christ of Latter-Day Saints, (No date was given) page 89.

**THWAITES, REUBEN GOLD**, Ed., "The Jesuit Relations and Allied Documents," The Travels of French Jesuit Missionaries Among the Indians of Canada and the Northern and Northwestern States of the United States, 1610-1791, (73 Volumes) in French, Latin and Italian, with an English translation, 1895, Reprint 1959, New York, Published 1960 by the Microcard Foundations, Washington D.C.

**VERREAU, H. A.**, "Les Veritables Motifs de Missieurs et Dames de La Societe de Notre-Dame," de Montreal pour la conversion des., de La Nouvelle-France, in Memoires des La Société historique de Montreal, Volume IX, Montreal, 1880.

**WALWORTH, ELLEN HARDIN**, "The Life and Times of Kateri Tekakwitha," the Lily of the Mohawks, 2nd ed., Albany, New York, 1929.

**ZEISBERGER, DAVID**, "Diary of David Zeisberger," A Moravian Missionary Among the Indians of Ohio, 1721-1808, Published at St. Clair Shores, Michigan, by Scholarly Press, 1972. Originally published in Cincinnati, Ohio, by Robert Clarke, 1885.

## ARCHIVES, COLLEGES, LIBRARIES AND MUSEUMS

The Public Archives of Canada is at 395 Wellington Street, Ottawa, Ontario, Canada, K1A ON3. Reference Sources: The Ontario Archives, Annual Report of the American Historical Association, by Alexander Fraser, 1913, pages 353-362. "The Ontario Archives: Records and Research Methods," by J. Bryan Gilchrist, Volume 15, No. 4, Fall 1976, pages 168-176. The address of the Ontario Provincial Archives is 77 Granville, Toronto, Ontario, M-5S1-B3. Reference Sources: "The City of Toronto Archives," by R. Scott James "OGS Family," Volume, 17, No. 3, Summer 1978, Pages 109-113. "Toronto Area Archivists Group Guide to Archives in the Toronto Area," (Toronto, 2nd Ed., 1978). A published guide is available to the Regional Collection to the University of Western Ontario. The Archives Nationales du Quebec is located at St. Foy, Quebec, Canada, GIV 4N1, P.O. Box.

The Family History Library of the Church of Jesus Christ of Latter-Day Saints (Mormon) is the largest genealogy library in the world. The main library is located in Salt Lake City, Utah. The Library has branch libraries in the United States and throughout the world. Over ninety percent of the holdings of the main library is available on loan to their branch libraries on microfilm and microfiche. A small nominal cost for the loan of the microfilms and microfiche is involved. The FHLC Catalog (Family History Library Center Catalog) is available on microfiche or computer. The FHLC Catalog is the guide to the library's entire holdings. It is divided into four major sections, Author/Title, Locality, Subject and Surname. The key to effectively using the library lies in the knowledge that everything within the four major catalog sections is arranged in alphabetical order. Finding out what Native Canadian material is available in the catalog is just a matter of good research procedures. Start by searching the Locality Section. The easy-to-use locality section is arranged from the largest to the smallest geographical area in alphabetical order. Look for the largest geographical division to be listed under the title Canada/Native Races. Review the types of records available in this section. To learn more about the availability of specific records extend your search in the locality section to include geographical subdivisions in Canada such as a province, county, city or town. The example would be, Ontario/Native Races, Ontario/Native Races/Brant County or Ontario/Native Races/ Brant County/City of Brantford. When using the subject catalog consider the name of the tribe as your subject. Look for records in the subject section on native tribes in North and South America to be listed in alphabetical order such as Cayuga, Chippewa then Mohawk. The surname section is arranged in alphabetical order by individual or family surname. Search this section for family histories. Researchers use the Author/Title Section to find out if a book or manuscript has been deposited in the main library. In order to use this section, you need to know the author's name or the title of the book. If you know the author's name, search in alphabetical order first by the author's surname then the given name such as Prevost, Toni Jollay. If you do not know the author's name but know the book title, search in alphabetical order by title such as "Delaware and Shawnee Adopted by the Cherokee." Two computerized indexes, the International Genealogical Index (I.G.I.) & Ancestral File also contain Native American information. Compiled and arranged from the Computer Catalog of the Family History Library is the "Register of Native American Indians," United States and Canada. This register is available on microfiche number 60449508. It is arranged in Alphabetical order by states. It lists the library's film call numbers for Native American material. The Native American Directory, Alaska, Canada, United States," published by the National Native American Co-operative, San Carlos, Arizona is a comprehensive directory that provides the addresses for reserves from Alaska to the Mexican border. Also included, are the addresses of native newspapers, colleges and many other related facilities. The library has the July 1982 copy available on microfiche number 6048689. See: "The Library," A Guide to the LDS Family History Library, Edited by Johni Cerny & Wendy Elliott, Ancestry Publishing, Salt Lake City, Utah, Chapter 14, "Dominion of Canada," pages 359-384. The Library publishes research guides for Canadian provinces. For further information about branch LDS Libraries in Canada and the United States write to the following: The Family History Library of the Church of Jesus Christ of Letter-Day Saints, 35 North West Temple, Street, Salt Lake City, Utah, 84150.

The American Genealogy Lending Library loans and sells microfilms and microfiche to public libraries, genealogy groups and individual members. They have microfilm copies of the Draper Manuscripts and United States Bureau of Indian Affairs Rolls from 1885. For more information about their Canadian holdings write to: The American Genealogy Lending Library, P.O. Box 329, Bountiful, Utah, 84011-0329.

Tribal Museums in Ontario and Quebec include: The Chapel of the Mohawks, Brant Historical Museum (Brant County), Woodland Indian Cultural Education Centre, Brantford, Brant County, Ontario, Joseph Brant Museum in Burlington, Ontario, Chiefswood and the Six Nations Indian Reserve is located at Brantford. Indian material can also be found at the Royal Ontario Museum, Toronto, The Museum of Indian Archaeology and Pioneer Life, University of Western Ontario and Brock University. The North American Indian Traveling College operates out of Cornwall Island, Ontario, Canada (Mohawks). Museums in Quebec include: Chief Poking Fire Indian Reservation, Caughnawauga, Kanien Kehaka Raotitiohkwa Cultural Center, Mc Cord Museum, Mc Gill University, Montreal and the Musee de Quebec, Quebec City. Source: "Atlas of the North American Indian," by Carl Waldman, Facts on File Publications, 1985, page 265.

## CANADIAN CENSUS RECORDS

A wealth of genealogy and family information can be found in Canadian Census Records. French Canadian Censuses (Quebec) are called recensements. The column headings for the recensements are in French. The 1881 recensements may mention that an individual is an Allemande (German) Irlandais (Irish) Ecossais or an Ecosse (Scottish) and Etats-Unis or an Americain (United States or American). Abbreviations are often used in French Canadian Census for given names. Ant., is an abbreviation for Antoine, Arch., for Archange, Cath., for Catherine, Elisa for Elisabeth, Eust., for Eustache, Frs., for Francois, Frse., for Francoise, Ls., for Louis, Lse., for Louise, M., for Marie, Marg., for Marguerite, Nic., for Nicolas, Pl., for Paul, Pi., for Pierre and Jean-Bte., for Jean-Baptiste. In the 1881 Canadian Census ethnic origins and religious affiliations are identified. Expect to find such terms as Indian, Indien, Savage or Sauvage to describe Native Canadians. The tribal origin for individual Indians is usually not provided. Canadian census records were taken every ten years. The original Canadian Censuses for certain years have been microfilmed and made available by the Canadian Archives for research. You can obtain microfilm copies of these census records through the following: 1. Your local public library interlibrary loan system from the Canadian Archives. 2. The Church of Jesus Christ of Latter-Day Saints (Mormon) Family History Library Centers. 3. Check with the American Genealogy Lending Library. For further information write to the Public Archives of Canada. The "Catalogue of Census Returns on Microfilm 1666-1881," by Thomas A. Hillman has been published by: Printing and Publishing Supply and Services Canada, Mail Order Service, 45 Scre Coeur, Hull, Quebec, K1A OS9 Canada (Public Archives of Canada, 1981).

## MILITARY SOURCES

British and Canadian military records can yield a wealth of historical and genealogical information. They may provide the locality of a soldiers former residence in the United States, place of birth, date of death, maiden name of wife and children's names. Another type of record is called Confiscation Records. These records contain information about men who once lived in the colonies before the Revolution. They left property that was confiscated because they joined a Loyalist regiment. Sources: "The Confiscations, Albany, Charlotte & Tryon Counties, New York," by H. C. Burleigh, Toronto,

Canada, Ontario United Empire Loyalists Association, 11 Pages, 1970. The originals are in the New York State Library. "The Lyman Copeland Draper Manuscripts," Sir William Johnson Papers and Joseph Brant Papers, Wisconsin Historical Society. "Guide to the Contents of the Public Record Office," Volume II London (England): 1963, List and Indexes Volume XVIII and spp. series. "The Researcher's Guide to American Genealogy," by Val D. Greenwood, Genealogy Publishing Company, Inc., Baltimore, Maryland, 1988. Chapter 21, "Colonial Wars and the American Revolution," pages 440-444. This book Includes a bibliography of printed Loyalists sources for the United States & Canada, "Canadian Military Institute," Officers of the British Forces in Canada During the War of 1812-15, by L. Homfray Irving, Librarian, Welland Tribune Print, 1908, pages 208-220. Loyalists Gazette: Published by the United Empire Loyalists of Canada, 23 Prince Arthur Avenue, Toronto 180, Canada. "Enquiry into the Losses and Services in Consequence of Their Loyalty;" Evidence in the Canadian Claim (2 Volumes), United Empire Loyalists, Toronto: Ontario Archives (1904-5).

## LANGUAGE

Language Sources: "Algonkian Languages," In International Encyclopedia of Linguistics, by Ives Goddard, edited by William Bright, 1:44-48, New York: Oxford University Press, 1992. "A Dictionary of the Ojibway Language, Frederic Baraga, first published as "A Dictionary of the Otchipwe Language by Beauchemin & Valois, Montreal 1878, 1880, Reprint by the Minnesota Historical Society, 1992. "Mohawk For Beginners," Tapes & Book by Josie Horne or "Kanien 'Keha: Ka Owenna 'Shon," (Dictionary). Write to the Kanien Kehaka Raotitiohkwa Cultural Centre, Kahnawake, Quebec, Canada. "The Records of the Moravian Mission among the Indians of North American," in English and German, Research Publications, 1969, New Haven, Connecticut. The originals are in the Archives of the Moravian Church, Bethlehem, Pennsylvania. These records include many Indian Language dictionaries (See Box 3383, Indian Languages, Mohawk).

## OTHER RESERVES IN ONTARIO & QUEBEC

In 1881 The Munsee, Delaware and Oneida Reserve was located in Middlesex County, Ontario, Canada. The Moravian Delaware were in Kent County, Ontario. Source: "The Delaware and Shawnee Admitted to Cherokee Citizenship," and the Related Wyandotte and Moravian Delaware, by Toni Jollay Prevost, Heritage Books, Inc., Bowie, Maryland, 1993. The surnames found among the Moravian Delaware who resided in Kent County, Ontario, Canada included: Anthony, Clingersmith, Fish, Hendricks, Hill, Hopkins, Jacobs, Lacell, Lastnight, Lewis, Logan, Mac Donald, Noah, Peters, Pheasant, Snake, Stonefish, Timothy, Tobias, Tomice, Wampun and Whiteye. Sources: The 1881 Canadian Census. "The Delaware Indians," A History: by C. A., Weslager, Rutgers University Press, New Brunswick, New Jersey, Copyright 1909, pages 22-24, 320, 352.

Many Chippewa or Ojibway have reserves in Ontario. Source: "Atlas of the North American Indian," by Carl Waldman, Facts on File Publications, New York, New York, 1985, pages 242-243. The Potawatomi, Chippewa, and Ottawa were part of the Three Fires Confederacy. The Potawatomi live today in Kansas, Oklahoma, Wisconsin and Ontario,

Canada. Today a group of Chippewa, Potawatomi and Ottawa live at Wallaceburg, Ontario, Canada. Sources: "Walpole Island," the struggle for Self-Sufficiency: A Panel Presentation," by Sheila M. Van Wych., Ed., Walpole Island Research Centre, Wallaceburg, Ontario. "Speaking Together: Canada's Native Women," Toronto, 1975. This source includes, interviews with Canadian Indian woman, especially with Potawatomi women from Walpole Island. For a reference source for the Parry Island including the Christian Island Chippewa see: "Ojibwa Indians of Parry Island," (Chippewa & Potawatomi) Their Social and Religious Life. by Diamond Jenness, Bulletin No. 78, Anthropological Series N. 17, Ottawa, National Museum of Canada, 1935. "Notes on the Ojibwa and Potawatomi of Parry Island Reservation, Ontario," 1929, Article by Joseph Karol, "American Ecclesiastical Review," 129, December 1953, pages 361-67. Minnesota Historical Collection, Volume XVII, page 136. The Sombra Reserve was located in Lambton County, Ontario in the 1881 Canadian Census. Many of the Pottawatomi Indians in this area came to Canada from the United States during the War of 1812. The following surnames appeared among the Indians who resided in Lambton County, Ontario in 1881. The census taker listed the tribal membership of each family member. Many were Chippewa, Potawatomi and Ottawa mixed. Altman (Chippewa) Ashquih, Blackbird (Ottawa), Blesset? or Basset? Brigham (Potawatomi) Buckwheat (Ottawa) Charlo (Chippewa) Compo or Campeau, Crow, David, Day (Chippewa/Potawatomi) Ermatinger (Chippewa) George, Greenbird (Chippewa) Henry, Hiyoshk or Heyoshk (Chippewa) Isaac (Potawatomi) Jackson (Potawatomi) Johnson (Chippewa) Jones (Ottawa) Knaggs (Chippewa/Potawatomi) Kicknosway (Chippewa) Konoosh-Mah-Qua (Chippewa) Kow-Sod (Potawatomi) Lewas, Makomehsh (Chippewa) Minadone, Miskokomon (Chippewa) Moneish (Potawatomi) Moses (Potawatomi) Nahda or Nahdu (Chippewa) Nah-Dotosnce? (Ottawa) Nah-Wa-Ko-Do (Potawatomi) Nomgesis (Ottawa) Omasader (Potawatomi) Penance (Chippewa) Pe-Shah-Na (Potawatomi) Pewash, Pyne (Potawatomi) Rye (Chippewa) Rapp (Potawatomi) Riley (Chippewa) Sands (Chippewa) Salimis (Chippewa) Scotchman (Chippewa) Shawina, Shawkias, Smith (Chippewa) Solomon (Chippewa) Thomas (Chippewa/Potawatomi) Warner (Chippewa) Waucaush, White (Potawatomi) Williams (Potawatomi/Ottawa) Willis (Chippewa) Wilson (Ottawa) and Wolf. This census abstracts begin with M2-Basanquet Township, Pages 1-70, starting with page 65 is a listing of Indian children who attended school. The Indians who resided in Bruce County, Ontario, Canada were enumerated in District Number 144, Amabal Division in the 1881 Canadian census.

In the 1881 Canadian census the Indians residing in Algoma District, Ontario, were enumerated in District Number 182, including Algoma Township for Burpee, Robinson and Barrie Island on pages 1-24. The following surnames appeared among the Indians found in Algoma District: Abice, Abram, Ace, Angus, Baptist, Batice, Bebomsa, Beboning, Bebosa, Bennet, Corbier, Debosiga, Francis, Goolah, Kadaw, King, Lewis, Reboan, Shallow, Simpson, Chief Solomon, Turkey, Madice, Manzanquit, Megose, Mucketygiosh, Ninawuska, Paul, Pinamic, Waubano, Wawbungee.

The Abenaki (Abanaka) were divided into two parties one was in Upper Canada (Ontario) at Queenstown and Beaver Dams, the other was at Chateauquay. Some live in Vermont (Swanton). Becancour is located on the eastern side of the St. Lawrence Seaway above Montreal. In 1881 The Abenaki Reserve at Becancour was enumerated in, District 2, page

17, Nicole County, Quebec in the Canadian Census. Surnames found among the Abenaki at Becancour included: Bernard, Denis, Gagne, Inaivometh? Le Fault? Metzalabenleth?, Onarenhillon, Thomas, Thubune? Servoid, Vincent, Pakikin and Nepton or Neptune. The Passamaquoddy and Malecite of Maine belong to the Abnaki group. Some live in New Brunswick, Canada. The Penobscot of Maine were also members of the Abnaki Confederacy. Source: "Abenaki Win Religious Freedom Case," (Vermont) Shaman's Drum Magazine, Number 24, Summer 1991, page 16, Submitted by Judy Wells, "Spirit of Crazy Horse, May-June 1991." "Indian American," A Traveler's Companion, by Eagle/Walking Turtle, John Muir Publications, 1989, Santa Fe, New Mexico, pages 164-167. "The Penobscot Indian Nation, Indian Island, Maine, Tribal Census List for the Year 1970." Major Surnames among the Penobscot & Passamaquoddy are: Akin, Alamanas, Attean, Archambaud, Benedict, Bernard, Dana, Francis, Mitchell, Neptune, Paul, Polchies, Ranco, Sapiel, Sappier, Sockalexis, Sockabeson, Soctomah, Thomas and Tomer.

## NEW YORK RESERVES

The Six Nations Indians in the United States reside or have tribal offices at the following localities: Versailles, New York (The Cayuga Nation), at Nedrow, New York (The Onondaga Nation), at Oneida, New York (The Oneida Nation), at Irving, New York (The Seneca Nation), at Hogansburg, Franklin County, New York (The St. Regis Mohawk), at Basom, New York (The Tonawanda Band of Seneca), at Lewiston, New York (The Tuscarora Nation), at Irving, New York (The Allegany Cattaraugus Oil Springs Seneca Reserves), at Southampton and Mastic on Long Island in Suffolk County New York (The Shinnecock/Poospatuck Reserves), at Oneida, Wisconsin (The Oneida of Wisconsin ) and at Miami, Oklahoma (The Seneca/Cayuga in Oklahoma).

Matrilineal descent among the New York Iroquois can present special problems. Most, but not all of the Iroquois, Zuni and Hopi Indians had matrilineal societies. Matrilineal descent means that tribal membership was based on the mother's tribe. An example would be, all of the children of a Mohawk father and an Onondaga mother would belong to the Onondaga. If an Onondaga son of this marriage married an Oneida woman his children would all be members of the Oneida. Source: "Man's Rise to Civilization," As Shown by the Indians of North America, by Peter Farb, E. P. Dutton & Co., Inc., New York, pages 82, 97, 99.

The surnames among the Cayuga Indians who resided on the Cattaraugus Reservation in New York in 1886 included: Armstrong, Bennett, Billy, Bone, Brooks, Charles, Crow, Doxtator, George, Gordon, Griffin, Ground, Jackson, Jimison, John, Johnnyjohn, Johnson, Joshua, Kenjockety, Lay, Logan, Parker, Patterson, Pierce, Seneca, Snow, Snyder, Spring, Stafford, Sundown, Tallchief, Taylor, Thompson, Turkey, Warrior, Wheelbarrow and Wilson. Source: The 1886 United States Bureau of Indian Affairs Rolls.

The surnames found among the Oneida residing on the Oneida Reservation in New York in 1887 included: Antone, Bread, Burning, Chrisjohn, Cornelius, Dana, Day, Doxtator, Elm, George, Gould, Honyost, John, Johnson, Jordon, Kennedy, Powels? or Powles? Scanadoah, Webster, Wheelock and White. Source: The 1886 United States Bureau of Indian Affairs Rolls.

Surnames found among the Onondaga residing on the Cattaraugus Reservation in New York in 1886 included: Jemison, Jackson, Jakey or Jake, Logan, Pierce, Patterson, Redeye, Stafford, Turkey, Yellowblanket. Surnames among the Onondaga Indians residing on the Allegany Reservation in New York in 1886 included: Bucktooth, Blacksnake, Crouse, Crow, Curry, Dolson, Gordon, Halftown, Halfwhite, Huff, Jackson, Jones, Jacob, Sampson, Pierce, Redeye, Snow, Thompson, Yellow Blanket. Surnames among the Onondaga residing on the Onondaga Reservation in New York in 1887 included: Adams, Beckman, Big Brav? Billing, Brown, Canada, Crouse, Crow, Cusick, Daxen? or Dixon? Day, Drake, Elm, Farmer, Fish, Frost, George, Gibson, Green, Griffin, Hill, Horner, Isaacs, Jacobs, Joe, John, Johnson, Jones, La Forte, Loft, Logan, Lyon, Obediah, Patterson, Pierce, Powles, Printup, Abram, Redeye, Reubin, Scannadoah, Smith, Chrisjohn, Thomas, Thompson, Varney, Webster, Wheelbarrow. Surnames among the Onondaga residing on the Tuscarora Reservation in New York in 1886 included: Cussick, Chin, Green, Garlow, Jacobs, Jack, Mt. Pleasant, Patterson, Pembleton, Printup, mith and Thompson. Source: The 1886 United States Bureau of Indian Affairs Census.

The surnames found among the Seneca residing on the Cattaraugus and Alleghany Reservation in New York in 1887 included: Abram, Armstrong Arnold, Bambery or Bombery, Barnum, Beaver, Bennett, Big Kettle, Billy, Bishop, Bone, Blacksnake, Blinkey, Blueye, Bluesky, Brooks, Buck, Bucktooth, Bullis, Butler, Button, Cayuga, Cook, Cooper, Cornfield, Cornplanter, Crouse, Crow, Crum, Curry, Davis, Dennis, Deer, Dickey, Doctor, Dolson, Dowdy, Doxtater, Doxtator, Dridley, Dyer, Eels, Fairchild, Falty, Farnum, Farmer, Fox, George, Gordon, Grant, Green, Halftown, Halfwhite, Harris, Hemlock, Hoag, Howe, Hudson, Huff, Isaac, Jacob, Jacobs, Jackson, Jemerson, Jimerson, Jimison, Jimmerson, Jack, Joe, John, Johnnyjohn, Johnson, Jonathan, Jonas, Jones, Junio, Kenjockety, Kennedy, Kettle, Killbuck, King, Lay, Lee, Lewis, Logan, Longfinger, Luke, Maybee, Mohawk, Moulton, Moses, Nephew, Newton, O' Bail, Parker, Patterson, Phillip, Phillips, Plumer, Pierce, Poodry, Pratt, Printup, Ray, Reed, Redeye, Rittenow, Russell, Sampson, Seely, Seneca, Scott, Scroggs, Shanks, Shongo, Silverheels, Sky, Smith, Smoke, Snow, Sprague, Spring, Steeprock, Synder, Sundown, Sutton, Stevens, Storey, Strong, Tandy, Tallchief, Taylor, Thomas, Thompson, Titus, Tommy, Turkey, Twoguns, Van Arnam? Wade, Wardell, Warrior, Watt, Washington, Washburn, Waterman, Wheeler, White, Williams, Wilson, Winnie, Yellowblanket, York and Young. Source: 1887 United States Bureau of Indian Affairs Census Rolls.

The surnames found among the Cayuga residing on the Cattaraugus Reservation in New York in 1886 included: Armstrong, Bennett, Billy, Bone, Brooks, Charles, Crow, Doxtator, George, Gordon, Griffin, Ground, Jackson, Jimison, John, Johnnyjohn, Johnson, Joshua, Kentjockety, Lay, Logan, Patterson, Parker, Pierce, Seneca, Snow, Snyder, Spring, Stafford, Sundown, Taylor, Thompson, Tallchief, Turkey, Warrior, Wheelbarrow and Wilson. Source: The 1886 Bureau of Indian Affairs Census Rolls.

The surnames found among the students attending the Quaker School for Indian children at Elko Township, Cattaraugus County, New York in 1900 included: Albuck, Button, Crouse, Curry, Dolson, Doxtator, Gordon, Jackson, Jameson, John, Kennedy, Logan, Mohawk, O'Brien, Patterson,

Pierce, Redeye, Scott, Snow, Tallchief, Thompson, Twoguns, Watt and White. Source: The 1900 United States Federal Census.

The surnames found among the Tonawanda Band of Seneca residing in New York in 1886 included: Abram, Alick, Bennett, Baptist, Bigfire, Billy, Black, Blackchief, Blacksquirrel, Blueye, Bluesky, Brooks, Carpenter, Charles, Clute, Cooper, Crow, David, Destroyon, Doctor, Doxtator, Fish, George, Green, Griffin, Ground, Hill, Hotbread, Hatch, Hiram, Infant, Jackson, Jemison, Johnyjohn, Johnson, Jones, Kennedy, Lindsley, Lone, Mason, Mc Pherson, Miller, Milton, Moses, Parker, Poodry, Printup, Reuben, Seneca, Scroggs, Shanks, Shongo, Silver, Silverheels, Skye, Smith, Snyder, Spring, Steeprock, Stone, Strong, Sundown, Taylor, Thomas, White and Wilson. Source: The United States 1886 Bureau of Indian Affairs Census Rolls.

The surnames found among the Tuscarora residing on the Tuscarora Reservation in Niagara County, New York in 1887 included: Anderson, Beaver, Bissel, Bones, Chew, Cusick, Douglas, Fish, Garlow, Gansworth, Greene, Henry, Hewitt, Hill, Isaac, Jacobs, Jack, Jemison, Johnson, Johnathan, Jones, Rackett, Martin, Miller, Mt. Pleasant, Nash, Pembleton, Parker, Patterson, Peter, Printup, Smith, Sylvester, Thompson, Williams and White. Source: The 1886 United States Bureau of Indian Affairs Census Rolls.

The surnames found among the St. Regis Mohawk residing in Franklin County, New York in 1900 included: Abrams, Adams, Angus, Armstrong (Stovepipe?) Arquette, Back, Barron, Beaubien, Benedict, Bevo, Bigtree, Bonapart, Bruce, Chubb, Cole, Bevo, Bovah, Billings, Bonspiel, Boots, Connors, Cook, Cornelius, Cree, Curood, David, Deer, De Lorimer, Deome, Dixon, Edwards, Ferguson, Francis, Friday, Gorrow, Gray, Hart, Herrin, Hill, Hops, Hoops, Isaac, Jackson, Jack, Jacobs, Jock, Johndrow, Johns, La France, Laughing, Lazor, Leaf, Loran, Lothridge, Martin, Miller, Mitchell, Mc Donald, Mc Donell, Mc Naughton, Oaks, Pappeneau, Pappineau, Paul, Peters, Philips, Price, Quart, Ransom, Rubado, Sandy, Saum? (Or Swamp) Sawyer, Sears, Seymour, Simons, Simmons, Smith, Smoke, Snow, Solomon, Stump, Squires, Swamp, Tarbell, Terance, Thomas, Thompson, Villeneauve, Webster, White, Williams and Wood. Source: The 1900 United States Federal Census.

The surnames found among the Shinnecock, Montauk and Poosepatuck who resided in Suffolk County, Long Island, New York in 1870 and 1900 included: Brewer, Bunn, Cuffy, Cuffey, Eleazor, Fowler, Harvey, Johnson, Kellis, Lee, Pharoah, Ryer, Swish, Thompson, Waters and Williams. Source: The 1870 and 1900 United States Federal Census.

## THE NANTICOKES FROM DELAWARE AND MARYLAND

Sometime after 1765 a small number of Nanticoke from upstate New York who were originally from Delaware and Maryland immigrated to Canada. This group eventually settled with the Six Nations. In Delaware the surnames found among the Nanticokes and a fringe group referred as Moors include: Burton, Clark, Coursey, Dean, Davis, Drain, Hanzer or Hansor, Harmon, Jackson, Johnson, Miller, Mosely, Peake, Ridgeway, Samson, Sockum, Morris, Norwood, Reed, Street and Wright. Sources: "Delaware's Forgotten Folk," The Story of the Moors & Nanticokes, by Clinton Alfred Weslager, University of Pennsylvania Press,

Philadelphia 1943. "The Nanticoke," by Frank W. Porter 111, Chelsea House Publishers, New York, New York, Copyright 1987, page 48.

## THE ONEIDA IN WISCONSIN
## AND THE SENECA/CAYUGA IN OKLAHOMA

The Oneida Reserve in Wisconsin is located near Oneida, Wisconsin, in Outagamie County. The Seneca-Cayuga are located near Miami, Oklahoma. Surnames among the Oneida in Wisconsin included: Adams, Anton, Archiquette, Baird, Beechtree, Bread, Charles, Chicks, Christjohn, Clinch, Cooper, Cornelious, Coulon, Danforth, Denny, Doxtator, Elm, George, Hart, Hass, Hayes, Hill, House, Huff, Island, Jacob, James, John, Johnson, Jordon, Jourdon, Kanandy or Kennedy, Kelly, Kick, King, Metoxin, Ninham, Parker, Parkhurst, Peters, Powless, Reed, Rhodes, Schmidt, Schyler, Sears, Sickles, Silas, Skanandore or Skenadoah, Skilar, Skyler, Smith, Somer or Summers, Stafford, Stephens, Stevens, Swamp, Thomas, Webster, Wheelock, Williams, White and Woodman. Source: The 1900 United States Federal Census.

The surnames found among the Cayuga, Seneca and Wyandotte (Huron) who resided on the Seneca/Cayuga Reserve in Northeastern Indian Territory (Oklahoma) included: Allen, Armstrong, Basset, Boofing? Captain, Carihoo, Cayuga, Charles, Hubard, Jamieson, Janes, Jneau, Johnson, Kingfisher, Lewis, Logan, Mingo, Nichols, Schripoter, Smith, Spicer, Splitlog, Standbone, Tsour, Turkey or Tinkey, Whitecrow, Whitetree, Winnie and Young. Source: The 1900 United States Federal Census.

## EMIGRATION/IMMIGRATION.

Many factors have contributed to Indian migration patterns between reservations, provinces, states and international boundaries. The 1900 United States Federal Census provides immigration information for Native Canadians who settled in the United States. Often the year of immigration was given. Since 1895 the United States Immigration and Naturalization Service has kept records on individuals who crossed the Canadian border from the Atlantic to the Pacific Ocean by foot, train or ship, and later by automobile. These records are called the St. Albans District manifest records. They contain an individual's name, age, physical descriptions, ethnic origins, place of birth and address in Canada. They often include the name and address of a relative the individual is visiting in the United States. The St. Albans District alphabetical index cards were arranged by surname. The United States Immigration and Naturalization Service has manifest records of aliens arriving at Detroit from 1906. Included are a few records for persons who entered the United States at Port Huron and Sault St. Marie, and other Michigan ports. Sources: National Archives Records Service, United States, St. Albans District manifest records arrivals at Canadian border ports from January 1895-195?, Washington, D.C., 937 microfilm reels, record numbers M1461, M1463, M1464, M1465. These records may be available on interlibrary loan from the National Archives. The Detroit District manifest records of arrivals in Michigan, 1906 to 195?, Washington, D.C., Immigration and Naturalization Service, Record Number M1478, are available on 117 reels of microfilm. These microfilms may be available through your local public library on interlibrary loan from the National Archives. The Church of Jesus Christ of Latter-Day Saints (Mormon) Family

History Centers also has microfilm copies of these records on interlibrary loan.

## BIOGRAPHICAL REFERENCES

**ALLEN, EBENEZER (OR INDIAN ALLEN):** Ebenezer Allen was a white man who served with the British during the American Revolution. He had several Indian children. After the war he removed to Ontario. Colonel Butler asked for a grant of land for Allen's Indian children at Genessee (New York). Source: "Lyman Copeland Draper Manuscripts," Treaties, Series Volume U/193/194, Wisconsin Historical Society. "History of Middlesex County, Ontario," originally published at Toronto and London, by W. A. & C. L. Goodspeed in 1889, introduction by Daniel J. Brock, facimile editon printed by Mika Studio, Belleville, Ontario, 1972, Chapter XIX, page 477, "The Life and Times of Sa-Go-Ye-Wat-Ha," or Red Jacket, by William L. Stone, Albany, New York, J. Munsell Publishing Company, 1866, pages 189, 192.

**ANTHONY FAMILY:** A Reverend Albert Anthony was a Delaware associated with the Tuscarora Mission Church in Brant County, Ontario. Sources: "Wilderness Christians," The Moravian Mission to the Delaware Indians, by Elma Gray, Toronto, Canada, Macmillan Company, Copyright 1956, page 320. "History of the Mission of the United Brethren Among the Indians in North America," George Loskiel, London 1794, Pt. 1, pages 125, 126.

**ASSANCE FAMILY:** The Assance surname was mentioned in "The History of Methodism in Canada," by George Frederick Playter, Published by A. Green, 1862, Page 350. An Indian family with that surname Assance was enumerated in the 1881 Canadian Census of Muskoka County, Ontario, District 131, among the Christian Island Indians.

**BEAVER, FAMILY:** The Beaver family is mentioned in the following source: "History of the County of Middlesex, Canada," Originally published at Toronto and London by W.A. & C. L. Goodspeed in 1889, introduction by Daniel J. Brock, facsimile edition printed by Mika Studio, Belleville, Ontario, 1972, Chapter 11, pages 20, 24, Chapter XIX page 480.

**BOWEN, WILLIAM:** A William Bowen was a Lieutenant in the British Six Nations Indian Department. Source: "Canadian Military Institute," Officers of the British Forces in Canada During the War of 1812-15, by L. Homfray Irving, Librarian, Welland Tribune Print, 1908, pages 208-220.

**BRANT, CATHERINE:** Catherine Brant John was a daughter of Joseph Brant. Source: "Lyman Copeland Draper Manuscripts," Wisconsin Historical Society, Volume 12/38.

**BRANT, ELLEN:** Ellen Brant was a grand daughter of Joseph Brant. She married a Joseph Lothridge. Sources: "Lyman Copeland Draper Manuscripts," Volume 14F/72 and Volume 13/F/191/1/191/2, Wisconsin Historical Society, The United Empire Loyalists Association, of Canada, "Loyalist Lineages Of Canada," 1783-1983, Toronto Branch, Generation Press, Copyright 1981, Ontario, Canada, page 81.

**BRANT, HENRY:** A reference for Henry Brant can be found in the following source: "The First Century of Methodism in Canada," Volume 1, 1775-1839, by J. E. Sanderson M. A., Toronto, William Briggs, 1908, Chapter 27, page 401.

**BRANT, ISAAC:** Isaac Brant was a son of Joseph Brant. Sources: "Lyman Copeland Draper Manuscripts," Volume 13/180, Wisconsin Historical Society. The United Empire Loyalist Association of Canada, "Loyalist Lineages of Canada," 1783-1983, (Toronto Branch) Generation Press, Copyright 1981, Ontario, Canada, pages 82-82.

**BRANT, JACOB:** Jacob Brant was a son of Joseph Brant. He married a daughter of Augustus Jones and his Mohawk wife. Source: "Lyman Copeland Draper Manuscript," Volume 13/14/14/1/14/2/14/3, Wisconsin Historical Society.

**BRANT, JOHN:** Lieut. John Brant was a son of Joseph Brant. Sources: "Canadian Military Institute," Officers of the British Forces in Canada During the War of 1812-1815, Homfray, L. Irving, Librarian, Welland Tribune Print, 1908, pages 210-212, "History of the County of Middlesex, Canada," Originally published at Toronto and London by W. A. & C. L. Goodspeed in 1889, introduction by Daniel J. Brock, facsimile edition printed by Mika Studio, Belleville, Ontario, 1972, Chapter 11, page 17, Indian residents from 1850-1888.

**BRANT, JOSEPH:** Joseph Brant was the brother of Mary (Molly) Brant the third wife of Sir William Johnson. He was a Mohawk who played a major role during the American Revolution in New York. He was educated by Sir William Johnson and had traveled on behalf of Sir William Johnson to England. He served the British during the Revolution. For his service to he received a land grant on both sides of the Grand River in Ontario, six miles square, near the present site of Brantford in the County of Brant in Ontario, Canada. Other Iroquois who had followed Chief Brant also crossed into Canada and settled on the Brant Reserve. Sources: "The Seneca People," by George H. J. Adams, Published by Indian Tribal Series, Phoenix, Arizona, Copyright 1979, page 32. "The Career of Joseph Brant Mohawk Indian," and the Trials of His People, by Harvey Chalmers, West to the Setting Sun, Toronto, Published by Macmillan 1944, 362 pages. "Life of Joseph Brant," Thayendangea, by George Dearborn and Company, 1838, New York, Two (2) Volumes. "Lyman Copeland Draper Manuscripts," Volume 15/F/14/14/1/14/2/14/3, Wisconsin State Historical Society. "Wilderness Messiah," The Story of Hiawatha and the Iroquois, by Thomas R. Henry, Bonanza Press, Copyright MCMLV, pages 219, 220, 221, 222, 234, 236. "History of Madison County, New York," by J.B. Mackenzie, page 62. "The Six Nations Indians in Canada," by Jean Newton, Mc Ilwraith, Toronto, The Hunter Rose Company 1896, pages 96, 97, "Sir Frederick Haldimand," 1718-1791, Toronto, Morange, Published 1910, in the Series "The Makers of Canada," Volume 6, 376 pages, "The History of Middlesex," Canada, by W. A. & C. L. Goodspeed, Originally published in 1889, introduction by Daniel J. Brock, facsimile edition Printed by Mika Studio, Belleville, Ontario, 1972, Chapter 11, Indian residents from 1580-1888, page 17. "The Loyalists in Ontario," The Sons of The American Loyalists of Upper Canada," William D. Reed, Hunterdon House, Lambertville, New Jersey, Copyright 1973. "The London Magazine," July 1776, London, England, "The Lyman Copeland Draper Manuscript Collection," State Historical Society of Wisconsin, Series F, Volumes 1-3, Joseph Brant Papers, Volumes 4-5 Brant Manuscripts 1778 (New York), Volume 12 Brant's later years and death (New York), Volumes 16-19 Brant Manuscripts, Notes and Letters, "Historical Sketch Of The

County of Brant," by W.C. Trimble, Brantford, printed in the Illustrated Historical Atlas of Brant County, Ontario, Toronto, Canada, 1875, pages 57-63.

**BRANT, MARGARET:** Margaret Brant was a daughter of Joseph Brant. She married Powless, Powless. Source: "Lyman Copeland Draper Manuscripts," Wisconsin Historical Society, Volume 13/32.

**BRANT, MARY (MOLLY):** Molly Brant was the sister of Mohawk Chief Joseph Brant. She was the third wife of Sir William Johnson and the mother of eight of his children. Sources: The Will of Sir William Johnson, written on the 27th of January 1774 & probated on the 25th of July 1774 in Surrogate Court, Old Tryon County, New York."Second Report of the Bureau of Archives for the Province of Ontario," by Alexander Fraser, Archivist, Printed by the Legislative Assembly of Ontario, 1904, page 472, Number 49/22/23, Montreal, the third of March 1788, The Report of Further Evidence on the Claim of the children of Mary Brant. Sir John Johnson son of Sir William Johnson testified that Mary Brandt had received compensation for her own losses. Seven of her children were living. A son Peter was deceased. He listed the land in detail in New York left to her children by Sir William Johnson. "Michigan Pioneers and Historical Collections," Volume IX, pages 423-424, Report of the Pioneer Society of Michigan, Lansing 1877, W.S. George and Co., Printers & Binders. Letter from Colonel Mc Kee (Indian Department) to General Haldimand at Quebec, 8th of April 1779. The letter mention's Joseph Brant's appreciations for the protection of his sister Molly and her children. "The Iroquois in the American Revolution," by Barbara Graymont," Syracuse University, Press, Copyright 1972, page 71. "The Story of Old Fort Johnson," by W. Max Reid, G. P. Putname & Sons, New York and London, The Knickerbocker Press, Copyright 1906, pages 2, 10, 11, 20, 22, 149. "The Lyman Draper Manuscripts," Volume 14/F/69, Wisconsin Historical Society. "The Loyalists In Ontario," The Sons and daughters of The American Loyalists of Upper Canada, by William D. Reed, Hunterdon House, Lambertville, New Jersey, Copyright 1973. "Ontario People," 1796-1803, by Norman K. Crowder, Genealogical Publishing Co., Incorporated, Baltimore, Maryland, 1993, page 125. "New York State Confiscations of Loyalists," Loyalists Society, Bay of Quente (Ontario) Branch.

**BURNHAM/DOXTADER FAMILY:** For a reference to the relationship between the Burnham and Doxtader family see the following Source: "Illustrated Historical Atlas of the County of Haldimand and Norfolk, Ontario," by H.R. Page & Company, Toronto, 1877-1879.

**BUTLER, COLONEL JOHN:** John Butler was listed as a Lieutenant Colonel in Butler's Rangers a Loyalist Regiment from New York during the American Revolution. For a relationship between the Butler and Doxtator family see the following source: "The Lyman Copeland Draper Manuscripts," Volume 13/F Series and Volume 11-12, Series U/103, Wisconsin, Historical Society, "Canadian Military Institute," Officers of the British Forces in Canada during the War of 1812-15, by L. Homfray Irving, Librarian, Welland Tribune Print, 1908, pages 208-220.

**CAMERON, JOHN:** A John Cameron was an interpreter for the Canadian Indian Department following the Revolutionary War. A Duncan Cameron also served in the Canadian Indian Department. Sources: "Canadian

Military Institute," Officers of the British Forces in Canada During the War of 1812-15, by L. Homfray, Irving, Librarian, Welland Tribune Print, 1908, pages 208-220. "The History of Methodism in Canada," by George Frederick Playter, Published by A. Green, 1862, pages 347-348.

**CAYUGA, NICOLAS:** Some members of the Cayuga and Kingfisher family removed to Indian Territory (Oklahoma) in the United States. Nicolas Cayuga was born in 1863 in English Canada of Cayuga parents. He immigrated in 1886. His cousins James and Mary Kingfisher (Both Cayuga) were also born in English Canada. They immigrated in 1880 and 1892 respectively. Source: The 1900 United States Census, Indian Territory, District 61, Seneca Reserve, E.D. 3, page 173A, Household 83.

**CLINCH/CLENCH/JOHNSON FAMILY:** A Ralph Clinch was listed as both a Lieutenant an a Colonel in Butler's Rangers. A Ralph Clinch married Elizabeth Johnson a granddaughter of Sir William Johnson and Molly Brant. "Pioneer Collections" Report of the Pioneer Society of the State of Michigan, Lansing Michigan, W. S. George & Company Printers, 1877, Volume 13, pages 92, 93. Source: "A History of Brant County, Ontario," page 686. "Lyman Copeland Draper Papers," Volume 13/F/184, Wisconsin Historical Society. "Loyalists In Ontario," "The Sons and Daughters of The American Loyalists of Upper Canada, by William D. Reed, Hunterdon House, Lambertville, New Jersey, Copyright 1973.

**CUSICK FAMILY:** The surname Cusick can be found among the Tuscarora. Nicholas Cusick served as a Lieutenant during the American Revolution as Lafayette's body guard. Joseph Cusick a descendent served in the War of 1812. Sources: "A Brave Indian's Services," Chicago Times, 1888. "Lyman Copeland Draper Manuscripts," Series U, Volume 8, 11-12, Wisconsin Historical Society, War of 1812 Pension Papers for Joseph Cusick in the National Archives, Washington, D.C. "Ancient Society," by Henry Lewis Morgan, Published 1877, first printing, reprinted July 1969 as the third printing, page 128. Indians in Pennsylvania," by Paul A. W. Wallace, Published by Pennsylvania Historical and Museum Commission, pages 160, 161.

**DAVIDS FAMILY:** A David Davids was wounded in a battle in 1814 at Grand River. Source: "Canadian Military Institute," Officers of the British Forces in Canada During the War of 1812-15, by L. Homfray Irving, Librarian, Welland Tribune Print, 1908, pages 220, 221.

**DAVIS, THOMAS:** Thomas Davis was an Indian who served in the Revolutionary War and possibly the War of 1812. Sources: Canadian Archives, Series C., Volume 261, pages 27-31. "Canadian Military Institute," Officers of the British Forces in Canada During the War of 1812-15, by L. Homfray Irving, Librarian, Welland Tribune Print, 1908, page 220. "The First Century of Methodism in Canada," Vol., 1, 1775-1839, J. E. Sanderson M A., Toronto, William Briggs, 1908, page 167.

**DE LORMIER, GEORGE:** George De Lorimer was a Mohawk Chief at Caughnawaga in the 1830's. Sources: "The History of the County of Huntingdon (Quebec) and the Seigniories of Chateaugay and Beauharnois," by Robert Sellar, Huntingdon, (Quebec) the Canadian Gleaner, 1888, Chapter XVIII, page 513.

**DEE/SMITH/BRANT FAMILY:** A Mrs. Dee was a grand daughter of Joseph Brant according to the following source: "Lyman Copeland Draper Manuscripts," Volume 13/18, Wisconsin Historical Society.

**DESERONTO OR MOHAWK, FAMILY:** John Mohawk, Alias Deseronto or Odiserundy was a Mohawk Chief during the Revolutionary War. Source: "Dictionary of the American Indians," by John Stoutenburgh, Jr., Copyright 1960, Published by Philosophical Library Inc., page 293.

**DILK/JOHNSON FAMILY:** A Mrs. Dilk was a great grand daughter of Sir William Johnson according to the following source: "Lyman Copeland Draper Manuscripts," Wisconsin Historical Society, Volume 13/183/183/2/183/3.

**DOLSON FAMILY:** The surname Dolson is found among the Delaware. Sources: "Wilderness Christians," The Moravian Mission to the Delaware Indians, by Elma E. Gray, Toronto, Canada, Macmillan Company, 1956, page 320. "The Delaware Indians," A History: by C. A. Weslager, Rutgers University Press, New Brunswick, New Jersey, Copyright 1909, pages 22-24, 320, 352.

**DOXTATOR/DOCKSTEDER/DOCKSTADER/LOTHRIDGE FAMILY:** The Doxtator family is supposedly descended from a German by that name who married an Indian woman. Sources: "Lyman Copeland Draper Manuscripts," Series U, Volume 11-12, Wisconsin Historical Society. "New York State Confiscations of Loyalists," United Loyalists Society, Bay of Quinte Branch. "The Iroquois in the American Revolution," by Barbara Graymont, Syracuse University Press, Copyright 1972, pages 133, 146. A John Dockstader was listed as a Lieutenant in the British Six Nations Indian Department at the time of the American Revolution or shortly after. Polly Mytop, was a Delaware who married a Doxtator who was an Oneida. In 1834 she moved with the Oneida to Wisconsin, near Green Bay. Source: Green Bay Associate, Newspaper, December 21th 1882, Article entitled "A Notable Death". A Joseph Doxtator married a Lothridge who was a grand daughter of Chief Joseph Brant. Sources: "Lyman Copeland Draper," Manuscripts, Volume 13/F/41, Volume 13/F/ & Vol., 11-12 Series U, Wisconsin Historical Society. A John Dockstader who served in the American Revolution obtained land in Brant County & Haldimand County, Ontario. Source: "History of the County of Middlesex," Canada Originally published at Toronto and London by W. A. & C. L. Goodspeed in 1889 introduction by Daniel J. Brock, facsimile edition printed by Mika Studio, Belleville, Ontario, 1972, page 18. Other sources: "Illustrated Historical Atlas of the County of Haldimand and Norfolk," H.R. Page & Company, Toronto, 1877-1879. "County of Haldimand in the Days of Auld Lang Syne," by Robert Bertram Nelles, M.A., Chaplain, Haldimand Old Boys Association of Toronto, The Hambly Press Book Printers, Port Hope, Ontario, 1905. pages 11, 13.

**DUCHARME, DOMINIQUE:** Dominique Ducharme was a Captain at Two Mountains (Deux Montagnes or Oka) in the Canadian Indian Department following the Revolutionary War. French-Canadian traders Dominique, Charles, Jacque and John B. Ducharme are mentioned in: "The Indians of Illinois," by Helen Cox Tregillis, Heritage Books, Inc., Copyright 1983, Reprint 1991, page 116.

**EGG, JAMES:** A James Egg was mentioned in the Indian marriages recorded by Ezra Adams of the Wesleyan Methodist Church in the 1830's. "History of Middlesex County, Canada," Originally published at Toronto and London by W. A. & C. L. Goodspeed in 1889, introduction by Daniel J. Brock, facsimile edition printed by Mika Studio, Belleville, Ontario, 1972, Chapter 11, page 25.

**EARL/JOHNSON FAMILY:** Hugh Earl served as a Captain in the British and Canadian Indian Department. Sources: "County of Haldimand in the Days of Auld Lang Syne," by Rev. Robert Bertram Nelles, M.A., Chaplian, Haldimand Old Boys Association of Toronto, Port Hope, Ontario, The Hamly Press Book Printers, 1905, page 12. "Lyman Copeland Draper Manuscripts," Wisconsin Historical Society, Volume 14/S/53.

**FARLEY/JOHNSON FAMILY:** A daughter of Sir William Johnson and Molly Brant (Mohawk) married a Mr. Farley. Source: "Lyman Copeland Draper Manuscripts," Wisconsin Historical Society, Volume 14/S/53.

**FISH-CARRIER FAMILY:** Fish Carrier was a Cayuga warrior on the British side during the American Revolution. Source: "The Iroquois in the American Revolution," by Barbara Graymont, Syracuse University Press, Copyright 1972, page 225. "American Heritage Magazine & Books, Article entitled "Cornplanter Can You Swim," by Alvin M. Josephy Jr., December 1968, pages 8, 9.

**FRADENBURGH/DOCHSTADER FAMILY:** For a reference to relationship between the Fradenburgh and Dochstader family see the following source: "Illustrated Historical Atlas," of Counties, of Haldimand and Norfolk, Published by the H.R. Page & Company, Toronto, 1877-1879.

**FUNN/BRANT FAMILY:** A member of the Funn family married a descendant of Joseph Brant. Source: The United Empire Loyalist Association of Canada, "Loyalist Lineages Of Canada," 1783-1983, (Toronto Branch) Generation Press, Copyright 1981, Ontario, Canada, page 82.

**GIVENS, JAMES:** James Givens was a Major and interpreter in the Canadian Indian Department. In 1825 when the Mississauga (Ojibwa or Chippewa) received annual payment for their exchange of their land at Credit in Ontario the Indian agent in charge was a Colonel Givens. Source: "The History of Methodism in Canada," by George Frederick Playter, published by A. Green, Toronto, Canada, 1862, pages 212, 250. "Canadian Military Institute," Officers of the British Forces in Canada During the War of 1812-15, by L. Homfray Irving, Librarian, Welland Tribune Print, 1908, pages 208-220.

**GRAY JOHN:** A John Gray was a Muncy Warrior in the Canadian Indian Department. Source: "Canadian Military Institute," Officers of the British Forces in Canada During the War of 1812-15, by L. Homfray Irving, Librarian, Welland Tribune Print, 1908, pages 208-220.

**HALF-KING, TANACHARISON:** Tanacharison or the Half King was an Oneida chief born about 1700. Source: "The Indian Chiefs of Pennsylvania," by C. Hale Sipe, Arno Press & The New York Times Reprint Edition 1971 from a copy in the Pennsylvania State Library, originally printed by the Ziegler Company, Inc. Butler, Pennsylvania, Copyright 1927, Chapter XIII, "Tanacharison, the Half King," pages 179-212.

**HALFMOON FAMILY:** A native named Halfmoon is mentioned in the following source: "History of the County of Middlesex," Canada, Originally published at Toronto and London by W.A. & C. L. Goodspeed in 1889, introduction by Daniel J. Brock, facsimile edition printed by Mika Studio, Belleville, Ontario, 1972, page 19.

**HENDRICK, CAROLINE:** Caroline Hendrick (A Mohawk) was Sir William Johnson's second wife. They had three children, Charlotte, Caroline and Teg-Che-Un-To or William of Canajohaire also known as William Johnson. Source:"The Story of Old Fort Johnson," by Max Reid, Published by G.P. Putname & Sons, New York and London, The Knickerbocker Press, Copyright 1906, pages 11, 20, 22.

**HENRY FAMILY:** The surname Henry is found among the Delaware. Sources: "The Delaware Indians," A History: by C. A. Weslager, Rutgers University Press, New Brunswick, New Jersey, Copyright 1909, pages 22-24, 320, 352.

**HERKIMER, WILLIAM:** In 1832 William Herkimer a native toured Michigan for the Methodist Church. Source: "The First Century for Methodism in Canada," by J. E. Sanderson M. A., Volume 1, 1775-1839, Published by William Briggs, Toronto, 1908, Chapter 21, page 286.

**HILL, CATHERINE:** A Catherine Hill was a granddaughter of Captain John and Joseph Brant according to the following source: "Lyman Copeland Draper Manuscripts," Volume 14/S/52, Wisconsin Historical Society. "The Loyalists In Ontario," The Sons and Daughters of the American Loyalists of Upper Canada, by William D. Reed, Hunterdon House, Lambertville, New Jersey, Copyright 1973.

**HILL, FAMILY:** For a reference to the relationship between the Brant and Hill family see the following sources:"The Iroquois in the American Revolution," by Barbara Graymont, Syracuse University Press, Copyright 1972, pages 226, 239. "Lyman Copeland Draper Manuscripts," Wisconsin Historical Society, Volume 13/29, Volume 13/33 and Volume 14/S/62/63-1/63-2. "Canadian Military Institute Officers of the British Forces in Canada During the War of 1812-15," by L. Homfray Irving, Librarian, Welland Tribune Print 1908, page 220."The Sons and Daughters of the American Loyalists of Upper Canada, by William D. Reed, Hunterdon House, Lambertville, New Jersey, Copyright 1973. The United Empire Loyalist Association of Canada, "Loyalist Lineages of Canada 1783-1983," (Toronto Branch) Generation Press, Copyright 1981, Ontario, Canada, page 81."The History of Methodism in Canada," by George Frederick Playter, published by A. Green, 1862, page 216.

**ISLAND FAMILY:** For a reference for the Island family see the Indian ministers returns of 1850. Source: "History of Middlesex County," Canada, Originally published at Toronto and London by W. A. & C. L. Goodspeed in 1889, introduction by Daniel J. Brock, facsimile edition printed by Mika Studio, Belleville, Ontario, 1972, Chapter 11, page 26.

**JACOBS FAMILY:** The Jacobs surname is often found among the Delaware. Sources: "Wilderness Empire," A Narrative, by Allan W. Eckert, Published 1969, Little, Brown and Company, Boston, Toronto, pages 406, 407, 422, 423. "Wilderness Christians" The Moravian Mission to the

Delaware, by Elma E. Gray, Toronto, Canada, Mac Millan Publishing Company, 1956, page 275. "Journals of Major Robert Rogers," by J. Allen, London Printed MDCCLXV, the account of the French and Indian War, Published in London in 1765, pages 31, 109. "Indians In Pennsylvania, Pennsylvania, by Paul A.W. Wallace, Historical and Museum Commission, 1989.

**JAQUETTE, PETER:** Peter Jaquette was a leading Chief of the Oneida who was taken to be educated in France by the Marquis de la Fayette after the revolution. Source: "The Life & Times of Sa-Go-Ye-Wat-Ha or Red Jacket," by William L. Stone, Albany, New York, J. Munsell Publishing, 1866. page 192.

**JEMISON, THOMAS:** Thomas Jemison was a son of Mary Jemison the white captive. Sources: "Loyalist Lineages of Canada," 1783-1983, (Toronto Branch) The United Empire Loyalist Association of Canada, Published by Generation Press, Ontario, Canada, Copyright 1981, page 343. "A Narrative of the Life of Mary Jemison," (1743-1833) the White Woman of the Genesee, by James Everett Seaver, New York, American Scenic and Historic Preservation Society, 1942.

**JOHN/JOHNS/BRANT FAMILY: (OR DESERONTYON)** Captain John alias Deserontyon served in the British and Canadian Indian Department. For the relationship between the John and Brant family see the following sources: "Lyman Copeland Draper Manuscripts," Wisconsin Historical Society, Volume 14/S/53. "The Loyalists In Ontario" "The Sons and Daughters of The American Loyalists of Upper Canada. by William D. Reed, Hunterdon House, Lambertville, New Jersey, Copyright 1973.

**JOHNSON, BRANT:** A Brant Johnson served as a Lieutenant in the British Six Nations Indian Department. Source: "Canadian Military Institute," Officers of the British Forces in Canada During the War of 1812-15, by L Homfray Irving, Librarian, Welland Tribune Print, 1908, pages 208-220.

**JOHNSON, CAROLINE:** Caroline Johnson was a daughter of Sir William Johnson an his second wife Caroline Henrick (Mohawk). She married to a man named Byrne and after his death a British officer named Mc Kim. Source: "The Story of Old Fort Johnson," by W. Max Reid, G. P. Putname & Sons, New York and London, The Knickerbocker Press, Copyright 1906, pages 11, 22.

**JOHNSON, CHARLOTTE:** Charlotte Johnson was a daughter of Sir William Johnson an his second wife Caroline Henrick (Mohawk). She married a British officer named Randall. Source: "The Story of Old Fort Johnson," by W. Max Reid, G.P. Putnam & Sons, New York and London, The Knickerbocker Press, Copyright 1906, page 22.

**JOHNSON, JOHN (SMOKE):** John "Smoke" Johnson was a Mohawk Chief who served on the British side during the War of 1812. Sources: "History of the County of Middlesex," Canada, Originally published at Toronto and London by W. A. & C. L. Goodspeed in 1889, introduction by Daniel J. Brock, facimile edition printed by Mika Studio, Belleville, Ontario, 1972, page 17. "Lyman Copeland Draper Manuscripts," Volume 15/S/10 and Volume 15/F/19, Wisconsin Historical Society.

**JOHNSON, JOHN:** John Johnson served as a Captain in the British Six Nations Indian Department. Source: "Canadian Military Institute," Officers of the British Forces in Canada During the War of 1812-15, by L. Homfray Irving, Welland Tribune Print, 1908, pages 208-220.

**JOHNSON, MAGDELENE:** A Colonel John Ferguson married Magdelene Johnson a daughter of Sir William Johnson and Molly Brant (Mohawk). Sources: "Lyman Copeland Draper Manuscripts," Wisconsin Historical Society, Volume 14/S/53. "The Loyalists In Ontario," The Sons and Daughters of The American Loyalists of Upper Canada, by William D. Reed, Hunterdon House, Lambertville, New Jersey, Copyright 1973.

**JOHNSON, PETER:** Peter Johnson was a son of Sir William Johnson and Molly Brant (Mohawk). He served for the British during the Revolutionary War. Source: "The Iroquois in the American Revolution," by Barbara Graymont, Syracuse University Press, Copyright 1972, page 71.

**JOHNSON, SIR WILLIAM:** Sir William Johnson was born in Ireland about 1715. He was employed by his uncle Peter Warren in 1738 to manage his New York estate's. These estate's included a large tract of land in the Mohawk Valley. His first wife was a white woman named Catherine Weisenburg by whom he had three children, Sir John Johnson, Baronet, Anna Johnson and Mary Johnson. After the death of his first wife he took as his second wife Caroline Henrick a Mohawk Indian by whom he had three children. After the death of Caroline Henrick he married Mary (Or Molly) Brant a Mohawk sister of Joseph Brant. Sources: "Lyman Copeland Draper Manuscript," Sir William Johnson Papers, Series F, Volumes 13-15, Wisconsin Historical Society, "The Story of Old Fort Johnson," by W. Max Reid, G.P. Putname & Sons, New York and London, The Knickerbocker Press, Copyright 1906, Pages 2, 10, 11, 20, 22, 54. New York Historical Society, "The Register Book of Baptisms, Marriages & Funerals," by Henry Barclay, of Fort Hunter," 1734-. The original register book is in the Library of New York, Historical Society. Source: Surrogate Court, Old Tryon County, New York, "Will of Sir William Johnson," dated 27, January 1774. Compiled Guide, "Records of the British Colonial Office," Class 5, Linda Womanski, Frederick, Maryland, University Publications of America, 1972. (53 microfilm reels). These films are selected records from volumes of transcripts in the Manuscript Room of the Library of Congress, Washington D.C. The library has three printed guides to the films. The records are divided into five parts. Part one includes "Indian Affairs out letters," 1766-1768 & "Indian Affairs in Letters," 1768-1771. Also included is "Indian Affairs records for 1756." Part Three includes records concerning the French and Indian War. Part five includes British records concerning the American Revolution, 1772-1784.

**JONCAIRE, FAMILY:** M. Charbert De Joncarie was a Frenchman who worked for the French about 1750 at a Seneca Mission near the site of Lewiston, New York. He married a Seneca woman. Two of his sons were Chaubert and Clauzonne. Sources: "Our County and Its People," A Descriptive Work On Erie County, New York, Edited by Truman C. White, Boston History Company, Publishers, 1898, Chapter IV, Pages 60, 70. "Dictionnaire Genelogique des familles du Quebec," By Rene Jette, 1983, University of Montreal Press, Montreal, Quebec, Canada.

**JONES, FAMILY:** Augustus Jones was a white man who had two Indian wives. One wife was a Mississauga Chippewa (Ojibway). His other wife was a Mohawk at the Six Nations Reserve. Source: "Lyman Copeland Draper Manuscripts," Volume 13/14/14/1/14/2/14/3, Wisconsin Historical Society. Mary (Polly) Jones was a daughter of Augustus Jones. She married Jacob Brant the son of Joseph Brant. Source: "Lyman Copeland Draper Manuscripts," Volume 13/14/14/1/14/2/14/3, Wisconsin Historical Society. Peter Jones was a son of Augustus Jones. His mother was a Mississauga (Chippewa). He was educated at an English school in Ontario. He worked as a missionary among the Indians of Ontario in the late 1820's and 1830's. He was presented to the King and Queen of England. His married Eliza Fields who was born in England. Sources: Brant County, Ontario Genealogical Society transcripts of "The New Credit United Church (Methodist) Cemetery Records," "The First Century of Methodism in Canada," Volume 1, 1775-1839, by J. E. Sanderson, M.A., Copyright in Canada, 1908, by William Briggs. Chapter 6, page 131, Chapter 11, pages 154, 169, Chapter 18, page 239. "The History of Methodism in Canada," by George Frederick Playter, Published by A. Green, Toronto, 1862, page 218.

**KERR/BRANT/FARLEY FAMILY:** A William J. Kerr was a Captain in the Canadian Indian Department. A William Kerr married Elizabeth Brant a daughter of Joseph Brant. Source: "Lyman Copeland Draper Manuscript," Volume 13/F/182/182/1/183/2, Volume 14/S/81/82, Volume 14/S/53, Volume 14/S/81/82 and Volume 17/1. Wisconsin Historical Society. A Robert Kerr married Miss Farley a grand daughter of Sir William Johnson and Molly Brant. Sources: "Lyman Copeland Draper Manuscripts," Wisconsin Historical Society, Volume 13/F/182/182/1/182/2 and Volume 15/191/191/2. "The First Century of Methodism in Canada," Volume 1, 1775-1839, by J. E. Sanderson, M.A., Toronto, Published by William Briggs 1908, Chapter 22, page 343. A Robert Kerr was a Captain (Surgeon) in the Indian Department. "Canadian Military Institute," Officers of the British Forces in Canada During the War of 1812-15, by L. Homfray Irving, Welland Tribune Print, 1908, pages 209-220.

**KILLBUCK FAMILY:** John Henry Killbuck was a Delaware whose family migrated from Canada to Kansas. He became a minister in the Moravian Church. "The Moravian Mission to the Delaware Indians," by Elma E. Gray, Toronto, Canada, Macmillan Company, 1956, pages 316 & 317.

**LA CLAIR, ISAAC:** Isaac La Claire was an Indian Agent for the St. Regis Mohawk (Franklin County, New York) in 1820. "The History of the County of Huntingdon and the Seigniories of Chateaugay and Beauharnois," by Robert Sellar, Huntingdon, Quebec, the Canadian Gleaner, 1888, page 172.

**LE RONDE/LA RONDE FAMILY:** Members of the La Ronde family from Montreal were living in Simcoe County, Ontario in 1861. See the following census entry, Simcoe County, Canada West, Ontario, Township of Tiny and Tay, before page nine. Mary La Ronde (Indian) age 80 born in Montreal. She was listed on the same page the family of Ezekiel Solomon (Indian) age 49 born on Drummond Island, Ontario. Source: The 1861 Canadian Census.

**LEFERTS/CLINCH/JOHNSON FAMILY:** A Mrs. J. Clinch Leferts was a great granddaughter of Sir William Johnson. Source: "Lyman Copeland Draper Manuscripts," Volume 14/1/1/1/1/5, Wisconsin Historical Society.

**LEFFERTY/JOHNSON/BRANT FAMILY:** A Mrs. Johnson Lafferty or Lefferty was a grand daughter of Sir William Johnson and Molly Brant. Sources: "Lyman Copeland Draper Manuscripts," Volume 13/F/184, Wisconsin Historical Society, Volume 13/F/184. "The Loyalists In Ontario," The Sons and Daughters of The American Loyalists of Upper Canada, by William D. Reed, Hunterdon House, Lambertville, New Jersey, Copyright 1973.

**LEWIS/POWLESS/BRANT FAMILY:** For a reference to the relationship of the Lewis, Powless and Brant family see the following source: "Lyman Copeland Draper Manuscripts," Wisconsin Historical Society, Volume 13/32, Volume 14/S/57/57/1/57/2/57/3, Volume 15/F/34/34/1.

**LOGAN FAMILY:** A Indian whose surname was Logan may have been descended from Muncey and Mohicans according to the following source: "History of the County of Middlesex," Canada Originally Published at Toronto and London by W.A. & C. L. Goodspeed in 1889, introduction by Daniel J. Brock, facsimile edition printed by Mika Studio, Belleville, Ontario, 1972, Chapter 11, Indian residents from 1580-1888, page 19.

**LORIMER FAMILY:** Chevalier Lorimer was a Lieutenant in the Canadian Indian Department. "Canadian Military Institute," Officers of the British Forces in Canada During the War of 1812-15, by L Homfray Irving, Librarian, Welland Tribune Print, 1908, pages 208-220.

**LOTHRIDGE FAMILY:** A Robert Lothridge was a Captain in the British Six Nations Indian Department. A Joseph Lothridge married Ellen Brant a granddaughter of Joseph Brant. Sources: "Journals of Major Robert Rogers," London, Printed MDCCLXV, by J. Allen, And account of the French and Indian War, Published in London 1765, pages 127-130. "Loyalist Lineages of Canada, 1783-1983," The United Empire Loyalists Association of Canada, Generation Press, Copyright 1981, (Toronto) page 81. "New York State Confiscations of Loyalists," United Loyalists, Bay of Quinte (Ontario) Branch.

**MARICLE/LOTHRIDGE/BRANT FAMILY:** A Mr. Maricle a Mohawk doctor married a Lothridge who was a great grand daughter of Joseph Brant. Source: "Lyman Copeland Draper Manuscripts," Volume 13/F/41. Wisconsin Historical Society.

**MARTIN/HILL FAMILY:** A Mrs. Lydia Martin was a grand daughter of Captain Isaac Hill a Mohawk. Source: "Lyman Copeland Draper Manuscripts," Volume 13/33, Wisconsin Historical Society.

**MAYBEE FAMILY:** A Mr. Maybee kept an Indian Store at Cattaraugus about 1788. "Our County and Its People," A Descriptive Work On Erie County, New York, page 126, Edited by Truman C. White, Volume 1, The Boston History Company, Publishers, 1898.

**MC GEE, FAMILY:** Thomas Mc Gee was Indian missionary for the Methodist Church. Source: "History of the County of Middlesex," Canada, Originally published at Toronto and London, by W. A. & C. L. Goodspeed in 1889, introduction by Daniel J. Brock, facsimile edition printed by Mika Studio, Belleville, Ontario, 1972, page 22. Source: "The First Century of Methodism in Canada," Volume 1 1775-1839, by J.E. Sanderson, M.A., Toronto, William Briggs, 1908, Chapter 21, page 286.

**MISKOKOMAN FAMILY:** Miskokoman was a Chippewa (Ojibwa) who served during the War of 1812. Source: "History of the County of Middlesex," Canada, originally published at Toronto and London, by W.A. & C.L. Goodspeed, Publishers in 1889, intrduction by Daniel J. Brock, Facsimile edition printed by Mika Studio, Belleville, Ontario, 1972, Chapter 11, Indian residents from 1580-1888, page 20.

**MONTOUR, ANDREW:** Andrew Montour sometimes referred to as Henry Montour was a Indian trader and diplomat concerning Indian affairs from New York to Ohio and for Pennsylvania and Virginia. Sources: "British Colonial Office Records of the British Office of Indian Affairs," Class 5, Fairfax County, Virginia 15th of May 1753. "The Indians Chiefs of Pennsylvania," by C. Hale Sipe, Arno Press & The New York Times Reprint Edition 1971, from a copy in the Pennsylvania State Library, originally printed by the Ziegler Company Inc., Butler, Pennsylvania, Copyright 1927, "Madam Montour and Her Son, Andrew Montour," Chapter XX, pages 310-324. "Souvenir Historical Book Sesqui-Centennial Celebration of Huntingdon County, Pennsylvania," by the Huntingdon County, Historical Society 1787-1937, Chapter 4, article "Indian Trails," page 18, gives the estimated location of the residence of Andrew Montour in 1752.

**MONTOUR, ELIZABETH COUC:** Elizabeth Montour or Couc was the daughter of Pierre Lafleur Couc and Marie Miteouamigoukoue. She married a Germaneau. Source: "Dictionnaire Genealogique des familles du Quebec," by Rene Jette, 1983, University of Montreal Press, Montreal, Quebec, Canada.

**MONTOUR, FRENCH MARGARET:** French Margaret Montour was mentioned as the daughter of Madam Montour. "The Indian Chiefs of Pennsylvania," By C. Hale Sipe, Arno Press & The New York Times, Reprint Edition 1871, from a copy in the Pennsylvania State Library, originally printed by The Ziegler Company Inc., Butler, Pennsylvania, Copyright 1927, Chapter XX, pages 311, 312.

**MONTOUR, JACOB:** A Jacob Montour supposedly married Joseph Brant's daughter Christiana. Source: "Lyman Copeland Draper Manuscripts," Wisconsin Historical Society, Volume 13/F/41, Wisconsin Historical Society.

**MONTOUR, JEAN BAPTISTE COUC:** Jean Baptiste Montour or Couc was the son of Pierre La Fleur Couc and Marie Miteouamigoukoue. He married an Abenaki Indian. Source: "Dictionnaire Genealogique des familles du Quebec," by Rene Jette, 1983, University of Montreal Press, Montreal, Quebec, Canada.

**MONTOUR, JOHN:** John Montour was supposedly a son of Andrew or Andre Montour of mixed Indian and French-Canadian ancestry. He served as a Captain on the American side during the Revolution. He attended college in 1754 at William & Mary in Virginia. Sources: William and Mary Quarterly., 1st series, Volume 6, page 188. Service card number

391226999, National Archives, Washington, D.C. Captain John Montour or Mountour a Indian received a Bounty Land Warrant number 1572-300 for a Captain on the 24th day of October 1789. Also Bounty Land Warrant Number 301-300 for Indian Captain Moutour. "Index to Revolutionary War Pension and Bounty Land Records of the Veteran's Administration Archives," The National Archives, Washington, D.C., Volume 1, Supplement to "The National Genealogical Society Quarterly." "Pocahontas's People," The Powhatan Indians of Virginia Through four Centuries, by Helen C. Roundtree, Copyright 1944, Reprint 1990, by University of Oklahoma Press, pages 170 & 336, No. 304. The "History of Livingston County, New York," by L., Doty, 1854, Chapter 111, Chapter 111, page 61, Chapter IV, page 86. "The King's Rangers," by John Brick, Published by Doubleday and Company Inc., page 46.

**MONTOUR, LOUIS COUC:** Louis Montour was a son of Pierre La Fluer Couc and Marie Miteouamigoukoue. He went by the name of Montour. He married Jeanne Quiquetigoukoue an Algonquin. Sources: Report of the Pioneer Society of Michigan, "Michigan Pioneer and Historical Collections," Lansing (Michigan) 1877. W.S., George and Company, Printers and Binders. (Mentions Capt. Montour and Louis and John Montour). "The Jesuit Relations and Allied Documents," Published 1858, Reprint 1959, New York, published 1960 by Microcard, Foundations, Washington, D.C. "Dictionnaire Genealogique des familles du Quebec," by Rene Jette, 1983, University of Montreal Press, Montreal, Quebec, Canada.

**MONTOUR, MARGARET:** Margaret Montour was a mentioned as a niece of Madam Montour who married a Iroquois. She may also have been French Margaret. She has been said to have lived in Ohio, Pennsylvania and New York. Sources: Lewis Evans "Map of The Middle British Colonies, in America," Including Virginia, Maryland, Delaware, Pennsylvania, New Jersey, New York, Connecticut, and Rhode Island, and Part of New-France (Canada) 1755. This map shows the location of Hockhocking (River) or French Margarets in Ohio. Source: The Church of Jesus Christ of Latter-Day Saints (Mormon) Family History Center has a copy of this map available on microfilm. "Indians in Pennsylvania," by Paul W. A. Wallace, Pennsylvania Historical and Museum Commission, Harrisburg, 1989, page 174.

**MONTOUR, MARGUERITE COUC:** Marguerite Couc or Montour was the daughter of Pierre LaFleur Couc. She married Jean Fafard. Jean Fafard was an interpreter to the Indians at Detroit. Source: "Dictionnaire Gnealogique des familles du Quebec," by Rene Jette, 1983, University of Montreal Press, Montreal, Quebec, Canada.

**MONTOUR, MICHAEL:** Michael Montour and Joseph Montour were mentioned in the following Source: "Library of New York Historical Society," "The Register of Baptism, Marriages & Funerals," of Fort Hunter (New York) 1734.

**MONTOUR, NICHOLAS:** Nicholas Montour signed a memorial petition to Lord Dochester from the merchants of Montreal trading with the Indians of the Upper County. Sources: "Michigan Pioneers and Historical Collections," Report of the Pioneer society of Michigan, Lansing 1877, W. S. George and Company, Printers, Chapter 24, page 16. "Dictionnaire Genealogique des Familles Du Quebec," by Rene Jette, 1983, University of Montreal Press, Montreal, Quebec, Canada. "The Jesuit Relations and

Allied Documents, published 1858, reprint 1959, New York, published 1960 by Microcard, Foundations, Washington, D.C.

**MONTOUR, PIERRE LA FLEUR COUC:** The surname Montour or Monture is found among many different native groups. The surname supposedly stems from Pierre La Fleur Couc (Montour) who was born in Saintes Saintonge France. He served in Canada as an interpreter to the Indians at Three Rivers in Quebec. In 1657 at Three Rivers he married Marie Miteouamigoukoue an Algonquin. Some of his children adopted the surname Montour. Source: "Dictionnaire Genealogique des Familles du Quebec," by Rene Jette, 1983, University of Montreal Press, Montreal, Quebec, Canada. "The Jesuit Relations and Allied Documents," Published 1858, Reprint 1959, New York, Published 1960 by Microcard, Foundations, Washington, D.C.

**MONTOUR, ROLAND:** A Roland Montour was born about 1740 in Pennsylvania and died in Canada. A Captain Rowland Montour was at the head of a party of Delaware Indians during the Revolutionary War. Sources: "The Iroquois in the American Revolution," by Barbara Graymont, Syracuse University Press, Copyright 1972, page 204. "Loyalist Lineages of Canada," 1783-1983, Toronto Branch, "The United Empire Loyalists" Association of Canada, Published by Generation Press, Ontario, Canada, Copyright 1981, page 461.

**MONTURE, MADAM:** Madam Monture was supposedly a daughter of Pierre Couc or Monture who had lived at Mackinac (Michigan) and Detroit. She was Involved in Indian trade. One source mentions that she married an Oneida chief and lived in Pennsylvania. Another source reports that she married a Seneca. Sources: "Indians in Pennsylvania," by Paul A. W. Wallace, Pennsylvania Historical and Museum Commission, 1989, page 178. "Lyman Copeland Draper Manuscripts," Volume 13/F/41, Wisconsin Historical Society. "The Indian Chiefs of Pennsylvania," by C. Hale Sipe, Arno Press & The New York Times, Reprint Edition 1871, from a copy in the Pennsylvania State Library, originally printed by the Ziegler Company, Inc. Butler, Pennsylvania, Copyright 1927, Chapter XX, page 310

**MONTURE, MADELINE COUC:** Madeline Montour or Couc was a daughter of Pierre LaFleur Couc who married Maurice Menard. Maurice Menard was an interpreter at Michilimakinac (Michigan). Source: "Dictionnaire Genealogique des familles du Quebec," by Rene Jette, 1983, University of Montreal Press, Montreal, Quebec, Canada.

**MONTOUR, MARIE-ANGELIQUE COUC:** Marie-Angelique Montour or Couc was the daughter of Pierre LaFleur Couc who married Francois Delpe. Source: "Dictionnaire Genealogique des familles du Quebec," by Rene Jette, 1983, University of Montreal Press, Montreal, Quebec, Canada.

**MOSES FAMILY:** The surname Moses is found in the following Sources: "Loyalist Lineages of Canada," 1783-1983, (Toronto Branch) "The United Empire Loyalist Association of Canada, Generation Press, Copyright 1981, Ontario, Canada, page 82.

**NELLES ROBERT:** A Robert Nelles was a Lieutenant in the British Six Nation Indian Department. Sources: "Loyalist Lineages of Canada," 1783-1983 (Toronto Branch) The United Empire Loyalists Association of

Canada, Generation Press, 1983. Source: "Lyman Copeland Draper Manuscripts," Volume 13/F/182/182/1. "Canadian Military Institute," Officers of the British Forces in Canada During the War of 1812-15, by L. Homfray Irving, Librarian, Welland Tribune Print, 1908, pages 208-220.

**NINHAM FAMILY:** The surname Ninham is found among the Indian marriages performed during the 1840's. Source: "History of Middlesex County," Canada, Originally published at Toronto and London by W. A. & C. L. Goodspeed in 1889, introduction by Daniel J. Brock facimile edition printed by Mika Studio, Belleville, Ontario, 1972, Chapter 111, page 26.

**OSBORN/KERR FAMILY:** A Mrs. Kate Osborn was mentioned as the granddaughter of Joseph Brant. Source: "Lyman Copeland Draper Manuscripts," Wisconsin, Historical Society, Volume 14/F/4/4/1/4/2/4/3 and Volume 14/S/81/82.

**PETERS FAMILY:** The surname Peter or Peters is found among the Delaware and the Six Nations. Sources: "The Delaware Indians," A History: By C. A. Weslager, Rutgers University Press, New Brunswick, New Jersey, Copyright 1909, pages 22-24, 320, 352. "Canadian Military Institute Officers of the British Forces in Canada during the War of 1812-15," by L. Homfray Irving, Librarian, Welland Tribune Print 1908, page 220.

**POWLESS/BRANT FAMILY:** Powless Powless married Margaret Brant a daughter of Joseph Brant. Sources: "Lyman Copeland Manuscripts," Volume 13/32, Wisconsin Historical Society. "The Oneida People," by Cara E. Richards, published by Indian Tribal Series, Phoenix, 1974.

**RANDALL/KING/JOHNSON FAMILY:** Charlotte Randall was a grand daughter of Sir William Johnson and his second wife Caroline Henricks. She married a George King. Source: "The Story of Old Fort Johnson," by W. Max Reid, Published by G.P. Putnam & Sons, New York and London, The Knickerbocker Press, Copyright 1906, pages 11, 20, 22.

**RILEY, FAMILY:** John Riley was a Chief at Upper Muncey. Source: "History of the County of Middlesex," Canada, by W.A. & C.L. Goodspeed, Publishers, 1889, facsimile edition printed by Mika Studio, Belleville, Ontario, 1972, Chapter 11, page 20.

**RUGGLES FAMILY:** A Mrs. Ruggles was the grand daughter of Sir William Johnson Molly Brant. Sources: "Lyman Copeland Draper Manuscripts," Volume 13/F/184, Wisconsin Historical Society, "The Loyalists In Ontario," The Sons and Daughters of The American Loyalists of Upper Canada, by William D. Reed, Hunterdon House, Lambertville, New Jersey, Copyright 1973.

**SAWYER, FAMILY:** David Sawyer was a native Methodist missionary. Source: "The First Century of Methodism in Canada," Volume 1, 1775-1839, by J.E. Sanderson, M.A., Toronto, Published by William Briggs, 1908. Chapter 21, page 282.

**SCHMITD OR SMITH, PETER KLINGLES (OR WHITE-PETER):** Peter Klingles Smith or Schmitd was a white captive who lived at the Grand River Settlement. Source: "County of Haldimand in the Days of Auld Lang

Syne," by Rev. Robert Bertram Nelles, M.A., Port Hope, Ontario, The Hamly Press, Book Printers, 1905, pages 59-60.

**SCHUYLER, MOSES:** A Moses Schuyler was an Oneida Chief about 1840. Sources: "History of the County of Middlesex," Canada, originally published by W.A. & C. L. Goodspeed, Publishers, 1889, introduction by Daniel J. Brock, facsimile edition printed by Mika Studio, Belleville, Ontario, 1972, Canadiana Reprint Series No. 36, Chapter 11, page 18. "The Iroquois in the American Revolution," by Barbara Graymont, Syracuse, University Press, Copyright 1972, pages 226 & 239.

**SENECA, FAMILY:** John Seneca was a Muncey Indian. Source: "History of the County of Middlesex," Canada, Originally published at Toronto and London by W.A. & C. L. Goodspeed in 1889, introduction by Daniel J. Brock, facsimile edition printed by Mika Studio, Belleville, Ontario, 1972, page 24.

**SERO/BRANT FAMILY:** For a reference to a relationship between the Sero (Cero) family and the Brant Family see the following source: "Loyalist Lineages Of Canada," 1783-1983 (Toronto Branch) The United Empire Loyalists Association of Canada," Generation Press, Copyright 1981, page 82.

**SICKLES/LOTHRIDGE FAMILY:** The Sickles family married into the Lothridge Family. Source: "Lyman Copeland Draper Manuscripts," Volume 14/S/72, Volume 13/32 and Volume 14/F/72, Wisconsin Historical Society.

**SIMPSON, JOHN:** A John Simpson an Indian was involved with the Methodist Mission. Source: "The First Century of Methodism in Canada," by J. E. Sanderson, M.A., Volume 1, 1775-1839, Chapter 27, Toronto, Published by William Briggs, 1908.

**SKENANDO/SKINADO/SCANADOAH FAMILY:** The Skenando family stems from a famous Oneida by that name. His daughter was said to have been the first wife of Joseph Brant. Sources: "Lyman Copeland Draper Manuscripts," Series U, Volume 11 and Volume 12, Wisconsin Historical Society. "Wilderness Empire," A Narrative, by Allan W. Eckert, Published 1969, by Little, Brown and Company, Boston, Toronto, page 637. "The Life & Times of Sa-Go-Ye-Wat-Ha- or Red Jacket, by William L. Stone, Albany, New York, J. Munsell Publisher, 1866, Speech of John Skenando, Appendix G., pages 495, 496.

**SMITH, FAMILY:** A Thomas Smith a Indian worked at the Methodist Mission Schools in Ontario. Source: "The First Century of Methodism in Canada," Volume 1, 1775-1839, by J. E. Sanderson, M.A., Toronto, William Briggs, 1908, Chapter 16, page 231. W. K. Smith from New York settled early in Brant County, Ontario. He had a Indian daughter. Source: "History of Brant County, Ontario, Canada," by W. K. Smith, page 178. Charlotte Brant a grand daughter of Joseph Brant married a Mr. Smith. Source: "Lyman Copeland Draper Manuscripts," Volume 14/S/57/57/1/57/2/57/3, Wisconsin Historical Society.

**SNAKE FAMILY:** The surname Snake is found among the Delaware. Source: "Wilderness Christians," The Moravian Mission to the Delaware Indians, by Elma E. Gray, Toronto, Canada, Macmillan Company, Copyright 1956.

"The Delaware Indians," by C. A. Weslager. Rutgers University Press, New Brunswick, New Jersey, Copyright 1909, pages 22-24, 320, 352.

**STUART OR STEWARD/JOHNSON FAMILY:** Mrs. Alexander Johnson Stuart was a grand daughter of Molly Brant and Sir William Johnson. Source: "Lyman Copeland Draper Manuscripts," Wisconsin Historical Society, Volume 13/F/184, Volume 13/38.

**SUMMERFIELD, FAMILY:** A Mr. Summerfield a native was a member of the Methodist Mission at Credit (Ontario) in 1835. "The First Century of Methodism in Canada," by J. E. Sanderson, M. A., Toronto, William Briggs, 1908, Volume 1, 1775-1839, Chapter 22, page 343, Volume 1, Chapter 27, 1836, page 389.

**SUNDAY, JOHN:** John Sunday was a native who was as a member of the Methodist Mission at Credit (Ontario). Source: "The First Century of Methodism In Canada," by J.E. Sanderson, M.A., Volume 1, 1775-1839, Toronto, William Briggs, 1908, Chapter 16, pages 234-235.

**THOMAS, FAMILY:** The surname Thomas was mentioned among the native marriages performed in 1834 by Rev. Ezra Adams, of the Wesleyan Methodist Church. "History of Middlesex County," Canada, Originally published at Toronto and London by W. A. & C. L. Goodspeed in 1889, introduction by Daniel J. Brock, facsimile edition printed by Mika Studio, Belleville, Ontario, 1972.

**TURKEY, GEORGE:** About 1826 George Turkey worked with the Methodist among the Indians in Ontario. "The First Century of Methodism in Canada," by J. E. Sanderson, M.A., Toronto, William Briggs, 1908, Volume 1, 1775-1839, page 156, Copyright 1908, Toronto, Canada.

**WADDILOVE, FAMILY:** W. J. Waddilove was a chief at Munceytown. "History of the County of Middlesex," Canada, Originally published at Toronto and London by W. A. & C. L. Goodspeed in 1889, introduction by Daniel J. Brock, facsimile edition printed by Mika Studio, Belleville, Ontario, 1972, Chapter 11, page 24.

**WAHCOSH, FAMILY:** The Wahcosh family were Muncey. "History of Middlesex County," Canada, Originally published at Toronto and London by W. A. & C. L. Goodspeed in 1889, introduction by Daniel J. Brock, facsimile edition printed by Mika Studio, Belleville, Ontario, 1972, Chapter 11, page 26.

**WAWANOSH FAMILY:** Wawanosh served during the War of 1812. Source: "History of the County of Middlesex," Canada, Originally published at Toronto and London by W. A. & C. L. Goodspeed in 1889, introduction by Daniel J. Brock, facsimile edition printed by Mika Studio, Belleville, Ontario, 1972, page 21.

**WHITELOON FAMILY:** The name White Loon is mentioned among the Chippewa of Michigan. "History of the Late War," In the Western Country, by Robert Breckinridge Mc Agee, Published by Worsley and Smith, 1816, page 35.

**WILLIAMS FAMILY:** A Reverend Eleazer Williams was a Caughnawaga (Mohawk) Indian who was educated in Connecticut for the Episcopal

Ministry. He was said to have been descended from a family that was taken prisoner by the Indians at Deerfield, Massachusetts. He ministered among the Indians at Green Bay, Wisconsin. Sources: "The History of the County of Huntingdon and the Seigniories of Chateaugay and Beauharnois," by Robert Sellar, Huntingdon, Quebec, "The Canadian Gleaner," 1888, Chapter IX, page 168. "Genealogical Index to "Historical Sketches of Franklin County (New York)," by Frederick J. Seaver, New York, State, pages 580, 581, 583. "Dictionnaire Genealogique des familles du Quebec," by Rene Jette, 1983, University of Montreal Press, Montreal, Quebec, Canada, page 1,133.

**WOMPUM OR WAMPUM FAMILY:** The surname of Wompum or Wampum is listed among the Muncey. Source. "History of the County of Middlesex," Canada, Originally published at Toronto and London by W. A. & C. L. Goodspeed in 1889, introduction by Daniel J. Brock, facsimile edition printed by Mika Studio, Belleville, Ontario, 1972, Chapter 11, page 26.

**YOUNG FAMILY:** A Mr. Young was an officer who served in the Indian Department. He married a Mohawk. "History of Brant County," by W. K. Smith, page 127.

**YOUNG KING:** Young King was in alliance with the United States during the War with England in 1812-15. Source: "The Life & Times of Sa-Go-Ye-Wat-Ha," or Red Jacket, by William L. Stone, Albany, New York, J. Munsell, Publishing, 1866, page 247.

## BRANT COUNTY, ONTARIO, CANADA
## HISTORICAL NOTES

Brant County is located in the southern part of Ontario, Canada west of Lake Ontario. About 1780 Joseph Brant the Mohawk leader was given land by the British in Ontario near the Grand River in the area of Brant and Haldimand County for his services during the American Revolution. The Mohawks lived on the north. Other native groups such as the Cayuga, Oneida, Missisauga Chippewa (Ojibwa), Munsie, Seneca and Tuscarora lived nearby. In 1796 the "Home District" included Haldimand and Brant Counties. The original district town was Niagara. In 1800 the Niagara region was called the "Niagara District." Gore District later covered what is now Halton, Waterloo, Wellington, Wentworth including Brant and Haldimand Counties. District records contain the Grand River Tract Indian Land Recordings. In 1840 the Mississauga Chippewa lived on the Credit River near Toronto. In 1847 the Six Nations Councils gave them land on the Grand River Reserve. Tuscarora and Onondaga Township was included in this reserve.

Townships in Brant, County included: Dumfries South parts one, two and three, Oakland,. Brantford, the town of Burford, Burford, Onondaga, Tuscarora and the Village of Paris. Towns in Brant County included: Brantford, Mt. Pleasant, Paris and. Scotland. A small portion of Oneida Township extended into Haldimand County, Ontario. Eagle's Nest was a peninsular tract of land surrounded by the Grand River near the town of Brantford. The Mohawk Mission School land was located at the Eagle's Nest tract. Oxbow Bend was a bend in the Grand River located in Brantford Township just west of the River. Smith's Creek was a tributary of the Grand River located north the town of Paris. Cayuga Village and Indiana were settlements in the Townships of North or South Cayuga and Seneca Township in Haldimand County near the Grand River. Monteagle was a township in Hastings County, Ontario. Napanee was a village listed in Lennox and Addington County, Ontario. Walpole Township was in Haldimand County. Woodstock was a township located in Oxford County, Ontario. Amhurstburg is a town located in Essex County, Ontario. The Thames River flows through Chatam in Kent County and London in Middlesex County, Ontario. The town of Lewiston is in Niagara County, New York. A Tuscarora Reserve is located in Niagara County, New York. Near the end of the Revolutionary War some Mohawks waited to move to Canada on the American side of the Niagara River at a place called "The Landings," (Now called Lewiston). Sources: "Lovell's Gazetteer of British North American," Montreal 1881, Published at Quebec, by John Lovell and Son, "National Archives of Canada," National Map Collection Number 5541, (A Map of Gore District), "Ontario Archives Ontario Land Index." "Ontario People," 1796-1803, Transcribed and Annotated by E. Keith Fitzgerald, Home District, pages 180-215, With an Introduction and Index by Norman K. Crowder, Genealogical Publishing Co., Inc., Copyright 1993. "Illustrated Historical Atlas of the County of Brant, Ontario," Page & Smith, Toronto, 1875, Historical Sketch of the County of Brant, By W.C. Trimble, pages 57, 87. This book includes a map of Tuscarora Township showing individual Indian names and the locations of their property in 1875.

## RESEARCH SOURCES

**THE RECORDS OF ST. JOHN'S CHURCH AND ST. PETERS CHRIST CHURCH BAPTISM, MARRIAGES & DEATHS FROM 1829, "ANGLICAN CHURCH OF CANADA."** These original church records have been made available on microfilm in Canada. They contain Indian baptisms, marriages and deaths for the Middlesex and Brant County, Ontario area. To obtain a copy of these records: 1. Consult your public library interlibrary loan system. 2. Consult the Canadian Archives. 3. The Church of Jesus Christ of Latter-Day Saints (Mormon) Family History Library Centers has a copy available on interlibrary loan

**BRANT COUNTY, GENEALOGY SOCIETY (BRANT COUNTY CEMETERY RECORDS).** The Brant County Genealogy Society has compiled the following Indian Cemetery Records in Brant County, Ontario, Canada: Bethany Mission Cemetery, Christ Church Anglican Cemetery, Delaware Mission Cemetery of the Delaware United Church Cemetery, First Line Cemetery, Jamieson Cemetery, St. John's Mission, New Credit Reserve Cemeteries, Garlow Baptist Reserve, the Pentecostal Church Cemeteries of the Six Nations Indian Reserve, Salvation Army Cemetery and the Grand River Mission United Church Cemetery. Also the records of the "Mohawk Chapel Cemetery" on six pages and "Indian Burial Sites," which includes sites in Tuscarora, Onondaga and Oneida Township have been compiled on four pages, including a map.

The cemetery records for Brant County, Ontario have been published. To find these published records 1. Try your local public library interlibrary loan system. 1. Contact the Canadian Archives. 2. Write the Brant County Genealogy Society. 3. A microfiche copy is available on interlibrary loan through the Church of Jesus Christ of Latter-Day Saints (Morman) Family History Library Centers.

A notation found in the 1851 Census of Brant County mentions that there existed on the Indian Reservation a Church built of wood capable of holding about one hundred and fifty persons under the control of the New England Society (Onondaga Township, Part 2, District 2).

# BRANT COUNTY, ONTARIO 1851 CENSUS ABSTRACT

The 1851 Canadian Census did not provide the relationships between family members. Married couples and children with similar surnames were enumerated and grouped together. Sometimes an individual will appear within a family group with a different surname. This person may have been an adopted child, a step child or a grandparent. These individuals were listed separately in this census abstract. The name of the family group or person they appeared to be living with was included after their entry. This census abstract should not take the place of any government or tribal records. For more information write the tribal offices.

**ACO, JACOB:** (Indian) Age 27 born (About 1824) at Onondaga, a member of the Church of England, Hannah age 22 born at Onondaga, age 22, Kayennehsondo (Female) age five months born at Onondaga. Tuscarora Township, District 22, Page 43/43, Numbers 20-22.

**ACO, THOMAS F:** (Indian) Age 60 born (About 1791) at Cayuga, Elizabeth age 60 born (About 1791) in New York State (United States) Ellen age 30 born at Onondaga, Mathew age 40 born at Lewiston (New York?) James age 13, born at Onondaga, Lucy age 5, born at Onondaga, Mark age 3, born at Onondaga, Mary age 1, born at Onondaga, Hannah age 13, born at Onondaga, Esther age 8, born at Onondaga, Peter age 4, born at Onondaga. Tuscarora Township, District 21, Page 41/41, Numbers 26-33.

**ACO, THOMAS:** (Indian) Age 16 born (About 1835) at Onondaga, Catharine age 34 born (1817) at Onondaga, Dehhaghsennontye (Male) age 13 born at Onondaga, Tsyawens (Female) age 8 born at Onondaga, Waterryakon (Male) age 7 born at Onondaga, Konwatyense? (Female) age 4 born at Tuscarora. Tuscarora Township, District 29, Page 57/27, Numbers 16-21.

**ADAMS, MOSES:** (Indian) Age 28 born (About 1823) at Onondaga, A member of the Methodist Church. Tuscarora Township, District 12, Page 23/1, Number 11.

**AGETONCE, MARY:** (Indian) Age 60 born (About 1791) at Credit River, a member of the Methodist Church. Tuscarora Township, Page 67/53, Number 13.

**AGHNOHHON?:** (Male Indian) Age 47 born (About 1804) at Onondaga, Dehhennonhsokotha (Male) age 14 born at Onondaga, Nikarondasa (Male) age 30 born at Brantford. Tuscarora Township, District 20, Page 39/39, Numbers 43-45.

**AJAKDATYE:** (Male Indian) Age 48 born (About 1803) at Onondaga, Kanoskenra (Female) age 40 born at Onondaga, Atsdaja (Male) age 10 born at Tuscarora, Onyehdanoron (Male) age 7, Yohhahowanen (Female) age 5, Aghhonwanentake? (Female) age 3. Tuscarora Township, District 26, Page 51/29, Numbers 50-53.

**AKWAKE, ISAAC:** (Indian) Age 60 born (About 1791) at Lewiston (New York?) a member of the Church of England, Elizabeth age 60 born at Onondaga. Tuscarora Township, District 24, Page 47/35, Numbers 9, 10.

**ALVIS, JOHN:** (Indian) Age 21 born (About 1830) in New York State (United States) Catherine age 18 born at Onondaga, Lucy age 16 born at Onondaga. Tuscarora Township, District 21, Page 41/41, Numbers 42-44.

**ALVIS, LUCY:** (Indian) Age 17, born (About 1834) at Tuscarora, a member of the Church of England, Stephen age 12, Susan age 10. District 5, Tuscarora Township, District 5, Page 9/61, Numbers 11-13.

**ANDERSON, CORNELIUS:** (Indian) Age 47 born (About 1804) in Canada West, a member of the Church of England, Jinny (Female) age 48, born in the United States, William age 16 born in Canada West, Amos age 12 born in Canada West, John age 4 born in Canada West. Onondaga Township, Part 11, Page 67, Numbers 2-6.

**ANOTYENAN:** (Male Indian) Age 45 born (About 1806) in New York State (United States) a member of the Church of England, Tsyononioti? (Female) age 28 born at Brantford, Honwanyende (Male) age 3 born at Tuscarora, Kahakentyo (Female) age 1. Tuscarora Township, District 20, Page 39/39, Numbers 20-23.

**AUHQWAKE, ANN:** (Indian) Age 48 born (About 1803) at Onondaga, Isaac age 22 born at Onondaga, William age 15 born at Onondaga. Tuscarora Township, District 18, Page 35/49, Numbers 30-32.

**AWENNARATYS:** (Male Indian) Age 22 born (About 1829) at Seneca, a member of the Church of England. Tuscarora Township, District 22, Page 43/43, Number 9. See the family of John Jack on the same page.

**BABCOCK, MARY:** (Indian) Age 9, born (About 1842) in New York (United States) a member of the Church of England, Brantford Township, Fifth Ward, Page 155/2, Number 35. See the family of Peter Powles.

**BAPTISE, CATHARINE:** (Indian) Age 24, born (About 1827) at Oxbow, a member of the Church of England. Tuscarora Township, District 5, Page 9/61, Number 33.

**BATIST, ISAAC:** (Indian) Age 4 born (About 1847) at Brantford. Tuscarora Township, District 17, Page 33/11, Number 11.

**BEACHTREE, LUCY:** (Indian) Age 20 born (About 1831) in New York State (United States) a member of the Methodist Church. Tuscarora Township, District 16, Page 31/9, Number 5.

**BEARFOOT, DAVID:** (Indian) Age 16 born (About 1835) at Tuscarora, Samuel age 14 born at Tuscarora. Tuscarora Township, District 10, Page 19/71, Number 45, 46.

**BEAVER, JABUS?:** (Indian) Age 40 born (About 1811) at Credit River, a member of the Methodist Church, Catharine age 40, John age 17, Louise age 16, Eliza age 14, George age 10. All were born at Credit River. (Credit Indians) Tuscarora Township, District 35, Page 69/17, Numbers 16-21.

**BEAVER, JOSEPH:** (Indian) Age 11 born (About 1840) at Grand River. Tuscarora Township, District 15, Page 29/7, Number 43. See the family of Sarah Longfish.

**BLACKNOSE, DAVID:** (Indian) Age 26, born (About 1825) at Tuscarora, a member of the Church of England, Nancy age 18, born in Paris, Catherine age 66 born in Cayuga. Tuscarora Township, District 4, Page 7/57, Numbers 23-25.

**BLIND, JOSEPH:** (Indian) Age 38 born (About 1813) at Credit River, a member of the Methodist Church. (Credit Indian) Tuscarora Township, District 35, Page 69/17, Number 45.

**BLUEJAY, SAPPHIRE:** (Female Indian) Age 16 born (About 1835) in Upper Canada (Ontario), a member of the Methodist Church. (Credit Indian) Tuscarora Township, District 35, Page 69/17, Number 4.

**BOMBARY, GEORGE:** (Indian) Age 9, born (About 1842) at Grand River, A member of the Methodist Church. Tuscarora Township, District 36, Page 71/47, Number 13. See the family of Henry Jones.

**BOMBERY, BETSEY:** (Indian) Age 52 born (About 1799) in Upper Canada (Ontario) a member of the Church of England. Tuscarora Township, Brant, District 1, Page 1/71, Number 11.

**BOMBY, MARY:** (Indian) Age 8, born (About 1843) in Canada a member of the Church of England, George age 3. Tuscarora Township, District 1, Page 1/71, Numbers 28, 29. See the family of Susan Lewis.

**BOMPARY, DAVID:** (Indian) Age 12 born (About 1839) at Oxbow. A member of the Methodist Church. Tuscarora Township, Twelfth Township, Brant County, Ontario, Page 23/1, Number 20.

**BOMPARY (OR POMPARY?) JOHN:** (Indian) Age 31 born (About 1820) at Paris, a member of the Church of England, Margret BOMPARY age 32, born at Paris, John BOMPARY age 7, born at Grand River, Esther HOUSE age 11, born at Green Bay, Alexander BOMPARY age 4, born at Grand River, Levi BOMPARY age 2, born at Grand River, Mary BOMPARY age 1, born at Grand River, Peter BOMPARY age 25, born at Paris. Tuscarora Township, District 24, Page 47/35, Numbers 45-52. This name was spelled on the census as Pompary?

**BOMPARY, JOSEPH:** (Indian) Age 20, born (About 1831) at Tuscarora, a member of the Methodist Church, Seth age 28, born at Tuscarora, Elizabeth age 22, born at Onondaga, Lydia age 6, born at Tuscarora, Betsey age 3, born at Tuscarora, Catharine age 2, born at Tuscarora. Tuscarora Township, District 9, Page 17/69, Numbers 24-29.

**BOMPARY, JOSEPH:** (Indian) Age 14 born (About 1837) at Grand River. A member of the Methodist Church. Tuscarora Township, District 11, Page 21/15, Number 4. See family of Augustus Jones.

**BOMPARY, MARGRET:** (Indian) Age 32, born (About 1819) at Johnson's Settlement, a member of the Church of England. Tuscarora Township, District 13, Page 25, Number 34.

**BRANT, HENRY:** (Indian) Age 63 born (About 1788) at Grand River, a member of the Church of England, Betsy age 37, Mary age 11. Tuscarora Township, District 30, Page 59/19, Numbers 35-37.

**BRANT, HENRY:** (Indian) Age 63 born (About 1788) at Grand River, a member of the Church of England. Tuscarora Township, District 7, Page 13/65, Number 48.

**BRANT, ISAAC:** (Indian) Age 20 born (About 1831) at Grand River, a member of the Church of England. Tuscarora Township, District 30, Page 59/19, Number 38.

**BRANT, JOHN:** (Indian) Age 20, born (About 1831) at Tuscarora. Tuscarora Township, District 25, Page 49/37, Numbers 11.

**BRANT, JOHN:** (Indian) Age 40 born (About 1811) at Grand River, a member of the Methodist Church, Mary (Indian) age 30 born at Scotland John age 17 born at Credit River, Ramon? a male age 16 born at Credit River, Elizabeth age 8 born at Credit River, Joseph age 3 born at Credit River, Lucy age 7 months born at Credit River. (Credit Indians) Tuscarora Township, District 35, Page 69/17, Numbers 22-28.

**BRANT, LYDIA:** (Indian) Age 14 born (About 1837) at Tuscarora, William age 12, Christina age 10, Elizabeth age 8, Peter age 6, Thomas age 4. Tuscarora Township, Page 39/7, Numbers 28-33. These are the children of either Seth Brant or Catharine Docks on the same page.

**BRANT, MARGRET:** (Indian) Age 12 born (About 1839) at the Bay of Quinty, a member of the Methodist Church. Tuscarora Township, District 9, Page 17/69, Number 43. See the family of William Hill.

**BRANT, POLLY:** (Indian) Age 47, born (About 1804) at Stoney Creek, a member of the Methodist Church, Eliza age 15 born at Credit River, Henry? age 6 born at Credit River. Tuscarora Township, District 19, Page 71/47, Numbers 15-17.

**BRANT, MARY:** (Indian) Age 17, born (About 1834) at Onondaga, a member of the Church of England. Tuscarora Township, District 5, Page 9/61, Number 37.

**BRANT, SETH:** (Indian) Age 36 born (About 1815) at the Bay of Quinty, a member of the Church of England, Catharine age 30 born in New York State (United States). Tuscarora Township, District 16, Page 31/9, Numbers 25, 26.

**BUCK, ABRAHAM:** (Indian) Age 18 born (About 1833) at Onondaga, a member of the Church of England. Tuscarora Township, District 22, Page 43/43, Number 10.

**BUCK, GEORGE:** (Indian) Age 40 born (About 1811) at Onondaga, Peggy age 25 born at Indiana, Wdorahkwansa? (Male) age 14 born in Indiana. Tuscarora Township, District 22, Page 43/43, Numbers 48-50.

**BUCK, JOHN:** (Indian) Age 28 born (About 1823) at Onondaga, Mary age 21 born at Brantford, Kanonsann (Female) age 4. Tuscarora Township, District 18, Page 35/49, Numbers 50-52.

**BUCK, PETER:** (Indian) Age 40 born (About 1811) at Onondaga, a member of the Church of England, Karihhokenserondo (Female) age 30 born at Onondaga, Ekshaha (Female) age 15, Ekshaha (Female) age 2 born at

Tuscarora. Tuscarora Township, District 22, Page 43/43, Numbers 15-18.

**BULL, POWLESS:** (Indian) Age 16 born (About 1835) at Grand River, a member of the Church of England. Tuscarora Township, District 16, Page 39/7, Number 48.

**BURNING, JEMIMA:** (Indian) Age 19 born (About 1832) at Onondaga, a member of the Church of England, Lydia age 2 born at Tuscarora. Tuscarora Township, District 3, Page 5/55, Numbers 33, 34.

**BURNING, JOHN:** (Indian) Age 55, born (About 1796) in Canada, a member of the Methodist Church. Tuscarora Township, District 9, Page 17/69, Number 21.

**BURNING, LEAH:** (Indian) Age 18 born (About 1833) at Johnson's Settlement, a member of the Church of England. Tuscarora Township, District 3, Page 5/55, Number 45.

**BURNING, NICHOLAS:** (Indian) Age 40 born (About 1811) at Bunnel Wharf, a member of the Methodist Church, Margret age 39, born at Salt Springs, John H., age 12, born at Salt Springs, Janet age 10, born at Salt Springs, Augustus age 8, born at Tuscarora, Eve age eight months, born at Tuscarora. Tuscarora Township, District 9, Page 17/69, Numbers 8-13.

**BURNING, THOMAS:** (Indian) Age 29 born (About 1822) at Onondaga, a member of the Church of England. Tuscarora Township, District 4, Page 7/57, Number 2.

**BURNINGS, ISAAC:** (Indian) Age 60 born (About 1791) at Cayuga, Sarah age 50 born at Tuscarora, Peter age 27 born at Tuscarora, Sampson age 24 born at Tuscarora, Timothy age 19 born at Tuscarora. Tuscarora Township, District 3, Page 5/55, Numbers 23-27.

**BURNINGS, NICHOLAS:** (Indian) Age 37 born (About 1814) at Upper Canada (Ontario), a member of the Church of England, Mary age 31 born at Grand River, Augustus age 13 born at Tuscarora, Abraham age 4 born at Tuscarora, Betsy age 4 months born at Tuscarora. Tuscarora Township, District 3, Page 5/55, Numbers 18-22.

**BUTLOR, JOHN:** (Indian) Age 22, born (About 1829) at Tuscarora, a member of the Church of England. Tuscarora Township, District 5, Page 9/61, Number 10.

**BUZZAR, JEMIMA:** (Indian) Age 13 born (About 1838) at Grand River, a member of the Church of England, Nelly age 16 born at Grand River. Tuscarora Township, District 36, Page 71/47, Numbers 20, 21.

**CAMP, CATHARINE:** (Indian) Age 97 born (About 1704) in New York (United States) a member of the Church of England. Tuscarora Township, District 11, Page 21/75? Number 7.

**CANNON, JEMIMA:** (Indian) Age 3 born (About 1848) at Brantford. Tuscarora Township, District 21, Page 41/41, Number 22. See Elizabeth Silver on the same page.

**CARPENTER, ABRAHAM:** (Indian) Age 44 born (About 1807) in Brantford Township, a member of the Methodist Church, Ann age 48, Bayler? or Benj? age 19, Yehaze (Male) age 16, Susan age 18, K? (Female) age 7, Betsey age 4. Tuscarora Township, District 2, Page 3/54? Numbers 3-9.

**CARPENTER, GEHAZE?** (Indian) Age 17 born (About 1834) in Upper Canada (Ontario). He was a member of the Methodist Church. Onondaga Township, Part 11, Page 31, The census indicated however that he resided in Tuscarora (Township?).

**CARPENTER, JACOB:** (Indian) Age 42, born (About 1809) at Oxbow, a member of the Church of England, Elias age 7? born at Tuscarora. Tuscarora Township, District 8, Page 15/67, Numbers 32, 33.

**CARPENTER, JOSEPH:** (Indian) Age 44 born (About 1807) in Canada, a member of the Methodist Church, Magrette? age 43, Margrette? age 21, Sabre? (Female) age 18, Catherine age 16, Edgerton age 13, Joseph age 11, Mary age 9, John age 7, Harper age 5, Phe? Ann age 2, Tuscarora Township, District One, Township One, Page 1/71, Numbers 42-50. Harper Carpenter and Phe? Ann Carpenter were listed on the following page.

**CARRIER, WILLIAM:** (Indian) Age 28 born (About 1823) in Canada West, a member of the Church of England, Hanah age 26, George age 8, Hulet? (Male) age 6, Simon age 4, James age 1, Elizabeth CARRIER age 60 born in the United States, a member of the Church of England. Onondaga Township, Part 11, District 2, Page 67, Numbers 7-13.

**CASE, MARY:** (Indian) Age 22 born (About 1829) in New York (United States) a member of the Church of England. Brantford Township, District 5, Page 155/2, Number 37.

**CATY:** (Female Indian) Age 30 born (About 1821) at Onondaga, Arahkwis (Male) age 4 born at Tuscarora, Kanonhwayentha (Female) age 2 born at Tuscarora. Tuscarora Township, District 25, Page 49/37, Numbers 17-19.

**CHEEK, SAMUEL:** (Indian) Age 28 born (About 1823) at Grand River. A member of the Church of England. Tuscarora Township, District 11, Page 21/75? Number 40.

**CISKUM, ELIZABETH:** (Indian) Age 43, born (About 1808) in New York (United States) Mary age 27, born in Onondaga, Catharine age 9, born in Tuscarora, Albert age 7, born in Tuscarora, Cyrus age 4, born in Tuscarora. Tuscarora Township, District 32, Page 63/23, Numbers 19-23.

**CISKUM, JULIA ANN:** (Indian) Age 40, born (About 1811) in New York (United States) a member of the Church of England, Susanah age 10, born in Onondaga. Tuscarora Township, District 32, Page 63/23, Numbers 17, 18.

**CISKUM, JULIA:** (Indian) Age 40, born (About 1811) in New York (United States) a member of the Church of England, Catharine age 19 born at Tuscarora, Tuscarora Township, District 5, Page 9/61, Numbers 8, 9.

**CLAUSE, CHARLOTTE:** (Indian) Age 15 born (About 1836) at Oxbow, a member of the Church of England, Margaret age 12, born at Oxbow, Thomas age 9, born at Oxbow, Catharine age 7, born at Tuscarora, John age 4, born at Tuscarora, Mary age 1, born at Tuscarora. Tuscarora Township, District 10, Page 19/71, Numbers 23-28. See the family of John Clause on the same page.

**CLAUSE, HANNAH:** (Indian) Age 68, born (About 1783) at Grand River, a member of the Methodist Church, Mary age 11 born at Grand River. Tuscarora Township, District 36, Page 71/47, Numbers 29, 30.

**CLAUSE, ISAAC:** (Indian) Age 30 born (About 1821) at Grand River, Sarah age 26 born at Bay of Quinty, a member of the Methodist Church, Elizabeth age 9 born at Grand River, William age 5 born at Grand River, A male Child age 2 born at Grand River. Tuscarora Township, District 36, Page 71/47, Numbers 44-48.

**CLAUSE, JOHN:** (Indian) Age 66, born (About 1785) at Onondaga, a member of the Church of England, Tuscarora Township, District 5, Page 9/61, Number 36.

**CLAUSE, JOHN:** (Indian) Age 43 (About 1808) born at Grand River, a member of the Church of England, Daby? of Gaby? age 31, John age 14? Mary age 12, Joseph age 5. Tuscarora Township, District 13, Page 25, Numbers 42-46.

**CLAUSE, JOHN:** (Indian) Age 42 born (About 1809) at Onondaga, a member of the Church of England, Mary age 38 born at Mohawk Village. Tuscarora Township, District 10, Page 19/71, Numbers 19/20.

**CLAUSE, JOSEPH:** (Indian) Age 46 born (About 1805) at Onondaga, a member of the Methodist Church, Polly age 43 born at New York State (United States) Thomas age 17, born at Onondaga, Jonah age 11, born at Onondaga, Alexander age 8, born at Onondaga. Tuscarora Township, District 10, Page 19/71, Numbers 13-17.

**CLAUSE, PETER:** (Indian) Age two months born at Tuscarora, Tuscarora Township, District 13, Page 25, Number 20. See Margret Stots? on the same page.

**CLAUSE, PETER:** (Indian) Age 49 born (About 1802) at the Bay of Quinty, a member of the Methodist Church, Elizabeth age 46 born at the Bay of Quinty, Peter age 19, born at the Bay of Quinty, James age 17, born at the Bay of Quinty, Betsey age 12, born at Grand River, Joseph age 8, born at Grand River, Jemima age 6, born at Grand River, Catharine age 14, born at Grand River. Tuscarora Township, District 16, Page 31/9, Numbers 6-13.

**CLAUSE, SETH:** (Indian) Age 23 born (About 1828) at the Bay of Quinty, a member of the Methodist Church, Cornelious (Female) age 25. Tuscarora Township, District 16, Page 31/9, Numbers 3, 4.

**CLAUSE, SUSAN:** (Indian) Age 17, born (About 1834) at Onondaga, a member of the Church of England, Hannah age 4 born in Tuscarora. Tuscarora Township, District 5, Page 9/61, Numbers 38, 39.

**CLAUSE, WIDOW:** (Indian) Age 34 born (About 1817) at the Bay of Quinty, a member of the Church of England. Tuscarora Township, District 8, Page 15/67, Number 4.

**CLINCH, HENRY:** (Indian) Age 32 born (About 1819) at Ancaster, a member of the Methodist Church, Ellen age 30 born at Onondaga, Henry Jr., age 12 born at Johnson's Settlement, Amos age 3 born at Tuscarora, Joseph age 2, born at Tuscarora. Tuscarora Township, District 3, Page 5/55, Numbers 13-17.

**COFFEE, CHARLOTTE:** (Indian) Age 3 born (About 1848) at Tuscarora Township. Tuscarora Township, District 13, Page 25, Number 38. See the household of Margret Bompary on the same page.

**COFFEE, DABY:** (Female Indian) Age 10 born (About 1841) at Brantford, a member of the Church of England. Tuscarora Township, District 7, Page 13/65, Number 31.

**COFFEE, SAMUEL:** (Indian) Age 42 born (About 1809) at Mohawk Village, a member of the Methodist Church, Margret age 42 born at Mohawk Village, Rachael age 28 born at Tuscarora, Abraham age 2 born at Tuscarora. Tuscarora Township, District 13, Page 25/3 Numbers 1-4.

**COFFEE, SAMUEL:** (Indian) Age 23 born (About 1828) at Onondaga, Elizabeth age 15 born at Brantford. Tuscarora Township, District 17, Page 33/11, Numbers 12, 13.

**COFFEE, THOMAS:** (Indian) Age 46 born (About 1805) at Mohawk, a member of the Methodist Church, Margret age 24 born at Bay of Quinty, Abednego age 3 born at Tuscarora, Tuscarora Township, District 2, Page 2/59, Numbers 32-34.

**COMMONTURE, JOHN:** (Indian) Age 27 born (About 1824) at Brantford, a member of the Church of England. Tuscarora Township, District 22, Page 43/43, Number 4.

**CONJECTON? MOSES:** (Indian) Age 21, born (About 1830) in the United States, a member of the Church of England. Onondaga Township, Part 11, Page 35, Number 36.

**CRAWFORD, ADAM:** (Indian) Age 60 born (About 1791) at Paris, a member of the Church of England. Tuscarora Township, District 7, Page 13/65, Number 49.

**CRAWFORD, ADAM:** (Indian) Age 77, born (About 1773) in Canada, and resided in Tuscarora Township, a member of the Church of England, Brantford Township, District 5, Page 183/16, Number 40.

**CRAWFORD, DAVID:** (Indian) Age 19 born (About 1832) at Onondaga, a member of the Methodist Church. Tuscarora Township, District 29, Page 57/27, Number 26.

**CRAWFORD, JOSEPH:** (Indian) Age 10 born (About 1841) at Oneida, a member of the Church of England. Tuscarora Township, District 30, Page 59/19, Number 41. See the family of Jacob Williams.

**CRAWFORD, MARY:** (Indian) Age 40 born (About 1811) at Indiana? (Or Onondaga?) a member of the Church of England, Joseph age 12 born at Seneca (A township in Haldimand County) Stephen CISKUM age 12 born at

Onondaga. Tuscarora Township, District 32, Page 63/ 23, Numbers 14-16.

**CRAWFORD, NELLY:** (Indian) Age 25 born (About 1826) at Brantford, a member of the Church of England. Moses age 4 born at Mohawk Village. Tuscarora Township, Page 11/63, Numbers 37, 38.

**CULP, MOSES:** (Indian) Age 58 born (About 1793) at Clinton (New York?) Mary age 56 born at Ancaster, William age 26 born at Clinton, Margret age 19, no birthplace given. All were members of the Methodist Church. Twenty Ninth Township, Brant County, Ontario, Page 57/27?,

**CULP, MOSES:** (Indian) Age 58 born (About 1803) at Clinton (New York?), a member of the Methodist Church, Mary age 56 born at Ancaster, William age 26 born at Clinton, Margaret age 19 place of birth was not given. Tuscarora Township, District 29, Page 57/27, Numbers 22-25.

**CURLEY, CHARLOTTE:** (Indian) Age 12 born (About 1839) at Grand River. A member of the Church of England. Tuscarora Township, Township, District 15, Page 29/7. See the family of David Jameson.

**DAKWENWISARERENH:** (Male Indian) Age 20 born (About 1831) at Brantford, Good Lumber (Female) age 20 born at Indiana, Tsidontha? or Lsidontha? (Female) age 3, Niyakaah (Female) age eight months born at Tuscarora. Tuscarora Township, District 25, Page 49/37, Numbers 29-32.

**DANGERFIELD, PEGGY:** (Indian) Age 56 born (About 1795) in Canada, a member of the Church of England. Tuscarora Township, District 1, Page 1/71, Number 18.

**DAVID, JOHN:** (Indian) Age 35, born (About 1816) at Credit River, a member of the Methodist Church. Tuscarora Township, District 34, Page, 67/53, Number 12.

**DAVIDS, HELEN:** (Indian) Age 20, born (About 1831) in New York (United States) a member of the Church of England. Brantford Township, District 5, Page 155/2, Number 36.

**DAVIDS, MARGRET:** (Indian) Age 40 born (About 1811) at Brantford, a member of the Methodist Church, Tuscarora Township, District 26, Page 51/29, Number 26. See the entry for Tkakowihhe? or Shakowihhe? on the same page. He may be the husband of Margret Davids.

**DAVIS, ELIAS:** (Indian) Age 22, born (About 1829) at Tuscarora, a member of the Church of England, George age 17, John age 29. Tuscarora Township, District 5, Page 9/61, Numbers 16-18,.

**DAVIS, ESTHER:** (Indian) Age 50 born (About 1801) at Grand River. A member of the Church of England. Tuscarora Township, District 13, Page 25, Number 47.

**DAVIS, GEORGE:** (Indian) Age 16 born (About 1835) at Indiana, David age 11 born at Tuscarora, Elizabeth age 6 born at Tuscarora, Peter age 3 born at Tuscarora. Tuscarora Township, District 29, Page 57/27, Numbers 44-47.

**DAVIS, JACOB:** (Indian) Age 20 born (About 1831) at Tuscarora, a member of the Methodist Church, Hannah age 18, born at Tuscarora, Mary age 16, born at Tuscarora, Elizabeth age 14, born at Tuscarora, Henry age 12, born at Tuscarora, Catharine age 10, born at Tuscarora, John age 8, born at Tuscarora, Lydia age 6, born at Tuscarora, William age 2, born at Tuscarora, James age 1, born at Tuscarora. Tuscarora Township, District 26, Page 51/29, Numbers 27-36.

**DAVIS, JACOB:** (Indian) Age 25 born (About 1826) at Grand River, a member of the Church of England, Christian (Female) age 23 born at Brantford Township. Tuscarora Township, District 17, Page 33/11, Numbers 39, 40.

**DAVIS, MARY JANE:** (Indian) Age 3 born (About 1848) at Brantford Township, Joseph age 1 born at Brantford Township. Tuscarora Township, District 17, Page 33/11, Numbers 42, 43. See the entry for Jacob Davis on the same page

**DAVIS, SUSANAH:** (Indian) Age 26 born (About 1825) at Grand River, a member of the Church of England, Richard age four hours old. Tuscarora Township, District 13, Page 25, Numbers 40, 41.

**DAVIS, WILLIAM:** (Indian) Age 50 born (About 1801) at Lewiston (New York?) Mrs. Davis age 40 born at Credit, Rodenwade (Female) age 6 born at Tuscarora. Tuscarora Township, District 29, Page 57/27, Numbers 48-50.

**DAYMY? JOHN:** (Indian) Age 45 born (About 1806) at Oneida, a member of the Baptist Church, Susannah age 41 born at Tuscarora, Mary age 3 born at Tuscarora. Tuscarora Township, District 17, Page 35/49, Numbers 23-25.

**DEHANONDEJI:** (Male Indian) Age 32 born (About 1819) at Brantford. Tuscarora Township, District 25, Page 49/37, Number 46.

**DEHHANONYANIHTHA:** (Male Indian) Age 30 born (About 1821) at Onondaga, Kahendisaks (Female) age 26 born at Onondaga, Wesorenh (Female) age 17 born at Onondaga, Kanadaah (Male) age 17 born at Onondaga, Dehnynnenth (Male) age 10 born at Onondaga, Nadakenwahtha (Male) age 8 born at Onondaga, Tharonhyonarens (Male) age 6 born at Onondaga, Orahkwanoron (Female) age 2 born at Tuscarora. Tuscarora Township, District 29, Page 57/27, Numbers 8-15.

**DEHHASAREAHHANAHKWA:** (Male Indian) Age 38, born (About 1813) at Brantford, a member of the Church of England, Kahhendoratha (Female) age 20, born at Brantford, Thirty Second Township, Page 63/23, Numbers 37, 38.

**DEHONWADERYO:** (Male Indian) Age 45 born (About 1806) at Montrel (Montreal?) a member of the Baptist Church, Mary age 38 born at Rochester (New York?) Rowanih? (Female) age 13 born at Tuscarora, Konwakerih (Female) age 6 born at Tuscarora, Cyrus age 1 born at Tuscarora. Tuscarora Township, District 18, Page 35/49, Numbers 7-11.

**DEHORAHSARE:** (Male Indian) Age 50, born (About 1801) at Onondaga. a member of the Church of England, Tuscarora Township, Page 63/23, Number 36.

**DELAWARE, ABRAM:** (Indian) Age 4, born (About 1847) in Canada. See family of Jacob Johnson, Brantford Township, District 5, Page 163/6, Number 31.

**DEYOHJIKERAKEH:** (Male Indian) Age 28 born (About 1823) at Indiana, Niltadenhenraha? or Nihtadenhenraha? (Male) age 10 born at Indiana, Kahrakwas (Female) age 8 born at Indiana, Kanyendonkwas (Female) age 23 born at Indiana, Kanawide (Female) age 20 born at Indiana, Kahonwentha (Female) age 11 born at Indiana, Skahonware (Male) age 6, Kawenose (Female) age 2 born at Indiana. Tuscarora Township, District 29, Page 57/27, Numbers 31-38.

**DEYOTHOREHKWEN?:** (Male Indian) Age 76 born (About 1775) at Cayuga, Nihsuahskiriy? a female age 44 born at Indiana, Dewathaghhonhotha (Female) age 16, born at York. Tuscarora Township, District 20, Page 39/39, Numbers 2, 3, 4.

**DIXON, WILLIAM:** (Indian) Age 30 born (About 1821) at Onondaga. Tuscarora Township, District 21, Page 41/41, Number 34.

**DIXSON, PEGGY:** (Indian) Age 37 born (About 1814) at Tuscarora, Aaron age 19 born at Tuscarora, Dewadironhyonkohtha (Female) age 16 born at Tuscarora, Kayadonnens (Female) age 9 born at Tuscarora, Skawmnes (Female) age 6 born at Tuscarora, Dehhannyes (Male) age 1 born at Tuscarora. Tuscarora Township, District 26, page 51/29, Numbers 1-6.

**DOCKS, CATHARINE:** (Indian) Age 50 born (About 1801) in New York State (United States) a member of the Church of England. Tuscarora Township, District 19, Page 39/7, Number 27.

**DOCKS, PETER:** (Indian) Age 27 born (About 1824) in New York (United States), a member of the Church of England, Jemima age 25 born at Onondaga. Tuscarora Township, District 13, Page 25, Numbers 20, 21.

**DOCTOR, HENRY:** (Indian) Age 35 born at Grand River, a member of the Church of England. Tuscarora Township, District 30, Page 59/19, Number 1.

**DOCTOR, JOHN:** (Indian) Age 51, born (About 1800) at Tuscarora, a member of the Church of England. Tuscarora Township, District 5, Page 9/61, Number 14.

**DOCTOR, JOHN:** (Indian) Age 57, born (About 1804) at Tuscarora, a member of the Church of England. Tuscarora Township, District 5, Page 9/61, Number 14.

**DOCTOR, MARY:** (Indian) Age 15 born (About 1836) at Grand River, a member of the Methodist Church. Tuscarora Township, District 15, Page 29/7, Number 13.

**DOCTOR, SUSANNAH:** (Indian) Age 50? born (About 1801) at Grand River, a member of the Church of England, Joseph age 27, Philip age 5, ?

Doctor (Male) age one age a half. Tuscarora Township, District 30, Page 59/19, Numbers 2-5.

**DODGE, JOSEPH:** (Indian) Age 65 born (About 1786) at Credit River, a member of the Methodist Church (Credit Indian), Tuscarora Township, District 28, Page 55/33, Number 21.

**DOUGLAS, GEORGE:** (Indian) Age 44, born (About 1807) at Onondaga (Township?), Christeen age 40, born in Onondaga (Township?). All of the following were born in Tuscarora (Township?), Daniel age 14, William age 12, Isaac age 10, Amos age 6, Margret age 4. All were members of the Church of England. District 5, Tuscarora Township, District 5,, Page 9/61? or Page 9/51?, Numbers 19-25.

**DOUGLAS, GEORGE:** (Indian) Age 70 born (About 1781) in the State of New York (United States) a member of the Baptist Church, Peggy age 60 place of birth unreadable, Sarah age 18 born at Tuscarora, Henry age 16 born at Tuscarora, Susanah age ?, born at Tuscarora, Margret age ?, born at Tuscarora, James age ?, born at Tuscarora, Joseph age 5 born at Tuscarora. Tuscarora Township, District 31, Page 61/21, Numbers 21-28.

**DOUGLAS, HENRY:** (Indian) Age 26 born (About 1825) at Tuscarora, a member of the Baptist Church. Tuscarora Township, District 10, Page 19/71, Number 50.

**DOUGLAS, JOHN:** (Indian) Age 40 born (About 1811) at Onondaga, a member of the Baptist Church, Susanah age 34 born at Tuscarora, William age 16 born at Tuscarora, Peter age 10 born at Tuscarora, John age 6, born at Tuscarora, Isaac age 4, born at Tuscarora, Abram age 1, born at Tuscarora. Tuscarora Township, District 31, Page 61/21, Numbers 29-35.

**DOXSTADER, MARY:** (Indian) Age 7, born (About 1844) at Tuscarora, a member of the Church of England, Lydia age 4 born in Tuscarora. Tuscarora Township, District 2, Page 3/59, Numbers 21, 22. See the family of James Gevens.

**DOXTADER, DANIEL:** (Indian) Age 14 born (About 1837) in Onondaga, a member of the Methodist Church, Samuel age 12 born in Onondaga. Tuscarora Township, District 8, Page 15/67, Numbers 17, 18.

**DOXTADER, JOHN:** (Indian) Age 46 born (About 1805) at Grand River, a member of the Methodist Church, Lucy age 32 born at the Bay of Quinty, Charlotte age 5 born at Grand River, Joseph age 3, born at Grand River, George age 1, born at Grand River. Tuscarora Township, District 16, Page 39/7, Numbers 34-38.

**DOXTADER, SETH:** (Indian) Age 22 born (About 1829) at Grand River, a member of the Methodist Church. Tuscarora Township, Page 39/7, Number 39.

**DOXTADER, SUSAN:** (Indian) Age 16, born (About 1835) at Tuscarora, a member of the Methodist Church, Jonas age 12, born at Tuscarora, Betsey age 9, born at Tuscarora. Tuscarora Township, District 9, Page 17/69, Numbers 3-5.

**DOXTATOR, ISAAC?** (Indian) Age 26 born (About 1825) at Grand River, a member of the Methodist Church, Catharine age 25, Sarah age 5, James C. age 2, Catharine age 19 months, Betsey age 28, Peggy age 8, Tuscarora Township, District 15, Page 29/7, Numbers 1-7.

**DUNKIN, DAVID:** (Indian) Age 51 born (About 1800) in Canada, married, a member of the Church of England, Nancy age 51, Richard age 12, Elizabeth age 15, Catharine age 10. Brantford, District Number 5, Page 215/32.

**EKSHAHA:** (Male Indian) Age 38 born (About 1813) at Onondaga, a member of the Church of England, Waryh (Female) age 14 born at Onondaga, Kawennodas (Male) age 8 born at Onondaga, Akakewyon (Male) age 6 born at Onondaga, Kahenyakwas (Male) age 3 born at Onondaga, Dewatasaryake? (Male) age two months born at Onondaga, Rakshah (Male) age 2 born at Tuscarora. Tuscarora Township, District 22, Page 43/43, Numbers 23-28. See the family of Jacob Aco on the same page.

**ELLIOT, WILLIAM:** (Enumerated as a white man?) Age 35, born (About 1816) at Tronto?, (Toronto?) a member of the Church of England, Margret (Indian) age 27, born at Martins Settlement, George (Indian) age 17 months, born at Martins Settlement. Tuscarora Township, District 5, Page 9/61, Numbers 45-47.

**ENGLISH, WILLIAM:** (Indian) Age 28 born (About 1823) in Oneida Township, a member of the Church of England, Mary age 24 born in New York State (United States) William age 6 born in Tuscarora, John age 3 born in Tuscarora. Tuscarora Township, District 13, Page 25, Numbers 15-18.

**EVRITT, ISAAC:** (Indian, age not given) Born in New York State (United States) a member of the Church of England, Lydia age 21 born at Grand River, Solomon age 5 born at Grand River, George age 1 born at Grand River. Tuscarora Township, District 13, Page 25, Numbers 48-51.

**EVRITT? OR EVERETT? ISAAC:** (Indian age not given) Born in New York, Lydia age 21 born at Grand River, Solomon age 5 born at Grand River, George age 1 born at Grand River. All were members of the Church of England. Tuscarora Township, Thirteenth Township, Brant County, Ontario, Page 25.

**FAUM? FAWNN? OR FUNN? STEPHEN:** (Indian) Age 30 born (About 1821) at Credit River, a member of the Methodist Church, Nancy age 40, Saphire? age 13, Sarah Ann age 11, Marian (Female) age 8, Joseph age 2. (Credit Indians) Tuscarora Township, District 35, Page 69/17, Numbers 37-42.

**FIELDEN, JAMES:** (Indian) Age 39, (About 1812) born in the United States (All were born in the United States) Sarah J. age 27, Rachael age 5, James age 4. All were members of the Baptist Church. Brantford Township, Ward 1, Brant County, Ontario, Page 19.

**FINGER, LOUISE:** (Indian) Age 15? born (About 1836) at Credit River, a member of the Methodist Church, Mary age 14 born at Credit River, Jacob age 6 born at Credit River. Tuscarora Township, District 34, Page 67/53. See the family of Margret Wabanibe on the same page.

**FINGER, PAUL BEN:** (Indian) Age 30 born (About 1821) at Credit River, a member of the Methodist Church, Marget age 24 born at Credit River, Aaron age 2 born at Credit River. Tuscarora Township, District 34, Page 67/53, Numbers 41-43.

**FISH, SUSAN:** (Indian) Age 14, (About 1837) All were born in Tuscarora Township, Jacob age 11, David age 9, Becky age 5, Tuscarora Township, District 1, Township District 1, Page 1/71, Numbers 12-15. See the family of Betsey Bomberry?

**FISHCARRYER (OR FISHCARRIER) PETER:** (Indian) Age 40, born (About 1811) in New York (United States) a member of the Church of England, Sarah age 40 born at Tuscarora. Betsy age 15 born at Tuscarora, Tuscarora Township, District 4, Page 7/57, Numbers 34-36.

**FORSYTH, ALEXANDER:** (Indian?) Age 52, born (About 1799) in Scotland, Church of Scotland, Ann (White?) age 40, born in Scotland, Donald age 15, born in Scotland, Roderick age 17, born in Scotland, Alexander age 8, born in Scotland, Elizabeth age 18, born in Scotland, Catharine age 17, born in Scotland, Isabella age 10, born in Scotland. Note: The census may be in error for this family. Only Alexander age 52, Donald and Roderick were listed as Indians? The place of birth may be the town of Scotland in Brant County or the country of Scotland, Thirty Third Township, Page 65/25, Numbers 38-45.

**FRASIER, DAVID:** (Indian) Age 10 born (About 1841) at Tuscarora, a member of the Church of England. Tuscarora Township, District 6, Page 11/63, Number 36. See the family of Esther Hill.

**FRASIER, JOHN:** (Indian) Age 32 born (About 1819) at Grand River, a member of the Church of England, Mrs. Frasier age 32, Isaac age 12, Frasier Male Child age 8, Frasier Female Child age 6, Frasier Female Child age 4, Tuscarora Township, District 11, Page 21/75, Numbers 17-22.

**FRASIER, JOSEPH:** (Indian) Age 50 born (About 1801) at Grand River, a member of the Church of England, William age 20 born at Grand River. Tuscarora Township, District 7, Page 13/65, Numbers 32, 33.

**FRASIER, MARY:** (Indian) Age 20 born (About 1831) at Onondaga, a member of the Church of England. Tuscarora Township, District 8, Page 15/67, Number 38.

**FRASIER, WALTER:** (Indian) Age 58, born (About 1793) at Oxbow, a member of the Church of England. Tuscarora Township, District 4, Page 7/57, Number 5.

**FROMAN, JOHN:** (Indian) Age 70 born (About 1779) in New York State (United States) a member of the Methodist Church, Jonah age 18, born at Onondaga, Susan age 15, born at Onondaga, Jacob age 13, born at Onondaga. Tuscarora Township, District 7, Page 13/65, Numbers 34-37.

**FUND (OR FUNN?) ELIZABETH:** (Indian) Age 35, born (About 1816) in Canada, a member of the Church of England, Adam age 20, Brantford Township, District 5, Page 163/6, Numbers 32, 33.

**FUND, MARGARET:** (Indian) Age 6, born (About 1845) in Canada, a member of the Church of England, Christina FUND age 4, Brantford Township, District five, Page 163/6, Numbers 35, 36. See the family of Elizabeth Fund.

**FUNN, CORNELIUS:** (Indian) Age 4 born (About 1847) at Tuscarora. Tuscarora Township, District 8, Page 15/67, Number 47. This is possibly the child of Solomon Funn on the same page.

**FUNN, FRANCIS:** (Male Indian) Age 14 born (About 1837) at Onondaga, a member of the Methodist Church. Tuscarora Township, District 7, Page 13/65, Number 26. See the family of Esther Hill on the same page.

**FUNN, JAMES:** (Indian) Age 37 born (About 1814) at Smoky Hollow, a member of the Methodist Church, Esther age 29 born at Eagles Nests, Ellen age 5 born at Tuscarora, Elizabeth age 3 born at Tuscarora. Tuscarora Township, District 17, Page 33/11, Numbers 14, 17.

**FUNN, JOSEPH:** (Indian) Age 70, born (About 1779) in New York State (United States) a member of the Methodist Church, Susan age 40 born in New York State. Tuscarora Township, District 36, Page 71/47, Numbers 49, 50.

**FUNN, JOSHUA:** (Indian) Age 13 born (About 1838) at Smoky Hollow, a member of the Methodist Church. Tuscarora Township, District 7, Page 13/65, Number 10. See the family of Arcd. Lewis.

**FUNN, LYDIA:** (Indian) Age 7 born (About 1844) at Tuscarora. Tuscarora Township, District 7, Page 13/65, Number 12.

**FUNN, SOLOMON:** (Indian) Age 30 born (About 1821) at Onondaga, a member of the Methodist Church, Kezia age 20 born at Tuscarora. Tuscarora Township, District 8, Page 15/67, Numbers 41, 42.

**GARLOUGH, ABRAM:** (Indian) Age 31 born (About 1820) in New York (United States) a member of the Methodist Church, Betsy age 35 born in Brantford, Joseph age 11 born in Brantford, Margaret age 10 born in Brantford, Anthony age 8 born in Brantford, Abram age 8 months born in Tuscarora. Tuscarora Township, District 3, Page 5/55, Numbers 35-40.

**GARLOUGH, CHRISTOPHER:** (Indian) Age 28 born (About 1823) in New York State (United States) a member of the Methodist Church, Betsy age 16 born at Tuscarora. Tuscarora Township, District 9, Page 17/69, Numbers 22, 23.

**GARLOUGH, JOHN:** (Listed as a White man?) Age 69 born (About 1782) in New York State (United States) a member of the Church of England, Sarah (Indian) age 63 born in New York State. Tuscarora Township, District 16, Page 39/7, Numbers 23/24.

**GARLOUGH, PETER:** (Indian) Age 38 born (About 1813) in New York (United States) a member of the Methodist Church, Mary age 32 born at Grand River, Peter Jr., age 4 months born at Tuscarora. Tuscarora Township, District 3, Page 5/55, Numbers 41-43.

**GARLOUGH, PHEBE:** (Indian) Age 7 born (About 1804) at Tuscarora. Tuscarora Township, District 10, Page 19/71, Number 18. See the family of Joseph Clause on the same page.

**GARLOUGH, SOLOMON:** (Indian) Age 25 born (About 1826) in New York State (United States) a member of the Church of England, Hanah age 17 born at the Bay of Quinty, Elizabeth age 2 born at Tuscarora, Benjamin age five months born at Tuscarora. Tuscarora Township, District 16, Page 39/7, Numbers 19-22.

**GEORGE, PETER:** (Indian) Age 40 born (About 1811) at Grand River, a member of the Church of England, Victoria age 36 born at Grand River, Emily age 8 born at Tuscarora, Raksaha (Male) age 6 at Tuscarora Township, Ehsaha (Female) age 4 born at Tuscarora Township, Eksaha (Female) age 2 and a half born at Tuscarora Township, Raksaka (Male) age 1 born at Tuscarora Township. Tuscarora Township, Page 65/25, Numbers 31-37.

**GENERAL, PEGGY:** (Indian) Age 3 born (About 1848) at Grand River. Tuscarora Township, District 15, Page 29/7, Number 18. See Hannah Shaw on the same page.

**GEORGE, THOMAS:** (Indian) Age 27 born (About 1824) at Oxbow, member of the Church of England, Mary age 20 born at Onondaga, a George child age 2 born at Tuscarora Township. Tuscarora Township, District 12, Page 23/1, Numbers 1, 2.

**GEORGE, WILLIAM:** (Indian) Age 20 born (About 1831) at Onondaga, Kononyadon (Female) age 18 born at New York, Jaonhhi (Female) age 12 born at Onondaga, Kanhasawakhon (Female) age 17 born at Onondaga. Tuscarora Township, District 25, Page 48/37, Numbers 13-15.

**GEVENS, JAMES:** (Indian) Age 55 born (About 1796) at Mohawk, a member of the Methodist Church, Catharine age 55 born at Oxbow, Margret age 21 born at Oxbow, David age 18 born at Onondaga. Tuscarora Township, District 2, Page 3/54? Numbers 17-20.

**GIBSON, JOHN:** (Indian) Age 25 born (About 1826) at Onondaga, a member of the Church of England, Hannah age 27 born at Buffalo (New York?) George age 2 born at Onondaga. Tuscarora Township, District 22, Page 43/43, Numbers 1-3.

**GIBSON, MARY:** (Indian) Age 39 born (About 1812) at Grand River, a member of the Church of England. Tuscarora Township, District 30, Page 59/19, Number 18.

**GIBSON, SUSANNAH:** (Indian) Age 24 born (About 1827) at Grand River, a member of the Church of England, Margaret 22, Ellen 20, Peter 18, Christiana 16, Nicholas 14, Moses 12, Mary 10, William 8, Hannah 6. Tuscarora Township, District 30, Page 59/19, Numbers 18-27.

**GONE, RUBEL:** (Indian) Age 25 born (About 1826) at Lewiston (New York?) a member of the Baptist Church, Betsy age 34 born at Tuscarora, Albert age 9 born at Tuscarora. Tuscarora Township, District 21, Page 41/41, Numbers 9-11.

**GOOSE, ABRAHAM:** (Indian) Age 21, born (About 1830) in Canada, a member of the Church of England. Tuscarora Township, District 1, Page 1/71, Number 30.

**GREEN, ABRAM:** (Indian) Age 32 born (About 1819) at Grand River, a member of the Church of England, Susan age , born at Mohawk Village, Catherine age , born at Onondaga. Tuscarora Township, District 17, Page 33/11, Numbers 7-9.

**GREEN, ABRAM? D:** (Indian) Age 35 born (About 1816) at Grand River, a member of the Church of England, Ellen age 33 born at Grand River, Betsy age 1 born at Grand River. Tuscarora Township, District 14, Page 27/3, Numbers 48-50.

**GREEN, CATHARINE:** (Indian) Age 28 born (About 1823) in Canada, a member of the Methodist Church, Daniel age 6, Tuscarora Township, District 1, Page 1/71, Numbers 34, 35.

**GREEN, ELIZABETH:** (Indian) age 55 born (About 1796) at Paris, a member of the Church of England, Aaron age 40 born at Grand River. Tuscarora Township, District 7, Page 13/65, Numbers 50, 51.

**GREEN, ESTHER:** (Indian) Age 68 born (About 1783) at Oxbow, a member of the Methodist Church, John age 28 . Tuscarora Township, District 12, Ontario, Page 23/1, Numbers 17, 18.

**GREEN, HENRY?** (Indian) Age 10 born (About 1841) at Mohawk Village, John age 3 born at Tuscarora Township. Tuscarora Township, District 13. Page 25, Numbers 7, 8. See Mary Johnson on the same page.

**GREEN, JACOB:** (Indian) Age 48 born (About 1803) at Grand River, a member of the Methodist Church, Hanah age 55 born at Bay of Quinty, Hanah age 24 born at Bay of Quinty. Tuscarora Township, District 2, Page 3/59, Numbers 35-37.

**GREEN, JOHN:** (Indian) Age 40, born (About 1811) at Onondaga, a member of the Church of England. John Jr., age 24 born at Onondaga, Elizabeth age 35 born at Onondaga, Sarah age 15 born at Onondaga. Tuscarora Township, District 3, Page 5/55, Numbers 29-32.

**GREEN, JOSEPH:** (Indian) Age 9 born (About 1842) at Johnson's Settlement, a member of the Church of England. Tuscarora Township, District 7, Page 13/65, Number 17.

**GREEN, LYDIA:** (Indian) Age 23 born (About 1828) in Canada, a member of the Methodist Church. Tuscarora Township, District 1, Page 1/71, Number 37.

**GREEN, MARY:** (Indian) Age not given, born at Onondaga, a member of the Church of England. Tuscarora Township, District 5, Page 9/61, Number 40.

**GREEN, NICHOLAS:** (Indian) Age 38 born (About 1813) at Mohawk Village, a member of the Church of England, Hanah age 21 born at New York State (United States), Isaac age 13 born at Onondaga, Abram age 3 born at Blenhiem, John age 6 months, born at Tuscarora, Nancy age 14, born at

Onondaga, Julia age 4, born at Tuscarora. Tuscarora Township, District 10, Page 19/71, Numbers 6-12.

**GREEN, PETER:** (Indian) Age 37 born (About 1814) at Hamilton City, a member of the Church of England, Margret age 24, born at Onondaga, Edward age 8, born at Onondaga, Abram age 5, born at Smoky Hollow. Tuscarora Township, District 8, Page 15/67, Numbers 34-37.

**GREEN, PETER:** (Indian) Age 25, born (About 1826) at Grand River, a member of the Church of England, Mary age 29 born at the Bay of Quinty, Lydia age 12 born at Grand River, Catharine age 7 born at Grand River, Isaac age 1 born at Grand River, Christian (A female) age 4 born at Grand River. Tuscarora Township, District 36, Page 71/47, Numbers 1-6.

**GREEN, PETER:** (Indian) Age 53, born (About 1798) at Tuscarora, a member of the Church of England, Tuscarora Township, District 5, Page 9/61, Number 15.

**GREEN, WILLIAM:** (Indian) Age 35 born (About 1816) at Onondaga, a member of the Methodist Church, Hannah age 34 born at Onondaga, Margret age 14, born at Tuscarora, Peter age 12, born at Tuscarora, Catharine age 10, born at Tuscarora, George age 8, born at Tuscarora, Kahradohon (Male) age 5 born at Tuscarora, Dehratye (Male) age one and a half, born at Tuscarora. Tuscarora Township, District 26, Page 51/29, Numbers 37-44.

**GREEN, WILLIAM:** (Indian) Age 30, born (About 1821) at Onondaga, a member of the Church of England, Betsey age 29 born at Cayuga Village, Eliza age 11 born at Onondaga, Daniel age 7 born at Tuscarora, George age 3 born at Tuscarora, Susan age three months born at Tuscarora, Mary age 9 born at Tuscarora. Tuscarora Township, District 6, Page 11/63, Numbers 7-13.

**GREEN, WILLIAM:** (Indian) Age 21, born (About 1830) in Canada, single, a member of the Church of England, residence listed as Onondaga. Brantford, District Five, Page 215/32.

**GREEN, WILLIAM:** (Indian) Age 37, born (About 1814) at Canada West, a member of the Baptist Church, Elizabeth age 37, Nancy age 22, Onondaga Township Part 11, Page 37, Numbers 25, 26, 27.

**GROAT, JOHN:** (Indian) Age 38 born (About 1813) at Ancaster, a member of the Methodist Church, Hannah age 40 born at Brantford. Tuscarora Township, District 20, Page 39/39, Numbers 16, 17.

**HAHONTYOKDEN:** (Female Indian) Age three months born at Tuscarora. Tuscarora Township, District 25, Page 49/37, Number 49. See the family of Onakwadekha or Shahokenyatha she may have been the mother of the this child.

**HALFADAY, JOHN:** (Indian) Age 42 born (About 1809) at Credit River, a member of the Methodist Church, Adam age 8 born at Credit River, Mary age 10 born at Credit River. (Credit Indians) Tuscarora Township, District 35, Page 69/17, Numbers 34-36.

**HARIS? JOSEPH:** (Indian) Age 2 born (About 1849) at Tuscarora. Tuscarora Township, District 20, Page 39/39, Number 51. See Six Does on the same page this may be her child.

**HARRIS, CATHERINE:** (Indian) Age 18 born (About 1833) at Brantford, a member of the Church of England. Tuscarora Township, District 26, Page 51/29, Number 1.

**HARRIS, CHRISTIANA:** (Indian) Age 52 born (About 1799) at Oxbow, a member of the Methodist Church. Tuscarora Township, District 6, Page 11/63, Number 16.

**HARRIS, ESTHER:** (Indian) Age 7 born (About 1844) at Grand River, Nancy age 4. Tuscarora Township, District 19, Page 37/51, Number 51. See the family Jemima Hill? or Harris? on the same page.

**HARRIS, ISABELLA:** (Indian) Age 18 (About 1833) born at Tronto Township, a member of the Methodist Church. Tuscarora Township, District 35, Page 69/17, Number 12.

**HARRIS, JOSEPH:** (Indian) Age 35 born (About 1816) at Ancaster, a member of the Methodist Church. (Credit Indian) Tuscarora Township, District 35, Page 69/17, number 11.

**HENDAWAH:** (Male Indian) Age 27 born (About 1824) at Indiana. Tuscarora Township, District 25, Page 49/37, Number 47.

**HENHAWK, CHILDREN:** (Indians) Male Henhawk child age 6 born (About 1845) at Tuscarora, Male Henhawk child age 4, born at Tuscarora, Female Henhawk child age 2 born at Tuscarora. Tuscarora Township, District 8, Page 15/67, Numbers 5-7. These are possibly the children of Thomas Henhawk on the same page.

**HENHAWK, NANCY:** (Indian) Age 17 born (About 1834) in Canada, a member of the Church of England, Brantford Township, District 5, Page 183/16, Number 45.

**HENHAWK, THOMAS:** (Indian) Age 30 born (About 1821) at Grand River, a member of the Church of England, Jane age 26 born at Grand River. Tuscarora Township, District 8, Page 15/67, Numbers 1, 2.

**HENRY, ADAM:** (Indian) Age 23 born (About 1828) in Canada, a member of the Church of England, Elizabeth age 16, David age 1. Brantford Township, District five, Page 183/16, Numbers 42-44.

**HENRY, HANAH:** (Indian) Age 17? or 12? born at Credit River, a member of the Methodist Church (Credit Indian) Tuscarora Township, District 28, Page 55/33, Number 2. See Elizabeth Jackson.

**HENRY, JACOB:** (Indian) Age 35 born (About 1816) at Brantford, Mrs. Henry age 40 born at Tuscarora, Kanenoha age 6, born at Tuscarora, Shadekarenhes age 4, born at Tuscarora, Kawennaji (Male) age 2 born at Tuscarora. Tuscarora Township, District 23, Page 45/45, Numbers 39/43.

**HENRY, JOHN:** (Indian) Age 14 born (About 1837) at Smoky Hollow, a member of the Methodist Church, Tuscarora Township, District 2, Page 3/59, Number 23. See the family of James Gevens.

**HENRY, JOSEPH:** (Indian) Age 30 born (About 1821) at Brantford, Deyoah (Female) age 20 born at Onondaga, Kayonwade (Female) age 5 born at Tuscarora, Kawinnade (Female) age 2 born at Tuscarora. Tuscarora Township, District 18, Page 35/49, Numbers 40-43.

**HENRY, SALLY:** (Indian) Age 79 born (About 1771) in Upper Canada (Ontario) a member of the Methodist Church. (Credit Indian) Tuscarora Township, District 35, Page 69/17, Number 15.

**HEREN, JOHN:** (Indian) Age 52 born (About 1799) at Onondaga, a member of the Methodist Church, Hanah age 46, born at Martin's Settlement. Tuscarora Township, District 8, Page 15/67, Numbers 39, 40.

**HEREN, MARGRET:** (Indian) Age 18 born (About 1833) at Tuscarora, a member of the Methodist Church, Moses age 14, born at Tuscarora, Elizabeth age 10, born at Tuscarora, Isaac age 8, born at Tuscarora. Tuscarora Township, District 8, Page 15/67, Numbers 43-46. These are possibly the children of John Heren on the same page.

**HERKIMER, CHARLES:** (Indian) Age 26 born (About 1825) at Credit River, a member of the Methodist Church, Christian (Female) age 22 born at Credit River. (Credit Indians) Tuscarora Township, District 35, Page 69/17, Numbers 30, 31.

**HERKIMER, EDWARD:** (Indian) Age 23 born (About 1828) at Credit River, a member of the Methodist Church, Sally age 22 born at Onondaga. (Credit Indians) Tuscarora Township, District 27, Page 53/31, Numbers 1, 2.

**HERKIMER, GEORGE:** (Indian) Age 32 born (About 1819) at Credit River, a member of the Methodist Church, Charlotte age 18 born at Credit River. Tuscarora Township, Page 65/25, Numbers 14, 15.

**HERKIMER, LAWRENCE:** (Indian) Age 58 born (About 1793) at Credit River, a member of the Methodist Church, David age 10 born at Credit River. (Credit Indians) Tuscarora Township, District 27, Page 53/31, Numbers 3, 4.

**HERKIMER, WILLIAM:** (Indian Minister) Age 52 born (About 1799) at Credit River, a member of the Methodist Church, Betsy age 50 born at Credit River. (Credit Indians) Tuscarora Township, District 27, Page 53/31, Numbers 34, 35.

**HESS, ISAAC:** (Indian) age 35, born (About 1816) at Grand River, a member of the Methodist Church, Mary age 26, born at Grand River, David age 8, born at Grand River, Female HESS child age 6, Male HESS child age 4. Tuscarora Township, District 8, Page 15/67, Numbers 10-14.

**HESS, JOB:** (Indian) Age 20 born (About 1831) in Canada, a member of the Methodist Church, Abigale age 17 born in Canada, Eliza age 13 born in Canada, William age 9 born in Canada. Tuscarora Township, District 1, Page 1/71, Numbers 38-41.

**HESS, JOSEPH:** (Indian) Age 60, born (About 1791) at Oxbow, a member of the Methodist Church, Elector (Female) age 40, born in New York State (United States). Tuscarora Township, District 9, Page 17/69, Numbers 1, 2.

**HESS, MARGRET:** (Indian) Age 6 born (About 1845) at Tuscarora, John age 4, born at Tuscarora, Enoch age 2, born at Tuscarora, Sarah age ten months, born at Tuscarora. Tuscarora Township, District 8, Page 15/67, Numbers 19-22. These are possibly the children of Sampson Hess Jr., on the same page.

**HESS, NELSON:** (Indian) Age 30 born (About 1821) at Grand River, a member of the Church of England. Tuscarora Township, District 8, Page 15/67, Number 3.

**HESS, PETER:** (Indian) Age 60 born (About 1791) at Grand River, a member of the Methodist Church, Sarah age 50. Tuscarora Township, District 8, Page 15/67, Numbers 8, 9.

**HESS, SAMPSON JR:** (Indian) Age 32 born (About 1819) at Onondaga, a member of the Methodist Church, Mary age 33, born at Eagle's Nest. Tuscarora Township, District 8, Page 15/67, Numbers 15, 16.

**HESS, SAMPSON:** (Indian) Age 53 born (About 1798) in Canada, a member of the Methodist Church, Susanah age 49. Tuscarora Township, District 1, Page 1/71, Numbers 32, 33.

**HESS, SIMEON:** (Indian) Age four months? born at Tuscarora. Tuscarora Township, District 9, Page 17/69, Number 7. This is possibly the child of Joseph Hess on the same page.

**HILL, ABRAHAM:** (Indian) Age 40, born (About 1811) at Tuscarora, a member of the Church of England, Margret age 38, born in Onondaga, Augustus age 5, born in Tuscarora, Moses age 16 born in Tuscarora, Tuscarora Township, District 32, Page 63/23, Numbers 32-35.

**HILL, ABRAHAM:** (Indian) Age 10 born (About 1811) at Tuscarora, Thomas age 19 born at the Bay of Quinty. Tuscarora Township, District 9, Page 17/69, Numbers 44, 45. See the family of William Hill on the same page.

**HILL, AUGUSTUS:** (Indian) Age 24 born (About 1827) at Grand River, a member of the Church of England, Ellen age 25 born at Grand River, Abram age 4 born at Tuscarora. Tuscarora Township, District 8, Numbers 48-50.

**HILL, BETSEY:** (Indian) Age 15 born (About 1816) at Brantford Township, a member of the Church of England. Tuscarora Township, District 17, Page 33/11, Number 41.

**HILL, BETSEY:** (Indian) Age 6 born (About 1845) at Grand River, a member of the Church of England. Tuscarora Township, District 16, Page 39/7, Number 18.

**HILL, CATHARINE:** (Indian) Age 35 born (About 1816) at Onondaga, a member of the Church of England. Tuscarora Township, District 3, Page 5/55, Number 44.

**HILL, CATHERINE:** (Indian) Age 19 born (About 1832) in New York State (In the United States) a member of the Church of England, Mary Hill age four months born at Tuscarora. Tuscarora Township, District 17, Page 33/11, Numbers 3, 4.

**HILL, CATHERINE:** (Indian) Age 2 months, born at Tuscarora, John age 1, born at Tuscarora, Ellen age 19 months, born at Tuscarora. Tuscarora Township, District 10, Page 19/71, Numbers 1-3. These are possibly the children of Jacob Hill number 49 on the previous page.

**HILL, CATHERINE:** (Indian) Age 35 born (About 1816) at the Bay of Quinty, a member of the Methodist Church. Tuscarora Township, District 16, Page 39/7, Number 41.

**HILL, CATHERINE:** (Indian) Age 56 born (About 1795) in New York State (In the United States) a member of the Church of England. Tuscarora Township, District 11, Page 23/1, Number 42.

**HILL, CHARLOTTE:** (Indian) Age 10, born (About 1811) at Tuscarora, a member of the Church of England. Tuscarora Township, District 5, Page 9/61, Number 43.

**HILL, DAVID:** (Indian) Age 44, born (About 1807) at Tuscarora, a member of the Baptist Church, Catharine age 44 born at Onondaga, Susanah age 20 born at Tuscarora, Joseph age 15 born at Tuscarora, Simon age 13 born at Tuscarora, Moses age 10 born at Tuscarora, Jane age 8 born at Tuscarora, Alexander age 5 born at Tuscarora, Mary age 2 born at Tuscarora. Tuscarora Township, District 4, Page 7/57, Numbers 48-50. This family is extended to the top of the next census page. The page number is 9/61. Numbers 1-6 enumerates Joseph, Simon, Moses, Jane, Alexander and Mary Hill.

**HILL, DAVID:** (Indian) Age 50 born (About 1801) in Upper Canada (Ontario), a member of the Church of England, Eve age 48 born in Upper Canada, Nicolas age 10 born at Brantford Township, Elijah age 13 born at Tuscarora, George age 11 born at Tuscarora, Elizabeth age 5 born at Tuscarora, Mary age 3 born at Tuscarora. Tuscarora Township, District 17, Page 33/11, Numbers 28-34.

**HILL, DAVID:** (Indian) Age 45 born (About 1806) at Mohawk Village, a member of the Methodist Church, Catherine age 50. Tuscarora Township, District 17, Page 33/11, Numbers 45, 46.

**HILL, ELIZABETH:** (Indian) Age 10 born (About 1811) at Tuscarora, a member of the Church of England, Lucy age 8 born in Tuscarora Township, John Hill age seven months born at Tuscarora. District 3, Tuscarora Township, Brant County, Ontario, Page 5/55, Numbers 49, 50. John HILL was listed on the top of the next census page but was not enumerated as an Indian? See: Page Number 7/57, Number 1.

**HILL, ELLEN:** (Indian) Age 46 born (About 1805) at Johnson's Settlement, a member of the Church of England, Aaron age 21 born at

Brantford Township, Squire? age 19 born at Brantford, Peter age 15 born at Onondaga, Isaac age 4 born age Tuscarora. Tuscarora Township, District 13, Page 25, Numbers 26-30.

**HILL, ESTHER:** (Indian) Age 40 born (About 1811) at Onondaga, a member of the Methodist Church, Tuscarora Township, District 7, Page 13/65, Number 25.

**HILL, ESTHER:** (Indian) Age 57 born (About 1794) at Mohawk Village, a member of the Church of England, Aaron age 40 born at Brantford Township, Jacob age 28 born at Brantford Township, John age 19 born at Mohawk Village. Tuscarora Township, District 6, Page 11/63, Numbers 32-35.

**HILL, HANNAH:** (Indian) Age 38 born (About 1813) at Onondaga, a member of the Church of England. Tuscarora Township, District 26, Page 51/29, Number 19.

**HILL, ISAAC:** (Indian) Age 35 born (About 1816) at Oxbow, a member of the Church of England, Susannah age 30 born at Onondaga, Abigail age 10 born at Onondaga, Cojnus? (Male) age 8 born at Onondaga. Tuscarora Township, District 18, Page 35/49, Numbers 26-29.

**HILL, ISAAC:** (Indian) Age 57 born (About 1794) at Lower Canada (Quebec) age member of the Church of England, Susanah age 65 born in Ohio State (United States) Joseph age 21 born at Tuscarora, Catharine age 20 born at Brantford, Kadenhes (Female) age 3 born at Tuscarora. Tuscarora Township, District 26, Page 51/29, Numbers 20-24.

**HILL, ISAAC:** (Indian) Age 29 born (About 1822) at the Bay of Quinty, a member of the Methodist Church, Betsey age 15 born at Tuscarora. Tuscarora Township, District 10, Page 19/71, Numbers 4, 5 on the page.

**HILL, ISAAC:** (Indian) Age 34 born (About 1817) at Grand River, a member of the Church of England Mary age 30, Job age 10, Christiana age 7, Nancy age 5, Catherine age 3. Tuscarora Township, District 30, Page 59/19, Numbers 7-12.

**HILL, ISAAC:** (Indian) Age 20 born (About 1831) at Brantford. A member of the Methodist Church. Tuscarora Township, District 11, Page 21/75? Number 8.

**HILL, ISAIAH:** (Indian) Age 8 born (About 1843) at Grand River, a member of the Church of England, Isaac Hill age 5 born, Sarah Hill age 3. Tuscarora Township, Page 29/7, Numbers 45-47. See Mary Martin on the same page.

**HILL, JACOB SENR:** (Indian) Age 56 born (About 1795) in New York State (In the United States) a member of the Church of England, Jacob Hill Jr., age 23 born in Brantford Township, Tuscarora Township, District 12, Page 23/1, Numbers 40, 41.

**HILL, JACOB:** (Indian) Age 48 born (About 1803) at the Bay of Quinty, a member of the Methodist Church, Dorothy age 36, born in New York State, Charlotte age 15, born at Onondaga. Tuscarora Township, District 6, Page 11/63, Numbers 39-41.

**HILL, JACOB:** (Indian) Age 26 born (About 1825) at Indiana, a member of the Methodist Church, Magdelene age 23 born at Onondaga, Alexander age 6 born at Tuscarora, Lucy age 4 born at Tuscarora, Isaac age 2 born at Tuscarora. Tuscarora Township, District 23, Page 45/45, Numbers 5-9.

**HILL, JACOB:** (Indian) Age 27 born (About 1824) in New York (In the United States), a member of the Church of England, Hanah age 24 born at Cayuga Village. Tuscarora Township, District 13, Page 25, Numbers 10, 11.

**HILL, JACOB:** (Indian) Age 27 born (About 1824) at the Bay of Quinty, a member of the Methodist Church, Elizabeth age 23, born at the Bay of Quinty. Tuscarora Township, District 9, Page 17/69, Numbers 49, 50.

**HILL, JOHN:** (Indian) Age 27 born (About 1824) at Johnson's Settlement, a member of the Church of England, Lucy age 15 born at Onondaga, Samuel age 2 born at Tuscarora. Tuscarora Township, District 13, Page 25, Numbers 35-37.

**HILL, JOHN:** (Indian) Age 45 born (About 1806) at Onondaga, a member of the Methodist Church, Mary age 40 born at Onondaga, Israel age 21, born at Onondaga, Mary age 18, born at Onondaga, Margret age 15, born at Onondaga, Jemima age 10 born at Tuscarora, Hanah age 13 and a half born at Tuscarora, George age 1 born at Tuscarora, William age 9 born at Tuscarora, Joseph age 5 born at Tuscarora, Sarah age 12 born at Tuscarora, Catharine age 65 born at Tuscarora. Tuscarora Township, District 14, Page 27/3, Numbers 7-18.

**HILL, JOHN:** (Indian) Age 16 born (About 1835) at Johnson's Settlement, a member of the Church of England, Sarah Hill 13 born at Tuscarora. Tuscarora Township, District 17, Page 33/11, Numbers 1, 2.

**HILL, JOHN:** (Indian) Age 37 born (About 1814) at Brantford, a member of the Church of England, Lydia age 36 (Lydia was not listed as an Indian but she was counted as one) born at Brantford, John age 13, born at Mohawk Village, Joseph age 11, born at Salt Springs, Catharine age 9, born at Salt Springs, Susan age 7, born at Salt Springs, William age 5, born at Salt Springs, Isaac age 3, born at Salt Springs, James age ten months, born at Salt Springs. Tuscarora Township, District 7, Page 13/65, Numbers 39-47.

**HILL, JOHN:** (Indian) Age 80 born (About 1771) at Buffalo (New York?) a member of the Church of England, Catherine age 60, born at Montrel (Montreal?) Henry age 18, born at Onondaga, Moses age 17, born at Onondaga, Rakahsgontyon (Male) age 17. Tuscarora Township, District 20, Page 39/39, Numbers 24-28.

**HILL, JOHN:** (Indian) Age 52 born (About 1799) at Grand River, a member of the Church of England, Mary age 55. Tuscarora Township, District 11, Page 21/75? Numbers 38, 39.

**HILL, JOHN:** (Indian) Age 29 born (About 1822) in Canada West, a member of the Baptist Church, Jacob age 35, Elizabeth age 33, Nancy age 9, Margaret age 7, Samuel age 2. Onondaga Township, Part 11, Page 35, Numbers 21-26.

**HILL, JOHN:** (Indian) Age 7 mo. born in Tuscarora (Township?). He was a member of the Church of England. District 4, Tuscarora Township, Brant county, Ontario. Page 7.57, Number 1.

**HILL, JOSEPH:** (Indian) Age 29 born (About 1822) at Mohawk Village, a member of the Methodist Church, Jane age not given, born at Onondaga, Mary age 2 born at Tuscarora. Tuscarora Township, District 17, Page 33/11, Numbers 48-50.

**HILL, JOSEPH:** (Indian) Age 20 born (About 1831) at Grand River, a member of the Church of England, Mary age 19, Nancy age 11, John age 4. Tuscarora Township, District 19, Page 37/51, Numbers 47-50.

**HILL, JOSEPH:** (Indian) Age 15, (Born about 1836) Simon age 13, Moses age 18, Jane age 5, Alexander age 2. All were born in Tuscarora (Township?). All were listed as Baptist. District 5, Tuscarora Township, Brant County, Ontario, Page 9/61, Numbers on the Page 1-6.

**HILL, JOSEPH:** (Indian) Age 33 born (About 1818) at Oxbow, a member of the Methodist Church, Mary age 30 born at Oxbow, Marget age 9 born at Oxbow, Betsy age 5 born at Tuscarora, Joseph age 3 born at Tuscarora, George age 8 months born at Tuscarora. Tuscarora Township, District 12, Page 23/1, Numbers 24-29.

**HILL, JULIA:** (Indian) Age 44 born (About 1807) at Grand River, David age 23 born at Grand River. Members of the Church of England. Tuscarora Township, Fourteenth Township, Page 27/3, Numbers 35, 36.

**HILL, MAGDALEN:** (Indian) Age 72 born (About 1779) in Lower Canada (Quebec), a member of the Church of England. Tuscarora Township, District 30, Page 59/19, Number 19.

**HILL, MARY:** (Indian) Age 47 born (About 1804) at Grand River, a member of the Church of England. Tuscarora Township, District 13, Page 25, Number 33.

**HILL, MARY:** (Indian) Age 21 born (About 1830) at Grand River, a member of the Church of England. Tuscarora Township, District 30, Page 59/19, Number 6.

**HILL, MARY:** (Indian) Age 40, born (About 1811) in Canada West, a member of the Church of England. Onondaga Township, Part 11, Page 35, Number 4.

**HILL, MUDTURTLE:** (Male Indian) Age 36 (About 1815) born at Onondaga, a member of the Church of England, Caty age 34, born at Onondaga, Isaac age 17, born at Onondaga, Thomas age 15, born at Onondaga, Ellen age 7, born at Onondaga, Betsey age 1, born at Onondaga. Tuscarora Township, District 24, Page 47/35, Numbers 39-44.

**HILL, NICOLAS:** (Indian) Age 36 born at Onondaga, a member of the Church of England, Christiana age 36 born at Onondaga. Tuscarora Township, District 26, Page 51/29, Numbers 17, 18.

**HILL, PETER:** (Indian) Age 7 born at Tuscarora. Tuscarora Township, District 9, Page 17/69, Number 6. This is possibly the child of Augustus HILL.

**HILL, PETER:** (Indian) Age 8 born at Grand River. Tuscarora Township, District 16, Page 39/7, Number 40.

**HILL, SALLY:** (Indian) Age 20, born (About 1831) in Canada West, Levi? age 18, Mary age 16, Norris age 12, Susan age 9, Ellen age 6, Eliza age 1. Onondaga Township, Part 11, Page 35, Numbers 7-13.

**HILL, SARAH:** (Indian) Age 25 born at Whiteman's Creek, a member of the Church of England. Tuscarora Township, District 7, Page 13/65, Number 30.

**HILL, SARAH:** (Indian) Age 13, born at Tuscarora, a member of the Church of England. Tuscarora Township, District 3, Page 5/55, Number 28.

**HILL, SARAH:** (Indian) Age 18 born at Onondaga Township, a member of the Church of England, Lucy age 11 born at Tuscarora. Tuscarora Township, District 12. Page 23/1, Numbers 45, 46. These are possibly the children of Betsy Turkey or Susanah Maricle on the same page.

**HILL, WILLIAM:** (Indian) Age 50 born at the Bay of Quinty, a member of the Methodist Church, Lenah (Female) age 52, born at Bay of Quinty, Nelly age 30, born at Bay of Quinty. Tuscarora Township, District 9, Page 17/69, Numbers 40-42.

**HILL, WILLIAM:** (Indian) Age 32 born at Brantford Township, a member of the Church of England. Tuscarora Township, District 12, Page 23/1, Number 39.

**HILL, WILLIAM:** (Indian) Age 50 born at Grand River, a member of the Church of England, Lydia age 50, born at Grand River. Tuscarora Township, District 17, Page 33/11, Numbers 5, 6.

**HILL, WILLIAM:** (Indian) Age 28 born (About 1823) at Grand River, a member of the Church of England, Magdalene age 25 born at Grand River, John age 4, born at Grand River, Catharine age 1 born at Grand River. Tuscarora Township, District 14, Page 27/3, Numbers 31-34.

**HILL, WILLIAM:** (Indian) Age 14 born (About 1837) at Grand River, a member of the Church of England. Tuscarora Township, District 16, Page 39/7, Number 49.

**HILL? (OR HARRIS?) JEMIMA:** (Indian) Age 41 born (About 1810) in New York State (In the United States) a member of the Church of England. Tuscarora Township, District 19, Page 37/51, Number 46.

**HOBKINS, SARAH:** (Indian) Age 48 born (About 1803) at Tuscarora Township, a member of the Methodist Church (Credit Indians) Tuscarora Township, District 27, Page 53/31, Number 44.

**HOTTENBURG, JAMES:** (Indian) Age 25 born (About 1826) at Grand River, a member of the Church of England, Mrs. HOTTENBURG age 24, Miss HOTTENBURG age 4. Tuscarora Township, District 19, Page 37/51, Numbers 34-36.

**HOUSE, ESTHER:** (Indian) Age 11 born (About 1840) at Green Bay (Wisconsin?). Tuscarora Township, District 24, Page 47/35, Number 48. See the family of John Bompary on the same page.

**HOUSE, JOHN:** (Indian) Age 15 born (About 1836) at Grand River a member of the Church of England. Tuscarora Township, District 10, Page 19/71, Number 39.

**ISAAC, JACOB:** (Indian) Age 37 born (About 1814) at Onondaga, a member of the Methodist Church, Hannah age 36 born at Onondaga, Peggy age 7 born at Tuscarora, Mary age 4 born at Tuscarora. Tuscarora Township, District 23, Page 45/45, Numbers 13-16.

**ISAAC, MAGDELINE:** (Indian) Age 50 born (About 1801) at Onondaga, a member of the Methodist Church, Abraham age 19 born at Onondaga, Eliza age 8 born at Tuscarora. Tuscarora Township, District 23, Page 45/45, Numbers 10-12.

**ISAAC, NICHOLAS:** (Indian) Age 40 born (About 1811) at Onondaga. Tuscarora Township, District 20, Page 39/ 39, Number 18.

**ISAACS, JACOB:** (Indian) Age 60 born (About 1791) at Mohawk, a member of the Methodist Church, Sarah age 15, born at Brantford, Joseph age 12, born at Onondaga. Tuscarora Township, District 2, Page 3/59, Number 50 on the page 3/59 continued to Page 5/55, Numbers 1, 2.

**ISAACS, LEWIS:** (Indian) Age 24 born (About 1827) at Onondaga, a member of the Church of England, Lydia age 17, born at Tuscarora, Cyrous age 1, born at Tuscarora. Tuscarora Township, District Seven, Page 13/65, Numbers 5-7.

**ISAACS, SARAH:** (Indian) Age 40, born (About 1811) at Brantford (Township?) age 40, Joseph age 15, born in Onondaga (Township?). Both were members of the Methodist Church. District 3, Tuscarora Township, Brant county, Ontario, Page 5/55, Numbers 1, 2.

**JACK, JOHN:** (Indian) Age 22 born (About 1829) at Buffalo (New York?) a member of the Church of England, Hannah age 18 born at Seneca, Skarihwaksen (Male) age 4 born at Buffalo, Kayesonnihtha (female) Age 2 born at Tuscarora. Tuscarora Township, District 22, Page 43/43, Numbers 5-8.

**JACKSON, ALEXANDER:** (Indian) Age 40 born (About 1811) at Credit River, a member of the Methodist Church, Betsy age 38, Peter age 21 (Credit Indians) Tuscarora Township, District 28, Page 55/33, Numbers 3-5.

**JACKSON, ELIZABETH:** (Indian) Age 40 born (About 1811) at Credit River, a member of the Methodist Church (Credit Indian) Tuscarora Township, District 28, Page 55/33, Number 1.

**JACKSON, HENRY:** (Indian Interpreter) Age 30 born (About 1821) at Credit River, a member of the Methodist Church, Elizabeth age 18, born at Credit River. (Credit River Indians) Tuscarora Township District 27, Page 53/31, Numbers 36, 37.

**JACKSON, JACOB:** (Indian Teacher) Age 38 born (About 1813) at Credit River, a member of the Methodist Church, Betsy age 41 born at Credit River, John age 15 born at Credit River, Charlotte age 13 born at Credit River, Elizabeth age 5 born at Tuscarora, Catharine age 2 born at Tuscarora. (Credit Indians) Tuscarora Township, District 27, Page 53/31, Numbers 38-43.

**JACKSON, JOHN JR:** (Indian Lawyer) Age 32 born (About 1819) at Credit River, a member of the Methodist Church, Mary age 18 born at Credit River. (Credit Indians) Tuscarora Township, District 28, Page 55/33, Numbers 11, 12.

**JACKSON, JOHN:** (Indian) Age 44 born (About 1807) at Credit River, a member of the Methodist Church, Catharine age 44 born at Credit River. (Credit Indians) Tuscarora Township, District 35, Page 69/17, Numbers 32,33.

**JACOB, WILLIAM:** (Indian) Age 40, born (About 1811) at Indiana, a member of the Church of England. Tuscarora Township, District 32, Page 63/23, Number 13.

**JACOBS, SOLOMON:** (Indian) Age 18 born (About 1833) at Grand River, a member of the Church of England, Kayashinase (Female) age 5, Karahonde (Male) age 3. Tuscarora Township, District 15, Page 29/7, Numbers 23-26.

**JAMIESON, DAVID:** (Indian) Age not given, born at Grand River, a member of the Church of England, Susanah age 30. Tuscarora Township, District 15, Page 29/7, Numbers 36, 37.

**JAMIESON, JAMES:** (Indian) Age 68 born (About 1783) at Grand River, a member of the Church of England, Mrs. Jamieson age 42, Albert? (Male) age 20, Betsy age 22, George age 10. Tuscarora Township, District 30, Page 59/19, Numbers 13-17.

**JAMIESON, WILLIAM:** (Indian) Age 31 born (About 1820) at Grand River, a member of the Methodist Church, Catherine age 27, Augustus age 7, Lawrence age 4, Julia age 1. Tuscarora Township, District 36, Page 71/47, Numbers 24-28.

**JAMIESON, WILSON:** (Indian) Age 1 born (About 1850) at Grand River, Eunice JAMIESON age 1 born at Grand River. Tuscarora Township, District 15, Page 29/7, Numbers 39, 40. See David Jamieson on the same page.

**JOHN, BETSEY:** (Indian) Age 15 born (About 1836) at Grand River, a member of the Methodist Church. Tuscarora Township, District 15, Page 29/7, Number 12.

**JOHN, CATHARINE:** (Indian) Age 59, born (About 1792) in Canada. She was a member of the Church of England. Brantford Township, Fifth Ward, Page 159/4, Number 48.

**JOHN, CATHERINE:** (Indian) Age 18 born (About 1833) at Grand River, a member of the Methodist Church, Alexander Joseph age 6 months born at

Grand River. Tuscarora Township, District 15, Page 29/7, Numbers 19, 20.

**JOHN, DAVID:** (Indian) Age 44 born (About 1807) in Lower Canada (Quebec) a member of the Baptist Church, Mary age 44 born at Buffalo (New York?) Moses age 22, born at Buffalo, Mary age 19, born at Buffalo, Nicholas age 16, born at Buffalo, John age 15, born at Onondaga, Isaac age 13, born at Onondaga, Peter age 10, born at Onondaga, Ellen age 7, born at Onondaga, Margret age 4, born at Onondaga, David age six months, born at Onondaga, John age 8, born at Onondaga, Mary age 11, born at Onondaga. Tuscarora Township, District 24, Page 47/35, Numbers 20-32.

**JOHN, HANNAH:** (Indian) Age 1 born (About 1850) at Grand River. Tuscarora Township, District 24, Page 47/35, Number 19.

**JOHN, JOSEPH:** (Indian) Age 59 born (About 1792) at Grand River, a member of the Methodist Church, Margret age 54. Tuscarora Township, District 14, Page 29/7, Numbers 9, 10.

**JOHN, JOSEPH:** (Indian) Age 34 born (About 1817) in New York State (In the United States) a member of the Church of England. Tuscarora Township, District 7, Page 13/65, Number 29.

**JOHN, LUCY:** (Indian) Age 3, born (About 1848) at Tuscarora, Tuscarora Township, District 4, Page 7/57, Number 39. See the family of Peter Fishcarryer.

**JOHN, RACHEL:** (Indian) Age 13 born (About 1838) at Grand River, Tuscarora Township, District 15, Page 29/7, Number 14.

**JOHN, WILLIAM:** (Indian) Age 32, born (About 1819) in Canada, a member of the Church of England, Mary 39, Elizabeth age 11, Catharine age 5. Township of Brantford, District 5, Page 185/17, Numbers 46-50.

**JOHNS, POLLY:** (Indian) Age 64 born (About 1787) at Credit River, a member of the Methodist Church. Credit Indian, Tuscarora Township, District 28, Page 55/33, Number 20.

**JOHNS, WILLIAM:** (Indian) Age 50 born (About 1801) at Credit River, a member of the Methodist Church, Betsy age 42 born at Credit River, William age 20 born at Credit River, Sarah age 27 born at Credit River, Joshua age 18 born at Credit River, Zachariah age 14 born at Credit River, George Wesly age 2 born at Tuscarora Township. (Credit Indians) Tuscarora Township, District 28, Page 55/33, Numbers 13-19.

**JOHNSON, ABRAIM:** (Indian) Age 26 born (About 1825) at Johnson's Settlement, a member of the Church of England, Jacob age 20, born at Johnson's Settlement, Seth age 10, born at Onondaga, Hiram age 8, born at Onondaga. Tuscarora Township, District 6, Page 11/63, Numbers 1-4.

**JOHNSON, CATHARINE:** (Indian) Age 45, born (About 1806) at Johnson's Settlement, a member of the Church of England. Elizabeth age 22 born at Johnson's Settlement, Mary age 15, born at Johnson's Settlement. Tuscarora Township, District 5, Page 9/61, Numbers 48-50.

**JOHNSON, CHRISTIAN:** (Female Indian) Age 8 born (About 1843) at Mohawk. Tuscarora Township, District 13, Page 25, Number 9.

**JOHNSON, ELIJAH:** (Indian) Age 36 born (About 1815) at Grand River, a member of the Church of England, Hanah? age 36 born at Grand River, Isaac age 9 born at Tuscarora, Jacob age 5 born at Tuscarora, Mary age 2 born at Tuscarora. Tuscarora Township, District 14, Page 27/3, Numbers 19-23.

**JOHNSON, GEORGE M:** (Indian) Age 35 born (About 1816) in Canada West, a member of the Church of England. He was listed as a Clergyman. The household next to his was occupied by Reverend Adam ELLIOT (White) age 49, a clergyman born in England, a member of the Church of England, Mary ELLIOT (White) age 11, born in Canada West. Onondaga Township, Part 11, District 2, Numbers 22-24.

**JOHNSON, JACOB JR:** (Indian) Age 28 born (About 1823) in Canada, a member of the Church of England, Eliza (A white woman) age 27 born Canada, Sarah age 4, Nancy age 2 born Oneida. Brantford Township, Fifth Ward, Page 163/6. Numbers 37-40.

**JOHNSON, JACOB:** (Indian) Age 64, born (About 1787) in Canada, a member of the Church of England, Elizabeth age 49, Mary age 19, Susanah age 11, Nicolas age 20, Catherine age 18, Brantford Township, Fifth Ward, Page 163/6. Number 25-30.

**JOHNSON, JACOB:** (Indian) Age 26 born (About 1825) at Grand River, a member of the Church of England, Betsy age 24, Johnson male child age 6, Johnson male child age 4. Tuscarora Township, District 11, Page 21/75? Numbers 41-44.

**JOHNSON, JACOB:** (Indian) Age 30 born (About 1821) at Credit River, a member of the Methodist Church, Marian (Female) age 40 born at Credit River. Tuscarora Township, District 34, Page 67/53, Numbers 39, 40.

**JOHNSON, JAMES:** (Indian) Age 88? or 48? born (About 1763? or 1803?) at Credit River, a member of the Methodist Church, Lucy age 38 born at Credit River, William age 1 born at Tuscarora Township. Tuscarora Township, District 33, Page 65/25, Numbers 8, 9.

**JOHNSON, JOEL:** (Indian) Age 13 born (About 1838) at Johnson's Settlement, a member of the Church of England. Tuscarora Township, District 2, Page 3/59, Number 41. See the family of Joel Smith.

**JOHNSON, JOHN:** (Indian) Age 30 born (About 1821) at Credit River, a member of the Methodist Church, Mary age 35 born at Credit River. Tuscarora Township, District 34, Page 67/53, Number 1, 2 on the page.

**JOHNSON, MARY:** (Indian) Age 43 born (About 1808) at Mohawk Village, a member of the Church of England. Tuscarora Township, District 13, Page 25, Number 6.

**JOHNSON, THOMAS:** (Indian) Age 26 born (About 1825) in New York State, (In the United States) a member of the Baptist Church, Hanah age 28 born at Tuscarora, Cyrus age 6 born at Tuscarora, Eliza age 3, born at

Tuscarora Township. Tuscarora Township, District 31, Page 61/21, Number 17-20.

**JOHNSON, THOMAS:** (Indian) Age 10, born (About 1841) at Credit River. a member of the Methodist Church, Tuscarora Township, District 34, Page 67/53, Number 23. See the family of James Keshego on the same page.

**JOHNSON, WILLIAM:** (Indian) Age 56, born (About 1795) at Buffalo (In New York?), a member of the Baptist Church, Catherine age 55 born at Lewiston (In New York?), Elias age 12 born at Tuscarora. Tuscarora Township, District 4, Page 7/57, Numbers 18-20.

**JOHNSON, ZACK:** (Indian) Age 23 born (About 1828) at Onondaga, a member of the Church of England. Tuscarora Township, District 4, Page 7/57, Number 26.

**JOHNSON, ZECARIAH:** (Indian) Age 23 born (About 1828) in Canada West, a member of the Church of England, Margaret age 22. Onondaga Township, Part 11, District 2, Page 35, Numbers 5,6.

**JOHONWAH:** (Male Indian) Age 55, born (About 1796) at Brantford, a member of the Church of England, Tuscarora Township, District 32, Page 63/23, Number 39.

**JONES, AUGUSTUS:** (Indian) Age 32 born (About 1819) at Brantford, a member of the Methodist Church, Hanah age 48 born in England? (She was listed as an Indian) Sarah age 71 born at the Niagara. Tuscarora Township, District 11, Page 21/15, Numbers 1-3.

**JONES, CATHARINE:** (Indian) Age 11 born (About 1840) at Credit (River?), Elizabeth age 7 born at Credit (River?). Tuscarora Township, District 11, Page 21/75? Numbers 5, 6. See the family of Augustus Jones.

**JONES, HENRY:** (Indian) Age 44, born (About 1807) at Stoney? Creek, a member of the Methodist Church, Mary Ann age 45 born in Upper Canada (Ontario) Sarah age 16 born in Grand River, Charlotte age 10 born in Grand River, Emily age 5 born in Grand River, John age 3 born in Grand River. Tuscarora Township, District 36, Page 71/47, Numbers 7-12.

**JONES, PETER (REVEREND):** (Indian) Age 49, born (About 1802) in Canada, a Wesleyan Methodist Minister, Eliza age 39 (White woman of English ancestry) born in England, Charles (Indian) age 13 born in Canada (His residence listed as Lyma, New York) Frederick (Indian) age 11, born in Canada, Peter E. (Indian) age 9, born in Canada, George D. (Indian) age 5 born in Canada. Township of Brantford, District 5, Page 199/24.

**JONES, SETH:** (Indian) Age 24 born at Brantford Township, a member of the Methodist Church, Jane age 26 born in New York State, Susan age 4, born at Tuscarora, Charlotte age 3, born at Tuscarora, Peter age six months born at Tuscarora. Tuscarora Township, District 6, Page 11/63, Numbers 42-46.

**JORAHKWISON:** (Male Indian) Age 4 born (About 1847) at Tuscarora. Tuscarora Township, District 25, Page 49/37. See the family of Sugar on the same page.

**JORDON, NICOLAS:** (Indian) Age 35, born (About 1816) in New York State (In the United States) a member of the Methodist Church. Tuscarora Township, District 11, Page 21/75, Number 16.

**JOSEPH, DAVID:** (Indian) Age 16, born (About 1835) at Tuscarora, a member of the Church of England, Joseph age 4, born at Tuscarora, Nicholas age 3, born in Onondaga. Tuscarora Township, District 5, Page 9/61, Numbers 27-29.

**JYESAHTHA? OR IYESAHTHA?:** (Male Indian) Age 20 born (About 1831) at Grand River, a member of the Church of England. Tuscarora Township, District 32, Page 63/25, Number 46.

**KAHENYAKS:** (Female Indian) Age 30 born (About 1821) at Onondaga, a member of the Church of England. Tuscarora Township, District 22, Page 43/43, Number 19. See the family of Peter Buck on the same page.

**KAHHAWAHKWEN:** (Female Indian) Age 60 born (About 1791) at Cayuga, Yaonde (Female) Age 27 born at Cayuga, Dennyoh (Female) age 12 born in Indiana, Sennahase (Female) age 3 born in Indiana. Tuscarora Township, District 20, Page 39/39, Numbers 10-15.

**KAHSODES:** (Male Indian) Age 60 born (About 1791) at Indiana, Akwahekeh (Female) age 40 born at Indiana. Tuscarora Township, District 25, Page 49/37, Numbers 24, 25.

**KAKONDENAYON:** (Male Indian) Age 40 born (About 1811) at Onondaga, Caty? or Tcaby? (Female) age 37 born at Onondaga. Tuscarora Township, District 23, Page 45/45, Numbers 45, 46.

**KANADAHAGON:** (Male Indian) Age 60 born (About 1791) at Cayuga. Tuscarora Township, District 25, Page 49/37, Number 39.

**KANADAHSERE:** (Female Indian) Age 5 born (About 1846) at Indiana. Tuscarora Township, District 25, Page 49/37, Number 48. See the family of Onakwadekha on the same page.

**KANAHKWIYOHSTA:** (Female Indian) Age 40 born (About 1811) at Indiana, Thomas DAVIS age 18 born at Indiana, Kanehharhos (Female) age 10 born at Indiana, Konwih (Female) age 5 born at Indiana. Tuscarora Township, District 29, Page 57/27, Numbers 39-42.

**KANENDAYENHA:** (Male Indian) Age 70 born (About 1781) at Tuscarora. Tuscarora Township, District 29, Page 57/27, Number 4.

**KANONRARON:** (Male Indian) Age 55 born (About 1796) at Lower Canada (Quebec) a member of the Church of England, Kanwakasyon (Female) age 45 born at Onondaga, Kanonkwa (Female) age 30 born at Onondaga, Hannah age 12 born at Onondaga, David age 7 born at Onondaga, Peter age 3 born at Tuscarora, Isaac age 1 born at Tuscarora, John age 13 born at Onondaga. Tuscarora Township, District 20, Page 39/39, Numbers 35-42.

**KARONHYAKEH:** (Male Indian) Age 26, born (About 1825) in New York (In the United States) a member of the Church of England, Tuscarora Township, District 32, Page 63/23, Number 1.

**KASONHSAKSEN:** (Indian) Age 55, born (About 1796) at Brantford, a member of the Church of England, (Male Child) age 14, born in Tuscarora, (Male Child) age 6 born in Tuscarora, Iyesahtha (Male Child) age 4 ,born in Tuscarora, Yunonnent? or Nunonnent? age born in Tuscarora. Thirty Second Township, Page 63/23, Numbers 42-47.

**KASSOKWAKARRYS:** (Female Indian) Age 55. born (About 1796) in Ohio (In the United States) Kanyadrakera (Male) age 21, born in Tuscarora, Rone Gener Shakoyenha (Female) age 22, born in Brantford, Dehhaonhwajaweheoton? (Male) seven months old, born in Tuscarora. Thirty Second Township, Page 63/23, Numbers 6-11.

**KATHERADYTE:** (Male Indian) Age 36, born (About 1815) at Indiana, Church of England, Thirty Second Township, Page 63/23.

**KATHEYARONS:** (Female Indian) age 40, born (About 1811) at Indiana, Kahheryenentha (Female) age 18, born in Indiana, Kayadase (Female) age 16 born in Indiana, Kayahsodon (Male) age 13, born in Indiana, Dekanadoken (Female) age four months born in Indiana. Tuscarora Township, District 20, Numbers 5-9.

**KAYENAHSTA:** (Female Indian) Age 24 born (About 1827) at Indiana. Tuscarora Township, District 25, Page 49/37, Number 26.

**KAYENDATYE:** (Female Indian) Age 75 born (About 1776) at Indiana. Tuscarora Township, District 29, Page 57/37, Number 27.

**KEASSOKWAKARRYS:** (Indian) Age 55 born (About 1796) in Ohio State (In the United States) a member of the Church of England, Kanyadrakera (Male) Age 21 born at Tuscarora, Rone Gener Shakoyenha (Female) age 22 born at Brantford, Dehhaonhwajaweheston (Male) age seven months born at Tuscarora. Tuscarora Township, District 32, Page 53/25, Numbers 8-11.

**KERIKYEN:** (Female Indian) Age 21 born (About 1830) at Tuscarora. Tuscarora Township, District 18, Page 35/49, Number 12.

**KERR, ISAAC:** (Indian) Age 38 born (About 1813) at Mohawk Village, a member of the Methodist Church. Tuscarora Township, District 17, Page 33/11, Number 47.

**KESHEGO, BETSEY:** (Indian) Age 41? born (About 1810) at Credit River, a member of the Methodist Church, Nadah? (Female) age 24, Christian age 14, Mary age 12, Benjamin age 9. (Credit Indians) Tuscarora Township, District 27, Page 53/31, Numbers 29-33.

**KESHEGO, JAMES:** (Indian) Age 50 born (About 1801) at Credit River, a member of the Methodist Church, Mary age 50 born at Credit River. Tuscarora Township, District 34, Page 67/53, Numbers 21/22 on the page.

**KEY, PETER:** (Indian) Age 27 born (About 1824) at Onondaga, a member of the Church of England, Margret age 22, Kahonyont (Female) age 8, Walohariswaken? (Male) age 4, Kaharonnese (Female) age 1. Tuscarora Township, District 18, Page 35/49, Numbers 2-6.

**KHAIKORADON?:** (Female Indian) Age 35 born (About 1816) at Indiana. Tuscarora Township, District 20, Page 39/39, Number 1.

**KICK, JOSEPH:** (Indian) Age 19 born (About 1832) at Cayuga Village, a member of the Church of England, Nicholas age 14 born at Cayuga Village, Susan age 16 born at Cayuga. Tuscarora Township, District 13, Page 25, Numbers 12-14.

**KING, GEORGE:** (Indian) Age 38 born (About 1813) in Upper Canada (Ontario), a member of the Methodist Church, Susanah age 32, Aaron age 13, Sarah Ann age 9, Elizabeth age 3, Joseph Edward age 8 months. (Credit Indians) Tuscarora Township, District 35, Page 69/17, Numbers 5-10.

**KING, JOHN:** (Indian) Age 20 born (About 1831) at Credit River, Mary age 19, a member of the Methodist Church, born at Credit River, Jemima age 10 months born at Tuscarora Township. Tuscarora Township, District 33, Page 65/25, Numbers 11- 13.

**KONWAATS:** (Male Indian?) Age 50 born (About 1801) at Onondaga. Tuscarora Township, District 23, Page 45/45, Number 30.

**KONWAHHAWI:** (Male Indian) Age 40 born (About 1811) at Brantford. Tuscarora Township, District 25, Page 49/37, Number 45.

**KONWAHSANNAWY:** (Male Indian) Age 36 born (About 1815) at Brantford, Anokariksyon (Male) age 17 born at Onondaga, Dekayendon (Male) age 15 born at Onondaga. Tuscarora Township, District 23, Page 45/45, Numbers 48-50.

**LA FORM, CLARISY:** (Indian) Age 3 born (About 1848) at Tuscarora. Tuscarora Township, District 28, Page 55/33, Number 40. See the family of Moses Phadahquong.

**LAFORM, JOHN:** (Indian) Age 50 born (About 1801) at Credit River, a member of the Methodist Church, Betsy age 50, born at Credit River, James age 22 born at Credit River, John age 16 born at Credit River, Elizabeth age 12 born at Credit River, Angelic age 6 born at Credit River, David age 3 born at Credit River, Alexander age 1 born at Tuscarora Township. Tuscarora Township, District 34, Page 67/53, Numbers 24-31.

**LEWIS, ARCD:** (He was enumerated as both a Negro and an Indian on the census page?) Age 59 born (About 1792) in Virginia State (In the United States?) a member of the Methodist Church, Rocey? LEWIS (Female Indian) age 30 born in New York State (In the United States). Tuscarora Township, District 7, Page 13/65, Numbers 8, 9.

**LEWIS, ISAAC:** (Indian) Age 40 born (About 1811) at Grand River, a member of the Church of England, Susan age 40, Jacob age 21, Joseph age 19, Margret age 14, David age 4, Abraham age 2. Tuscarora Township, District 14, Page 27/3, Numbers. 37-43.

**LEWIS, JOSEPH:** (Indian) Age 20 born (About 1831) in Canada, a member of the Church of England. Brantford Township, District five, Page 181/15, Number 48.

**LEWIS, RICHARD:** (Listed as black?) Age 30 born (About 1821) at Grand River, a member of the Methodist Church, Margret (Indian) age 25 born at Grand River. Both were members of the Methodist Church, Tuscarora Township, Page 65/25, Numbers 6, 7.

**LEWIS, SUSAN:** (Indian) Age 36 born (About 1815) in Canada, a member of the Church of England, Betsey age 22, Christian age 18, Lucy age 12, Tuscarora Township, District 1, Page 1/71, Numbers 24-27.

**LICKERS, ABRAHAM:** (Indian) Age 40 born (About 1811) at Brantford, a member of the Methodist Church, Margret age 39 born at Seneca, Elijah age 14 born at Brantford, Catherine age 12 born at Brantford, Mary age 8, born at Brantford, Susannah age 2, born at Tuscarora. Tuscarora Township, District 23, Page 45/45, Numbers 23-29.

**LICKERS, HENRY:** (Indian) Age 47, born (About 1804) at Brantford, a member of the Methodist Church. Tuscarora Township, District 2, Page 3/59, Number 24.

**LICKERS, JOHN:** (Indian) Age 45 born (About 1806) in Brantford District, a member of the Methodist Church, Margaret age 44, born at Onondaga District, Mary age 19, born at Brantford, Charlotte age 17 born at Brantford, Daniel age 15 born at Brantford, Margaret age 8 born at Tuscarora, John age 6 born at Tuscarora, George age 2 born at Tuscarora, Township, District 2, Page 3/59, Numbers 42-49.

**LICKERS, JOSEPH:** (Indian) Age 19 born (About 1832) in Canada, a member of the Church of England, Brantford Township, District five, Page 183/16, Number 41.

**LICKERS, KEZIAH:** (Female Indian) Age 25 born (About 1826) in Canada, a member of the Methodist Church. Tuscarora Township, District 1, Page 1/71, Number 36.

**LICKERS, LUCY:** (Indian) Age 2 born (About 1849) at Grand River. Tuscarora Township, District 15, Page 29/7, Number 16. See Gaby Smith on the same page.

**LICKERS, NELLY:** (Indian) Age 12 born (About 1839) at Tuscarora, a member of the Methodist Church, Catharine age 7, born at Brantford. Tuscarora Township, District 3, Page 5/55, Numbers 3,4. See the family of Jacob Isaac's.

**LICKERS, PETER:** (Indian) Age 28 born (About 1823) in Brantford Township, a member of the Methodist Church. (Credit Indian) Tuscarora Township, District 35, Page 69/17, Number 29.

**LICKERS, SAMUEL:** (Indian) Age 42 born (About 1809) at Brantford, a member of the Methodist Church, Mary age 30, born at Onondaga, Abram age 6, born at Tuscarora, Betsey age 9, born at Tuscarora, Peter age 4, born at Tuscarora. Tuscarora Township, District 9, Page 17/69, Numbers 35-39.

**LOCK, CATHARINE:** (Indian) Age not given, born at Grand River, a member of the Church of England, Isaac age 25, born at Grand River, John age 22 born at Grand River, Lydia age 21 born at Grand River. Tuscarora Township, District 16, Page 31/9, Numbers 14-17.

**LOCK, WILLIAM:** (Indian) Age 2, born (About 1849) at Tuscarora Township. Tuscarora Township, District 12, Page 23/1, Number 23. See the family of Esther Thomas.

**LOFT, ADAM:** (Indian) Age 19, born in Canada, (About 1832) a member of the Church of England, residence the Bay of Quinty. Tuscarora Township, District 1, Page 1/71, Number 23.

**LOFT, SUSANAH M:** (Indian) Age 22 born (About 1829) in Canada, single, a member of the Church of England. Brantford, District Number 5, Page 199/24.

**LOFT, SUSANNAH:** (Indian) Age 23 born (About 1828) in Canada West, a member of the Church of England, Ellen age 21, Henry age 30, Mary age 19, Yaganoa? (A female) age 1. Onondaga Township, Part 11, Page 35, Numbers 46-50.

**LOGBOAT? (OR LONGBOAT) MARY:** (Indian) Age 28 born (1823) at Tuscarora, a member of the Baptist Church. Tuscarora Township, District 10, Page 19/71, Number 44.

**LONGBORD? (OR LONGBOAT?) ELIZABETH:** (Indian) Age 5 born (About 1846) at Tuscarora, a member of the Baptist Church. Tuscarora Township, District 10, Page 19/71, Number 47. See the family of Mary Logboat? or Longboat.

**LONGBORD? OR LONGBOAT? PETER:** (Indian) Age 2 born (About 1849) at Tuscarora. Tuscarora Township, District 10, Page 19/17, Number 49. See the family of Mary Logboat? or Mary Longboat.

**LONGFISH, JOSEPH:** (Indian) Age 43, born (About 1808) at Tuscarora, a member of the Baptist Church, Susan age 40, Simon age 15, Elizabeth age 12, Esther age 8, Adam age 4, Amy age 2. Tuscarora Township, District 4, Page 7/57, Number 27-33.

**LONGFISH, SARAH:** (Indian) Age 61 born (About 1791) at Buffalo (New York?) Adam Longfish age 63 born (About 1790) in New York State (United States), both were members of the Church of England. Tuscarora Township, District 15, Page 29/7, Numbers 41, 42.

**LONGFISH, WILLIAM:** (Indian) Age 37 born (About 1814) at Grand River, a member of the Church of England, Betsey age 35, Mary age 4. Members of the Church of England. Tuscarora Township, District 15, Page 29/7, Numbers 48-50.

**LOTHRIDGE, JACOB:** (Indian) Age 46 born (About 1805) at Grand River, a member of the Methodist Church, Lydia age 40 born at Bay of Quinty,

Joseph age 17 born at Tuscarora, Seth age 15 born at Tuscarora, Jemima age 12 born at Tuscarora, Mag? Ann? or Marg. Ann? age 10 born at Tuscarora, John age 5 born at Tuscarora. Tuscarora Township, District 2, Page 3/59, Numbers 25-31.

**LOTHRIDGE, JOE:** (Indian) Age 39 born (About 1812) in Canada. He was a member of the Church of England. Tuscarora Township, District 1, Page 1/71, Number 31.

**LOTHRIDGE, SARAH:** (Indian) Age 30 born (About 1821) in Canada, a member of the Church of England, Christiana age 7 born in Canada. Brantford Township, Fifth Ward, Page 159/4, Numbers 49-50.

**LOTTRIDGE, ISAAC:** (Indian) Age 22 born (About 1829) at Grand River, a member of the Methodist Church, Lydia age 20, born at Grand River. Tuscarora Township, District 6, Page 11/63, Numbers 26, 27.

**MAPLE-SUGAR, JOHN:** (Indian) Age 18 born (About 1833) at Onondaga. Tuscarora Township, District 25, Page 49/37, Number 20.

**MARACLE, DAVID:** (Indian) Age 48 born (About 1803) at the Bay of Quinty, a member of the Methodist Church, Jemima age 33 born at Brantford Township a member of the Church of England, James age ?, born at Onondaga, Margret age ?, born at Onondaga. Tuscarora Township, District 7, Page 13/65, Numbers 13-16.

**MARACLE, DAVID:** (Indian) Age 13? born (About 1838) at the Bay of Quinty, a member of the Church of England, Elias age 6, born at the Bay of Quinty. Children of David Maracle?

**MARACLE, ELLEN:** (Indian) Age 27 born (About 1824) at Onondaga, a member of the Church of England, Augustus age 5 born at Tuscarora, Phebe age 7 born at Tuscarora, Phebe Maracle was listed as member of the Methodist Church. Tuscarora Township, District 3, Page 5/55, Numbers 46-48.

**MARACLE, ELLEN:** (Indian) Age 11 born (About 1840) at Grand River, a member of the Church of England. Tuscarora Township, District 17, Page 33/11, Number 44.

**MARACLE, MARGARET:** (Indian) Age 34 born (About 1817) at Martin's Settlement, a member of the Church of England, Tuscarora Township, District 10, Page 19/71, Number 38.

**MARACLE, NICODEMUS:** (Indian) Age 10 born (About 1811) at Onondaga, a member of the Church of England, Aaron age 11? or 10? born at Tuscarora, Cornelius (Male) age 3, Susannah age two months born at Tuscarora. Tuscarora Township, District 7, Page 13/65, Numbers 11-21. See the family of David Maracle on the same page.

**MARACLE, POWLESS:** (Indian) Age 46 born (About 1805) at the Bay of Quinty, Margaret age 46 born at the Bay of Quinty, John age 22 born at the Bay of Quinty, Nelly age 24 born at the Bay of Quinty. Tuscarora Township, District 6, Page 11/63, Numbers 23-25.

**MARACLE, POWLESS:** (Indian) Age 15 born (About 1836) at Grand River, a member of the Methodist Church, Isaac MARACLE age 12 born at Grand River, Female MARACLE child age 4 born at Grand River, Male MARACLE child age 2 born at Grand River. Tuscarora Township, District 6, Page 11/63, Numbers 28-31. See the family of Powless Maracle on the same page.

**MARACLE, SARAH:** (Indian) Age 4 born (About 1847) at Tuscarora. Tuscarora Township, District 6, Page 11/63, Number 19. See the family of Christiana Harris.

**MARACLE, WILLIAM:** (Indian) Age 23 born (About 1828) at the Bay of Quinty, Daby (Female) age 27 born at Onondaga, Nelson age 6, born at Tuscarora, Hannah age 2, born at Tuscarora. Tuscarora Township, District 10, Page 19/71, Numbers 30-33.

**MARACLE, WILLIAM:** (Indian) Age 27 born (About 1824) at the Bay of Quinty, a member of the Methodist Church, Catharine age 22 born at Eagle's Nest. Tuscarora Township, District 17, Page 33/11, Numbers 20, 21.

**MARICLE, ABRAHAM:** (Indian) Age 38 born (About 1813) in Canada, a member of the Methodist Church, Leah (Female) age 38 born at Bay of Quinty, Susan age 12 born at Grand River, Abraham age 7 born at Grand River. Tuscarora Township, District 1, Page 1/71, Numbers 19-22.

**MARICLE, ABRAM:** (Indian) Age 23 born (About 1828) at the Bay of Quinty, a member of the Church of England, Susanah age 18, born at Oxbow. Tuscarora Township, District 10, Page 19/71, Numbers 21, 22.

**MARICLE, SUSANAH:** (Indian) Age 32 born (About 1819) at Onondaga. A member of the Church of England. Tuscarora Township, District 12, Page 23/1, Number 43.

**MARTIN, ADAM:** (Indian) Age 13 born (About 1838) at Grand River, a Baptist. Tuscarora Township, District 36, Page 71/47, Number 22.

**MARTIN, GEORGE:** (Indian) Age 87, born (About 1764) in the United States, a member of the Church of England, Tuscarora Township, Township District 1, Page 1/71, Number 9.

**MARTIN, JACOB:** (Indian) Age 50 born (About 1801) at Onondaga, a member of the Church of England, Susan age 42 born at Brantford, Moses age 24, born at Onondaga, Mary age 20, born at Onondaga, Adam age 16, born at Onondaga, Julia age 13, born at Onondaga, Lucy age 11, born at Onondaga, Joab age 8, born at Onondaga, Joel age 5, born at Onondaga. Tuscarora Township, District 8, Page 15/67, Numbers 23-31.

**MARTIN, MARY:** (Indian) Age 45 born (About 1806) at Grand River, a member of the Church of England. Tuscarora Township, District 15, Page 29/7, Number 44.

**MATOCK, GEORGE:** (Indian) Age 32 born (About 1819) at Brantford, a member of the Baptist Church, Elizabeth age 26 born at Onondaga, Thomas age 8 born at Onondaga, Jacob age 5 born at Tuscarora, Lydia age 3 born at Tuscarora, Joseph age 1 born at Tuscarora. Tuscarora Township, District 18, Page 35/49, Numbers 17-22.

**MC COLLUM, JOHN:** (Indian) Age 50 born (About 1801) at Credit River, a member of the Methodist Church, Catharine age 50, David age 14, Esther age 6. (Credit Indians) Tuscarora Township, District 28, Page 55/33, Numbers 28-31.

**MC COLLUM, JOSEPH:** (Indian) Age 25 born (About 1826) at Credit River, a member of the Methodist Church, Amanda age 29. Tuscarora Township, District 28, Page 55/33, Number 32, 33.

**MC DONALD, ALEXANDER:** (Indian?) age 32, born (About 1819) in Scotland, a member of the Church of Scotland, (All others were listed as white?) Mary age 19, born in Glengery, Elizabeth age 8, born in Glengery, Miss Mc Donald age?, born in Tuscarora Township, Roderick age 32?, born in Scotland, John age 30, born in Scotland, Kennith age 28, born in Scotland. Note: This census information may be in error. The birthplace mentioned as Scotland may be the country or the town of Scotland in Brant County, Thirty Three Township, Page 65/25, Numbers 46-52.

**MC DOUGAL, NICOLAS:** (Indian) Age 45 born (About 1806) at Credit River, a member of the Methodist Church, Christiana age 40, John age 18, Daniel age 16, Margaret age 14, Elijah? age 12, James age 10, Nicklas age 8, Sarah age 6, Baby? or Caty? age 4, Archie age 2 born at Tuscarora Township. (Credit Indians) Tuscarora Township, District 28, Page 55/33, Numbers 42-52.

**MIKE, CATY:** (Indian) Age 48 born (About 1803) at Upper Canada (Quebec) a member of the Methodist Church, Peter age 20, born at Upper Canada, John age 18, born at Upper Canada, Jane age 15, born at Upper Canada, Catherine age 5, born at Upper Canada. Tuscarora Township, District 27, Page 53/31, Numbers 47-50.

**MIKE, HENRY:** (Indian) Age 22 born (About 1829) at Grand River, a member of the Methodist Church, Ellen age 20 born at Grand River, James age 6 born at Tuscarora, Henry age 4 born at Tuscarora, Catherine age 2 born at Tuscarora. Tuscarora Township, District 33, Page 65/25, Numbers 1-5.

**MIKE, JOHN:** (Listed of Negro Ancestry?) age 50 born (About 1801) in Upper Canada (Quebec), a member of the Methodist Church. Tuscarora Township, District 27, Page 53/31, Number 46.

**MILLER, JOHN:** (Indian) Age 20, born (About 1831) at Grand River, a member of the Church of England, Mrs. Miller age 17, born at Grand River, Child (Female) age 1, born at Grand River, Tuscarora Township, District 32, Page 63/23, Numbers 48-50.

**MITTEN, JOHN:** (Indian) Age 55 born (About 1796) at Grand River, Christian (Female) age 53, Isaac age 22, James age 20, Jacob age 18, Mary age 15, Female age 14, Hanah age 12, Rachel age 10. Tuscarora Township, District 15, Page 29/7, Numbers 27-35.

**MONTURE, JACOB:** (Indian) Age 28 born (About 1823) at Grand River, a member of the Church of England, Ellen age 24 born at Grand River. Tuscarora Township, District 11, Page 21/75, Numbers 48, 49.

**MONTURE, JACOB:** (Indian) Age 27 born (About 1824) at Onondaga, a member of the Church of England. Tuscarora Township, District 13, Page 25, Number 5.

**MONTURE, PETER:** (Indian) Age 2 born (About 1849) at Tuscarora Township. Tuscarora Township, District 12, Page 23/1, Number 16. See the family of Noah Powless.

**MONTURE, WILLIAM:** (Indian) Age 40 born (About 1811) at Grand River, Mrs. MONTURE age 36, Miss Monture age 6, Miss MONTURE age 2. Tuscarora Township, District 19, Page 37/51, Numbers 41-44.

**MORAY, JOHN:** (Indian) Age 83 born (About 1768) in the United States (All were born in the United States) Hannah age 32, Cyrus age 38, Isaac age 24. All were members of the Baptist Church. Brantford Township, Ward 1, Brant County, Ontario, Page 19, Numbers 47-50.

**NASH, AARON:** (Indian) Age 61 born (About 1790) at Onondaga, a member of the Church of England, Eve age 30 born at Tuscarora, Mathew age 20 born at Tuscarora, James age 12 born at Tuscarora, Solomon age 9 born at Tuscarora, Mary age 7 born at Tuscarora, Pharon? or Pharoo age 1 born at Tuscarora. Tuscarora Township, District 4, Page 7/57, Numbers 41-47.

**NASH, ISAAC:** (Indian) Age 18, born (About 1833) at Onondaga, a member of the Church of England. Tuscarora Township, District 4, Page 7/57, Number 22.

**NASH, MATHEW:** (Indian) No age given, born at Grand River, a members of the Baptist Church. Tuscarora Township, District 36, Page 71/47, Number 23.

**NENDIKOOK, JAMES:** (Indian) Age 30 born (About 1821) at Indiana, Peggy age 30 born at Paris, Dehharihbrens? (Male) age 12 born at Grand River, Kanhodonkwas (Female) age 3 born at Grand River, Wennihhadaha (Female) age 9 born at Grand River. Tuscarora Township, District 24, Page 47/35, Numbers 34-38.

**NEWHOUSE, NICHOLAS:** (Indian) Age 37 born (About 1814) at Onondaga, a member of the Methodist Church, Catharine age 30 born at Martin's Settlement, Seth age 12 born at Tuscarora, Peter age 8 born at Tuscarora, Amos age 3 born at Tuscarora, Julia age 5 born at Tuscarora, Sampson age 9 weeks born at Tuscarora. Tuscarora Township, District 12, Page 23/1, Numbers 4-10.

**NEWHOUSE, SETH:** (Indian) Age 70 born (About 1791) at Lewiston (New York?), a member of the Church or England, Hannah age 69 born at Niagara. Tuscarora Township, District 7, Page 13/65, Numbers 27, 28.

**NIKARONDASA:** (Male Indian) Age 36 born (About 1815) at Onondaga, a member of the Church of England. Tuscarora Township, District 20, Page 39/39, Numbers 19.

**NILES? OR NELES? CATHERINE:** (Indian) Age 12 born (About 1839) at Tuscarora, a member of the Church of England. Tuscarora Township, District 4, Page 7/57, Number 40. See the Family of Peter Fishcarryer.

**NILES? OR NELES? AUGUSTUS:** (Indian) Age 4 born (About 1847) at Tuscarora, Tuscarora Township, District 4, Page 7/57, Number 38. See the family of Peter Fishcarryer.

**NOTTEN, JANE:** (Indian) Age 30 born (About 1821) at Onondaga, a member of the Church of England, Susannah age 30 born at Onondaga, Jemima age 28 born at Smoky Hollow, Margret age 24 born at Buffalo, George age 14 born at Onondaga, Jemima age 12 born at Onondaga, Catharine age 7 born at Onondaga, Nicholas age 4 born at Onondaga. Tuscarora Township, District 21, Page 41/41, Numbers 46-52.

**NOTTEN, PETER:** (Indian) Age 60 born (About 1791) at Buffalo (New York?), a member of the Methodist Church. Tuscarora Township, District 24, Page 47/35, Number 33.

**NUNONNENT? OR WNONNENT?:** (Female Indian) Age 30 born (About 1821) at Tuscarora. Tuscarora Township, District 32, Page 63/25, Number 47.

**OATS, JOHN:** (Indian) Age 20 born (About 1831) at Indiana, Iisdaneken? or Jisdaaneken? (Male) age 2. Tuscarora Township, District 25, Page 49/37, Numbers 27, 28.

**OBE, JOHN:** (Indian) Age 56 born (About 1795) at Brantford, a member of the Church of England, Jemima age 52, born at Brantford, Lawrence age 23 born at Grand River, John age 20 born at Grand River, Margaret age 16 born at Grand River, Catharine age 14 born at Grand River. Tuscarora Township, District 11, Page 21/75, Numbers 23-28.

**OBE, JOHN:** (Indian) Age 56 born (About 1795) in New York State (In the United States) a member of the Church of England. Tuscarora Township, District 10, Page 19/71, Number 29.

**OBEDIAH, JOHN:** (Indian) Age 68 born (About 1783) in the United States, a member of the Church of England, Sarah age 41 born in Canada West, Nancy age 14, Betsy age 9, Susan age 3, Dennis age 2. Onondaga Township, Part 11, Page 67, Numbers 15-19.

**OGHRADONHKWEN** (Male Indian) Age 48 born (About 1803) at Indiana. Tuscarora Township, District 29, Page 57/27, Number 28.

**OHONWADIRON:** (Male Indian) Age 32 born (About 1819) at Indiana, Konwahserory (Female) age 25 born at Indiana, Onwatyeronkway (Male) age 12 born at Tuscarora, Wendine (Female) age 10 born at Indiana, Waewennayeosa (Female) age 8 born at Indiana, Kondeusdakwe? (Female) age 6 born at Indiana, Kayatyenens (Female) age 2 born at Indiana. Tuscarora Township, District 22, Page 43/43, Numbers 34-40.

**OKAWENDA:** (Male Indian) Age 55 born (About 1796) at New York State (In the United States) Kanisonnentha (Female) age 50 born at Onondaga, Moses age 16 born at Onondaga, Shaiiyowane (Female) Age 13, Catherine age 11 born at Onondaga. Tuscarora Township, District 31, Page 61/21, Numbers 36-40.

**OKEDES:** (Female Indian) Age 21 born (About 1830) at Tuscarora. Tuscarora Township, District 23, Page 45/45, Number 44. See the family of Jacob Henry on the same page.

**OLDS, PETER:** (Indian) Age 80 born (About 1771) at Credit River, a member of the Methodist Church. (Credit Indians) Tuscarora Township, District 35, Page 69/17, Number 43.

**ONAKWADEKHA?** (Male Indian) Age 29 born (About 1822) at Cayuga, Youkweh? or Yonkweh? (Female) age 20 born at Indiana, Kayenhnshson (Female) age 3, Kayaltahston (Female) age 1 born at Tuscarora. Tuscarora Township, District 25, Page 49/37, Numbers 40-43.

**ONONSADKHA:** (Male Indian) Age 30 born (About 1821) at Onondaga, Christiana age 42 born at Brantford, Henry age 17 born at Brantford, Kanendoha (Female) age 13 born at Brandtford, Dawodakane (Male) age 8 born at Brantford. Tuscarora Township, District 18, Number 45.

**OTTER, DAVID:** (Indian) Age 19, born (About 1832) in Canada West, a member of the Church of England, residence Tuscarora (Township?). Onondaga Township Part 11, Page 37, Number 28.

**OTTER, ELLEN:** (Indian) Age 35, born (About 1816) at Tuscarora, a member of the Church of England. Tuscarora Township, District 5, Page 9/61, Number 44.

**OTTER, JOSEPH:** (Indian) Age 50, born (About 1801) at Grand River, a member of the Methodist Church, Mary age 40, William age 45, Henry? age 12, Ellen age 8, John age 4. Tuscarora Township, District 11, Page 21/75? Numbers 10-15.

**OTTER, WILLIAM:** (Indian) Age 22, born (About 1829) at Tuscarora, a member of the Church of England, Julia age 19 born at Tuscarora. District 5, Tuscarora Township, Page 9/61, Numbers 41, 42.

**OWEN, CORNELIUS:** (Indian) Age 38, born (About 1813) at Tuscarora, a member of the Church of England, Susanah age 31, born in Onondaga, Jesse age 15, born in Onondaga, Eunice age 10, born in Tuscarora, Jemima age 8, born in Tuscarora, Catharine age 6, born in Tuscarora, Stephen age 4, born in Tuscarora, Eliza age 1, born in Tuscarora. Tuscarora Township, District 32, Page 63/23, Numbers 24-31.

**PATTERSON, ISAAC:** (Indian) Age 14, born (About 1837) in New York (In the United States) a member of the Church of England. Tuscarora Township, District 4, Page 7/57, Number 37.

**PETER, CATHARINE:** (Indian) Age 40 born (About 1811) at Credit River, a member of the Methodist Church, John age 6, Jeremiah age 2. (Credit Indians) Tuscarora Township, District 28, Page 55/33, Numbers 6-8.

**PETER, PEGGY:** (Indian) Age 68 born (About 1783) at Credit River, a member of the Methodist Church, (Credit Indian) Tuscarora Township, District 27, Page 53/31, Number 45.

**PETER, POLLY:** (Indian) Age 58 born (About 1793) at Credit River, a member of the Methodist Church, Benjamin age 13, (Credit Indian) Tuscarora Township, District 28, Numbers 9, 10.

**PHADAHQUONG? MOSES:** (Indian) Age 46 born (About 1805) at Credit River, a member of the Methodist Church, Susan? age 21? or 2? born at Tuscarora, Clarisy LA FORM age 3 born at Tuscarora. (Credit Indians) Tuscarora Township, District 28, Page 55/33, Number 38-40.

**PHILIP, GARLOUGH:** (Indian) Age 22 born (About 1829) at Grand River, Julia age 20. Tuscarora Township, District 16, Page 39/7, Numbers 46, 47.

**POTER? OR PETER? JOSEPH:** (Indian) Age 17 born (About 1834) at Smoky Hollow, a member of the Methodist Church, Nocodemus age 11, born at Tuscarora, Lucy age 12, born at Smoky Hollow, Harriet age 14, born at Smoky Hollow. Tuscarora Township, District 3, Page 5/55, Numbers 8-11.

**POTER? OR PETER? HANNAH:** (Indian) Age 18 born (About 1833) at Smoky Hollow, a member of the Methodist Church. Tuscarora Township, District 3, Page 5/55, Number 6.

**POWLES, PETER:** (Indian) Age 12 born (About 1839) in Canada, a member of the Church of England, Brantford Township, Fifth Ward, Page 163/6, Number 34. See family of Elizabeth Fund.

**POWLES, PETER:** (Indian) Age 68 born (About 1783) in New York (In the United States) a member of the Church of England, Elizabeth age 70 born in New York. Fifth Ward, Brantford Township, Page 155/2, Number 33, 34.

**POWLES, POWLES:** (Indian) Age 73 (About 1778) born in Canada, a member of the Church of England. A comment was made that he boarded at the house of Wm. JOHN, Brantford Township, District 5, Page 181/15, Number 49.

**POWLESS, CHRISTIAN:** (Indian) Age 70 born (About 1781) at Brantford, Abram age? born at Johnson Settlement, William age? born at Johnson Settlement. Tuscarora Township, District 10, Page 19/71, Number 34-36.

**POWLESS, GEORGE:** (Indian) Age 40 born (About 1811) at Mohawk, a member of the Church of England, Susan age 36 born at Mohawk, Catharine age 13 born at Mohawk, Ellen age 8 born at Tuscarora, Lydia age 6 born at Tuscarora, Betsy age 4 born at Mohawk. Tuscarora Township, District 14, Page 27/3, Numbers 1-6.

**POWLESS, JACOB:** (Indian) Age 26 born (About 1825) at Grand River, a member of the Church of England, Margret age 53, Ellen age 30, Male Powless child age four months. Tuscarora Township, District 14, Page 27/3, Numbers 44-47.

**POWLESS, JAMES:** (Indian) Age 41 born (About 1810) at Grand River, a member of the Church of England, Ellen age 42, Isaac age 22, Charlotte age 16. Tuscarora Township, District 16, Page 39/7, Numbers 42-45.

**POWLESS, JOHN:** (Indian) Age 30 born (About 1821) at Johnson's Settlement, a member of the Methodist Church, Joseph age 19 born at Johnson's Settlement, Peter age 27 born at Johnson's Settlement, Ellen? age 24 born at Onondaga, Elizabeth age 23 born at Brantford Township, Mary age 28 born at Onondaga, Jacob age 6 born at Tuscarora, William age 3 born at Tuscarora, Peter age 3 born at Tuscarora. Tuscarora Township, District 12, Page 23/1, Numbers 30-38.

**POWLESS, JOSEPH:** (Indian) Age 28 born (About 1823) in New York State (In the United States), a member of the Church of England. Mary age 25 born at Grand River, Abraham age 1 born at Grand River, Tuscarora Township, District 11, Ontario, Page 21/75? Numbers 45-47.

**POWLESS, LYDIA:** (Indian) Age 1 born (About 1850) at Tuscarora, Peter Powless age 7. Tuscarora Township, District 17, Page 33/11, Numbers 18, 19. See Thomas Funn on the same page.

**POWLESS, MARY:** (Indian) Age 43 born (About 1808) at Mohawk Village, George age 20, born at Mohawk Village, Mary age 18, born at Mohawk Village, Elizabeth age 15, born at Onondaga, Peter age 14, born at Mohawk Village. Tuscarora Township, District 9, Page 17/69, Numbers 30-34.

**POWLESS, MARY:** (Indian) Age 24 born (About 1827) at Grand River, a member of the Methodist Church, Abram age 1 born in Tuscarora. Tuscarora Township, District 5, Page 11/63, Numbers 20, 21.

**POWLESS, NANCY:** (Indian) Age 5, born (About 1846) in Tuscarora Township. Tuscarora Township, District 2, Page 3/59, Number 38. See the family of Jacob Green.

**POWLESS, NOAH:** (Indian) Age 45 born (About 1806) at Oxbow, a member of the Methodist Church, Mary age 40 born Onondaga (Township?) Noah age 22 born at Oxbow. Tuscarora Township, District 12, Page 23/1, Number 15.

**RACEY? ELIZABETH:** (Indian) Age 4 born (About 1847) at the Grand River. Tuscarora Township, District 10, Page 19/71, Number 42. See the family of John Tome.

**RATHERADYTE:** (Indian) Age 36 born (About 1815) at Indiana, a member of the Church of England. Tuscarora Township, District 32, Page 63/25, Number 12.

**ROHSENNONNI:** (Male Indian) Age 37 born (About 1814) at Onondaga, Peggy age 37, Dewehnidsken (Male Indian) age 20. Tuscarora Township, District 29, Page 57/27, Numbers 5-7.

**ROUNDSKY, THOMAS:** (Indian) Age 46 born (About 1805) at Grand River, a member of the Church of England, Jemima? age 50, Solomon age 13. Tuscarora Township, District 11, Page 21/15, Numbers 35-37.

**RYAN, MAJOR:** (Indian) Age 40 born (About 1811) at Buffalo (New York?) Deyoah (Female) age 40 born at Buffalo, William age 15 born at Buffalo. Tuscarora Township, District 26, Page 51/29, Numbers 14-16.

**SAGE, PETER:** (Indian) Age not given, born at Grand River. Tuscarora Township, District 19, Page 37/51, Number 45.

**SAHKIDEAH:** (Female Indian) Age 40 born (About 1811) at Brantford, Adenadonni (Male) age 20 born at Brantford, Dehhanenharayen (Male) age 18 born at Brantford, Dayadekane (Male) age 11 born at Brantford, Kahendoah (Female) age 16 born at Brantford. Tuscarora Township, District 26, Page 51/29, Numbers 2-6.

**SAMPSON, THOMAS:** (Indian) Age 28 born (About 1823) in New York State (In the United States) a member of the Methodist Church, Mary age 25 born at the Bay of Quinty. Tuscarora Township, District 16, Page 31/9, Numbers 1, 2.

**SAWAT:** (Male Indian) Age 50, born (About 1801) in New York (In the United States) a member of the Church of England, Kasnonhsaksens (Female) age 55 born at Brantford, Thanattharen (Male) Age 14 born at Tuscarora, Child (Male) age 6, Child (Male) age 4. Tuscarora Township, District 32, Page 63/23, Numbers 41-45.

**SAWYER, JOHN:** (Indian) Age 35 born (About 1816) at Credit River, a member of the Methodist Church, Rachel age 34, born Credit River, Johnathan age 3, born Credit River, David age 2, born Credit River (Credit Indians) Tuscarora Township, District 35, Page 69/17, Numbers 46-49.

**SAWYER, JOHN?** (Indian) Age 65 (About 1786) born in Upper Canada (Ontario), a member of the Methodist Church, Nancy age 54 born in Upper Canada, Joseph age 27 born in Upper Canada. (Credit Indians) Tuscarora Township, District 35, Page 69/17, Numbers 1-3.

**SCHUYLER, JOHN:** (Indian) Age 28 born (About 1823) at Onondaga. Tuscarora Township, District 23, Page 45/45, Number 47.

**SECORD, JOHN:** (Indian) Age 56 born (About 1795) at Credit River, a member of the Methodist Church, Hannah age 58, Adam age 18, Nancy age 16, Sarah age 14, Albert age 13, Thomas age 8. Tuscarora Township, District 34, Page 67/53, Numbers 14-20.

**SENECA, DAVID:** (Indian) Age 30 born (About 1821) in Canada West, a member of the Church of England, Betsy age 30, Onondaga Township, Part 11, District 2, Page 51, Numbers 14, 15.

**SENECA, JOHN:** (Indian) Age 74, born (About 1777) at Mount Pleasant, a member of the Church of England, Tewatyadendons (Female) age 55, born in Onondaga, Atyadohtaronkwen (Male) age 19 born at Tuscarora, Anyawenrade (Male) age 17 born at Tuscarora, Kanonsahason (Female) age 20 born at Tuscarora, Rakashaha (Male) age ten days born at Tuscarora. Tuscarora Township, District 32, Page 63/25, Numbers 2-7.

**SENECA, REBECCA:** (Indian) Age 17 born (About 1834) in Canada West, a member of the Church of England, Hanah age 26, Cornelius age 5. Onondaga Township, Part 11, District 2, Page 35, Numbers 1,2,3.

**SENECA, THOMAS:** (Indian) Age 60 (About 1791) born in Canada West, a member of the Church of England, Sally age 59, William age 23 born in

Upper Canada. Onondaga Township, Part 11, District 2, Page 49, Numbers 48-50.

**SHADEYOYADONDON:** (Male Indian) Age 35 born (About 1816) at Brantford, Konwarihwawi (Female) age 32 born at Brantford, Dakahhende (Female) age 13 born at Tuscarora, Sakeniyo (Male) age 10 born at Tuscarora, Wadenyenden (Female) age 4 born at Tuscarora, Katsakentyon (Male) age 2 born at Tuscarora. Tuscarora Township, District 25, Page 49/37, Numbers 33-38.

**SHADINA:** (Male Indian) Age 37 born (About 1814) at Indiana. Tuscarora Township, District 29, Page 57/27, Number 29.

**SHAKOHHARWINEHTHA:** (Male Indian) Age 2 born (About 1849) at Tuscarora, Yohnyokwendon (Male) Age 6 born at Brantford, Konwayadorenhon (Female) age 1 born at Tuscarora. Tuscarora Township, District 29, Page 57/37, Number 1-3. These children do not appear to be connected with any adults. Possibly they are part of the Mc Collum family listed at the bottom of the previous page.

**SHAOKENYATHA:** (Female Indian) Age 22 born (About 1829) at Brantford. Tuscarora Township, District 25, Page 49/37, Number 44.

**SHAW, CATHARINE:** (Indian) Age 38 born (About 1813) in Upper Canada (Ontario), a member of the Church of England. Tuscarora Township, District 1, Page 1/71, Number 16.

**SHAW, MAGDELENE:** (Indian) Age 10 born (About 1811) at Grand River. Tuscarora Township, District 15, Page 29/7, Number 15.

**SHAW? HANNAH:** (Indian) Age 34 born (About 1817) at Grand River, a member of the Methodist Church. Tuscarora Township, Page 29/7, Number 17.

**SHEET? OR SHUT? JOHN:** (Indian) Age 57 born (About 1794) in the United States, a member of the Church of England. Onondaga Township, Part 11, Page 35, Number 20.

**SHODAKWARASON?** (Male Indian) Age 70 born (About 1781) at Brantford, a member of the Church of England. Tuscarora Township, District 18, Page 35/49, Number 1.

**SHOHENDOWANE:** (Male Indian) Age 45 born (About 1806) at Indiana. Tuscarora Township, District 29, Page 57/27, Number 43.

**SILVER, ELIZABETH:** (Indian) Age 50 born (About 1801) at Onondaga, a member of the Baptist Church, Jacob age 32, born at Onondaga, Terikyon (Female) age 30 born at Onondaga, Levi age 10, born at Tuscarora, Hannah age 9, born at Tuscarora, Abraham age 3, born at Tuscarora, Nelly age 10, born at Tuscarora, Solomon age 1, born at Tuscarora. Tuscarora Township, District 21, Page 41/41, Numbers 14-21. Numbers 14-18 on this page were listed as Negro. Numbers 19-21 were listed as Indians they may or may not be members of the same family.

**SILVER, JACOB:** (Indian) Age 20 born (About 1831) in New York State (In the United States). A member of the Methodist Church. Tuscarora Township, District 12, Page 23/1, Number 12.

**SILVER, JOSEPH:** (Indian) Age 49, born (About 1802) at Onondaga, a member of the Baptist Church, Sally age 46, born at Onondaga, James age 18, born at Onondaga, Mark age 12, born at Onondaga, Peter age 6, born at Tuscarora, Jacob age 4, born at Tuscarora, Powless age 1, born at Tuscarora, Eliza SILVER age 20, born at Tuscarora. Tuscarora Township, District 24, Page 47/35, Numbers 1-8.

**SILVER, SIMON:** (Indian) Age 9 born (About 1842) at Tuscarora, Alexander age 6 born at Tuscarora, Elizabeth SILVER age 50 born at Onondaga. Tuscarora Township, District 21, Page 41/41, Numbers 12-14. This family may be part of the Rubel Gone family on the same page.

**SILVERSMITH, HENRY:** (Indian) Age 41 born (About 1810) at Niagara Falls, a member of the Methodist Church, Krathathon? (Female) age 31 born at Onondaga, Dehharonnwendas (Female) age four and a half born at Tuscarora. Tuscarora Township, District 26, Page 51/29, Numbers 45-47.

**SILVERSMITH, JACOB:** (Indian) Age 30 born (About 1821) at Indiana, Mrs. Silversmith age 18 born at Onondaga, Kanyode (Female) age 1 born at Tuscarora, Akenhsajaha (Male) age 8 born at Tuscarora, Ronerahhere (Male) age 5 born at Tuscarora. Nancy (No last name given she may have been a Silversmith?) age 30 born at Onondaga, Deyonendaweron (Female) age 8 born at Tuscarora (Could have been a child of Nancy) Kayennayen (Male) age 1 (Could have been a child of Nancy) Tuscarora Township, District 23, Page 45/45, Numbers 31-35. The title Mrs. was crossed out in the name of Mrs. Silversmith.

**SIMON, ELIZABETH:** (Indian) Age 30, a member of the Church of England, born (About 1821) at Onondaga, Sarah, age 12 born at Tuscarora, Hanah age 8 born at Tuscarora. Tuscarora Township, District 5, Page 9/61, Numbers 30-32.

**SIMONS, LUCY:** (Indian) Age 4 born (About 1847) at Tuscarora. Tuscarora Township, District 10, Page 19/71, Number 48. See the family of Mary Logboat? or Mary Longboat.

**SIT DOWN:** (Female Indian) Age 50 born (About 1801) at Onondaga. Tuscarora Township, District 25, Page 49/37, Number 22.

**SIX DOES:** (Indian) Age 40 born (About 1811) in New York State (In the United States), Tuscarora Township, District 20, Page 39/39, Number 50.

**SMITH, AARON:** (Indian) Age 45 born (About 1806) at Grand River, a member of the Church of England, Electa age 45 born at Grand River, William age 10 born at Johnson's Settlement, Lucinda age 6 born at Grand River. Tuscarora Township, District 17, Page 33/11, Numbers 35-38.

**SMITH, DAVID:** (Indian) Age 24? born (About 1827) at Grand River, a member of the Methodist Church. Tuscarora Township, District 7, Page 13/65, Number 38.

**SMITH, ELIZABETH:** (Indian) Age 15, born (About 1836) in Upper Canada (All others born in Upper Canada) Mary age 11, Lucy age 8, Peter age 6, Charlotte age 3. All were members of the Methodist Church. Onondaga Township, Part 11, Page 31, Numbers 1-7.

**SMITH, GABY? OR DABY?** (Female Indian) Age 38 born (About 1813) at Grand River, a member of the Methodist Church. Tuscarora Township, District 15, Page 29/7, Number 11.

**SMITH, HENRY:** (Indian) Age 48 born (About 1803) at Brantford, Christiana age 42 born at Brantford, David age 23 born at Grand River, Abraham age 7 born at Grand River (A Female Smith Child) age 5, (A Female Smith Child) age 3. Tuscarora Township, District 11, Page 21/75, Numbers 29-34.

**SMITH, JOEL:** (Indian) Age 68, born (About 1783) at Grand River, a member of the Church of England, Elizabeth born at Mohawk, age 57. Tuscarora Township, District 2, Numbers 39, 40.

**SMITH, JOHN:** (Indian) Age 28 born (About 1823) at Credit River, Betsy age 30, Mary age 6. (Credit Indians) Tuscarora Township, District 27, Page 53/31, Numbers 26-28.

**SMITH, JOSEPH:** (Indian) Age 21 born (About 1830) at Green Bay (Wisconsin?) a member of the Church of England. Tuscarora Township, District 17, Page 33/11, Number 10.

**SMITH, PETER:** (Indian) Age 26, (About 1825) place of birth was not given, a member of the Methodist Church. Charlotte age 32 born in Canada West, Onondaga Township, Part 11, Brant County, Ontario, Page 35, Numbers 44, 45.

**SMITH, SUSAN:** (Indian) Age 2 born (About 1849) at Grand River, a member of the Methodist Church. Tuscarora Township, District 17, Page 33/11, Number 51. See Joseph Hill on the same page.

**SMITH, SUSANAH:** (Indian) Age 50 born (About 1801) at Brantford Township, a member of the Methodist Church. Tuscarora Township, District 6, Page 11/63, Number 48.

**SMITH, THOMAS JR:** (Indian) Age 46 born (About 1805) at Credit River, a member of the Methodist Church, Roseta age 36 born at Credit River, Joseph age 17 born at Credit River, Catharine age 3 born at Tuscarora Township, Esther age six months born at Tuscarora Township. (Credit Indians) Tuscarora Township, District 27, Page 53/31, Numbers 20-24.

**SMITH, THOMAS SR:** (Indian) Age 78 born (About 1773) at Credit River, a member of the Methodist Church. Tuscarora Township, District 27, Page 53/31, Number 24.

**SMITH, THOMAS:** (Indian) Age 35 born (About 1816) at Brantford, a member of the Church of England, Dekadas Smith (Female) age 30 born at

Brantford, Eksaha Smith (Female) age 3 born at Tuscarora Township. Tuscarora Township, District 30, Page 59/19, Numbers 42-44.

**SNOW, MARGARET:** (Indian) Age 10 born (About 1811) at Tuscarora, a member of the Methodist Church. Tuscarora Township, District 3, Page 5/55, Number 12. See the family of Salley Snow.

**SNOW, SALLEY W:** (Indian) Age 45, born (About 1806) at Cayuga, a member of the Methodist Church. Tuscarora Township, District 3, Page 5/55, Number 5.

**SPRINGS, WIDOW:** (Indian) Age 75 born (About 1776) in New York (In the United States) a member of the Church of England. Tuscarora Township, District 4, Page 7/57, Number 4.

**STARTS, BETSY:** (Indian) Age 4, born in Tuscarora Township, a member of the Church of England. Tuscarora Township, District 1, Page 1/17, Number 17. See the family of Catherine Shaw.

**STERLING, JOHN:** (Indian) Age 30 born (About 1821) at Credit River, a member of the Methodist Church, Julia age 25 born at Credit River, Jacob age 7 born at Credit River, William age 6 born at Credit River, Henry age 3 born at Credit River, John age 2 months born at Tuscarora Township. Tuscarora Township, District 34, Page 67/53, Numbers 32-37.

**STOATS, HENRY:** (Indian) Age 46 born (About 1805) at Grand River, a member of the Church of England, Sarah age 43, Henry Stoats Jr., age 15, William age 13, Joshua age 10, Isaac age 7, David age 5. Tuscarora Township, District 14, Page 27/3, Numbers 24-30.

**STOATS, JOHN:** (Indian) Age 25 born (About 1826) at Mohawk Village, Lydia age 18 born at Grand River. Tuscarora Township, District 13, Page 25, Numbers 31, 32.

**STOATS, WILLIAM:** (Indian) Age eight months, born at Tuscarora, Tuscarora Township, District 13, Page 25, Number 39. See family of Margret Bompary on the same page.

**STOTS? (OR STOATS?) MARGRET:** (Indian) Age 19 born (About 1832) at Johnson's Settlement, a member of the Church of England. Tuscarora Township, District 13, Page 25, Number 19.

**STUMP, CHARLOTTE:** (Indian) Age 17 (About 1834) born at Johnson's Settlement, a member of the Methodist Church. Tuscarora Township, District Number 3, Page 5/55, Number 7.

**SUGAR:** (Male Indian) Age 50 born (About 1801) at Onondaga, Peggy age 40 born at Onondaga, Kakhaghsyon (Female) age 15 born at Onondaga, Onadawanhde (Male) age 9 born at Tuscarora. Tuscarora Township, District Number 25, Page 49/47, Numbers 7-10.

**SUGAR:** (Male Indian) Age 60 born (About 1791) at Indiana. Tuscarora Township, District 25, Page 49/37, Number 23.

**SUMMERFIELD, JOHN:** (Indian) Age 13 (About 1838) born at Credit River, a member of the Methodist Church. (Credit Indian) Tuscarora Township, District 28, Page 55/33, Number 23. See the family of Mary Young.

**TEHRORENS:** (Male Indian) Age 60 born (About 1791) at Onondaga, Arisakwa (Female) age 50 born at Onondaga, Yorahhwadixon (Male) age 22 born at Onondaga, Dayohtharatye (Male) age 16 born at Onondaga, Dehadawenrye (Male) age 14 born at Onondaga, Wesayohha (Male) age 12 born at Onondaga, Ainenho? or Awenho?(Female) age 10 born at Tuscarora. Tuscarora Township, District 22, Page 43/43, Numbers 41-47.

**THAKOWIHHE:** (Male Indian) Age 30 born (About 1821) at Onondaga. Tuscarora Township, District 26, Page 51/29, Number 25. See Margret Davids on the same page. She is the possible wife of Thakowihhe.

**THOMAS, BETSY:** (Indian) Age 32, born (About 1819) at Oxbow. A member of the Methodist Church. Tuscarora Township, District 12, Page 23/1, Number 19.

**THOMAS, DAVID:** (Indian) Age 24 born (About 1827) at Onondaga, a member of the Church of England, Elizabeth age not given, born at Onondaga a member of the Methodist Church. Tuscarora Township, District 6, Page 11/63, Numbers 14, 15.

**THOMAS, DAVID:** (Indian) Age 41 born (About 1810) at Grand River, a member of the Church of England, Margret Thomas age 37, Susan age 14, Elizabeth age 7, Abram age 2, Jacob age two months. Tuscarora Township, District 17, Page 33/11, Numbers 22-27.

**THOMAS, ESTHER:** (Indian) Age 30 born (About 1821) at the Bay of Quinty, a member of the Church of England, Sarah age 15 born at Indiana Village, Mary age 14 born at Tuscarora, Isaac age 11, born at Tuscarora, William age 9, born at Tuscarora, Catharine age 4, born at Tuscarora, Betsey age 2, born at Tuscarora. Tuscarora Township, District 6, Page 11/63, Numbers 48-50. Isaac, William, Catharine, and Betsey Thomas were enumerated on the top of the next census page numbered 13/65.

**THOMAS, ISAAC:** (Indian) Age 40 born (About 1811) at Brantford, a member of the Methodist Church. Tuscarora Township, District 22, Page 43/43, Number 33.

**THOMAS, JACOB:** (Indian) Age 19, born (About 1832) at Tuscarora, a member of the Church of England, Tuscarora Township, District 4, Page 7/57. Number 21.

**THOMAS, JACOB:** (Indian) Age 52 born (About 1799) at Lewiston (In New York?), a member of the Baptist Church, Catherine age 50 born at Tuscarora, Thomas age 21, born at Tuscarora, Catharine age 30, born at Brantford, Susan age 8, born at Onondaga, Abram age 10, born at Tuscarora, George age 1, born at Tuscarora. Tuscarora Township, District 21, Page 41/41, Numbers 35-41.

**THOMAS, JOHN:** (Listed as a White man) Age 30 born (About 1821) in England, a member of the Baptist Church, Esther (Indian) age 28, born at Brantford, Mary age one and a half, born at Tuscarora. Tuscarora Township, District 18, Page 35/49, Numbers 13-15.

**THOMAS, LAWRENCE:** (Indian) Age 22 born (About 1829) at Grand River. A member of the Church of England. Tuscarora Township, District 11, Page 21/75? Number 50.

**THOMAS, NICHOLAS:** (Indian) Age 5 born (About 1846) at Onondaga, Joseph THOMAS age 2 born at Tuscarora. Tuscarora Township, District 6, Page 11/63, Numbers 17, 18. See the family of Christiana Harris.

**THOMAS, WIDOW:** (Indian) Age 55 born (About 1796) at Credit River, a member of the Methodist Church. (Credit Indians) Tuscarora Township, District 35, Page 69/17, Number 44.

**THOMAS, WILLIAM:** (Indian) Age 7 born (About 1844) at Tuscarora, Mary THOMAS age 5, born at Tuscarora. Tuscarora Township, District 6, Page 11/63, numbers 5, 6,.

**THOYENNOKEN:** (Male Indian) Age 42 born (About 1809) at Brantford. Tuscarora Township, District 25, Page 49/37, Number 50.

**TOBECO, HIRAM:** (Indian) Age 28 born (About 1823) at Credit River, a member of the Methodist Church, Mary Ann age 40. (Credit Indians) Tuscarora Township, District 27, Page 53/31, Numbers 5, 6.

**TOBECO, JAMES:** (Indian) Age 35 born (About 1816) at Credit River, a member of the Methodist Church, Sarah age 25 born at Credit River, John age 2 born at Tuscarora Township. Tuscarora Township, District 34, Page 67/53, Numbers 9-11.

**TOBECO, JOHN:** (Indian) Age 58 born (About 1793) at Credit River, Members of the Methodist Church, Betsy age 52, Elizabeth age ? (Credit Indians) Tuscarora Township, District 27, Page 53/31, Numbers 7, 8.

**TOBECO, SMITH:** (Indian) age 30 born (About 1821) at Credit River, a member of the Methodist Church, Elizabeth age 29, Sapphire? age 10, Joseph age 2. (Credit Indians) Tuscarora Township, District 27, Page 53/31, Numbers 9-14.

**TOBECO, WILLIAM:** (Indian) Age 44 born (About 1807) at Credit River, a member of the Methodist Church, Betsy age 44 born at Credit River, James age 6 born at Credit River, Mary age 3, born at Credit River. (Credit Indians) Tuscarora Township, District 27, Page 53/31, Numbers 15-18.

**TOBICE, ELIZABETH:** (Indian) Age 10, an orphan, born (About 1811) in Canada, a member of the Church of England. Brantford Township, District 5, Page 183/16, Number 46.

**TOM, JOHN:** (Indian) Age 17 born (About 1834) at Onondaga. Tuscarora Township, District 25, Page 49/37, Number 21.

**TOM, PETER:** (Indian) Age 40 born (About 1811) at Indiana, Kahwendaonho (Female) age 30 born at Indiana, Kahnaweksere (Female) Age 14 born at Indiana, John age 16 born at Indiana, Skentyonhkwadens (Male) age 15 born at Indiana. Tuscarora Township, District 25, Page 49/37, Numbers 2-6.

**TOME? JOHN:** (Indian) Age 55, born (About 1796) at Paris, a member of the Church of England. Tuscarora Township, District 10, Page 19/71, Number 37.

**TOWAH, JAMES? OR ISAAC?** (Indian) Age 50, born (About 1801) at Credit River, a member of the Methodist Church, Susan age 50 Francis (Male) 18, Frederick age 16, Joseph age 14, James age 10. Tuscarora Township, District 34, Page 67/53, Numbers 3-8.

**TURKEY, BETSY:** (Indian) Age 29 born (About 1822) at Brantford, a member of the Church of England. Tuscarora Township, District 12, Page 23/1, Number 44. See Sarah & Lucy Hill and Jesse? Turkey.

**TURKEY, JESSEE?** (A male Indian) Age 8 born (About 1843) at Tuscarora, Elijah age 6, Catharine age 4, John age 3, Elyelon? a female age 6 months. Tuscarora Township, District 12, Page 23/1, Numbers 47-51. See the entry for Betsy Turkey. She is possibly the mother of these children..

**TURKEY, JOSHUA:** (He was enumerated as a Negro?) Age 47, born (About 1804) in New York, (In the United States) a member of the Church of England, he resided at Onondaga, Tuscarora, Township, District 5, Page 9/61. Number 7.

**TWOFISH, JOSEPH:** (Indian) Age 56, born (About 1795) in Canada, a member of the Church of England, Hanah age 42 born in Canada, Christiana age 19 born in Canada, Catherine age 12 born in Canada, Benjamin age 9 born in Canada, Elizabeth age 5 born in Canada, William age 2 born in Canada. Brantford Township, District 5, Page 183/16, Numbers 33-39.

**WABANIBE OR WABANIBER, MARGRET:** (Indian) Age 48 born (About 1803) at Credit River, a member of the Methodist Church, Samuel age 7 born at Credit River. Tuscarora Township, District 34, Page 67/53, Numbers 44, 45.

**WAHBAHOOSA, POLLY:** (Indian) Age 79 born (About 1772) at Credit River, a member of the Methodist Church. Tuscarora Township, District 34, Page 69/53, Number 38.

**WAHODAHENNOKAGHE:** (Male Indian) Age 60 born (About 1791) at Cayuga. Tuscarora Township, District 25, Page 49/37, Number 1.

**WAHSIDENSEDO:** (Female Indian) Age 60 born (About 1791) at Onondaga, Karanyata (Female) age 15, born at Onondaga, Dehyorhawende (Female) age 8, born at Onondaga, Dehyonronwarate (Male) age 4, born at Tuscarora. Tuscarora Township, District 22, Page 43/43, Numbers 11-14.

**WAKARENNAHTON:** (Female Indian) Age 37 born (About 1814) at Indiana, a member of the Church of England, Thaweninake (Male) age 15 born at Indiana, Radenhenrehawe (Male) age 20 born at Indiana. Tuscarora Township, District 22, Page 43/43, Numbers 30-32.

**WAKONWADONKONTON:** (Male Indian) Age 32 born (About 1819) at Indiana, Dehawennakeh (Female) age 16 born at Indiana, Deyorahkose (Female) age 4 born at Indiana, Kahhindokha (Female) age 4 born at Indiana. Tuscarora Township, District 23, Page 45/45, Numbers 1-4.

**WALKER, DOROTHY:** (Indian) Age 50 born (About 1801) at Mohawk, a member of the Methodist Church, John age 17 born at Onondaga, Isaac age 74? or 17? born at Onondaga. Tuscarora Township, District 13, Page 25, Numbers 23-25.

**WALKER, MARGRET:** (Indian) Age 42, born (About 1809) at Onondaga, a member of the Church of England. Tuscarora Township, District 5, Brant County, Ontario. Page 9/61. Number 26.

**WALKER, MOSES:** (Indian) Age 29 born (About 1822) at Grand River, a member of the Methodist Church, Christiana age 26, Sarah age 24, Isaiah? age 9, Male Child age 7, Female age 3. Tuscarora Township, District 36, Page 71/47, Numbers 38-43.

**WAMPUN, MRS?** (Female Indian) Age 50 born (About 1801) at Grand River, a member of the Baptist Church, John age 50 born at Grand River, Elizabeth age 15 born at Grand River, Mary age 4 born at Grand River, Tuscarora Township, District 33, Numbers 27-30.

**WASHINGTON, GEORGE:** (Indian) Age 13 born (About 1838) at Woodstock. A member of the Methodist Church. Tuscarora Township, District 36, Ontario, Page 71/47, Number 14. See the family of Henry Jones.

**WEBSTER, THOMAS:** (Indian) Age listed as unknown, born in the United States, a member of the Baptist Church, residence Tuscarora, Margaret age listed as unknown, born in Canada West. Onondaga Township, Part 11, Page 37, Numbers 29, 30.

**WESLEY, MARY:** (Indian) Age 37 born (About 1814) at Credit River, a member of the Methodist Church, Sapphire? of Sapphios? (Female) age 14, Clary (Male) age 5. (Credit Indians) Tuscarora Township, District 28, Page 55/33, Numbers 25-27.

**WESLY, CHARLES:** (Indian) Age 25 born (About 1826) at Credit River, a member of the Methodist Church. Caroline age 22, born at Credit River. (Credit Indians) Tuscarora Township, District 35, Page 69/17, Numbers 13, 14.

**WHITBY, ISAAC:** (Listed as a Negro?) Age 45 (About 1806) born in Philadelphia (United States?), a member of the Baptist Church, Sarah (Indian) no age given. born at the Bay of Quinty. Tuscarora Township, District 36, Page 71/47, Numbers 18, 19.

**WHITE, GEORGE:** (Indian) Age 22 born (About 1829) in New York State (In the United States) a member of the Methodist Church, Mary age 23, born at Onondaga, Joseph age 7, born at Onondaga, Elizabeth age 2, born at Onondaga, John age four months born at Tuscarora. Tuscarora Township, District 23, Page 45/45, Numbers 17-21.

**WHITECOAT, JOHN:** (Indian) Age 85 (About 1766) born in New York (In the United States). He was a member of the Church of England. Tuscarora Township, District 4, Page 7/57, Number 3.

**WICKLEY, LOUISA:** (Indian) Age 13 born (About 1838) at Tuscarora, a member of the Methodist Church. Tuscarora Township, District 7, Page 13/65, Number 11. (See the family of Arc'd. Lewis)

**WILLIAM, SUSAN:** (Indian) Age 76, born (About 1777) in the United States, a member of the Church of England. Onondaga Township, Part 11, Page 35, Number 35.

**WILLIAMS, GEORGE:** (Indian) Age 25 born (About 1826) at Grand River, a member of the Church of England, Mrs. WILLIAMS age 24, born at Grand River, Miss WILLIAMS age 6, born at Tuscarora, Miss WILLIAMS age 2, born at Tuscarora. Tuscarora Township, District 19, Page 37/51, Numbers 37-40.

**WILLIAMS, JACOB:** (Indian) Age 36 born (About 1815) at Tuscarora, a member of the Baptist Church, Sarah age 31, Christiana age 4, born at Tuscarora, Nicholas age 8, born at Tuscarora, Eunice age 6, born at Tuscarora, Mary age 4, born at Tuscarora, David age 2, born at Tuscarora, Abraham age 23 born at Tuscarora. Tuscarora Township, District 21, Page 41/41, Numbers 1-8.

**WILLIAMS, JACOB:** (Indian) Age 40 born (About 1811) at Indiana, a member of the Church of England, Margret age 28 born at Onondaga Township. Tuscarora Township, District 30, Page 59/19, Numbers 39, 40.

**WILLIAMS, JOHN:** (Indian) Age 52 born (About 1799) in New York State (In the United States) Mary age 50 born in New York, John age 23 born in New York, Ellen age 17 born at Brantford, Kanononyadon (Female) age 1 born at Tuscarora Township, District 31, Page 61/21, Numbers 41-45.

**WILLIAMS, JOHN:** (Indian) Age 25, born (About 1826) at Tuscarora, a member of the Church of England, Mary age 25 born in Tuscarora Township, District 5, Page 9/61. Number 34, 35.

**WILLIAMS, JOSIAH:** (Indian) Age 10 born (About 1811) in Canada West, a member of the Church of England, Onondaga Township, Part 11, Page 35, Number 37. See the family of Moses Conjecton.

**WILLIAMS, JOSHUA:** (Indian) Age 27 born (About 1824) in the United States, a member of the Church of England. Mary age 27, born in Canada West. Onondaga Township, Part 11, District 2, Page 35, Numbers 18, 19.

**WILLIAMS, MARY:** (Indian) Age 76? or 16? born at Tuscarora. A member of the Methodist Church. Tuscarora Township, District 11, Page 21/75?, Number 9.

**WILLIAMS, MOSES:** (Indian) Age 30 born (About 1821) at Brantford, a member of the Church of England, Mrs. Williams age 58 born at Onondaga, a Williams son age 11 born at Onondaga, a Williams daughter age 9 born at Tuscarora. Tuscarora Township, District 20, Page 39/39, Numbers 46-49.

**WILLIAMS, MRS:** (Indian) Age 76, born (About 1777) in New York (In the United States) a member of the Baptist Church, Tuscarora Township, District 4, Page 7/57. Number 6.

**WILLIAMS, POWLESS:** (Indian) Age 30, born (About 1821) at the Bay of Quinty, a member of the Methodist Church, Elizabeth age 23, born at the Bay of Quinty, Ellen age 8, born at the Bay of Quinty. Tuscarora Township, District 9, Page 17/69, Numbers 46-48.

**WILLIAMS, RACHEL:** (Indian) Age 70 born (About 1781) in New York (All were born in New York) Eliza age 18, John age 16, Jonah B. age 12, George age 10. All were members of the Church of England. Tuscarora Township, District 31, Page 61, 21, Numbers 46-50.

**WILLIAMS, SAMPSON:** (Indian) Age 17 born (About 1834) in the United States. He was a member of the Church of England, James age 2, born in Upper Canada. Onondaga Township, Part 11, Page 31, Numbers 11, 12.

**WILLIAMS, SARAH:** (Indian) Age 50 born (About 1801) in New York State (In the United States). A member of the Baptist Church, Tuscarora Township, District 10, Page 19/71, Number 43.

**WILSON, JAMES:** (Indian) Age 45 born (About 1806) at Credit River, a member of the Methodist Church, Phebe age 40 born at Credit River, Julia Ann age 20 born at Credit River, Margret age 18 born at Credit River. (Credit Indians) Tuscarora Township, District 28, Page 55/33, Numbers 34-37.

**WILSON, JOHN:** (Indian) Age 50 born (About 1801) in New York (In the United States) a member of the Church of England, Betsey age 40 born at Grand River, James age 10 born at Grand River, John age 8 born at Grand River, Tuscarora Township, District 33, Page 65/25, Numbers 23-26.

**WING, WIDOW:** (Indian) Age 110, born (About 1742) in New York (In the United States) a member of the Church of England, Tuscarora Township, District 32, Page 63/23, Number 40.

**WINN, MARGARET:** (Indian) Age 28 born (About 1823) at Brantford, Tuscarora Township, District 18, Page 35/49, Number 16.

**WRIGHT, ALBERT:** (Indian) Age 18 born (About 1833) in Canada West, a member of the Baptist Church, Onondaga Township, Part 11, Page 35, Number 34.

**WRIGHT, JOHN:** (Indian) Age 75, born (About 1776) in the United States, a member of the Methodist Church. Barbara age 37 born in the United States, a member of the Baptist Church, Albert age 16 born in the United States, Timothy age 11 born in Canada West. Onondaga Township, Part 11, District 2, Page 35, Numbers 14-17.

**YELLOW, JOSEPH:** (Indian) Age 20 born (About 1831) at Onondaga, a member of the Church of England, Peter age 40, Elizabeth age 40, Mary age 14, Peter age 17, Jacob age 5. Tuscarora Township, District 19, Page 39/39, Numbers 29-34.

**YONHAWENJENHAWY:** (Female Indian) Age 34 born (About 1817) at Indiana. Tuscarora Township, District 29, Page 57/27, Number 30.

**YOUNG, PETER:** (Indian) Age 32 born (About 1819) at Onondaga. Tuscarora Township, District 18, Page 35/49, Number 44.

**YOUNGS, ELLEN:** (Indian) Age 45 born (About 1806) at Onondaga, a member of the Church of England, Abraham age 20 born at Onondaga, William age 15 born at Onondaga, Eksaha (female) age 7 born at Onondaga, Raksaha (Male) age 5 born at Tuscarora, Raksaha (Male) age 3 born at Tuscarora. Tuscarora Township, District 30, Page 59/19, Numbers 45-50.

**YOUNGS, MARIAH:** (Indian) Age 5 born (About 1846) at Credit River, a member of the Methodist Church. (Credit Indian) Tuscarora Township, District 35, Page 69/17, Number 50. See the family of John Sawyer on the same page.

**YOUNGS, MARY:** (Indian) Age 40 born (About 1811) at Credit River, a member of the Methodist Church, John SUMMERFIELD age 13 born at Credit River, Rachel YOUNG age 3 born at Credit River. (Credit Indians) Tuscarora Township, District 28, Page 55/33, Numbers 22-24.

**YOUNGS, THOMAS:** (Indian) Age 34 born (About 1817) at Credit River, a member of the Methodist Church, Mary age 20, Mariah age 5, Margret age 3. Tuscarora Township, District 34, Page 67/53, Number 49-52.

**YOWENHDE:** (Female Indian) Age 57 born (About 1804) at Buffalo (New York?). Tuscarora Township, District 26, Page 51/29, Number 7.

## ONONDAGA PART I

Onondaga County District Number One, Page One, in Brant County listed five Indians were on the page. They failed to check who they were. The author of this book has deemed that the family in question was probably that of John DAVIS age 23 born in Canada, A member of the Church of England, Dorothy age 20, born in Canada, a member of the Methodist Church, John age 5, Isaac age 25, Mary age 24. Page 1/1, Numbers 14-18.

In the 1851 Canadian Census surnames were presented on one page. On the next page columns were represented to check which individuals on the first page were colored, Indian or white. No checks were listed for the following pages. Only a column total represented how many Indians was listed on the proceeding pages. The pages involved included: Onondaga District Number 1, Page 7, seven Indians? Onondaga District Number 1, Page 9, 14 Indians? Onondaga District Number 1, Page 13, 17 Indians? Onondaga District Number 1, Page 19, 15 Indians? Onondaga District Number 1, Page 21, 10 Indians. These Indians were not included in this abstract.

# BRANT COUNTY, ONTARIO, MOHAWK INSTITUTE
## 1851 CENSUS ABSTRACT
## ONONDAGA PART II

Henry Hartman? or Hatman? a member of the Church of England was born in New Brunswick, Canada in 1808. He was enumerated in the 1851 Brant County, Ontario Census as the Superintendent of the Mohawk Institute. The census entry for this the Mohawk Institute was located in Brantford Township, District 5, Page 185/17, Numbers 1-7. All of the following students were born in Canada. Every student was enumerated as a member of the Church of England.

| THE MOHAWK INSTITUTE, 1851 CENSUS BRANT COUNTY, ONTARIO | | |
|---|---|---|
| BAREFOOT, ISAAC (Indian) | Age 13 | Number 15 |
| BATTICE, ELLEN (Indian) | Age 12 | Number 38 |
| BATTICE, ISAAC (Indian) | Age 11 | Number 19 |
| BRANT, JOHN (Indian) | Age 12 | Number 21 |
| CLAUSE, JOSEPH (Indian) | Age 9 | Number 26 |
| CLINCH, HENRY (Indian) | Age 13 | Number 28 |
| DIXON, JOHN (Indian) | Age 12 | Number 17 |
| GREEN, ELIZABETH: (Indian) | Age 9 | Number 39 |
| GREEN, ISAAC (Indian) | Age 10 | Number 32 |
| GREEN, NANCY (Indian) | Age 15 | Number 42 |
| HILL, ALEXANDER (Indian) | Age 7 | Number 27 |
| HILL, CATHARINE (Indian) | Age 12 | Number 43 |
| HILL, ELIAS (Indian) | Age 16 | Number 12 |
| HILL, JOSEPH (Indian) | Age 12 | Number 46 |
| HILL, SARAH (Indian) | Age 14 | Number 41 |
| HILL, SUSANAH (Indian) | Age 11? | Number 36 |
| ISAAC, GEORGE (Indian) | Age 8 | Number 20 |
| JACKET, AUGUSTUS (Indian) | Age 10? | Number 33 |
| JAMIESON, MARY (Indian) | Age 11 | Number 44 |
| JOHN, LUCY (Indian) | Age 14 | Number 40 |
| JOHN, PETER (Indian) | Age 9 | Number 25 |
| JOHN, WILLIAM (Indian) | Age 14 | Number 24 |

| | | |
|---|---|---|
| JOHNATHAN, LAWRENCE (Indian) | Age 11 | Number 23 |
| JOHNATHAN, MARY (Indian) | Age 15 | Number 35 |
| LEWIS, JACOB (Indian) | Age 18 | Number 10 |
| MARICLE, DAVID (Indian) | Age 13 | Number 16 |
| MARTIN, EMILY (Indian) | Age 11 | Number 37 |
| MARTIN, PETER (Indian) | Age 13 | Number 14 |
| MT. PLEASANT, THOMAS (Indian) | Age 12 | Number 18 |
| OWEN, JESSE (Indian) | Age 12 | Number 29 |
| STOTTS?, HENRY (Indian) | Age 16 | Number 13 |
| STOTTS, JOSHUA (Indian) | Age 10 | Number 22 |
| THOMAS, JOHN (Indian) | Age 17 | Number 11 |
| TURKEY, JESSE (Indian) | Age 9 | Number 34 |
| TURKEY, LUCY (Indian) | Age 11 | Number 45 |
| YOUNG, ISAAC (Indian) | Age 10 | Number 31 |
| YOUNG, JOHN (Indian) | Age 11 | Number 30 |

**NOTE:** Susanah HILL was crossed off the list. A note was included to indicate she died at age 13 on the 18th of December 1851 at George MARTINS house.

**NOTE:** Augustus JACKET was crossed off the list. A note was included that Augustus JACKET died at age 9 on the 4th of January 1852 at his father's house.

# BRANT COUNTY, ONTARIO 1881 CENSUS ABSTRACT

## SECTION ONE

### THE MOHAWK, DELAWARE AND TUSCARORA OF BRANT COUNTY, ONTARIO E-1 & E-2, 159 SOUTH BRANT, DISTRICT NUMBER TWO, TUSCARORA TOWNSHIP, INDIAN RESERVATION.

All of the following people were listed as Native Canadians unless otherwise noted. All of the children in each household has the same surname as the head of household unless otherwise noted. A surname was highlighted with capital letters in a family entry if the that surname was different from the surname of the head of household. A question mark was placed after a name that was in doubt. This census abstract should not take the place of any government or tribal records. For more information write the tribal office.

**ADAMS, MARY:** (Indian) Age 50, born (About 1831) in Ontario, a Methodist. Page 52, Household 319/324.

**ANTER? (OR ARTER?):** (Indian) Age 22, born (About 1859) in Ontario, a Baptist, Louise age 12, born in Ontario. Page 39, Household 235/238.

**BARE? (OR BARR?) JOHN:** (Indian) Age 19, born (About 1862) in Ontario, a Methodist, Betsy LICKEN age 25, born in Ontario. Page 51, Household 309/314.

**BENNETT, ERASTUS:** (Indian) Age 24, born (About 1857) in Ontario, A member of the Baptist Church, Catherine age 26, born in Ontario, a member of the Church of England, Sarah Ann age 3, born in Ontario, Lydia age 1, born in Ontario. Page 60, Household 373/378.

**BRESTIN? (OR BRESLIN?) FRANCIS:** (A male Indian) Age 20, born (About 1861) in Ontario, a member of the Church of England, Susana age 20, born in Ontario, Page 55, Household 333/348.

**BUCK, LUCY:** (Indian) Age 36, born (About 1845) in Ontario, no religion given, Cristine age 67, born in Ontario, Jacob OLYERS? OR SYERS? age 5, born in Ontario, ? BUCK age 13 (a female) born in Ontario, ? Buck, age 10 (a female) born in Ontario, ? Buck, age 6, (a female). Page 46, Household 279/284.

**BUCK, WILLIAM:** (Indian) Age 50, born (About 1831) no religion given, Curley Buck (female?) age 27, ? Buck (a female) age 9. Page 45, Household 276/281.

**BURNING, ARON:** (Indian) Age 25, born (About 1856) in Ontario, a member of the Church of England, Hannah age 20, born in Ontario, Joshua age 2, born in Ontario, Susannah DOUGLAS age 18, born in Ontario. Page 41. Household 249/253.

**BURNING? ISAAC:** (Indian) Age 28, born (About 1853) in Ontario, a member of the Church of England, Lucy age 26, born in Ontario, Charlotte age 8, born in Ontario, Elizabeth age 6, born in Ontario,

Mary age 4, born in Ontario, Katie age 2, born in Ontario. Page 41, Household 247/251.

**BURNHAM? (OR BARNHAM?) JOHN:** (Indian) Age 34, born (About 1847) in Ontario, no religion given, Lydia age 39, born in Ontario, Samuel age 12, born in Ontario. Page 47, Household 286/291.

**BURNHAM, JULIA:** (Indian) Age 47, born (About 1834) in Ontario, a member of the Universalist religion, Mary age 20, born in Ontario, Elizabeth age 18, born in Ontario. Page 40, Household 243/247.

**BURHAM? TIMOTHY:** (Indian) age 44, born (About 1837) in Ontario, a member of the Church of England, Lucy age 40, born in Ontario, Alex EUTOMLE? age 9, born in Ontario. Page 50, Household 305/310.

**CAPTAIN, WM:** (Indian) Age 35, born (About 1846) in Ontario, a Baptist, Julia age 24, born in Ontario, Annie age 2, born in Ontario, Francis (a male) abe five months, born in November in Ontario, Sussanah LONGFISH age 71, born in Ontario. Page 44, Household 273/277.

**CARPENTER, BENJAMIN:** (Indian) age 48, born (About 1833) in Ontario, a Methodist, Susan age 35, born in Ontario, Lizzie age 27, born in Ontario, Mary MC PHAIL (Indian) age 20, born in Ontario, Gahazes? (a male) Carpenter, age 34, born in Ontario. Page 52, Household 317/322.

**CARPENTER, JOHN:** Indian, age 34, born (About 1847) in Ontario, a Methodist, Elizabeth Carpenter, Indian, born in Ontario, age 25, a Methodist, Wesley born in Ontario, age 2. Page 65, Household 410/415.

**CARRIE, HANNAH:** (Indian) Age 55, born (About 1826) in Ontario, a member of the Church of England, Emily age 16, born in Ontario, Elizabeth age 20, born in Ontario, Ewel? age 35, born in Ontario, Seth CLAUSE, age 14, born in Ontario. Page 61, Household 381/386.

**CAUT? (OR CANT?) LUCY:** (Indian) Age 69, born (About 1812) in Ontario, no religion given. Page 41, Household 245/249.

**CLAUS, AARON:** (Indian) Age 29, born (About 1852) in Ontario, a member of the Church of England, Lucy age 24, born in Ontario, Jewell (a female) age 7, born in Ontario, John age 2, born in Ontario. Page 49, Household 297/302.

**CLAUS, ESTHER:** (Indian) Age 25, born (About 1856) in Ontario, a member of the Church of England, Levi age 3, born in Ontario. Page 40, Household 238/241.

**CLAUS, ISAAC:** (Indian) Age 20, born (About 1861) in Ontario, a member of the Church of England, Susie age 19, born in Ontario, Nancy BENNETT age 15, born in Ontario, age 15. Page 61, Household 377/382.

**CLAUS, ISAAC:** (Indian) Age 60, born (About 1821) in Ontario, a member of the Church of England, Esther age 62, born in Ontario, Sarah age 15, born in Ontario, Lawrence ? (a male) age 18, born in Ontario. Page 49, Household 296/301.

**CLAUS, JOHN:** (Indian) Age 30, born (About 1851) in Ontario, a Baptist, Louisa age 27, born in Ontario. Page 40, Household 237/240.

**CLAUS, MARGARET:** (Indian) Age 40, born (About 1841) in Ontario, a Methodist, George KICK, Indian, born in Ontario, age 10, Joseph HENRY, Indian, born in Ontario, age 2. Page 64, Household 406/411.

**CLAUS, THOMAS:** (Indian) Age 37, born (About 1844) in Ontario, Methodist, Lucy age 35, born in Ontario. Page 63, Household 399/404.

**CLAUS, WILLIAM:** (Indian) Age 34, born (About 1847) in Ontario, a member of the Church of England, Lucy age 31, born in Ontario, a member of the Church of England. Page 60, Household 376/381.

**CLINCH, AMOS:** (Indian) Age 32, born (About 1849) in Ontario, a member of the Church of England, Elizabeth age 37, born in Ontario, Maggie age 17, born in Ontario, Emma age 9, born in Ontario. Page 49, Household 299/304.

**CLINCH, CATHARINE:** (Indian) Age 23, born (About 1858) in Ontario, a Methodist, Joseph CLARK age 9, born in Ontario. Page 49, Household 300/305.

**CLINCH, HENRY:** (Indian), Age 60, born (About 1821) in Ontario, a Methodist, Ellen age 58, born in Ontario, John age 19, born in Ontario, Charles age 17, born in Ontario. Page 49, Household 299/304.

**CLINCH, (OR CLENCH) NELSON:** (Indian) Age 35, born (About 1846) in Ontario, a Methodist, Jane born in Ontario, age 25, Lily born in Ontario, age 6, Robert born in Ontario, age 4, a male Clinch (no first name given) age 2. Page 63, Household 397/402.

**CUSICK, JESSE:** (Indian) Age 23, born (About 1858) in Ontario, a member of the Church of England, Susannah age 20, born in Ontario, Moses age 8, born in Ontario, Edward age 4, born in Ontario, Katie age 1, born in Ontario. Page 41, Household 250/254.

**CUSICK, THOS:** (Indian) Age 24, born (About 1857) in Ontario, a member of the Baptist Church, Rebecca age 23, born in Ontario, Robert age 2, born in Ontario. Page 62, Household 392/397.

**DAVIS, FRANCIS:** (A Male Indian) Age 28, born (About 1853) in Ontario, a Methodist. Page 64, Household 408/413.

**DAVIS, RICHARD:** (Indian) Age 40, born (About 1841) in Ontario, a member of the Church of England, Mary age 42, born in Ontario. Page 60, Household 375/380.

**DAVIS, RICHARD:** (Indian) Age 29, born (About 1852) in Ontario, a member of the Church of England, Sarah? age 24, born in Ontario, R. Squire Lyman? Davis, age 5, born in Ontario, Margaret Mary age 4, born in Ontario, Jennie Ivey Davis, age 2, born in Ontario, E. G. Oswald Davis (a male) age nine months born in January in Ontario. Page 45, Household 274/279.

**DAVIS, WM:** (Indian) Age 34, born (About 1847) in Ontario, a member of the Church of England, Sarah age 32, born in Ontario, Elmer age 4, born in Ontario. Page 45, Household 273/278.

**DEE, ROBERT HILL:** (White/English) Age 51, born (About 1830) in Ontario, a member of the Church of England, born in England, A Medical Doctor, Kate Dee, age 23, (English) born in Ontario, Fanny Wade Dee, (English) age 21, born in Ontario, Charlotte SMITH (Indian) born in Ontario, a Baptist. Page 45, Household 275/280.

**DICKSON, JOHN:** (Indian) Age 34, born (About 1847) in Ontario, a Baptist, Unus (a female) age 39, born in Ontario, ? Dickson (a male) age 3, born in Ontario. Page 40, Household 240/243.

**DILION? (OR SILOES?) CATHERINE:** (Indian) Age 62, born (About 1819) in Ontario, no religion was given. Page 47, Household 288, 293.

**DUNCAN, ISAAC:** (Indian) Age 59, born (About 1822) in Ontario, a Methodist. Page 50, Household 304/309.

**DUNCAN, JOHN:** (White/Irish) Age 45, born (About 1836) in Ireland, a member of the Church of England, Cristine Duncan (Indian) age 43, born in Ontario, Elizabeth JOHNSON, age 17 (Indian) born in Ontario. Page 57, Household 360/365.

**ELLIOTT, MARGARET:** (Indian) Age 50, born (About 1831) in Ontario, a member of the Church of England, Augusta (a female) age 16, born in Ontario, George age 25, born in Ontario, James age 16? born in Ontario, John age 22, born in Ontario. Page 59, Household 370/375.

**FISH, CHARLES:** (Indian) Age 19, born (About 1862) in Ontario, a member of the Church of England, Carrie KEY? (Indian) age 78? or 8?, born in Ontario. Page 53, Household 328/333.

**FISH, DAVID:** (Indian) Age 37, born (About 1844) in Ontario, a member of the Church of England, Catharine DOXTATOR (age not given) born in Ontario. Page 53, Household 327/332.

**FISH, PETER:** (Indian) Age 27, born (About 1854) in Ontario, no religion given, Harriet age 31, born in Ontario, Daniel age 8, born in Ontario, Hannah age 6, born in Ontario, Lucy age 2, born in Ontario, John age 69, born in Ontario, no religion given. Page 36, Household 218/220.

**FRASER, JOHN:** (Indian) Age 48, born (About 1833) in Ontario, a Methodist, Charlotte born in Ontario, age 45, a Methodist, John born in Ontario, age 22, Joseph born in Ontario, age 20, Alex born in Ontario, age 18, Julia born in Ontario, age 9. Page 63, Household 395/400.

**FROMAN, JEMIMA:** (Indian) Age 21, born (About 1860) in Ontario, a Methodist, Hannah age three months, born in February. Page 40, Household 242/246.

**FROMAN, JONAS:** (Indian) Age ? born in Ontario, a Methodist, Charlotte age 37, born in Ontario, Sarah age 17, born in Ontario, John age 13, born in Ontario, Susanna age 11, born in Ontario, Daniel age 6, born in Ontario. Page 58, Household 361/366.

**FROMAN, PETNIGO:** (A Male Indian) Age 26, born (About 1855) in Ontario, a Methodist, Hanah age 27, born in Ontario, Susanah age 6, born in Ontario, Amos age 3, born in Ontario, Jake age 1. born in Ontario. Page 40, Household 241/245.

**GARLOW, CHRISTOPHER:** (Indian) age 62, born (About 1819) in Ontario, a member of the Church of England, Catherine age 19, born in Ontario, Albert ISLAND, age 6, born in Ontario. Page 55, Household 341/346.

**GARLOW, DAVID:** (Indian) Age 27, born (About 1854) in Ontario, a member of the Church of England, Julia age 8, born in Ontario, Jesse age 4, born in Ontario, Peter age 7, born in Ontario. Page 55, Household 342/347.

**GARLOW, LUCY:** (Indian) Age 30? or 57?, born in Ontario, a member of the Church of England, Sarah age 7, born in Ontario, Alex (a male) age 3, born in Ontario. Page 56, Household 352/357.

**GARLOW, LUCY:** (Indian) Age 18, born (About 1863) in Ontario, a member of the Church of England, Cristine age 15, born in Ontario, Margaret GENERAL age 14, born in Ontario. Page 55, Household 344/349.

**GARLOW, PETER:** (Indian) Age 68? born (About 1813) in Ontario, a Methodist, Mary age 60, born in Ontario. Page 51, Household 310/315.

**GARLOW, PETER JR:** (Indian) Age 30, born (About 1851) in Ontario, a Methodist, Mary A. POWLESS age 24, Chaucey Garlow (a male) age 3, born in Ontario. Page 51, Household 313/315.

**GENERAL, ESTHER:** (Indian) Age 82, born (About 1799) in Ontario, no religion given. Page 39, Household 229/232.

**GENERAL, ISAAC:** (Indian) Age 42, born (About 1839) in Ontario, no religion given, Ellen age 36, born in Ontario, Eliza Jane age 5, born in Ontario, Emeline age 1, born in Ontario. Page 37, Household 222/224.

**GENERAL, JOHN:** (Indian) Age 53, born (About 1828) in Ontario, no religion given, Jemima age 48, Mary age 20, born in Ontario, Elijah age 18, born in Ontario, Joseph age 16, born in Ontario, Susan age 16, born in Ontario, Nancy age 14, born in Ontario, Deborrah age 8, born in Ontario, Eliza age 6, born in Ontario. Page 58, Household 364/369.

**GENERAL, WILLIAM:** (Indian) Age 33, born (About 1848) in Ontario, no religion given, Lydia born in Ontario, age 22, David born in Ontario, age 12, Samon? or Damon? (a male) Indian, born in Ontario, age 10, Levi Indian, born in Ontario, age 8, a male General (no first name given) Indian, age 2. Page 63, Household 398/403.

**GENERAL, WILLIAM:** (Indian) Age 20, born (About 1861) in Ontario, a member of the Church of England, Charlotte MARTIN age 19, born in Ontario, Floretta? MIRACLE age 18, born in Ontario. Page 37, Household 223/225.

**GIBSON, GEORGE:** (Indian) Age 26, born (About 1855) in Ontario, no religion given, Annie age 22, born in Ontario, Charlotte age 1, born in Ontario. Page 42, Household 254/258.

**GIBSON, JOHN:** (Indian) Age 59, born (About 1822) in Ontario, a member of the Church of England, Hannah age 60, born in Ontario, Cornelius age 18, born in Ontario. Page 42, Household 253/257.

**GIBSON, JOHN:** (Indian) Age 31, born (About 1850) in Ontario, no religion given, Mary age 29, born in Ontario, Martha age 11, born in Ontario, Adam age 9, born in Ontario, Jemima age 7, born in Ontario. Page 42, Household 255/259.

**GIBSON, LEWIS:** (Indian) Age 33, born (About 1848) in Ontario, a member of the Church of England, Sarah age 35, born in Ontario. Page 42, Household 258/262.

**GIBSON, NICOLAS:** (Indian) Age 44, born (About 1837) in Ontario, a member of the Church of England, Margaret age 46, born in Ontario, Joseph age 6, born in Ontario, David age 1, born in Ontario. Page 36, Household 214/216.

**GIVERS? (OR GREEN?) DAVID:** (Indian) Age 48, born (About 1833) in Ontario, a Methodist, Lydia age 41, born in Ontario. Page 52, Household 316/321.

**GREEN, BETSY:** (Indian) Age 60, born (About 1821) in Ontario, a member of the Church of England, Edward age 20. Page 56, Household 353/358.

**GREEN, ISAAC:** (Indian) Age 25, born (About 1856) in Ontario, a Methodist, Deborah age 23, born in Ontario, Jesse age 6, born in Ontario, Peter age 4, born in Ontario, John age 3, born in Ontario, Hannah age one month, born in March in Ontario. Page 49, Household 302/307.

**GREEN, JOHN:** (Indian) Age 53, (About 1828) born in Ontario, a member of the Church of England, Betsy Green, age 44, born in Ontario, Abram age 18, born in Ontario, Jemima age 14, born in Ontario, George age 12, born in Ontario, Margaret age 10, born in Ontario. Page 59, Household 369/374.

**GREEN, JOHN:** (Indian) Age 42, born (About 1839) in Ontario, no religion given, Lucy age 35, born in Ontario. Page 47, Household 289/294.

**GREEN, JOSEPH:** (Indian) Age 45, born (About 1841) in Ontario, a member of the Church of England, Dennis WILLIAMS age 12, born in Ontario, William WILLIAMS age 2, born in Ontario. Page 61, Household 385/390.

**GREEN, JOSEPH:** (Indian) Age 35, born (About 1846) in Ontario, a member of the Baptist Church, Elizabeth age 35, born in Ontario, Carlyle (a male) age 3, born in Ontario, Wellington age 5 months, born in November. Page 60, Household 379/384.

**GREEN, KATIE:** (Indian) Age 57, born (About 1824) in Ontario, a Methodist, Daniel age 37, born in Ontario. Page 52, Household 320/325.

**GREEN, MARY:** (Indian) Age 31, born (About 1850) in Ontario, a Methodist, Maggie age 4, born in Ontario. Page 51, Household 312/317.

**GREEN, PETER:** (Indian) Age 60, born (About 1821) in Ontario, a Baptist. Page 40, Household 244.

**GREEN, PETER:** (Indian) Age 44, born (About 1837) in Ontario, a member of the Church of England, Katie age 34, born in Ontario. Page 36, Household 215/217.

**GRESIUM? JOHN:** (Indian) Age 30, born (About 1851) in Ontario (No religion was given) Elizabeth age 35, born in Ontario, Hannah DICKSON age 12, born in Ontario, Lucy WHISKEY age 3, born in Ontario, John WHISKEY age one month born in March in Ontario. Page 42, Household 252/256.

**HARRIS, JAMES:** (Indian) Age 49, born (About 1832) in Ontario (No religion was given) Catharine age 40, born in Ontario, William age 35, born in Ontario, Richard age 16, born in Ontario, Elijah Harris, age 12, born in Ontario, Louis age 9, born in Ontario, Betsy age 19, born in Ontario. Page 35, Household 211/213.

**HARRIS, MARY:** (Indian) Age 55, born (About 1826) in Ontario, a member of the Baptist Church, Katie JOSEPH age 18, born in Ontario, Joseph Harris, age 22, born in Ontario. Page 62, Household 393/398.

**HENHAWK, PETER:** (Indian) Age 45, born (About 1836) in Ontario (No religion was given) Ellen age 30, born in Ontario, Lucy age 17, born in Ontario, Jemima? age 11, born in Ontario, Ludia? age 9, born in Ontario, Peter age 7, born in Ontario, James age 5, born in Ontario, Elizabeth age 3, born in Ontario, a female age five months, born in Ontario in November not yet named. Page 62, Household 394/399.

**HESS? JOHN:** (Indian) Age ? born in Ontario, a Methodist, Cristine age 27, born in Ontario, Samson age 10, born in Ontario, Sussanah age 8, born in Ontario, Ellen age 3, born in Ontario, Isaac age 6 months, born in October in Ontario. Page 54, Household 331/336.

**HILL, ELIZABETH:** (Indian) Age 28, born (About 1853) in Ontario, a Baptist, Nathaniel CUSICK, age 8, born in Ontario, Foster Heming MARTIN age 2, born in Ontario. Page 39, Household 230/233.

**HILL, HANNAH:** (Indian) Age 48, born (About 1833) in Ontario, a Methodist, Mary GREEN, age 21, born in Ontario, James Green, age 18, born in Ontario, Sarah Green, age 13, born in Ontario. Page 49, Household 301/306.

**HILL, JOHN:** (Indian) Age 55, born (About 1826) in Ontario, a Baptist, Mary age 45, born in Ontario, Albert age 20, born in Ontario, David age 17, born in Ontario, Robert age 14, born in Ontario, Enos age 12, born in Ontario, Thomas Hill, age 9, born in Ontario, Hilton age 2, born in Ontario, Lydia GARLOW, age 30, born in Ontario. Page 48, Household 295/300.

**HILL, JOSIAH:** (Indian) Age 37, born (About 1844) in Ontario, a member of the Baptist Church, Nancy Age 36, born in Ontario, Simeon Roland

Hill, age 12, born in Ontario, Amelia, age 7, born in Ontario, Leopold, age 3, born in Ontario. Page 61, Household 386/391.

**HILL, RICHARD:** (Indian) Age 36, born (About 1845) in Ontario, a Baptist, Hannah age 45, born in Ontario, Susan age 12, born in Ontario, Mary age 8, born in Ontario, Leiala? (A female) age 3, born in Ontario, Frederick age 1, born in Ontario, Abram age 75, born in Ontario. Page 47, Household 290/295.

**HILL, ZACHARIAH:** (Indian) Age 32, born (About 1849) in Ontario, a Methodist, Hannah age 40, born in Ontario, Margaret age 20, born in Ontario, Samson CLAUSE, age 10, born in Ontario. Page 54, Household 332/337.

**HOPE, JOHN:** (Indian) Age 57, born in Ontario (About 1824) a Methodist, Eliza born in Ontario, age 53, a Methodist, Esther born in Ontario, age 25, born in Ontario, a Methodist. Page 64, Household 405/410.

**HOPE, POWLESS:** (Indian) Age 28, born (About 1853) in Ontario, a member of the Church of England, Mary age 50, born in Ontario, Elijah age 33, born in Ontario. Page 61, Household 383/388.

**HUSK, KATIE:** (Indian) Age 38, born (About 1843) in Ontario, a member of the Church of England. Page 61, Household 382/387.

**ISAAC, CYRUS? (OR lEYRIS?):** (Indian) Age 29, born (About 1852) in Ontario, a Methodist, Lucy age 21, born in Ontario. Page 50, Household 303/308.

**ISAAC, JOHN:** (Indian) Age 47, born (About 1834) in Ontario (No religion was given) Mary age 36, born in Ontario, Lydia age 16, born in Ontario, Jake age 14, born in Ontario, Hannah age 10, born in Ontario, Margaret age 7, born in Ontario, Robert age 5, born in Ontario, a Isaac child age five months was born in November in Ontario. Page 38, Household 228/231.

**ISAAC, JOSEPH:** (Indian) Age 42, born (About 1839) in Ontario, a member of the Church of England, Catherine age 40, born in Ontario, Jacob age 20, born in Ontario, Freeman age 12, born in Ontario, Jefferson age 5, born in Ontario, Alex (a male) age 3, born in Ontario. Page 55, Household 345/350.

**ISAAC, JOSEPH:** (Indian) Age 43, born (About 1838) in Ontario (No religion was given) Lydia age 30, born in Ontario, Martha age 7, born in Ontario, Catharine age 5, born in Ontario, Louisa age 2, born in Ontario, Robert age 13, born in Ontario, Lucy age 11, born in Ontario. Page 39, Household 227/229.

**ISAAC, PETER:** (Indian) Age 29, born (About 1852) in Ontario, a member of the Church of England, Lydia HILL age 11, born in Ontario. Page 39, Household 233/236.

**JACOB, ISAAC:** (Indian) Age 50, born (About 1831) in Ontario (No religion was given) Elizabeth age 48, born in Ontario, Betsy age 23, born in Ontario, George age 19, born in Ontario, David age 13, born in Ontario, Jacob age 11, born in Ontario, Sarah age 8, born in Ontario,

Martha age 5, born in Ontario, James CHARLES, age 4, born in Ontario. Page 37, Household 220/222.

**JAMIESON, AUGUSTUS:** (Indian) Age 36, born (About 1845) in Ontario, a member of the Baptist Church, Peter age 9, born in Ontario, Cecilia age 4, born in Ontario. Page 58, Household 362/367.

**JAMIESON, JACKSON:** (Indian) Age 34, born (About 1847) in Ontario, a member of the Church of England, Margaret age 26, born in Ontario, Sarah age 3, born in Ontario, Birdie (a female) age 1, born in Ontario. Page 61, Household 378/383.

**JAMIESON, JOHN:** (Indian) Age 38, born (About 1843) in Ontario (No religion was given) Susan age 30, born in Ontario, (Except for James Jamieson whose first names was listed all of the following children were females) ? Jamieson, age 16, born in Ontario, ? Jamieson, age 14, born in Ontario, ? Jamieson, age 11, born in Ontario, James Jamieson age 8, born in Ontario, ? Jamieson age 4, born in Ontario. Page 46, Household 278/285.

**JAMIESON, JOHN:** (Indian) Age 27, born (About 1854) in Ontario, a member of the Church of England. Page 38, Household 225/227.

**JAMIESON, WILLIAM:** (Indian) Age 63, born (About 1818) in Ontario, a member of the Church of England, Katie age 57, born in Ontario, Julia age 30, born in Ontario, William age 19, born in Ontario. Page 58, Household 363/368.

**JAMIESON, SOLOMON:** (Indian) Age 35, born (About 1846) in Ontario, a Baptist, Margaret HILL, age 29, born in Ontario, Elizabeth BEAVER, age 13, born in Ontario, Solomon Jamieson, age 5, born in Ontario. Page 39, Household 232/235.

**JAMISON, MARY:** (Indian) Age 39, born (About 1842) in Ontario, a member of the Church of England, Emily Ann DUNCAN, age 9, born in Ontario, Archie TURKEY, age 4, born in Ontario. Page 54, Household 333/338.

**JOHN, DAVID:** (Indian) Age 32, born (About 1849) in Ontario, a member of the Church of England, Esther JOHN age 29, born in Ontario, Emily John, age 13, born in Ontario, Catherine John, age 11, born in Ontario, Ellen John, age 7, born in Ontario, Clara John, age 2, born in Ontario. Page 39, Household 231/234.

**JOHN, KATIE:** (Indian) Age 41, born (About 1840) in Ontario, a member of the Church of England. Page 56, Household 351/356.

**JOHN, JOHN:** (Indian) Age 40, born (About 1841) in Ontario, a Baptist, Harriet age 25, born in Ontario, William age 5, born in Ontario, Sarah age 2, born in Ontario. Page 57, Household 357/362.

**JOHNSON, AUGUSTUS:** (Indian) Age 65, born (About 1816) in Ontario, a Baptist, Ellen age 50, born in Ontario, James age 18 born in Ontario. Page 43, Household 264/268.

**JOHNSON, DEBORAH:** (Indian) Age 61, born (About 1820) in Ontario, a Baptist, Page 39, Household 234/237.

**JOHNSON, FESTUS:** (Indian) Age 19, born (About 1862) in Ontario, a Baptist, Wm., age 21, born in Ontario, Mary age 21, born in Ontario. Page 43, Household 263/267.

**JOHNSON, GEORGE:** (Indian) Age 36, born (About 1845) in Ontario, no religion given, Elizabeth born in Ontario, age 19, a male Johnson born in Ontario, age 2. No first name was given for this child. Page 64, Household 401/406.

**JOHNSON, WILLIAM:** (Indian) Age ? born in Ontario, a member of the Church of England. Page 59, Household 371/376.

**JOHNSTON, CATHERINE:** (Indian) Age 76, born (About 1805) in Ontario, a member of the Church of England, Elizabeth age 50, born in Ontario, Jacob age 48, born in Ontario, Susan age 15, born in Ontario, Ellen age 14, born in Ontario. Page 59, Household 372/377.

**JONATHAN, LEVI:** (Indian) Age 46, born (About 1835) in Ontario, a Baptist, Hattie age 26, born in Ontario, Lincoln age 16, born in Ontario. Page 44, Household 271/275.

**JONES, SARAH JANE:** (Indian) age 40, born (About 1841) in Ontario, a Methodist. Page 63, Household 400/405.

**KEY, CHARLOTTE:** (Indian) Age 18, born (About 1863) in Ontario, a member of the Church of England. Page 41, Household 248/252.

**KEY? JACOB:** (Indian) Age 45, born (About 1836) in Ontario (No religion was given) Mary age 35, born in Ontario, Katherine YELLOW? or MELLOW? age 13, born in Ontario. Page 47, Household 284/289.

**KEY, THOMAS:** (Indian) Age 22, born (About 1859) in Ontario (No religion was given) Katie age 18, born in Ontario. Page 42, Household 244/248.

**KICK, ISAAC:** (Indian) Age 17, born (About 1864) in Ontario, a member of the Baptist Church. Page 62, Household 389/394.

**LEWIS, SUSANNA:** (Indian) Age ? born in Ontario, a member of the Church of England, Betsy age 50, born in Ontario, a member of the Church of England. Page 52, Household 323/328.

**LEWIS, WM:** (Indian) Age 41, born (About 1840) in Ontario, a member of the Church of England, Charlotte (White/Irish) age 23, Mary (White/Irish) age 10, Wm. Alex (White/Irish) age 6, Emma Jane (White/Irish) age 5, Margaret (White/Irish) age 3. Page 60, Household 374/379.

**LICKEN, GEORGE:** (Indian) Age 29, born (About 1852) in Ontario, a Methodist. Page 58, Household 365/370.

**LOMBARD? (OR LONBIRD?) GEORGE:** (Indian) Age 30, born (About 1851) in Ontario (No religion was given) Betsy age 30, born in Ontario, Thomas age four months was born in September.

**LONGFISH, JOSEPH:** (Indian) Age 72, born (About 1809) in Ontario, a Baptist. Page 44, Household 272/276.

**LOTTRIDGE, ISAAC:** (Indian) Age 50, born (About 1831) in Ontario, a member of the Church of England, Catherine age 19, born in Ontario, Albert ISLAND, age 6, born in Ontario. Page 55, Household 340/345.

**MIRACLE, ABRAM:** (Indian) Age 60, born (About 1821) in Ontario, a Methodist, Sussanah age 48, born in Ontario, Mary age 21, born in Ontario, Esther age 17, born in Ontario, Charlotte age 11, born Ontario, Powless age 8, born in Ontario, Peter age 8 months, born in July in Ontario, Ellen GREEN, age 7 months, born in August in Ontario. Page 56, Household 349/354.

**MIRACLE, ABRAM:** (Indian) Age 35, born (About 1846) in Ontario, a member of the Church of England, Annie age 32, born in Ontario, Susanna age 11, born in Ontario, Solomon age 8, born in Ontario, Margaret age 7, born in Ontario, Jeremiah age 4, born in Ontario, Archie age 2, born in Ontario, George STOUT, age 18, born in Ontario. Page 53, Household 324/329.

**MIRACLE, DANIEL:** (Indian) Age 25, born (About 1856) in Ontario (No religion was given) Mary age 20, a Methodist, William age 3, born in Ontario. Page 59, Household 366/371.

**MIRACLE, ELLEN:** (Indian) Age 37, born (About 1844) in Ontario, a Methodist, Joseph MARTIN, age 9, born in Ontario, Catherine HESS? age 9, born in Ontario. Page 56, Household 347/352.

**MIRACLE, JOSEPH:** (Indian) Age 29, born (About 1852) in Ontario, a Methodist, Susanna age 23, born in Ontario, Joab age 6, born in Ontario, Peter age 4, born in Ontario. Page 52, Household 321/326.

**MIRACLE, SAMUEL T:** (Indian) Age 25, born (About 1856) in Ontario, a Baptist, Hannah age 19, born in Ontario. Page 59, Household 368/373.

**MIRACLE, WILLIAM:** (Indian) Age 62, born (About 1819) in Ontario, a member of the Baptist Church, Catherine age 52, born in Ontario, Peter age 18, born in Ontario, Jemima age 11, born in Ontario. Page 59, Household 367/372.

**MIRACLE, WILLIAM:** (Indian) Age 26, born (About 1855) in Ontario, Methodist, Susie age 20, born in Ontario, Alfred age 1, born in Ontario, age 1. Page 56, Household 350/355.

**MARTIN, ALIX:** (Indian) Age 60, born (About 1821) in Ontario, a member of the Church of England, Eva? age 46, born in Ontario, George age 29, born in Ontario, Mark age 15, born in Ontario, Maggie age 20, born in Ontario, Sarah age 18, born in Ontario, Ellen age 12, born in Ontario, Carrie age 8, born in Ontario. Page 51, Household 314/319.

**MARTIN, EDWARD:** (Indian) Age 23, born (About 1858) in Ontario, a member of the Church of England, Hanah born in Ontario, age 20, a member of the Church of England, a male Martin, born in Ontario, age 4, a male Martin born in Ontario, age 2. Only the childrens surnames were given. Page 64, Household 402/407.

**MARTIN, WM:** (Indian) Age 47, born (About 1834) in Ontario, a member of the Church of England, Henrietta (White/Irish) age 45, born in Quebec Province, (All the following were listed as Indians) Robert age 21, born in Ontario, Henry age 19, born in Ontario, David age 16, born in Ontario, Wm. Jr., age 14, born in Ontario, Lily age 12, born in Ontario, Albert age 5, born in Ontario. Page 53, Household 330/335.

**MC NAUGHTON, MARY:** (Indian) Age 35, born (About 1846) in Ontario, a member of the Church of England, Daniel age 14, born in Ontario, Janet age 4, born in Ontario, Alix age 9, born in Ontario, James age 7, born in Ontario, George E. age 4, born in Ontario. Page 52, Household 322/327.

**MILLER, ANTHONY:** (White/French) Age ? born in Ontario, a member of the Church of England, Sarah Miller (Indian) age 34, born in Ontario, (all of the following were listed as French) Elizabeth Miller, age 16, born in Ontario, Lucinda? Miller, age 13, born in Ontario, Susanna Miller, age 8, born in Ontario, Samuel Miller, age 6, born in Ontario, David Darsey? Miller, age 3, born in Ontario. Page?

**MILLER, ANTHONY P.** (White/French) Age 77, born (About 1804) in Quebec, a member of the Church of England, Cristene? Miller (Female Indian) born in Ontario, age 72, a member of the Church of England. Page 64, Household 404/409.

**MILLER, HIRAM:** (Indian) Age 18, born (About 1863) in Ontario, a member of the Church of England. Page 44, Household 268/272.

**MILLER, JOHN:** (Indian) Age 25, born (About 1856) in Ontario, Age 25, a member of the Church of England, Elizabeth age 19, born in Ontario, Frank age 2, born in Ontario, Frederick age eight months, born in Ontario in August. Page 44, Household 267/271.

**MILLER, JOSIAH:** (White/French) Age 37, born (About 1844) in Ontario, a member of the Church of England, Margaret Miller (Indian) born in Ontario, age 34, a member of the Church of England, Peter Miller (White/French) born in Ontario, age 13, Rebecca Miller, (White/French) born in Ontario, age 5, Elliot Miller (White/French) born in Ontario, age 3, Page 64, Household 403/408.

**MILLER, PETER:** (White/French) Age 50, born (About 1831) in Ontario, a member of the Church of England, Jemima Miller (Indian) age 33, born in Ontario, Angeline Miller, age 16, born in Ontario, William Miller, age 15, Joshua Miller, age 14, born in Ontario, Francis Miller (A Male) age 10, born in Ontario, Jemima Miller, age 8, born in Ontario, Katie Miller, age 6, born in Ontario, Amy Miller, age 5, born in Ontario, Robert Miller, age 3, born in Ontario. Page 37, Household 224/226.

**NASH, ISAAC:** (Indian) Age ? born in Ontario, a member of the Church of England, Henry POWLESS age 22, a member of the Baptist Church, born in Ontario. Page 61, Household 387/392.

**NEWHOUSE, MARGARET:** (Indian) Age 25, born (About 1856) in Ontario, a member of the Church of England, Mary Jane age 7, born in Ontario,

Lizzie age 4, born in Ontario, Charlotte age 2, born in Ontario. Page 54, Household 335/340.

**NEWHOUSE, NICOLAS:** (Indian) Age 57, born (About 1824) in Ontario, a member of the Church of England, Catharine age 56, born in Ontario, a Methodist, Sarah age 16, born in Ontario. Page 54, Household 334/339.

**NEWHOUSE, SETH:** (Indian) Age? born in Ontario, a member of the Church of England, Elizabeth SILVERSMITH age? born in Ontario, a member of the Church of England. Page 53, Household 329/334.

**OBADIAH, SARAH:** (Indian) Age 71, born (About 1810) in Ontario, a member of the Church of England. Dennis HILL age 35, born in Ontario. Page 62, Household 390/395.

**OBADIAH, WILLIAM:** (Indian) Age 20, born (About 1861) in Ontario, a Baptist, Jemima BOMBERY age 25, born in Ontario, Thomas age 4, born in Ontario, Lucy THOMAS age 7, born in Ontario, Peter Thomas age 6, born in Ontario. Page 40, Household 236/239.

**OTTER, JOHN:** (Indian) Age 32, born (About 1849) in Ontario, a Methodist. Page 56, Household 348/353.

**PORTER? (OR POSTER?) JOSEPH:** (Indian) Age 47, born (About 1834) in Ontario, a Baptist, Catherine age 45, born in Ontario. Page 48, Household 292/397.

**PORTER, JOSEPH:** (Indian) Age 22, born (About 1859) in Ontario, a Baptist, Lucy age 23, born in Ontario, Susanna Mary age 12, born in Ontario, Henrietta age 5, born in Ontario. Page 49, Household 293/298.

**PORTER? NICODEMUS:** (Indian) Age 37, born (About 1844) in Ontario, a Baptist, Annie age 35, born in Ontario, Lucy age 17, born in Ontario, Charles age 12, born in Ontario, Hardy age 4, born in Ontario, Susanah POWLESS age 70, born in Ontario, a member of the Church of England, Alfred STYERS? age 7, born in Ontario. Page 47, Household 291/296.

**POWLESS, ABRAHAM:** (Indian) Age 32, born (About 1849) in Ontario, a Methodist, Esther HENRY (Indian) born in Ontario, age 36, a Methodist. Page 64, Household 407/412.

**POWLESS, ELIZABETH:** (Indian) Age 45, born (About 1836) in Ontario, a member of the Church of England. Page 42, Household 259/263.

**POWLESS, GEORGE:** (Indian) Age 50? or 30?, born in Ontario, a member of the Church of England, Carrie age 26, born in Ontario, E. Earnest age 3, born in Ontario, Page 42, Household 260/264.

**RACHETT, DAVID:** (Indian) Age 36, born (About 1845) in Ontario, a member of the Baptist Church, Susie age 32, born in Ontario, Sarah age 12, born in Ontario, Laura age 10, born in Ontario. Page 62, Household 391/396.

**RANKIN, SAMUEL:** (Indian) Age 57, born (About 1824) in Ontario, a Methodist. Page 47, Household 285/290. Page 47, Household 285/290.

**RANKIN, SARAH:** (Indian) Age 40, born (About 1841) in Ontario, a Methodist. Page 63, Household 396/401.

**SENECA, DAVID HILL:** (Indian) Age 77, born (About 1804) in Ontario, a Baptist, Catherine age 77, born in Ontario, Enoch age 33, born in Ontario, Seba? JOHN (A Female) age 13, born in Ontario, Wilson BUTLER age 12, born in Ontario, Betsy John, age 11, born in Ontario. Page 48, Household 294/299.

**SENECA, JOHN:** (Indian) Age 30, born (About 1851) in Ontario, Hanah age 28, born in Ontario, William age 12, born in Ontario. Page 47, Household 287/292.

**SENECA, WM:** (Indian) Age 49, born (About 1832) in Ontario, A Baptist, Sarah age 53, born in Ontario, Amos BEAVER age 8, born in Ontario. Page 57, Household 359/364.

**SERO? (OR CERO?) DOROTHEA:** (Indian) Age 78, born (About 1803) in Ontario, a Methodist, Sarah GREEN age 4, born in Ontario. Page 54, Household 337/342.

**SERO? (OR CERO? OR SENO?) ISRAIL:** (Indian) Age 42, born (About 1839) in Ontario, a Methodist, Jemima age 39, born in Ontario. Page 52, Household 318/323.

**SHERRY, ALEXANDER:** (Indian) Age 35, born (About 1846) in Ontario, a Baptist, Catherine age 35, born in Ontario, Gilbert age 14, born in Ontario, Alfred age 12, born in Ontario, Margaret age 7, born in Ontario, Levia age 9 months, born in Ontario in August. Page 57, Household 358/363.

**SILVER, CORNELIUS:** (Indian) Age 38, born (About 1843) in Ontario, a member of the Baptist Church, Catherine age 31, born in Ontario, Annie age 12, born in Ontario, Herman age 6, born in Ontario, Lena age 1, born in Ontario, James WEBSTER, age 12, born in Ontario. Page 57, Household 356/361.

**SILVERSMITH, ALEX:** (Indian) Age 32, born (About 1849) in Ontario (No religion was given) Hannah age 66, born in Ontario, Mary age 11, born in Ontario, Emily age 7, born in Ontario, Alie? (A Male) age 6, born in Ontario, Robert age 2, born in Ontario. Page 36, Household 219/221.

**SILVERSMITH, BETSY:** (Indian) Age 26, born (About 1855) in Ontario, a member of the Church of England, born in Ontario. Page 55, Household 346/351.

**SILVERSMITH, JOHN:** (Indian) Age 38, born in Ontario, no religion given, Mary age 50, born in Ontario, Alex DOCTOR, age 15, born in Ontario, John DOCTOR, age 14, born in Ontario, Susannah Doctor, age 13, born in Ontario. Page 45, Household 277/282.

**SILVERSMITH, JOHN:** (Indian) Age 34, born in Ontario, a member of the Church of England, Julia age 30, born in Ontario, William age 3, born in Ontario, ? Silversmith (a male) age 1, born in Ontario. Page 36, Household 217/219.

**SKY, CATHARINE:** (Indian) Age 80, born (About 1801) in Ontario, no religion given. Page 47, Household 283/288.

**SKY, CHARLES:** (Indian) Age 40, born in Ontario, a member of the Church of England, May (or Mary?) age 39, born in Ontario, Cristine age 11, born in Ontario. Page 46, Household 280/285.

**SKY, DAVID:** (Indian) Age 31, born in Ontario, no religion given, Mary age 30, born in Ontario, Sarah age 11, born in Ontario, Nancy age 8, born in Ontario, Andrew age 7, born in Ontario, David age 6, born in Ontario, Rosa age 2, born in Ontario, Sepa? (a female) age 1, born in Ontario. Page 46, Household 282/287.

**SKY, JAMES:** (Indian) Age 38, born in Ontario, no religion given. Page 46, Household 281/286.

**SKY, JAMES:** (Indian) Age 23, born in Ontario (No religion was given) Julia JOHNSON age 17, born in Ontario. Page 42, Household 256/260.

**SMITH, JOHN A:** (Indian) Age 50, born in Ontario, a Methodist, Eliz Marie age 49, born in Ontario, John Wesly Smith, age 23, born in Ontario, Fred Albert Smith, age 22, born in Ontario. Page 270/274.

**SMITH, PETER:** (Indian) Age 26, (Born about 1855) a member of the Methodist Church, Charlotte age 32 born in Canada West. Onondaga Township Part 11, Township 1? Page 35, Number 44, 45.

**SMITH, PETER:** (Indian) Age 53, born (About 1828) in Ontario, a Methodist, David age 21, born in Ontario, Henry age 13, born in Ontario, Peter age 10, born in Ontario, Elizabeth age 10, born in Ontario, Lawrance age 7, born in Ontario, Joseph age 4, born in Ontario. Page 51, Household 311/316.

**SNAKE, HENRY:** (Indian) Age 38, born (About 1843) in Ontario, a member of the Church of England. Page 40, Household 239/242.

**SNOW? SARRAH:** (Indian) Age 85, born (About 1804) in Ontario, a Methodist, Ellen TWOFISH born in Ontario. Page 50, Household 307/312.

**SNOW, SISSIE:** (Female Indian) Age 27, born (About 1854) in Ontario, a Methodist. Page 64, Household 409/414.

**STYEN? GEORGE:** (Indian) Age 81, born (About 1800) in Ontario, a member of the Church of England, ? Styen (a male) age 29, born in Ontario. Page 44, Household 269/273.

**STYEN? (OR STYERS?) SAMUEL:** (Indian) Age 34, born (About 1847) in Ontario, a member of the Church of England, Elizabeth age 25, born in Ontario, Robert age 3, born in Ontario, John age 45, born in Ontario. Page 43, Household 265/269.

**THOMAS, DAVID:** (Indian) Age 50, born (About 1831) in Ontario, a member of the Church of England, Daniel age 21, Eliza Jane age 20, Israel age 18, Cristine age 10, Joseph BENNETT age 9. Page 56, Household 355/360.

**TWOFISH, MARGARET:** (Indian) Age 39, born in Ontario, Simon age 13, born in Ontario, Lucy age 6, born in Ontario, Esther age 3, born in Ontario. Page 50, Household 308/313.

**VANEVERY? (OR DOUSVERY?) JAMES:** (Indian) Age 25, born (About 1856) in Ontario (No religion was given) Mary age 19, born in Ontario, George age 3, born in Ontario, Alexander age 2, born in Ontario. Page 38, Household 230.

**WALKER, KATIE:** (Indian) Age 20, born (About 1861) in Ontario, a member of the Church of England, Lucy age 12, born in Ontario. Page 53, Household 326/331.

**WHITE, CRISTINE:** (Indian) Age 24, born (About 1857) in Ontario, a member of the Church of England, John age 1, born in Ontario, George GREEN, age 30, born in Ontario. Page 56, Household 354/359.

**WILLIAM, ALIX:** (Male Indian) Age 23, born (About 1858) in Ontario, a member of the Baptist Church, Sophia age 25, born in Ontario. Page 61, Household 380/385.

**WILLIAMS, JACOB:** (Indian) Age 72, born (About 1809) in Ontario, a member of the Baptist Church, Ellen age 61, born in Ontario, Jemima age 22, born in Ontario, Sarah age 18, born in Ontario, Enoch age 15, born in Ontario. Page number difficult to read.

**WILLIAMS, JOSHUA:** (Indian) Age 40, born (About 1841) in Ontario, a member of the Church of England, Mary age 50, born in Ontario, Elijah age 33, born in Ontario. Page 61, Household 384/389.

**YELLOW, ELIZA:** (Indian) Age 17, born (About 1864) in Ontario, a member of the Church of England, Augustus YELLOW age 15, born in Ontario, Emma KEY, age 7, born in Ontario. Page 36, Household 216/218.

| CROSS INDEX TO 1881 CENSUS OF BRANT COUNTY, ONTARIO PART I LISTED ABOVE ||
|---|---|
| **SURNAME CROSS INDEX** | **HEAD OF HOUSEHOLD** |
| **BEAVER,** Amos | Wm. SENECA |
| **BEAVER,** Elizabeth | Solomon JAMIESON |
| **BENNETT,** Joseph | David Thomas |
| **BENNETT,** Nancy | Isaac CLAUSE |
| **BOMBERY,** Jemima | William OBADIAH |
| **BUTLER,** Wilson | David Hill SENECA |
| **CHARLES,** James | Isaac JACOBS |
| **CLARKE,** Joseph | Catherine CLINCH |
| **CLAUS,** Seth | Hannah CARRIE |

| | |
|---|---|
| **CLAUSE,** Samson | Zachariah HILL |
| **CUSICK,** Nathaniel | Elizabeth HILL |
| **DICKSON,** Hanah | John GRESIUM? |
| **DOCTOR,** Alex | John SILVERSMITH |
| **DOUGLAS,** Sussanah | Aaron BURNING |
| **DOXTATOR,** Catherine | David Fish |
| **DUNCAN,** Emily Ann | Mary JAMIESON |
| **EUTOMLE?,** Alex | Timothy BURNING |
| **GARLOW,** Lydia | John HILL |
| **GENERAL,** Margaret | Lucy GARLOW |
| **GREEN,** Ellen | Abram MIRACLE |
| **GREEN,** George | Cristine WHITE |
| **GREEN,** Mary | Hanah HILL |
| **GREEN,** Sarah | Dorothea SERO? OR CERO? |
| **HENRY,** Esther | Abraham POWLESS |
| **HENRY,** Joseph | Margaret CLAUSE |
| **HESS,** Catherine | Ellen MIRACLE |
| **HILL,** Dennis | Sarah OBADIAH |
| **HILL,** Margaret | Solomon JAMIESON |
| **HILL?,** Lydia | Peter ISAAC |
| **ISLAND,** Albert | Isaac LOTTRIDGE |
| **ISLAND,** Albert | Christopher GARLOW |
| **JOHN,** Esther | David JOHN |
| **JOHN,** Seba? | David Hill SENECA |
| **JOHNSON,** Elizabeth | John DUCAN |
| **JOHNSON,** Julia | James SKY |
| **JOSEPH,** Katie | Mary HARRIS |
| **KEY,** Emma | Elias YELLOW |
| **KEY?,** Carrie | Charles FISH |
| **KICK,** George | Margaret CLAUSE |
| **LICKEN,** Betsy | John BARE? OR BARR? |

| | |
|---|---|
| **LONGFISH**, Sussannah | Wm. CAPTAIN |
| **MARACLE**, Foloretta? | William GENERAL |
| **MARTIN**, Charlotte | William GENERAL |
| **MARTIN**, Foster Heming | Elizabeth HILL |
| **MARTIN**, Joseph | Ellen MIRACLE |
| **MC PHAIL**, Mary | Benjamin CARPENTER |
| **OLYERS OR SYERS**, Jacob | Lucy BUCK |
| **POWLESS**, Henry | Isaac NASH |
| **POWLESS**, Mary A. | Peter GARLOW Jr. |
| **POWLESS**, Sussanah | Nicodemis PORTER |
| **SILVERSMITH**, Elizabeth | Seth NEWHOUSE |
| **SMITH**, Charlotte | Robert Hill DEE |
| **STOUT? OR STOAT**, George | Abraham MIRACLE |
| **STYERS**, Alfred | Nicodemis PORTER |
| **THOMAS**, Lucy | William OBADIAH |
| **TURKEY**, Archie | Mary JAMIESON |
| **TWOFISH**, Ellen | Sarah SNOW |
| **WEBSTER**, James | Cornelius SILVER |
| **WHISKEY**, John | John GRESIUM? |
| **WHISKEY**, Lucy | John GRESIUM? |
| **WILLIAMS**, Dennis | Joseph GREEN |
| **WILLIAMS**, William | Joseph GREEN |
| **YELLOW**, Katherine | Jacob KEY |

## BRANT COUNTY, ONTARIO 1881 CENSUS ABSTRACT
### SECTION II
### SOUTH BRANT COUNTY, TUSCARORA RESERVE.

**ARRON, JOHN:** (Indian) Age 55, born (About 1826) in Ontario, Lydia Aaron age 45, Henry age 22, Lucy age 16, Jeremiah age 11, Catherine age 9, Page 37, Household 210/210

**AARON, THOMAS:** (Indian) Age 27, a member of the Church of England. Page 42, Household 241/241.

**ACKLEY? ABIGAIL:** (Indian) Age 42?, born (About 1839) in Ontario, a Baptist, Joseph age 11, Rosa age 5, Stephen age 2. Page 31, Household 173/173.

**ADAMS, HENRY:** (Indian) Age 50 (About 1831) born in Ontario, a Baptist, Henry age 21. Page 3, Household 12.

**ADAMS, MOSES:** (Indian) Age 50, born (About 1831) in Ontario, a member of the Church of England, Joseph MARTIN age 14. Page 4, Household 17.

**ANTHONY, ALEXANDER:** (Indian) Age 28, born (About 1853) in Ontario, a Baptist, Elizabeth age 23, Frances (female) age 3, Solomon age 1. Page 33, Household 183.

**BAREFOOT, DAVID:** (Indian) Age 45, born (About 1836) in Ontario, a Baptist, Elizabeth age 44, Peter age 18, Henry age 16, Charles age 13, Sylvester age 10, Clara age 8, Mary BRANT age 76, born in Ontario, a Methodist. Page 17, Household 98.

**BATTEESE, JONAS:** (Indian) Age 14, born (About 1867) in Ontario, a member of the Church of England, Christina age 12. Page 43, Household 250/250.

**BATTESE? (PATTESE?) POWLESS:** (Indian) Age 50, born (About 1831) in Ontario, a member of the Church of England, Christeen age 55, Jacob age 23, Richard age 23. Page 29, Household 160/160.

**BEAVER, GEORGE:** (Indian) Age 60, born (About 1821) in Ontario, a Baptist, Susannah age 60, born in Ontario, a Baptist, Eliza CARRIER age 10, Levi CARRIER age 8, John CARRIER age 4, Eli NASH age 12, Levi WHIPLY age 10, Josephine WHIPLY age 7, Simeon SILVER age 13, Levi NASH age 6. Page 20, Household 114.

**BEAVER, PETER:** (Indian) Age 21, born (About 1860) in Ontario, a Baptist, Abbey WILLIAMS age 16, born in Ontario, a member of the Church of England. Page 20, Household 115.

**BOMBERRY, JAMES:** (Indian) Age 30, born (About 1851) in Ontario, a member of the Church of England, Ellen age 22, Lewis age 4, Walter age five months, born in November. Page 48, Household 288/288.

**BOMBERRY, JEMIMA:** (Indian) Age 20, a Baptist, Vanloon CALVIN? or Calvin VANLOON? age 23. Page 34. Household 191/191.

**BOMBERRY, THOMAS:** (Indian) Age 24, born (About 1857) in Ontario, a Baptist, Lucey age 23, born in Ontario. Page 42, Household 243/243.

**BOMBERRY, MARY:** (Indian) Age 48, born (About 1833) in Ontario, a member of the Church of England, Marey? Hess age eleven months, born in May. Page 10, Household 55/55.

**BOOTY, CRENEWS?:** (Indian) Age 27, born (About 1854) in Ontario, a member of the Church of England, Elizabeth age 27, Marey age 5, Ellen born in March. Page 7, Household 36/36.

**BOWDEN, EMMY:** (Indian?) Age 24, born (About 1857) in the United States, a Baptist, (all others listed as Indians) Johey? Bowden (male) age 11, Jully Bowden (female) age 6, Charles Bowden age 2. Page 46, Household 268/268.

**BRANT, HENRY:** (Indian) Age 36, born (About 1845) in Ontario, a member of the Church of England, Elizabeth age 35, Peter age 8, Mary age 5, Margaret age 2, Page 36, Household 203/203.

**BRANT, MARY:** (White/Scotch) Age 54, born (About 1827) in Scotland, a member of the Presbyterian Scotch Church. (All others listed as Indians). Robert D. age 19, Maggy age 21, Sidney age 17, Jacob WALTON age 7, C. E. WALTON age one month born in March. Page 23, Household 126.

**BROWN, JAMES:** (Indian) Age 28, born (About 1853) in Ontario, a Methodist, Janet age 27, born in Ontario. Page 52, Household 311/311.

**BUMBRY? (BOMBERY?) WILLIAM:** (Indian) Age 41, born (About 1840) in Ontario, a member of the Church of England, Elizabeth age 17, Malinda age ten months, born in June. Page 11, Household 61/61.

**BURNING, ELIZABETH:** (Indian) Age 26, born (About 1855) in Ontario, a member of the Church of England, Ely age 5. Page 13, Household 76/76.

**BURNING, EZEKIAL:** (Indian) Age 21 (Born about 1860) a Methodist, Martha age 22, James age 2. Page 36, Household 204/204.

**BURNING, MAGGY:** (Indian) Age 21, born (About 1860) in Ontario, a member of the Church of England. Page 41, Household 231/231.

**BURNING, NICHOLAS:** (Indian) Age 71, born (About 1810) in Ontario, a member of the Church of England. Page 17, Household 94.

**BURNING, SARAH:** (Indian) Age 39, born (About 1842) in Ontario, a member of the Church of England, Julia age 18, Magdalane age 7, Jeremiah age seven months, born in October. Jane LONG? or SONG? Page 49, Household 294/294.

**CANADA, WILLIAM:** (Irish?) Age 44, born (About 1837) in Ontario, a member of the Church of England, Catherine FRENCH (Indian) age 50. Page 50, Household 297/297.

**CARPENTER, JACOB:** (Indian) Age 68, born (Aout 1813) in Ontario, a member of the Church of England. Page 17, Household 97.

**CARPENTER, JOHN:** (Indian) Age 60, born (About 1821) in Ontario, a member of the Church of England, Eliza age 47, Hester age 44, Margaret age 39. Page 48, Household 285/285.

**CARPINTER (CAPENTER) CATRINE:** (Indian) Age 51, born (About 1830) in Ontario, a member of the Church of England. Page 40, Household 227/227.

**CERO, DENNIS:** (Indian) Age 45, born (About 1836) in Ontario, Lucey? age 24. Page 47, Household 276/276.

**CERO, JACOB:** (Indian) Age 49, born (About 1832) in Ontario, a member of the Church of England, Ann age 40, Mary Jane age 11. Page 10, Household 56/56.

**CHUP? or CHUB? SARAH:** (Indian) Age 57, born (About 1824) in Ontario, a Methodist, Joseph age 17, John GREENE age 28, Eliza GREENE age 24. Page 21, Household 21.

**CLAUSE, HESTOR:** (Indian) Age 55, born (About 1826) in Ontario, a member of the Church of England, Elizabeth FANN? or FUNN? age 29, Ellen age 2. Page 9, Household 51/51.

**CLAUSE, JAMES:** (Indian) Age 26, born (About 1855) in Ontario, a Baptist, Betsy age 20. Page 8, Household 42/42.

**CLAUSE, JOSEPH:** (Indian) Age 35, born (About 1846) in Ontario, a member of the Church of England, Emley age 9, Methew age 7, Deborah age 60? Page 13, Household 77/77.

**CLAUSE, PETER:** (Indian) Age 46, born (About 1835) in Ontario, a Baptist, Margaret age 40, Jemima age 16, Isaac age 14, Henry age 11, Sussanah age 7. Page 8, Household 41/41.

**CLAUSE, SETH:** (Indian) Age 51, born (About 1830) in Ontario, a Baptist, Margaret LEWEN? or LEWIS? age 35, Catherine? age 11. Page 8, Household 40.

**COOK, JOHN:** (Indian) Age 45, born (About 1836) in Ontario, Nancy age 66, Elias age 23, William age 12, David age 12, Abba (female) age 9, John age 6. Page 4, Household 15.

**COPELAND, DEBORAH:** (Indian) Age 43, born (About 1838) in Ontario, a member of the Church of England, Margaret age 18, born in Ontario, Martha age 16, born in Ontario, John age 15? born in Ontario, Sarah age 11, born in Ontario, Elizabeth age 7, born in Ontario, Hiram age 4, born in Ontario. Page 51, Household 302/302.

**CORNELIUS, JOHN:** (Indian) Age 40, born (About 1841) in Ontario, a member of the Church of England, Lamada? (A Female) age 37, Senian? (A Male) age? and Ranson FOSTER age 6. Page 51, Household 304/304.

**CRAIN, WILLIAM:** (Indian) Age 30, born (About 1851) in Ontario, a Methodist, Adline age 21, William age 10. Page 30, Household 170/170.

**CRAWFORD, ABRAHAM:** (Indian) Age 58, (Born about 1823) a member of the Church of England, Sussanah age 53, Noah POWLIS age 51, born in Ontario. Page 11, Household 60/60.

**CRISTEEN, JOHN:** (Indian) Age 23, born (About 1858) in Ontario. Page 51, Household 303/303.

**CURLEY, JOHN:** (Indian) Age 22, born (About 1859) in Ontario, a Baptist, Nancy age 18, Eliza age two months, born in February. Page 16, Household 92.

**CURLEY, SAMUEL:** (Indian) Age 47, born (About 1834) in Ontario, a Baptist, Sarah A. age 45 (White/German) Allice age 20, George age 19, Mary Ann age 18, Sarah age 17, Charlotte age 13, Matilda age 10, Robert age 8, William age 6, Anas? age 3, Arthur age 2, Nelly age one month born in March. Page 18, Household 102.

**CUSIC, (CUSICK?) JOSEPHUS:** (Indian) Age 28, born (About 1853) in Ontario, a Baptist, Ellen age 20, Cornelius age 1. Page 19, Household 108/108.

**DAVIS, CHARLES:** (Indian) Age 49, born (About 1832) in Ontario, a member of the Church of England, Ann (White/English) age 56, Darel (male) age 24, Ann HARRIS (White/Irish) age 11. Page 45, Household 263/263.

**DAVIS, JACOB:** (Indian) Age 56, born (About 1825) in Ontario, a member of the Church of England, Cristeen age 52, John age 23, Sarah age 19, Lawrence age 17, Jacob age 15, Joseph age 13, Frances (female) age 11. Page 5, Household 28/28.

**DAVIS, JOHN:** (Indian) Age 40, born (About 1841) in Ontario, a Methodist, John David age 21, Andrew age 19? Mathew age 11, Mary age 8, William age 5, Josiah age 3. Page 30, Household 171/171.

**DAVIS, PETER:** (Indian) Age 48, born (About 1833) in Ontario, a member of the Church of England, Susan age 51, Mary age 10. Page 5, Household 24/24.

**DENNEY, JOHN:** (Indian) Age 74, born (About 1807) in Ontario, a member of the Church of England, Hannah DOXTATOR age 70, born in Ontario. Page 46, Household 273/273.

**DOCTOR, ISICK:** (Indian) Age 49? born (About 1832?) in Ontario, a Baptist, Elizabeth age 53, Albert age 20, Ellen age 17, Thomas age 10, Josephine ANTONY? or ANTHONY? age 9, Jane ANTONY? age 6. Page 18, Household 103/103.

**DOCTOR, JOSEPH:** (Indian) Age 27, born (About 1854) in Ontario, a member of the Church of England, Jemima age 20, Eddy age 4, Susannah age seven months, born in October. Page 39, Household 221/221.

**DOCTOR, JOSIAH:** (Indian) Age 56, born (About 1825) in Ontario, a member of the Church of England, Mary age 41, John Doctor age 19, Mary age 15, Wm. Chambrie Doctor age 10, Julia Ann age 7, Margarett age 4. Page 39, Household 220/220.

**DOXTATOR, CHARLES:** (Indian) Age 21, born (About 1860) )in Ontario, a Methodist. Page 44, Household 257.

**DOXTATOR, DANEL:** (Indian) Age 45, born (About 1836) in Ontario, a Methodist, Elizabeth age 25, Dannel (male) age 22, Juley age 14 (female), Joab age 12, Marey age 11. Page 11, Household 65/65.

**DOXTATOR, LEVINA:** (Indian) Age 40, born (About 1841) in Ontario, a Baptist, Mathew NASH? age 11. Page 46. Household 266/266.

**DOXTATOR, SETH:** (Indian) Age 25, born (About 1856) in Ontario, a Baptist, Elizabeth ATKINS age 20, John J. DOXTATOR age 25, Catharine DOXTATOR age 13, Lydia Doxtator age 11. Page 35, Household 194/194.

**DREDGE, WILLIAM:** (White/English) Age 42, born (About 1839) in England, a Methodist, Sarah Dredge (Indian) age 38, (All others listed as Indians) Susan MC DUGAL age 9, Sarah MC DUGAL age 7, Aeda? MC DUGAL (female) age 4. Page 27, Household 150.

**ELLIOTT, WILLIAM:** (Indian) Age 35, born (About 1846) in Ontario, a member of the Church of England, Hestor age 32, born in Ontario, Eliza age 10, born in Ontario, John age 4, born in Ontario. Page 52, Household 307/307.

**ENGLISH, WILLIAM:** (Indian) Age 34, born (About 1847) in Ontario, a member of the Church of England, Minney age 24, born in Ontario. Page 46, Household 274/274.

**EVERETT, GEORGE:** (Indian) Age 29, born (About 1852) in Ontario, a Baptist, Lucy age 29, Isaac age 8, John age 3, Charlotte age 5, John DOXTATOR (Indian) age 24, Elizabeth DOXTATOR (White/ English) age 22. Page 14, Household 80/80.

**EVERETT, SOLOMON:** (Indian) Age 33, born (About 1848) in Ontario, a member of the Church of England, Elizabeth age 33, Sarah age 3, Ellen age 1. Page 12, Household 71/71.

**EVERETTE, JOHN:** (Indian) Age 55, born (About 1826) in Ontario, a member of the Plymouth Brethren Church, Susannah age 40, Lydia age 24, William age 22, Sussanah age 18, Elizabeth age 15, Julia age 13, Peter age 10, George age 8. Page 3, Household 11.

**FOWLER, SAMUEL:** (Indian) Age 67, born (About 1814) in Ontario, a member of the Church of England. Page 10, Household 53/53.

**FRASIER, WILLIAM:** (Indian) Age 21, born (About 1860) in Ontario, a member of the Church of England. Page 42, Household 244/244.

**FRASURE, ELIZA:** (White/Scotch) Age 30, born (About 1851) in Ontario, a member of the Church of England, Mary Ann Frasure (Indian) age 14, Charety Frasure (Indian) age 11. Page 7, Household 34.

**FRASURE, JOHN:** (Indian) Age 65, born (About 1816) in Ontario, a member of the Church of England, Ann age 57? born in Ontario, Ellen age 18, Lydia age 17. Page 5, Household 26/26.

**FROMAN, JOSEPH:** (Indian) Age 40, born (About 1841) in Ontario, a member of the Church of England, Joseph age 3, Francis (A Male) age 11, Peter age 8, Isaac age 6, Ann age 3. Page 35, Household 195/195.

**FUNN?, (FRUM?) ELIZABETH:** (Indian) Age 70, born (About 1811) in Ontario, a member of the Church of England, Jacob HILL age 12. Page 29, Household 163/163.

**GARLOW, BENJAMIN?:** (Indian) Age 28 (Born about 1853) a Baptist, Phepe? (A Female) age 3, Levi age 1, Mary LOFT age 26. Page 38, Household 158/158.

**GARLOW, ISICK:** (Indian) Age 24, born (About 1857) in Ontario, a member of the Church of England, Sarah age 22, Mary age 5, Edward age 3, Catharine age nine months. Page 29, Household 164/164.

**GARLOW, JAMES:** (Indian) Age 28, born (About 1853) in Ontario, a member of the Church of England, Louisa age 20, Francis (male) age 1. Page 14, Household 84/84.

**GARLOW, PHIP?:** (Indian) Age 51, born (About 1830) in Ontario, a Baptist, Julia age 49. Page 14, Household 83/83.

**GENERAL, ALEXANDER:** (Indian) Age 23, born (About 1858) in Ontario, Eliza age 21, Walter age 2, Lottie age one month, born in March. Page 42, Household 239/239.

**GENERAL, JEMIMA:** (Indian) Age 54, born (About 1827) in Ontario, Jacob age 21, George age 19, Sarah age 14, James age 12. Page 45, Household 261/261.

**GENERAL? or PLENERAL? ADAM:** (Indian) Age 25 (Born about 1856) Catrine age 19? Joseph age 2, Elizabeth age two months, born in February. Page 9, Household 47/47.

**GIBSON, PETER:** (Indian) Age 50, born (About 1831) in Ontario, a member of the Church of England, Sarah age 40, Nancy age 20, Jessy age 16, Ellen age 12, Eliza age 7, Sarah age 5, William age 2. Page 3, Household 14.

**GOOD, THOMAS:** (White/Irish) Age 40, born (About 1841) in Ontario, Juley Good age 30 (Indian) born in Ontario, a member if the Church of England, (Everyone else listed as Irish) Josephine Good age 12, Ida Good age 7, Elizabeth Good age 3, Edith Good age 2. Page 11, Household 58/58.

**GREEN, CORNELIUS:** (Indian) Age 20, born (About 1861) in Ontario, a member of the Church of England, Marey age 15, Mallase? or Wallace? age 1, Ana or Anna SKILLER age 50, born in Ontario, Catey FUNN age 20, born in Ontario, William GREEN age 20. Page 15, Household 87.

**GREEN, DANIEL:** (Indian) Age 27, born (About 1854) in Ontario, a member of the Church of England, Martha age 22, George age 4, Andrew age 1. Page 38, Household 217/217.

**GREEN, GEORGE:** (Indian) Age 35 born (About 1846) in Ontario, a member of the Church of England, Ann age 38, Eliza age 8, Abraham age 6, Lottie age three months, born in January. Page 33, Household 186/186.

**GREEN, HANAH:** (Indian) Age 50 born (About 1831) in Ontario, a member of the Church of England, Josiah age 17, Ann R. age 11, William age 5. Page 29, Household 165/165.

**GREEN, HENRY:** (Indian) Age 40, born (About 1841) in Ontario, a member of the Church of England, Lydia age 28, Joseph age 8. Page 9, Household 52/52.

**GREEN, JAMES:** (Indian) Age 24, born (About 1857) in Ontario, a member of the Church of England, Catrine Green (White Irish) age 24. Page 15, Household 86.

**GREEN, JOHN Mc K.?** (Indian) Age 64, born (About 1817) in Ontario, a member of the Church of England. Page 46, Household 271/271.

**GREEN, JOHN:** (Indian) Age 25, born (About 1856) in Ontario, a Baptist, Ann age 19, Elizabeth age three months, born in January. Page 34, Household 193/193.

**GREEN, MARY:** (Indian) Age 41, born (About 1840) in Ontario, a member of the Church of England, Isick age 22, Sussanah age 20, Joab age 18, Elizabeth age 16, Charlotte age 14, John age 11, Marey age 1. Page 13, Household 78/78.

**GREENE, ARON:** (Indian) Age 27, born (About 1854) in Ontario, a Baptist, Elizabeth age 23. Page 29, Household 162/162.

**GREENE, CATHERINE:** (Indian) age 30 (Born about 1851) a member of the Church of England, Lucy Greene age 14, Henry HILL age 21. Page 34, Household 188/188.

**GROAT, CHRISTINE:** (Indian) Age 50, born (About 1831) in Ontario, a Baptist, Sarah Groat age 14, Solomon Groat age 11, Mary Groat age 8, Ida Groat age 5, Leah BAREFOOT age 2. Page 38, Household 215/215.

**GROAT, HENRY:** (Indian) Age 34, born (About 1847) in Ontario, a Baptist, Nancy age 32, Marthy age 6, Andrew age 2, James age one month, born in March. Page 20, Household 116.

**GROAT, MIKEL:** (Indian) Age 26, born (About 1855) in Ontario, a Methodist, Emily age 24, Sarah age 3, Henry age 2, Sarah CRYSLY? (African/Origins) age 9, born in Ontario. Page 32, Household 178/178.

**GROAT, SAMSON:** (Indian) Age 32, born (About 1849) in Ontario, a Baptist, Charlotina? HILL age 24, Joseph HILL age 43, born in Ontario a member of the Church of England. Page 20, Household 111.

**HENHAWK, GEORGE:** (Indian) Age 29, born (About 1852) in Ontario, a member of the Church of England, Sussanah HOUSE age 28, Robert Henhawk age nine months, born in July. Page 11, Household 59/59.

**HENHAWK, NELSON:** (Indian) Age 28, born (About 1853) in Ontario, a member of the Church of England, Elizabeth age 28. Page 37, Household 208/208.

**HENRY, GEORGE:** (Indian) Age 46, born (About 1835) in Ontario, a Baptist, Mary age 40, Clarry age 16 Francis (male) age 13, Alfred age 4. Page 24, Household 132.

**HENRY, JOHN:** (Indian) Age 29, born (About 1852) in Ontario, Julia age 21, born in Ontario, Fagan (male) age 1. Page 36, Household 205/205.

**HENRY, JOSEPH:** (Indian) Age 49, born (About 1832) in Ontario, a member of the Church of England, Hester age 30, William age 20. Page 41, Household 236/236.

**HERKIMER, DANIEL:** (Indian) Age 43, born (About 1838) in Ontario, a Methodist, Harriet Jane age 28, Haddy May age 9, Charlotte Ann age 6, Augustus Jane age 3, Daniel W. age 1. Page 25, Household 138.

**HERKIMER, DAVID:** (Indian) Age 38, born (About 1843) in Ontario, a Methodist, Rachel age 28, Reuben age 10, Berthy age 4. Page 25, Household 143/143.

**HERREN, MOSES:** (Indian) Age 40, born (About 1841) in Ontario, a member of the Church of England, Sarah age 37, John HENCELY age 24. Page 17, Household 95.

**HERRIN, ELIZABETH:** (Indian) Age 40, born (About 1841) in Ontario, a member of the Church of England, Margaret age 50, Eve age 11. Page 43, Household 252/252.

**HERRIN, LEVINA:** (Indian) Age 66, born (About 1815) in Ontario, a Baptist. Page 47, Household 269/269.

**HESS, NELSON:** (Indian) Age 26, born (About 1855) in Ontario, a member of the Church of England, Haner (female) age 26, Jacob age ten months, born in June. Page 29, Household 161/161.

**HILL, ABRAHAM:** (Indian) Age 32, born (About 1849) in Ontario, a member of the Church of England, Ellen age 30, Alpheus (male) age 11? Thomas age 8, Henryetta age 4. Page 2, Household 8.

**HILL, ABRAHAM:** (Indian) Age 41, born (About 1840) in Ontario, a member of the Church of England. Page 6, Household 31/31.

**HILL, AUGUSTUS:** (Indian) Age 53, born (About 1828) in Ontario, a member of the Church of England, Ellen age 53, Augustus W? age 21, Mary GARLOUGH age 8. Page 5, Household 21.

**HILL, DAVID:** (Indian) Age 28, born (About 1853) in Ontario, a member of the Church of England, Hestor age 22, William age 5, Charlotte age 3, Page 5, Household 27/27.

**HILL, DAVID:** (Indian) Age 81, born (About 1800) in Ontario, a Baptist, Eve Hill age 79, born in Ontario, Powless HENHAWK age 38, Elizabeth

HENHAWK age 33, Lucy HENHAWK age 13, Jacob Hill age 20, Margaret Hill age 17. Page 34, Household 190/190.

**HILL, ELIJAH:** (Indian) Age 42, born (About 1839) in Ontario, a member of the Church of England, Elizabeth age 44, Elizabeth age 18, Allice age 14, George age 12, Unis age 8, Nicholas age 6, Joseph TWOFISH age 86, born in Ontario, William TWOFISH age 35, born in Ontario. Page 37, Household 209/209.

**HILL, ELIZABETH:** (Indian) Age 50, born (About 1831) in Ontario, a member of the Church of England, Nicholas age 33, Thomas age 23, Joseph age 20, Eliza age 17. Page 45, Household 259/259.

**HILL, GEORGE:** (Indian) Age 29, born (About 1852) in Ontario, a member of the Church of England, John age 25, Abram age 22. Page 12, Household 70/70.

**HILL, GEORGE:** (Indian) Age 31, born (About 1850) in Ontario a member of the Church of England, Mary age 72, born in Ontario, Margaret age 40, William age 36. Page 1, Household 2.

**HILL, ISAAC S.:** (Indian) Age 51, born (About 1830) in Ontario, a Baptist Ellen age 48. Page 33, Household 184/184.

**HILL, ISAAC J.:** (Indian) Age 64, born (About 1817) in Ontario, a Baptist, Mary age 60, born in Ontario, Isaac age 15, Sophia age 10, Elliot age 4. Page 41, Household 235/235.

**HILL, ISICK:** (Indian) Age 53, born (About 1828) in Ontario, a Baptist, Andrew age 19, Catherine age 21, William age 3, Hestor WAKER? or WALKER age 18. Page 8, Household 43.

**HILL, ISICK:** (Indian) Age 53, born (About 1828) in Ontario, a member of the Church of England, Mary age 25, John age 9? Jane age 7, Ann age 5, Ellen age 3, Page 8, Household 44/44.

**HILL, JAMES:** (Indian) Age 40, born (About 1841) in Ontario, a Baptist, Lydia age 30, Jemima age 5, Annie age 3, Jane age 1. Page 52, Household 306/306.

**HILL, JAMES:** (Indian) Age 21, born (About 1860) in Ontario, a member of the Church of England, Mary age 20, born in Ontario, Josephine age 1. born in Ontario. Page 52, Household 306/306.

**HILL, JAMES:** (Indian) Age 30, born (About 1851) in Ontario, a member of the Church of England, Susanah age 27, James age 4, Victoria age 2. Page 41, Household 231/231.

**HILL, JEMIMA:** (Indian) Age 78, born (About 1803) in Ontario, a Baptist, Simon HARRIE? age 28, born in Ontario. Page 42, Household 240/240.

**HILL, JOAB:** (Indian) Age 36, born (About 1845) in Ontario, a Baptist, Mary age 33, Edward age 15, Lucey age 13, Sharlotte age 9, John age 4. Page 41, Household 234/234.

**HILL, JOHN:** (Indian) Age 34, born (About 1845) in Ontario, a member of the Church of England, Lydia age 32, Mary age 9, Isaac age 8, Joseph age 8? William age 3, Christeen (A Female) age 2, Ann age 2. Page 10, Household 54/54.

**HILL, JOHN:** (Indian) Age 50, born (About 1831) in Ontario, a member of the Church of England, Elizabeth age 40, Clara age 8, William age 2. Page 13, Household 73/73.

**HILL, JOHN:** (Indian) Age 25, born (About 1856) in Ontario, a member of the Church of England, Mary age 20. Page 46, Household 272/272.

**HILL, JOSEPH:** (Indian) Age 30, born (About 1851) in Ontario, a member of the Church of England, Mary age 30. Page 48, Household 289/289.

**HILL, LYDIA:** (Indian) Age 70, born (About 1811) in Ontario, a member of the Church of England, Joseph age 40, Jacob age 23. Page 41, Household 233/233.

**HILL, MARY:** (Indian) Age 63, born (About 1818) in Ontario, a Baptist, Caroline THOMAS age 83? born in Ontario, James JONSON or JOHNSON? age 16. Page 43, Household 247/247.

**HILL, MATHEW:** (Indian) Age 24, born (About 1857) in Ontario, a member of the Church of England, Sarah age 26, Mary Ann age 3. Page 12, Household 68/68.

**HILL, PETER:** (Indian) Age 42, born (About 1839) in Ontario, a member of the Plymouth Brethren Church, Eunice age 32, Sampson age 16, Eli age 13, Louise age 10, Myles age 6, Alberty (A Female) age 4, Wilbert age 2, Elen age five months, born in October. Page 1, Household 6.

**HILL, PETER:** (Indian) Age 38, born (About 1843) in Ontario, a member of the Church of England, Sussanah age 33, Polly age 12, William age 9, Emily age 7. Page 34, Household 189/189.

**HILL, SAMUEL:** (Indian) Age 29, born (About 1852) in Ontario, a member of the Plymouth Brethren Church, Mary age 24, Oliver age 6, Persia? E. (Male) age 4, Catharine WILLIAMS age 17. Page 36, Household 202/202.

**HILL, SILAS:** (Indian) Age 31, born (About 1850) in Ontario, a Baptist, Betsy age 30. Page 20, Household 113.

**HILL, WILLIAM:** (Indian) Age 44, born (About 1837) in Ontario, a member of the Church of England, Christeen age 40, William age 18, Eliza age 6, Catrine HENHAWK age 50. Page 7, Household 35/35.

**HILL, WILLIAM:** (Indian) Age 20, born (About 1861) in Ontario, Mary Hill age 25, George BOMBERY age 7, Joseph BOMBERRY age 1, Catherine JACOB age 70, born in Ontario. Page 38, Household 218/218.

**HILL, WILLIAM:** (Indian) Age 57, born (About 1824) in Ontario, a member of the Church of England, Magdaline age 55, Christeen (female) age 18. Page 6, Household 29/29.

**HURCAMER (OR HERKIMER?) ELIZABETH:** (Indian) Age 48, born (About 1833) in Ontario, a Methodist, Stinson age 17, David age 12, Rachel age 10, Matildy age 5, Mary C. age 3. Page 24, Household 134.

**HUSK, JOHN:** (Indian) Age 44, born (About 1837) in Ontario, Ellen age 52, James age 21, John age 18? Sussanah age 10, Harriet age 10, George age 7. Page 49, Household 293/293.

**ISAAC, NICHOLAS:** (Indian) Age 55, born (About 1826) in Ontario, a member of the Plymouth Brethren Church, Charlotte age 45. Page 43, Household 248/248.

**JACOB, CATHERINE:** (Indian) Age 38, born (About 1843) a Baptist, Mary Jacob age 24, Ida Jacob age 19? Lucy Jacob age 16, Edward DOXTATOR age 8. Page 34, Household 192/192.

**JACOB, JAMES:** (Indian) Age 26, born (About 1855) in Ontario, Betsy age 55, a Baptist, Jemima age 13, Page 18, Household 101.

**JACOB, JOSEPH:** (Indian) Age 25, born (About 1856) in Ontario, Nancy HARRIS age 19, John HARRIS age 1. Page 38, Household?

**JACOB, PETER:** (Indian) Age 28, born (About 1853) Jemima age 24, Marthy age 6, Ely age 3, Sampson GREEN age 18, Mary GREEN age 10. Page 17, Household 100.

**JACOB, WILLIAM:** (Indian) Age 44, born (About 1837) in Ontario, Hester Jacob age 45, Peter JAMIESON age 20, Eliza BILL? or BELL? age 11. Page 48, Household 290/290.

**JAMESON, DAVID:** (Indian) Age 60, born (About 1821) in Ontario, a member of the Church of England, Lucretia age 55, born in Ontario, Ann age 20, born in Ontario. Page 52, Household 309/309.

**JAMESON, HAWLOW:** (Indian) Age 27, born (About 1854) in Ontario, a Baptist, Minnie HAWLOW age 25, born in Ontario, Mallissa Jameson age 5, born in Ontario, Jesse CLAUSE (Male) age 15, born in Ontario. Page 52, Household 310/310.

**JAMIESON, ELIZABETH:** (Indian) Age 54, born (About 1827) in Ontario. Page 48, Household 286/286.

**JAMIESON, JOHN:** (Indian) Age 38, born (About 1843) in Ontario, a member of the Church of England, Susanah age 35, Elias D. age 16, Mary age 11, Heatty age 9, Catharine age 7, John age 5, Chancer? or Chauncer age 3, Lydia age five months, born in November. Page 39, Household 223/223.

**JEMERSON, CHRISTEEN:** (Indian) Age 48, born (About 1833) in Ontario, a member of the Church of England, Archey age 21, Alexander age 19, Hatty age 12, George age 9, Alfred age 7. Page 46, Household 260/260.

**JEMERSON, JACOB:** (Indian) Age 60, born (About 1821) in Ontario, Baptist, Sarah age 40, Lucy age 16, David age 14, Susan age 10, Alexander age 8, Marget? age 6, Austin age 3, Christopher age eight months, born in August, Sampson age 22. Page 15, Household 90.

**JOHN, JOSEPH:** (Indian) Age 25, born (About 1856) in Ontario, a member of the Church of England. Page 1, Household 4.

**JOHN, THOMAS:** (Indian) Age 20, born (About 1861) in Ontario, Mary age 17. Page 43, Household 246/246.

**JOHNSON, ARON:** (Indian) Age 55, born (About 1826) in Ontario, a member of the Church of England, Elizabeth age 44, Levi age 23, Julia Ellen age 17, John age 14, Charline (female) age 12, Susannah age 10, George age 8, Charlotte age 6. Page 6, Household 32/32.

**JOHNSON, ELIJAH:** (Indian) Age 68, born (About 1813) in Ontario. Page 52, Household 308/308.

**JOHNSON, JOHN H.:** (Indian) Age 83, born (About 1798) in Ontario, a member of the Church of England. Page 5, Household 23/23.

**JOHNSON, JOHN:** (Indian) Age 28, born (About 1853) in Ontario, a Methodist, Elizabeth age 29. Page 22, Household 121.

**JONES, ALFRED:** (Indian) Age 40, born (About 1841) in Ontario, a Methodist (He was listed as a school teacher) Elizabeth age 31, Allice age 9, Mebel? age 4. Page 27, Household 151/151.

**JONES, JASPER:** (African) Age 50, born (About 1831) a Baptist, Susan (Indian) age 40, Mary age 18, Isick age 16, Joseph age 14, Sophia age 9. Page 47, Household 281/281.

**JOSEPH, WILLIAM:** (Indian) Age 50, born (About 1831) in Ontario, a member of the Church of England, Hester age 34, William age 17, Elam age 10, Peter age 9, Osborne age 6, Walter age seven months, born in September. Page 18, Household 104.

**KEY, JOHN:** (Indian) Age 70, born (About 1811) in Ontario, Mary age 60. Page 43, Household 254/245.

**KING, ALFRED A.:** (Indian) Age 25, born (About 1856) in Ontario, a Methodist, Nancey age 21, Joseph age 4, Sussanah age eight months, born in August. Page 24, Household 131.

**KING, JOSEPH:** (Indian) Age 29, born (About 1852) in Ontario, a Methodist, Elizabeth age 20. Page 30, Household 169/169.

**KING, JULIUS:** (Indian) Age 24, born (About 1857) in Ontario, a member of the Church of England, Nancy age 21, Joseph age 5, Julius age 3, Charlotte age 1. Page 26, Household 146/146

**KING, MRS. GEORGE:** (Indian) Age 50, born (About 1831) a Methodist, Edward age 17, Sussanah age 15, George age 12. Page 27, Household 152/152.

**LA FORM, ALEXANDER:** (Indian) Age 29? born (About 1852) in Ontario, a Methodist, Nancy age 29, Samuel age 12, John age 10, Mary age 8, Angeline age 5, Ann age 4. Page 50, Household 296/296.

**LA FORM, JAMES:** (Indian) Age 26, born (About 1855) in Ontario, a Methodist. Page 32, Household 179/179.

**LA FORM, CAROLINE:** (Indian) Age 40, born (About 1841) in Ontario, a Methodist, James age 52, Dannel age 23. Page 25, Household 141/141.

**LA FORM, JOHN:** (Indian) Age 18, born (About 1863) in Ontario, a Methodist Lydia age 20. Page 25, Household 140.

**LA FORM, JOHN:** (Indian) Age 47, born (About 1834) in Ontario, a member of the Church of England, Christine age 37, Loososy? or Tracy? age 77, born in Ontario, Page 24, Household 133.

**LA FORM? JOHN:** (Indian) Age 78, born (About 1803) in Ontario, a Catholic, Betsy age 77, a Methodist, Elizabeth age 16. Page 50, Household 295/295.

**LA FORME, JAMES:** (Indian) Age 26, born (About 1855) a Methodist, Mary age 28. Page 26, Household 145/145.

**LA FORME, JOSEPH:** (Indian) Age 28, born (About 1853) in Ontario, a Methodist, Betsy age 18, Peter age 2. Page 27, Household 154/154

**LA FORME, CHESTER:** (Indian) Age 24, born (About 1857) in Ontario, a Methodist, Lydia age 25, Agnes age 5, Phepe age 1. Page 25, Household 139.

**LA FORME, JOHN:** (Indian) Age 18, born (About 1863) in Ontario, a Methodist, Lydia age 20. Page 25, Household 39.

**LA FORME, DAVID:** (White/French) Age 37, born (About 1844) in Ontario, Lydia La Forme (Indian) age 30, (All others were listed as French). Lucy La Forme age 11, Betsy La Forme age 9, David La Forme age 6, Emily La Forme age 3, Melie? La Forme (A Female) age 1. Page 28, Household 156/156.

**LEWEN? (OR LEWIS?) ADAM:** (Indian) Age 37, born (About 1844) in Ontario, a member of the Church of England, Christina age 34, Thomas age 9, Richard age 6, Walter age 4. Page 4, Household 18.

**LEWIS, ABRAM:** (Indian) Age 30, born (About 1851) in Ontario, a member of the Church of England, Abram age 16? Page 36, Household 207/207.

**LEWIS, CHARLOTTE:** (Indian) Age 44, born (About 1837) in Ontario, a member of the Church of England, Lydia age 19, Cristina age 16, Sussanah age 14, Jacob age 12. Page 14, Household 82/82.

**LEWIS, JOSEPH:** (Indian) Age 23, born (About 1858) in Ontario, a member of the Church of England, Elizabeth age 18, Page 9, Household 46.

**LEWIS, SIAS? (OR LIAS):** (Male Indian) Age 28, born (About 1853) in Ontario, a member of the Church of England, Lydia HILL age 26, Cristain Lewis age 1. Page 1, Household 5.

**LICKENS, JOHN:** (Indian) Age 38, born (About 1843) in Ontario, Elizabeth age 24, Deborah age 8, Josiah? age 5, Sarah age eight months, born in July. Page 48, Household 291/291.

**LICKERS? (LICKENS?) MARY:** (Indian) Age 50, born (About 1831) in Ontario, a member of the Church of England, Sussanah age 5. Page 38, Household 216/216.

**LICKERS? (OR LICKENS?) SAMUEL:** (Indian) Age 66, born (About 1815) in Ontario, a Methodist, Sussanah age 65, Edward age 11. Page 12, Household 67/67.

**LOFT, GEORGE:** (Indian) Age 45, born (About 1836) in Ontario, a member of the Church of England, Mary age 42, William age 18, John P. age 14. Page 6, Household 33/33.

**LOTERRIDGE, HESTER:** (Indian) Age 39, born (About 1842) in Ontario, a member of the Church of England, Willison age 13, James age 3. Page 9, Household 49/49.

**LOTREDGE, (LOTHRIDGE) LYDIA:** (Indian) Age 77, born (About 1804) in Ontario, a Methodist. Page 44, Household 255/255.

**LOTRIDGE, (LOTHRIDGE) SETH:** (Indian) Age 42, born (About 1839) in Ontario, a Methodist, Mary age 30, Magdalene age 8, Nancy age 5, Jacob age 3, John age 1. Page 44, Household 256/256.

**LOTTRIDGE, SARAH:** (Indian) Age 60, born (About 1821) in Ontario, a member of the Church of England. Page 5, Household 20.

**MARACLE, JOHN:** (Indian) Age 57, born (About 1824) in Ontario, a Baptist, Margaret age 34, Myers age 11, David age 9, Peter age 5, Charles age 1. Page 49, Household 292/292.

**MARACLE, POWLIS:** (Indian) Age 70, born (About 1811) in Ontario, a member of the Church of England, Marey age 60, Lusey age 17. Page 14, Household 79/79.

**MARACLE, THOMAS:** (Indian) Age 30, born (About 1851) in Ontario, a member of the Church of England, William age 28, born in Ontario, age 28. Page 39, Household 222/222.

**MARACLE, WILLIAM:** (Indian) Age 22, born (About 1859) in Ontario, a member of the Church of England, Mary J. age 26, Sarah age 7, Henry age 4, Mary age 3, George age eleven months, born in May. Page 9, Household 50/50.

**MARGRET?:** (Indian) Age 76, born (About 1805) in Ontario, a member of the Church of England. Page 45, Household 264/264.

**MARTIN, ADAM:** (Indian) Age 44, born (About 1837) in Ontario, a member of the Plymouth Brethren Church, Sarah age 40, Uriah age 17, Adolphas age 12, Eunice age 10, Lucinda age 8, Ida age 6, Robert age 4, Matilda age 2. Page 2, Household 9/9.

**MARTIN, ADAM:** (Indian) Age 23?, born (About 1858) in Ontario, a member of the Church of England, Charlotte age 28. Page 15, Household 88/88.

**MARTIN, CHARLES:** (Indian) Age 28, born (About 1853) in Ontario, a member of the Church of England, Sarah age 23, Josephine age 5, Norman age 3. Page 12, Household 69/69.

**MARTIN, CHARLOTTE:** (Indian) Age 27, born (About 1854) in Ontario, a member of the Church of England, Charles age 5, Preston age 2. Page 44, Household 254/254.

**MARTIN, JAMES:** (Indian) Age 33, born (About 1848) in Ontario, a member of the Church of England, Phoebe age 30, Christana age 3. Page 12, Household 66/66.

**MARTIN, JOEL:** (Indian) Age 34, born (About 1847) in Ontario, a Methodist, Sarah age 17. Page 11, Household 64/64.

**MARTIN, JOHN:** (Indian) Age 28, born (About 1853) in Ontario, a Baptist, Charlotte age 33, Andrew age 8, Francis age 6, Eliza age 4, Ella? or Ailly? (A Female) age two months, born in January, Joseph RUSSEL, age 18, Claber RUSSEL age 18 (male) Wilson RUSSEL age 14, John RUSSEL age 12, Sarah RUSSEL age 10. Page 16, Household 93.

**MARTIN, MOSES:** (Indian) Age 53, born (About 1828) in Ontario, a member of the Plymouth Brethren Church, Caroline age 11. Page 11, Household 63/63.

**MARTIN, PETER:** (Indian) Age 25, born (About 1856) in Ontario, a member of the Church of England, George age 53, Christine age 48, Peter age 21, George age 18? Joseph age 17, Eva age 14, Henry age 11, Albert age 8, Mary age 5. Page 44, Household 253/253.

**MARTIN, SARAH:** (Indian) Age 45, born (About 1836) in Ontario, a member of the Church of England, Edward age 22. Page 48, Household 284/284.

**MARTIN, SUSSANAH:** (Indian) Age 79, born (About 1802) in Ontario, a member of the Plymouth Brethren Church, Leah (A Female) age 40, Joab age 38. Page 11, Household 62/62.

**MARTIN? CHARLES C.:** (Indian) Age 21, born (About 1860) in Ontario, a member of the Church of England, Ellen TWOFISH age 28. Page 17, Household 96.

**MC DOUGAL, NICOLAS:** (Indian) Age 24, born (About 1857) in Ontario, a Baptist. Page 26, Household 144/144.

**MC DOUGLE, ALONZO:** (Indian) Age 25, born (About 1856) in Ontario, a Methodist, Mary Mc Dougle age 27, Augusta Mc Dougle age one month (female) Margaret PAHTAHQUAQ? age 17. Page 32, Household 177/177.

**MC GEE?, ANDREW:** (Indian) Age 23, born (About 1858) in Ontario, a Methodist, George FARMER age 30, Pheope FARMER age 19, Pheope WILSON age 65, born in Ontario. Page 22, Household 124.

**MILLER, MARY:** (Indian) Age 42, born (About 1839) in Ontario, a member of the Church of England, Jacob age 20, Mary age 17, James age 14, Thomas age 10, Minnie age 7. Page 15, Household 89.

**MILTEN?, (MITTEN) JAMES:** (Indian) Age 48, born (About 1833) in Ontario, a Baptist, Mary age 44, Samuel age 17, Jemima age 10, Margaret age 7. Page 42, Household 238/238.

**MONTURE, (MONTOUR) PETER:** (Indian) Age 31, born (About 1850) in Ontario, a member of the Church of England, Eliza age 29, John age 9, Henry age 3, Christine age nine months, born in June. Page 40, Household 225/225.

**MONTURE, ISAAC:** (Indian) Age 26, born (About 1855) in Ontario, a member of the Church of England, Sarah age 24, Victoria age four months, born in December. Page 51, Household 305/305.

**MONTURE, JOSEPH:** (Indian) Age 27 (Born about 1854) a Methodist, Mary E. age 24, Emily age 4. Page 47, Household 282/282.

**MONTURE, WILLIAM:** (Indian) Age 75? or 25? born in Ontario, a Methodist, Ann age 30, Cornelius age 21, Eliza age 19, Jane age 16, Lawson? (male) age 14, Josiah age 12, Dannel? (male) age 10, Jemerson age 8, Eliza age 6, Emmy age 4. Page 47, Household 283/283.

**MOSES, CATHERINE:** (Indian) Age 80, born (About 1801) in Ontario, a member of the Church of England, Isaac BATTESSE? age 24, born in Ontario. Page 37, Household 211/211.

**MOUNTURE, (MONTURE) JOHN:** (Indian) Age 52, born (About 1829) in Ontario, a Methodist, Marthy age 24. Page 47, Household 277/277.

**MURDOCK, GEORGE:** (Indian) Age 60, born (About 1821) in Ontario, a member of the Church of England, Eliza age 33, Thomas RANCIER (White/German) age 14. Page 13, Household 74/74.

**MURDOCK, JOHN:** (Indian) Age 24, born (About 1857) in Ontario, a member of the Church of England, William age 22. Page 13, Household 75/75.

**NASH, EVE:** (Indian) Age 70, born (About 1811) in Ontario, a member of the Church of England, Solomon age 44, born in Ontario, a Baptist, Nechotimas? Johnathan Nash age 11. Page 19, Household 109/109.

**NASH, JAMES:** (Indian) Age 45, born (About 1836) in Ontario, a Baptist, Rachel age 40. Page 20, Household 112.

**NASH, LOT:** (Indian) Age 20, born (About 1861) a Baptist, Sarah SILVER age 56, Elam Nash age 14. Page 26, Household 147/147.

**NASH, LOVINA:** (Indian) Age 30, born (About 1851) in Ontario, a Baptist, Caroline age 12, Wallice age 6, Walter age one month, born in March, Lydia JACOB age 45, born in Ontario, a Baptist. Page 21, Household 117.

**NEWHOUSE, PETER:** (Indian) Age 40, born (About 1841) in Ontario, a member of the Church of England, Elizabeth age 39, Ezekel age 20, William age 11, Ellen age 9. Page 44, Household 258/258.

**NOAH, PHAROAH:** (Indian) Age 31, born (About 1850) in Ontario, a Baptist, Sarah Noah age 81, Baptist, born in Ontario, William SETH age 7. Page 36, Household 201/201.

**PETERS, JOHN N.:** (Indian) Age 21, born (About 1860) in Ontario, a member of the Church of England, Mary age 24, born in Ontario. Page 51, Household 301/301.

**PETERS, JOHN:** (Indian) Age 44, born (About 1837) in Ontario, a member of the Church of England, Sarah age 38, born in Ontario, Daniel age 20, born in Ontario, Mary age 15, born in Ontario, Benjamin age 12, born in Ontario. Page 51, Household 300/300.

**POWLES, PETER:** (Indian) Age 36, born (About 1845) in Ontario, a member of the Church of England, Catharine age 30, Isac age 10, Elizabeth age 8, Peter age 6, William age twenty-four months? born in April. Page 38, Household 224/224.

**POWLESS, CHARLOTTE:** (Indian) Age 21, born (About 1860) in Ontario, a member of the Church of England, Sussanah age 18, born in Ontario, a member of the Church of England. Page 2, Household 10.

**POWLESS, JOSEPH:** (Indian) Age 51, born (About 1830) in Ontario, a member of the Church of England, Joseph age 20, Elizabeth age 15, Sarah age 12, Nelson MILLER age 26, Charlotte MILLER age 23. Page 14, Household 81/81.

**POWLESS, MARGARET:** (Indian) Age 33, born (About 1848) in Ontario, a member of the Church of England, Nicklis age 15, Naomi age 3. Page 47, Household 280/280.

**RAP? (OR REEP?) WILLIAM:** (Indian) Age 23, born (About 1858) in Ontario a member of the Church of England. Page 1, Household 3.

**ROUNDSKY, THOMAS:** (Indian) Age 30 (Born about 1851) a member of the Church of England, Mary age 30, Isaac age 11, George age 6, Nancy age 4, Thomas ROUNDSKY SR., age 73, a member of the Church of England. Page 37, Household 213/213.

**SALT?, PETER:** (Indian) Age 34, born (About 1847) in Ontario, a Methodist, Clara age 33, Allan age 11, Rufus age 9, Charles age 7, Walter age 5, Mary age 1, James KESHEGOO age 90, born in Ontario, a Methodist. Page 26, Household 148/148.

**SAWER? (OR SAWYER?) DAVID:** (Indian) Age 30, born (About 1851) in Ontario, a Methodist. Page 24, Household 135.

**SCOTT, LUCINDA:** (Indian) Age 46, born (About 1835) in Ontario, a Baptist, Andrew age 21, Ellen age 18, Elizabeth age 16, Amelia age 13, Joab age 11, Edwin age 8. Page 28, Household 159.

**SCUNADY, CATHERINE:** (Indian) Age 48 (Born about 1833) a Methodist, Sussanah MARTIN age 20, Ida MARTIN age 13, Augustus MARTIN age 17. Page 35, Household 196/196.

**SECORD, ADAM:** (Indian) Age 40, born (About 1841) in Ontario, a Methodist, Mary age 43. Page 28, Household 157/157.

**SECORD, THOMAS:** (Indian) Age 45, born (About 1836) in Ontario, a Methodist, Catherine age 60, born in Ontario. Page 24, Household 136.

**SECORD, ZACARIAH:** (Indian) Age 21, born (About 1860) in Ontario, a Methodist, Sophia age 36, George age 13, Charity age 11, John age 8, William age 5. Page 22, Household 125.

**SETH, STEWART:** (Indian) Age 22, born (About 1859) in Ontario, a Baptist, Abigle? (female) age 19, Ezakriah? (male) age 2. Page 46, Household 265/265.

**SILVER, MARK:** (Indian) Age 40, born (About 1841) in Ontario, a Baptist, Elizabeth age 33, Jackson age 14, Delily? (female) age 4. Page 46, Household 267/267.

**SILVERSMITH, ALEXANDER:** (Indian) Age 40, born (About 1841) in Ontario, Margaret age 26, Julia age four months, born in December. Page 38, Household 214/214.

**SILVERSMITH, JOSEPH:** (Indian) Age 65, born (About 1816) in Ontario, Mary age 40, Joseph age 23, James age 22, Peter age 19, Joab age 10, Hester age 30. Page 33, Household 185/185.

**SKILER, HENRY:** (Indian) Age 47, born (About 1834) in Ontario, a Baptist, Lucey age 36, Ellen age 9, Caterine age one month. Page 46, Household 270/270.

**SMITH, ALEXANDER:** (Indian) Age 34, born (About 1847) in Ontario, a member of the Church of England (He was listed as the Indian Interpreter) Mary age 32, Hattie age 9, Mary age 7, Lilly age 5, Alexander age 2. Page 40, Household 225/225.

**SMITH, DEBORAH:** (Indian) Age 75, born (About 1806) in Ontario, a member of the Church of England, Page 17, Household 99.

**SMITH, WILLIAM:** (Indian) Age 39, born (About 1842) in Ontario, a member of the Church of England, Charlotte age 33, Marcy? or Mary? age 15, William age 13, James age 8, Alfred age 4, Frederic age 1. Page 1, Household 1.

**SPENCER, EDWARD:** (Indian) Age 50, born (About 1831) in Ontario, a Baptist, Hestor age 40, Solomon age 20, William age 28, Lucey age 22. Page 31, Household 172/172.

**STERLING, JOHN:** (Indian) Age 59, born (About 1822) in Ontario, a Methodist, Juley age 53, Benson age 26, Joseph age 15, Thomas age 11. Page 26, Household 149/149.

**STERLING, WILLIAM:** (Indian) Age 34, born (About 1847) in Ontario, a Methodist, Mary age 37, Sarah age 5, Charlotte age 3, Catharine JACKSON age 17. Page 25, Household 142/142.

**STOATS? (OR STOTS) HENRY:** (Indian) Age 44, born (About 1837) in Ontario, a member of the Church of England, Catherine age 44, William H., age 23, Andrew age 21, Sophia age 18, Thomas age 17 Lydia age 15, Mary J. age 13, Sarah age 10, Cristeen age 7. Page 10, Household 57/57.

**STOATS? (OR STOTS?) WILLIAM:** (Indian) Age 41, born (About 1840) in Ontario, a member of the Church of England, Catherine age 44, Lucy age 4, Thomas age 6. Page 12, Household 72/72.

**STOT, WILLIAM:** (Indian) Age 36, born (About 1845) on Ontario, a member of the Church of England, Sussanah age 26, Samuel age 9, Robert A., age 8, Ann age 6, Hirma age 4, Cary (female) age seven months, born in June. Page 15, Household 85.

**STOTS, HENRY:** (Indian) Age 77, born (About 1804) in Ontario, a member of the Church England, Betsy age 58, Sampson age 17. Page 9, Household 48/48.

**STOTS, JOHN:** (Indian) Age 56, born (About 1825) in Ontario, a member of the Church of England, William CARPENTER age 26, Caroline CARPENTER age 19, Robert CARPENTER age 16. Page 40, Household 228/228.

**STOTS, JOSHUA:** (Indian) Age 36, born (About 1845) in Ontario, a member of the Church of England, Mary age 30, Francis (Male) age 14, James age 13, Lucey age 11, Martha age 6, Isic age 9, Eddy age 4, Jeremia age 2. Page 43, Household 251/251.

**SUMMERS? (SUMNERS?) JOHN:** (Indian) Age 35, born (About 1836) on Ontario, a Methodist, Sarah age 45, George age 15, Ann age 10, Mary age 6. Page 33, Household 187/187.

**THOMAS, ABRAHAM:** (Indian) Age 28? or 23? born in Ontario, a member of the Church of England, Caroline age 20, Joseph age eight months, born in July, Hester BLAKE age 15. Page 4, Household 16.

**THOMAS, ADAM:** (Indian) Age 18, born (About 1863) in Ontario, a Baptist, Emma age 20. Page 36, Household 200/200

**THOMAS, HENRY:** (Indian) Age 28, born (About 1853) in Ontario, a Baptist, Catharine age 60, born in Ontario, a Baptist, Arthur MILLER age 8. Page 35, Household 197/197.

**THOMAS, THOMAS:** (Indian) Age 20, born (About 1861) in Ontario, a Baptist, Phobey age 22. Page 19, Household 107.

**THOMPSON, WILLIAM:** (Indian) Age 37, born (About 1844) in Ontario, a member of the Church of England, Elizabeth age 37, Lucey age 14, Joseph age 11. Page 4, Household 19/19.

**THOMPSON, THOMAS:** (Indian) Age 56 (Born about 1825) a Baptist, Sharlotte age 43, Thomas age 3, Lucy HOUSE age 15. Page 8, Household 45/45.

**TEBECO, DANIEL:** (Indian) Age 21, born (About 1860) a Methodist, Caroline age 43, James TAHWAH age 17, born in Ontario. Page 23, Household 130.

**TOBICO, HIRAM:** (Indian) Age 52, born (About 1829) in Ontario, a Methodist, Mary Ann age 49, Charles age 20. Page 30, Household 166/166.

**TOBICO, JAMES:** (Indian) Age 55, born (About 1826) in Ontario (A Methodist Minister) Mary age 34, James age 25, Edward age 16, Hiram age 12, Walter age one month, born in March. Page 22, Household 123.

**TOOLITTLE, JOHN:** (Indian) Age 55, born (About 1826) in Ontario, a member of the Plymouth Brethren Church, Sussanah age 30. Page 43, Household 249/249.

**TURKEY, JOHN:** (Indian) Age 35, born (About 1846) in Ontario, a Baptist, Dolly age 35, Elizabeth age 5, Peter age 4. Page 7, Household 39/39.

**TURKEY, MOSES:** (Indian) Age 40, born (About 1841) in Ontario, a member of the Church of England (He was listed as the Forest Baliff) Elizabeth age 32, William age 2, Lucy age 8. Page 40, Household 230/230.

**TWOFISH, ABRAM:** (Indian) Age 60, born (About 1821) in Ontario, a member of the Church of England, Mary age 50. Page 37, Household 212/212.

**TWOFISH, SUSSANAH:** (Indian) Age 82, born (About 1799) in Ontario. Page 36, Household 206/206.

**VENERY, GEORGE:** (Indian) Age 70, born (About 1811) in Ontario, a member of the Church of England, Nancy age 48, Sussanah age 22, Joseph age 20, Peter age 18, David age 16, Noah age 14, Lydia age 12, Samuel age 9. Page 3, Household 13.

**VYSE?, PHEOPE?:** (Indian) Age 36, born (About 1845) in Ontario, a Baptist, William Vyse? age 5, David Vyse age ten months, Dorty BURKE (Irish white female) age 13. Page 32, Household 181/181.

**WALKER, AUGUSTUS:** (Indian) Age 32, born (About 1849) in Ontario, a Baptist, Ellen age 22, Edward age 4, Martha age 3, Christina age three months. Page 32, Household 182/182.

**WALKER, LUCEY:** (Indian) Age 19, born (About 1862) in Ontario, a member of the Church of England. Page 42, Household 237/237.

**WALKER, MRS.:** (Indian) Age 70, born (About 1811) in Ontario, a Methodist. Page 35, Household 199/199.

**WEDGE, WILLIAM:** (Indian) Age 55, born (About 1826) in Ontario, a member of the Church of England, Catharine age 52. Page 48, Household 287/287.

**WESLEY, CHARLES:** (Indian) Age 50, born (About 1831) in Ontario, a Methodist, Caroline age 40. Page 22, Household 120.

**WILLIAMS, ADAM:** (Indian) Age 26, born (About 1855) in Ontario, a Baptist, Lucey age 25, Elcey age 5, Walter age one month, born in March. Page 19, Household 106.

**WILLIAMS, ELIZABETH:** (Indian) Age 50, born (About 1831) in Ontario, a Baptist, David age 14. Page 7, Household 37/37.

**WILLIAMS, GEORGE:** (Indian) Age 53, born (About 1828) in Ontario, a Methodist. Page 47, Household 278/278.

**WILLIAMS, JANE:** (Indian) Age 80, born (About 1801) in Ontario, a member of the Church of England. Page 47, Household 279/279.

**WILLIAMS, JOHN:** (Indian) Age 34, born (About 1847) in Ontario, a Baptist, Nancy Williams age 34, Elizabeth Williams age 12, Alpheus? Williams age 9, Martha Williams age 7, Catherine JOHN age 5, Lucinda JOHN age ten months, born in June. Page 50, Household 299/299.

**WILLIAMS, THOMAS:** (Indian) Age 48, born (About 1833) in Ontario, a Baptist, Rebecca age 43, Isiah age 16, Mary Ann age 24, Matilda CUSICK age 8, Frederick NASH age 4, Catherine MARICLE age 1. Page 19, Household 105.

**WILSON, BETSY:** (Indian) Age 80, born (About 1801) in Ontario. Page 47, Household 275/275.

**WILSON, JAMES:** (Indian) Age 40, born (About 1841) in Ontario, a Methodist, Philipine age 35, Jerimiah age 9. Page 30, Household 168/168.

**WOOD, JAMES A.:** (Indian) Age 39, born (About 1842) in Ontario, a Methodist, Harriet Jane age 37, James MC LEAN, age 15, Harriet Jane Wood age 10, Rebecca Wood age 8, Gordon Oliver Wood age 6, Betsy Lillian Wood age 3. Page 34, Household 137.

**WOODRUFF, ROSANNA:** (White/Irish) Age 50, born (About 1831) in Ireland, a Roman Catholic, (All other members of the Woodruff family were listed as Indians) Joseph Woodruff age 20, James Woodruff age 24, Thomas Woodruff age 18, Thomas WHITMAN age 62, (White/English) born in England, a member of the Church of England, John WILSON age 33, born in Ontario (Indian?), a Roman Catholic. Page 30, Household 167/167.

**WRIGHT, TIMOTHY:** (Indian) Age 41, born (About 1840) in Ontario, a Baptist, Mary age 29, Barby (female) age 13, John age 12, Albert age 8, Melchy (male) age 5, Anny age 2, George DOUGLAS age 28. Page 19, Household 110/110.

| CROSS INDEX TO 1881 CENSUS OF BRANT COUNTY, ONTARIO-PART II LISTED ABOVE ||
|---|---|
| SURNAME CROSS INDEX | HEAD OF HOUSEHOLD |
| ANTONY? OR ANTHONY, Jane | Isick DOCTOR |
| ANTONY? OR ANTHONY, Josephine | Isick DOCTOR |
| ATKINS, Elizabeth | Seth DOXTATOR |
| BAREFOOT, Leah | Christine GROAT |
| BILL? OR BELL?, Eliza | William JACOB |
| BLAKE, Hester | Abraham THOMAS |
| BOMBERRY, George | William HILL |
| BOMBERRY, Joseph | William HILL |
| BRANT, Mary | David BAREFOOT |
| BURKE, Dorty? or Doty? | Pheope? or Phebe? VYSE? |
| CARPENTER, Caroline | John STOTS |
| CARPENTER, Robert | John STOTS |
| CARPENTER, William | John STOTS |
| CARRIER, Eliza | George BEAVER |
| CARRIER, John | George BEAVER |
| CARRIER, Levi | George BEAVER |
| CLAUSE, Jesse | Jamieson HAWLOW? OR HARLOW? |
| CRYSLY?, Sarah | Mikel GROAT |
| CUSICK, Matilda | Thomas WILLIAMS |
| DOUGLAS, George | Timothy WRIGHT |
| DOXTATOR, Edward | Catharine JACOB |
| DOXTATOR, John | George EVERETT |
| FARMER, George | Andrew Mc GEE? |
| FARMER, Pheope (Pheobe?) | Andrew Mc GEE? |
| FOSTER, Ranson | John CORNELIUS |
| FUNN, Catey | Cornelius GREEN |
| FUNN, Elizabeth | Hestor CLAUSE |
| GARLOUGH, Mary | Augustus HILL |

| | |
|---|---|
| **GREEN**, Eliza | Srah CHUB? or CHUP? |
| **GREEN**, John | Sarah CHUB? or CHUP? |
| **GREEN**, Mary | Peter JACOB |
| **GREEN**, Sampson | Peter JACOB |
| **HARIE?**, Simon | Jemima HILL |
| **HARRIS**, Ann | Charles DAVIS |
| **HARRIS**, John | Joseph JACOB |
| **HARRIS**, Nancy | Joseph JACOB |
| **HENCELY**, John | Moses HERREN |
| **HENHAWK**, Catrine | William Hill |
| **HENHAWK**, Elizabeth | David HILL |
| **HENHAWK**, Lucy | David HILL |
| **HILL**, Charlotina | Samson GROAT |
| **HILL**, Henry | Catherine GREENE |
| **HILL**, Jacob | George EVERETT |
| **HILL**, Joseph | Samson GROAT |
| **HILL**, Lydia | Sias? LEWIS |
| **HOUSE**, Lucy | Thomas THOMPSON |
| **HOUSE**, Sussanah | George HENHAWK |
| **JACKSON**, Catherine | William STERLING |
| **JACOB**, Catherine | William HILL |
| **JACOB**, Lydia | Lovina NASH |
| **JAMIESON**, Peter | William JACOB |
| **JOHN**, Catherine | John WILLIAMS |
| **JOHNSON? OR JONSON?**, James | Mary HILL |
| **JONSON? OR JOHNSON**, James | James JONSON? or JOHNSON? |
| **KESHEGOO**, James | Peter SALT |
| **LEWEN? OR LEWIS**, Margaret | Seth CLAUSE |
| **LOFT**, Mary | Benjamin GARLOW |
| **LONG? OR SONG?**, Jane | Sarah BURINING |
| **MARICLE**, Catherine | Thomas WILLIAMS |

| | |
|---|---|
| **MARTIN**, Augustus | Catherine SCUNADY |
| **MARTIN**, Ida | Catherine SCUNADY |
| **MARTIN**, Joseph | Moses ADAMS |
| **MARTIN**, Sussanah | Catherine SCUNADY |
| **MC DUGAL**, Aeda | William DREDGE |
| **MC DUGAL**, Sarah | William DREDGE |
| **MC DUGAL**, Susan | William DREDGE |
| **MC LEAN**, James | James A. WOOD |
| **MILLER**, Arthur | Henry THOMAS |
| **MILLER**, Charlotte | Joseph POWLESS |
| **MILLER**, Nelson | Joseph POWLESS |
| **NASH**, Frederick | Thomas WILLIAMS |
| **NASH**, Levi | George BEAVER |
| **NASH**, Mathew | Levina DOXTATOR |
| **PAHTAHQUAQ?**, Margaret | Alonzo Mc DOUGLE |
| **POWLIS**, Noah | Abraham CRAWFORD |
| **RANCIER**, Thomas | George MURDOCK |
| **RUSSELL**, Claber | John MARTIN |
| **RUSSELL**, John | John MARTIN |
| **RUSSELL**, Joseph | John MARTIN |
| **RUSSELL**, Sarah | John MARTIN |
| **RUSSELL**, Wilson | John MARTIN |
| **SILVER**, Sarah | Lot NASH |
| **SILVER**, Simeon | George BEAVER |
| **SKILLER**, Anna | Cornelius GREEN |
| **TAHWAH**, James | Daniel TEBECO |
| **THOMAS**, Caroline | Mary HILL |
| **THOMAS**, Caroline | Mary HILL |
| **TWOFISH**, Ellen | Charles C. MARTIN? |
| **TWOFISH**, Joseph | Elijah HILL |
| **TWOFISH**, William | Elijah HILL |

| | |
|---|---|
| **VAN LOON,** Calvin | Jemima BOMBERRY |
| **WAKER? OR WALKER,** Hestor | Isick HILL |
| **WALTON,** C. E. | Mary BRANT |
| **WALTON,** Jacob | Mary BRANT |
| **WHIPLEY,** Josephine | George BEAVER |
| **WHIPLEY,** Levi | George BEAVER |
| **WHITMAN,** Thomas | Rosanna WOODRUFF |
| **WILLIAMS,** Abbey | Peter BEAVER |
| **WILLIAMS,** Catherine | Samuel HILL |
| **WILSON,** John | Rosanna WOODRUFF |
| **WILSON,** Pheope | Andrew Mc GEE? |

# HALDIMAND COUNTY, ONTARIO
## HISTORICAL NOTES

Haldimand County was once part of "The Haldimand Grant." This grant covered over 300,000 acres. In 1784 Sir Frederick Haldimand Governor Chief of Canada granted to the Six Nations parts of lands in what is now Haldimand and Brant Counties. The County of Haldimand was incorporated in 1800. The Chippewa or Ojibway were the original inhabitants of Haldimand County. The Six Nations Reserve, in Brant County, Ontario is extended over into Haldimand County in Oneida Township. In 1832 by treaty the Indians surrendered townships in Haldimand County, Ontario and removed up the river to the Township of Tuscarora in the County of Brant. In 1847 the Mississaugas (Chippewa or Ojibwa) from the River Credit were offered by the Six Nations a portion of their reserve to live on. They accepted and removed to the south-east corner of the reservation. The Townships in Haldimand County include Canborough, Dunn,. Moulton, Sherbrooke, North Cayuga, Oneida, Rainham, Seneca, South Cayuga and Walpole. Seneca was a Township located in the north west corner of Haldimand County along the Grand River. The land that makes up the Township of South Cayuga was not surrendered by the Six Nations Indians until 1832. The Township of Walpole borders Oneida Township in Haldimand County and Tuscarora township in Brant County. One early settlement was Indiana, along the Grand River. Several large tracts of land were part of the Nelles Settlement. This land was granted along the Grand River. Another tract was the Young Settlement. Sources: Centennial Historical Committee, "The Township of Seneca, History," Centennial Year, 1867-1967, pages 3, 5, 12. "Illustrated Atlas of the Counties of Haldimand and Norfolk," H.R. Page & Co., Toronto, 1877-1879. Nelles, Rev. Robert Bertram, M.A., Chaplain, Haldimand Old Boys," Association of Toronto "County of Haldimand in the Day of Auld Lang Syne," Port Hope, Ontario, The Hamly Press Book Printers, 1905.

## CAYUGA & MOHAWK 1851 HALDIMAND COUNTY, ONTARIO
## CENSUS ABSTRACT

The 1851 Canadian Census did not provide the relationships between family members. Married couples and children with similar surnames were enumerated and grouped together. Sometimes an individual will appear within a family group with a different surname. This person may have been an adopted child, a step child or a grandparent. In this census abstract the author of this book listed these people separately. The name of the family group or person they appeared to be living with was included after their entry. A question mark was placed after a name that was in doubt. This census abstract should not take the place of any tribal or government records. For more information write the tribal office.

**ABRAHAM, JAMES:** (Indian) Age 25 born (About 1826) in Upper Canada, Jane age 30, Mary 10, Nancy 8, Eliza 5, Margaret 4. Oneida Township, District 2, Page 103/29, Numbers 34-38.

**ANTHONY, GEORGE:** (Indian) Age 45, born (About 1806) in Upper Canada, Jane 35, Albert 13, Silve? 13. Oneida Township, District 2, Page 71/11, Number 44-47.

**ANTHONY, HANAH:** (Indian) Age 17, born (About 1834) in Upper Canada. Oneida Township, District 1, Page 40/20, Number 41.

**BILL, JOHN:** (Indian) Age 26 born (About 1825) in Upper Canada. Oneida Township, District 2, Page 107//32, Number 50.

**BURNAM, WILLIAM:** (Indian) Age 20, born (About 1831) in Upper Canada, Ann age 17. Oneida Township, District 2, Page 71/11, Numbers 48, 49.

**CAYUGA, JOHN:** (Indian) Age 24 born (About 1827) in Upper Canada, Mary age 18, James age 3. Oneida Township, District 2, Page 107/32, Numbers 45-47.

**COOK, SUSAN:** (Indian) Age 40 born (About 1811) in South Cayuga, George age 21, William age 15, John age 14, James age 9, Mary age 6, Laney? age 11. Township of Cayuga, District 2, Page 19, Numbers 39-45.

**CORNELIUS, JOHN:** (Indian) Age 56 born (About 1795) in Upper Canada, District 1, Page 40.20, Number 46.

**CORNELIUS, MINTIN?** Age 70 born (About 1781) in Upper Canada, Mary age 68. Oneida Township, District 1, Page 40/20, Numbers 43, 44.

**CRAFORD (OR CRAWFORD) ABRAHAM:** (Indian) Age 30 born (About 1821) in Upper Canada, Susan age 25, Nancy age 4, Eliza age 1. Oneida Township, District 2, Page 103/29, Numbers 23-26.

**CURLEY, ELIZABETH:** (Indian) Age 45, born (About 1806) in C. W. (Canada West), Elizabeth age 27, George age 22, Samuel age 18, James age 3. Township of Cayuga, North, District 1, Page 53/27, Numbers 1-5.

**CURLEY, WILLIAM:** (Indian) Age 39, born (About 1822) in Upper Canada, Margaret age 40, Sally, Eliza, Susan, Nancy, James. Oneida Township, District 2, Page 103/29, Numbers 44-45.

**BULL, RICHER?** (Indian) Age 16, born in Upper Canada, Betsy age 6. Oneida Township, District 1, Page 40/20, Numbers 33, 32.

**DIXON, JAMES:** (Indian) Age 45 born (About 1806) in Upper Canada, Margaret age 40. Oneida Township, District 2, Page 103/29, Numbers 21, 22.

**DRAKE, HENRY:** (Indian) Age 12, born (About 1839) in Upper Canada. Oneida Township, District 1, Number 42.

**EVERYDAY, JOHN:** (Indian) Age 60, born (About 1791) in Upper Canada, James age 6, Elizabeth age 40, Susan age 38, Nancy age 35, Margt age 30, Mary age 28. Oneida Township, District 2, Page 103/29, Numbers 14-20.

**FISH, WILLIAM:** (Indian) Age 30, born (About 1821) in Upper Canada, Susan age 28, John age 9, Samuel age 7, Thomas age 5. Oneida Township, District 2, Page 103/29, Numbers 39-43.

**GILSON, SARAH:** (Indian) Age 23 born (About 1828) in Upper Canada, Thomas age 5, Nancy age 3. Oneida Township, District 2, Page 89/20.

**HARIS, JOHN:** (Indian) Age 45 born (About 1806) in Upper Canada, Ann age 40, Mary age 8, Sally age 3, James age 10, John age 1. Oneida Township, District 2, Page 103/29, Numbers 27-32.

**HIGHFLYER, BETSEY:** (Indian) Age 75 born (About 1776) in Upper Canada. Oneida Township, District 2, Page 107/32, Numbers 49.

**HILL, JOHN:** (Indian) Age 35 born (About 1816) in Upper Canada, Ann age 28. Oneida Township, District 2, Page 89/20.

**HILL, SAMUEL:** (Indian) Age 8 born (About 1843) in Upper Canada, Susan age 6, John age 3. Oneida Township, District 2, Page 89/20.

**HORN, HANAH:** (Indian) Age 25, born (About 1826) in Upper Canada, Nancy age 5, Mary age 2, Ann age 1. Oneida Township, District 1, Page 40/20, Numbers 22-24.

**HUFF, DAVID:** (Indian) Age 16, born (About 1835) in Upper Canada. Oneida Township, District 1, Page 40/20, Number 30.

**HUFF, HANAH:** (Indian) Age 50, born (About 1801) in Upper Canada. Oneida Township, District 1, Page 40/20, Number 21.

**JACKSON, CHARLES:** (Indian) Age 5, born (About 1846) in Upper Canada. Oneida Township, District 1, Page 40/20, Number 37.

**JACKSON, THOMAS:** (Indian) Age 8, born (About 1830) in Upper Canada. Oneida Township, District 1, Page 40/20, Number 45.

**JOHNSON, YOUNG:** (Indian) Age 22 born (About 1829) in Upper Canada, Nancy age 40, Thomas age 4, Mary age 12, James age 75, Cathren age 50, Susan age 30, Margaret age 32, Kelly age 28, Nelly age 18, Elina? age 9, John age 13, Ann age 6. Oneida Township, District 2, Page 103/29, Numbers 1-13.

**LATHAM, ALEXANDER:** (Indian) Age 4, born (About 1847) in Upper Canada. Oneida Township, District 1, Page 40/20, Number 39.

**LATHAM, WILLIAM:** (Indian) Age 24, born (About 1827) in Upper Canada, Polly age 25, Oneida Township, District 1, Page 40/20, Number 35, 36.

**LOCK, GEORGE:** (Indian) Age 50, born (About 1801) in Upper Canada. Oneida Township, District 1, Page 40/20, Number 29.

**MONTORE? MARGT:** (Indian) Age 20 born (About 1831) in Upper Canada. Oneida Township, District 2, Page 107/32, Number 25.

**MONTORE, THOMAS:** (Indian) Age 46 born (About 1805) in Upper Canada, James age 25, Margaret age 24, George age 5. Oneida Township, District 2, Page 107/32, Numbers 31-34.

**MOSES, CORNELIUS:** (Indian) Age 50, born (About 1801) in Upper Canada, Mary age 50, Margaret Moses age 16, Oneida Township, District 1, Page 40/20, Numbers 15-16.

**MOSES, ELIZABETH:** (Indian) Age 52, born (About 1799) in Upper Canada. Oneida Township, District 1, Page 40/20, Number 40.

**PETERS, WILLIAM:** (Indian) Age 49, born (About 1802) in Upper Canada, Helen age 50, Oneida Township, District 1, Page 40/20, Numbers 31, 32.

**SILVERSMITH, WITHER?** (Indian) Age 45 born (About 1806) in Upper Canada, William 28, James 24, Margaret 16, John 13, Stephen 11, Thomson 6. Oneida Township, District 2, Page 107/32, Numbers 35-41.

**SIMON, JACOB:** (Indian) Age 30, born (About 1821) in Upper Canada, Eliza age 28, Daniel age 3. Oneida Township, District 1, Page 40/20, Numbers 18-20.

**SIXPENCE, JOHN:** (Indian) Age 40, born (About 1811) in Upper Canada. Oneida Township, District 2, Page 107/32, Number 42.

**SMOKE, HANNA:** (Indian) Age 7, born (About 1844) in Upper Canada. Oneida Township, District 2, Page 107/32, Number 48.

**SMOKE, JOHN:** (Indian) Age 56 born (About 1795) in Upper Canada (Ontario) Gatonis? age 40, Oneida Township, District 2, Page 107/32, Numbers 43, 44.

**SNAKE, GEORGE:** (Indian) Age 29, born (About 1822) in C.W.F., Mrs. Snake age 28. Township of Cayuga North, Page 79/40, Numbers 27-28 on Page.

**STYERS, HANNA:** (Indian) Age 40 born (About 1811) in Upper Canada, Joseph age 16. Oneida Township, District 2, Page 107/32, Numbers 23, 24.

**STYERS, ISAAC:** (Indian) Age 13 born in Upper Canada, David age 11, Stephen age 8, John age 5, Ann age 1. Oneida Township, District 2, Page 107/32, Numbers 26-30.

**WAMPUN, JOHN:** (Indian) Age 50, born (About 1801) in Upper Canada (Ontario) Eliza age 49, Maunhas? age 10, Chenny? age 2. Oneida Township, District 1, Page 40/20, Numbers 25-28.

**WILLIAMS, MARGARET:** (Indian) Age 26, born (About 1825) in C.W.F., Adam Williams age 26, Members of the Episcopal Church, Township of Cayuga North, District 1, Page 79/40, Numbers 25, 26 on the Page.

## HALDIMAND COUNTY, ONTARIO 1881 CENSUS ABSTRACT
## THE CAYUGA AND MOHAWK OF HALDIMAND COUNTY

The Cayuga formerly occupied the area of Cayuga Lake, New York. At the beginning of the American Revolution a part of the tribe removed to Canada. Others in New York lived among the tribes of the Six Nations Confederacy. Some Cayuga went to Ohio where they joined a group of Seneca. They were known as the Seneca of the Sandusky. This group later moved to Indian Territory (Oklahoma). Some Cayuga also joined the Oneida in Wisconsin. Source: "Indian American," A Traveler's Companion, By Eagle Walking Turtle, pages 170, 171, published in 1989, by John Muir Publications, Santa Fe, New Mexico, 1989.

This census abstract begins with District-146-E, Cayuga Village, Pages 1-34 and continues to F-2-Township, Oneida, Pages 1-43. All of the following people in this census abstract were listed as Native Canadians unless otherwise noted. All of the children in each household had the same surname as the head of that household unless otherwise noted. A surname was highlighted with capital letters in a family entry if that surname was different from the surname of the head household. A question mark was placed after a name that was in doubt. This census abstract should not take the place of any gorvernment or tribal records. For more information write the tribal office.

**ALVIS, STEVEN:** (Indian) Age 41, born (About 1840) in Ontario, a member of the Church of England, Ellen age 46. District Number 146, S. District, Division Number 1 of Oneida, Page 72, Household 351/352.

**ANTHONY, MICHAEL:** (Indian) Age 40, born (About 1841) in Ontario, a member of the Church of England, Susan age 56, Charles age 14, Thomas age 12, Direkle? (Male) age 9, Lucy age 4. District Number 146, S. District, Page 71, Household 348/349.

**BARON, ANTHONY:** (Indian) Age 66, (About 1815) born in Quebec, Catholic, Margaret age 58, born in Quebec. Page 35, Household 162.

**BARON, CHARLES:** (White/French) Age 67, born (About 1814) in Quebec, Catholic, Mary (Indian) age 55, born in Quebec, Catholic. (All others were listed as French) Lewis age 18, Peter age 14, William age 16, born in Ontario. Anthony age 36, born in Quebec, Angus age 40 born in Quebec, Christeen age 28, born in Quebec. Page 38, Household 168/180.

**BEAVER, JAMES:** (Indian) Age 30 born (About 1851) in Ontario, a member of the Church of England, Lyda age 22, Emma age 7, Fredrick age 4, Rourie (A Female) age 2. District Number 146, S. District, S. Division, Number 2, Oneida, Page 40, Household 177/188.

**BEAVER, JOHN A:** (Indian) Age 37, born (About 1844) in Ontario, A member of the Church of England, Jemima age 37, District Number 146, S. District, S. Division, Number 2, Oneida, Page 40, Household 179/192.

**BILL, ALEXANDER:** (Indian) Age 23, born (About 1858) in Ontario, Astin age 15, Anne age 21, Lehgasdee? (Female) age 20, Lewis age 14, Dawaco (A Female) age 11, Deepinwater (A Female) age 5, Kinesqiuaw? (A

155

Female) age 14. District Number 146, S. District, Division Number 2, Oneida, Page 34, Household 156.

**BILL, JOHN:** (Indian) Age 58, born (About 1823) in Ontario, Susana age 50, District Number 146, S. District, S. Division Number 2, Oneida, Page 34, Household 153/155.

**BILL, WILLIAM:** (Indian) Age 47 born (About 1834) in Ontario, Catherine age 19, Jack age 18, Thomas age 13, Lucy age 11. District Number 146, S. District, Division Number 2, Oneida, Page 41, Household 183/196.

**CACK, RITCHARD:** (Indian) Age 22, born (About 1859) in Ontario, Mary age 22, John age 2. District Number 146, S. District, Division Number 1, Oneida, Page 70, Household 339/340.

**CAYUGA, NICHOLAS:** (Indian) Age 20, born (About 1861) in Ontario, Kate CURLEY age 75, born in Ontario, John STIRE age 43, born in Ontario, Mary STIRE age 40. District Number 146, S. District, Division Number 2, Oneida, Page 36, Household 161/170.

**CHEBOCK, JOHN:** (Indian) Age 47 born (About 1834) in Ontario, a Methodist, Sarah age 34, Emelia (Female) age 25, John age 16, Fanney age 15, Catharine CHEBBOCK age 78, born in Ontario. District Number 146, S. District Number 1, Oneida, Page 61/62, Household 242.

**CHIEF, CAWASS (OR CHIEF CAWASS):** (Indian) Age 80 born (About 1801) in Ontario, Louisa age 40, Peter age 20, Luyse (A Female) age 12, Fred age 10. District Number 146, S. District, S. Division, Number 2, Oneida, Page 42, Household 187/198.

**CONSTON, CATHERINE:** (Indian) Age 36, born (About 1845) in Ontario, Nancy age 5, Levi age 1. District Number 146, S. District, Divisional Number 1, Oneida, Page 71, Household 343/344.

**CRAWFORD, GIBSON:** (Indian) Age 20, born (About 1861) in Ontario, a member of the Church of England, Peter age 16, James age 14, Lucyann age 4, Church of England. District Number 146, S. District, S. Division, Number 2, Oneida, Page 33, Household 148/150.

**CRAWFORD, PETER:** (Indian) Age 35 (Born about 1846) Katy age 25, born in Ontario, Peter HILL age 22, Parting HILL (A Female) age 15, born in Ontario, District Number 146, S. District, Division Number 2, Oneida, Page 37, Household 169/174.

**CRAWFORD, WILLIAM:** (Indian) Age 28 born (About 1853) in Ontario, a member of the Church of England, Susan age 20 born in Quebec, Mary age eight months, born in February, Susan LEWIS? CRAWFORD age 6. District Number 146, S. District, S. Division, Number 2, Oneida, Page 40, Household 181/194.

**CRAWFORD, WILLIAM:** (Indian) Age 28 born (About 1853) in Ontario, a member of the Church of England, Eliza age 1. District Number 146, S. District, Number 2, Oneida, District Number 146, S. District, Division Number 2, Oneida, Page 37, Household 168/175.

**CURLEY, JOHN:** (Indian) Age 74 born (About 1807) in Ontario, Margret GARLOW age 66, District Number 146, S. District, Division Number 1, Oneida, Page 70, Household 338, 339.

**CURLEY, JOHN SR:** (Indian) Age 40 born (About 1841) in Ontario, Betsey age 50, John Jr., age 17, William age 15, Thomas age 13, George age 10, Laures? or Lewis age 8, Alexander age 6. District Number 146, S. Division, Number 2, Oneida, Page 41, Household 185/198.

**CURLEY, MARGARET:** (Indian) Age 28 born (About 1853) in Ontario, William age 12, District Number 146, S. District, S. Division, Number 2, Oneida, Page 39, Household 173/186.

**CURLEY, MARY:** (Indian) Age 38 born (About 1843) in Ontario, Lucy age 18, Lidy age 16, William age 12, George age 10, District Number 146, S. District, Division Number 2, Oneida, Page 42, Household 186/199.

**DAVIE ROBERT:** (Indian) Age 22, born (About 1859) in Ontario, Jane age 15, Eliza age 1. District Number 146, S. District, Number 2, Oneida. Page 42, Household 189/202.

**DAVY, ROBERT:** (Indian) Age 20, born (About 1861) in Ontario, Mary age 20, Hattie age 1, Margaret age 50, District Number 146, S. District, Division Number 2, Oneida, Page 37, Household 165/170.

**DAVY, JACOB:** (Indian) Age 50, born (About 1831) in Ontario, Jane age 33, Lewis age 20, Charlotte age 16, Mc Lean age 11, Susan age 3. District Number 146, S. Division, Number 2, Oneida, Page 33, Household 147/149.

**DAVY, ROBERT:** (Indian) Age 20, born (About 1861) in Ontario, Mary age 20, Hattie age 1, Margaret age 50. Page 37, Household 165/170.

**DAVY, ROBERT:** (Indian) Age 26, born (About 1855) in Ontario, Lucy age 22, Robert Jr., age 5, District Number 146, S. Division, Number 2, Oneida, Page 39, Household 174/186.

**DOCKSTADER, HENRY:** (Indian) Age 53, born (About 1828) in Ontario, a member of the Church of England, Sarah (White/English) age 48 born in England, John H. age 23, FLate? or Hote? (A Female) age 19, Nellie age 14, Albert ANTHONY age 42. District Number 146, S. District, Division Number 2, Oneida, Page 40, Household 180/193.

**DOCKSTEDER, JAMES (OR DOCKSTEDER JAMES?):** (Indian) Age 47, born (About 1834) in Ontario, a member of the Church of England, Ellen (White) age 33, (All others were listed as Canadian Indians) Jessy (A Female) age 13, Assy (A Male) age 10, Cate age 7, Maggie age 4, Jenny age 2. District Number 146, S. District, Divisional Number 1, Oneida, Page 71, Household 345/345.

**FISH, DAVID:** (Indian) Age 30 born (About 1851) in Ontario, District Number 146, S. Division, Number 2, Oneida, Page 42, Household 190/203.

**FISH, JAMES:** (Indian) Age 25, born (About 1856) in Ontario, Snallheaueu? (A Female) age 20, born in Ontario, Ellen age one month born in March. District Number 146, S. District, Number 2, Oneida, Page 37, Household 170/175.

**FISH, WILLIAM:** (Indian) Age 62 born (About 1819) in Ontario, Nelly age 50, (A Female Indian) no name age 19, (A Female Indian) no name age 12, Jacob age 11? or 16. District 146, S. District, S. Division, Number 2, Oneida, Page 42, Household 189/202.

**FISH, WILSON:** (Indian) Age 52 born (About 1829) in Ontario, Female no name age 35, Female no name age 17, Mitchel age 14, Mary age 11, Distant Cloud (A Male) age 8. District Number 146, S. Division, Number 2, Oneida, Page 39, Household 171/183.

**FISHCARRICK, JOHN:** (Indian) Age 46, born (About 1835) in Ontario, a member of the Church of England, Orner (A Female) age 45, Nancy age 23, Mary age 17, Margaret age 3, William 14, John age 11, Robert age 8. District Number 146, S. Division, Number 2, Oneida, Page 34, Household 15150/152..

**GARLOW, ANGUS:** (Indian) Age 28, born (About 1853) in Quebec, Catholic, Mary Charlotte age 23, born in Quebec, Agnes age 6, Anna? age 3. District Number 146, S. District, S. Division, Number 2, Oneida, Page 35, Household 161.

**GROAT, HENRY?** (Indian) Age 56 born (About 1825) in Ontario, a member of the Methodist, Eleanor (Whit) born in England, age 26, Peter age 22, Margret age 19, John age 17, Ellen age 15. District 146, S. District Number 1, Oneida, Page 62.

**HARRIS, RICHARD:** (Indian) Age 50, born (About 1831) in Ontario. Page 70, Household 340/341.

**HERKIMER, CHARLES:** (Indian) Age 50 born (About 1831) in Ontario, a member of the Methodist Church, Christiana age 48, Sarah age 26, Agusta age 22, Lawrence age 20, Lahtan (Male) age 16, Maggie age 14, District 146, S. District, Division Number 1, Oneida, Page 61.

**HESS, LIDDY:** (Indian) Age 20? born (About 1861) in Ontario, James age 21, Agness age eight months born in August, Chariety age 8, (All were members of the Church of England) District Number 146, S. District, S. Division, Number 2, Page 36, Household 171.

**HEY? (OR KEY?) PETER:** (Indian) Age 40, born (About 1841) in Ontario, a member of the Church of England, Cecelia age 30, Margaret age 3, born in Ontario, a member of the Church of England. Page 33, Household 152/153.

**HOAG, GEORGE?** (Indian) Age 57, born (About 1824) in Ontario, William age 22, Elizabeth age 21, Peter age 19, Ann age 17, Margret age 15, Cathrine age 14, Jane age 12, Margaret RITCHERD age 47. District Number 146, S. District, Division Number 1, Oneida, Page 70, Household 334.

**HUSS? (OR HESS?) JOHN::** (Indian) Age 60, born (About 1821) in Ontario, Margaret age 50, Mary age 30, Louise age 20, Susana THOMAS age 18,

Lucy THOMAS age 16. District Number 146, S. Division, Number 2, Oneida, Page 35, Household 157/162.

**HUTT, JOHN:** (Indian) Age 45 born (About 1836) in Ontario, Margaret age 40, Julia age 12, John age 4, District Number 146, S. District, S. Division, Number 2, Oneida, Page 35, Household 155/158.

**JACOB, JACKSON:** (Indian) Age 40, born (About 1841) in Ontario, Lucy age 36, Sophia age 1, Isaac HESS age 30, born in Ontario, a member of the Church of England. District Number 146, S. District, S. Division, Number 2, Oneida, District Number 146, S. District, S. Division, Number 2, Oneida, Page 36, Household 159/168.

**JAMIESON, ALEXANDER:** (Indian) Age 30, born (About 1851) in Ontario, a member of the Church of England. District Number 146, S. District Number 2, Oneida, Page 34, Household 152/154.

**JOHN, DAVID:** (Indian) Age 50 born (About 1831) in Ontario, a member of the Church of England, Mary age 40, Margaret CRAWFORD age 22, Mary JOHN age 20, Hannah HILL age 10, Christian CUSICK age 3. District Number 146, S. Division, Number 2, Oneida, Page 41, Household 182/195.

**JOHN, PETER:** (Indian) Age 46, born (About 1835) in Ontario, Liddy age 45, William age 19, Joseph age 14, Anne age 11, John age 9. District Number 146, S. District, Division, Number 2, Oneida, Page 39, Household 175/188.

**JOHNSON, DAVID:** (Indian) Age 50, born (About 1831) in Ontario, Mary age 45, (A Female Indian) no name age 15, (A Female Indian) no name age 13, (A Female Indian) no name age 11, (A Female Indian) no name age 9, Rodgers age 7, (A Female Indian) no name age 5. District Number 146, S. District, Division Number 2, Oneida, Page 39, Household 172/185.

**JOHNSON, JAMES:** (Indian) Age 24, born (About 1857) in Ontario, Lucy age 22, James age 2. District Number 146, S. Division, Number 2, Oneida, Page 38, Household 170/182.

**JOHNSON, JOSEPH:** (Indian) Age 25, born (About 1856) in Ontario, Sarah age 23, Agnes age 3. District Number 146, S. Division, Number 2, Oneida, Page 36, Household 161/165.

**JOHNSON, SUSANA:** (Indian) Age 50 born (About 1831) in Ontario, District Number 146, S. District, Division Number 2, Oneida, District Number 146, S. District, Division Number 2, Oneida, Page 39, Household 172/184.

**JOHNSON, WILLIAM:** (Indian) Age 34, born (About 1847) in Ontario, Hadanewaks? (A Male) age 16, born in Ontario, Sagaatance (A Male) age 13. District Number 146, S. District, Division Number 2, Oneida, Page 37, Household 166/171.

**JOHNSTON, GEORGE:** (Indian) Age 40, born (About 1841) in Ontario, Ellen age 35, Abraham age 12? Sharlote age 13, Archibald age 10, Maggie age 3? Mary age 2, District Number 146, S. District, Number 1, Oneida, Page 70, Household 337/338.

**KEY, PETER:** (Indian) Age 40 born (About 1841) in Ontario, Cecelia age 30, Maragret age 3. District Number 146, S. Division, Number 2, Oneida, Page 34, Household 149/151.

**KICK, NICHOLAS:** (Indian) Age 40, born (About 1841) in Ontario, Betsy FISH age 30, Nicholas KICK JR., age 1, James FISH age 6, Jane FISH age 4. District Number 146, S. Division, Number 2, Oneida, Page 38, Household 172/17?

**LATHAM, GEORGE:** (Indian) Age 26, born (About 1855) in Ontario, a member of the Church of England, District Number 146, S. District, Division Number 1, Oneida, Page 70, Household 336/337.

**LONGBEARD? OR LONGBOAT?, GEORGE:** (Indian) Age 25, born (About 1856) in Ontario, Charlotte age 30, William age 9, Frank age 11, Joseph age 4, District Number 146, S. District, S. Division, Number 2, Oneida, Page 37, Household 167/172.

**LONGBOAT, JOHN:** (Indian) Age 28 born (About 1853) in Ontario, Nancy age 23, Nancy Jr. age 3. District Number 146, S. District, Division Number 2, Oneida, Page 41, Household 184/197.

**LONGBOAT, THOMAS:** (Indian) Age 23 born (About 1858) in Ontario, Mary age 20, John age 5, Jack age 2, District Number 146, S. District, Division Number 2, Oneida, Page 40, Household 178/191.

**MARTIN, JOSEPH:** (Indian) Age 23, born (About 1858) in Ontario, a member of the Church of England, Christeen (White/French) age 22, born in Quebec, George age 1 (Indian). District Number 146, S. District, Division Number 2, Oneida, Page 37, Household 170/179.

**MC KAY, JOHN:** (White/Scotch) Age 60, born (About 1821) in Scotland, a Presbyterian, Margaret (Indian) age 45, born in Ontario, (All others were listed as Indians) Mary age 24, Donald age 22, John age 16, Christeen age 11, Thomas J. HARDY age 4, John HUTT age 45, Margaret HUTT age 40, Julia HUTT age 12, John HUTT age 4. Page 35, Household 154/157.

**MONTORE? (OR MONTURE?) EMELY:** (Indian) Age? Catharine age 36, Nancy age 5, Levi age 1. Page 71, Household 343/343.

**MONTURE, JAMES:** (Indian) Age 56, born (About 1825) in Ontario, a member of the Church of England, Liddy age 20, Mary age 15. Page 33, Household 146/148.

**MOONTORE, (OR MONTORE?) MARY:** (Indian) Age 40? or 20? Peter JOHN age 40? or 20? Lucinda MONTORE age 9, Emely age 1. District Number 146, S. District, Divisional Number 1, Oneida, Page 70/71, 342/343.

**MOONTURE? (OR MONTURE?) PETER:** (Indian) Age 40 (Born about 1841) Susan age 40, James age 8, Margaret age 6. District Number 146, S. District, Division Number 1, Oneida Page 70, Household 341/342.

**MOONTORE (OR MONTURE) SARAH:** (Indian) Age 86 born (About 1795) in Ontario, District Number 146, S. District, Division 1, Oneida, Page 71, Household 339/346.

**MOSES, CORNELIUS:** (Indian) Age 60, born (About 1821) in Ontario, Joshua age 12, Cornelia age 10. Page 71, Household 346/346.

**MOSES, PAVIA? OR TAVIA?** (A Male Indian) Age 25 (Born about 1856) Hariot age 22, July age 2, John age 1, Nelson age 21. District Number 146, S. District, Number 1, Oneida, Page 71, Household 347/348.

**MUARTSON? WILLIAM:** (Indian) Age 56, born (About 1825) in Ontario, William age 22, Bresalla (A Male) age 20, Ephrim age 9. Page 72, Household 352/353.

**NOAB? JOHN:** (Indian) Age 28, born (About 1853) in Ontario, Margaret age 27, Yetel? (A Female) age 2. District Number 146, S. District, Division Number 1, Oneida, Page 72, Household 350/351.

**RUSSELL, AMOS:** (White/English) Age 58, born (About 1823) in Ontario, Mary (White) age 54, Mary age 25 (Indian) Emerd? (A Female Indian) age 18, William 15 (A male Indian) District Number 146, S. District, Number 1, Onedia, Page 72, Household 353/354.

**SALT, WILLIAM:** (Indian) Age 55, born (About 1826) in Ontario, a member of the Methodist Church, Susan age 19, District 146, S. District, Division Number 1, Oneida, Page 63, Household 299.

**SANDY, DAVID:** (Indian) Age 40, born (About 1841) in Ontario, (A Female Indian) no name given age 37, born in Ontario, a member of the Church of England, Robert age 19, Lucy age 16, Betsy age 12, James age 8, William age 3. District 146, S. District Division, Number 2, Oneida, Page 34 Household 151/153.

**SAWYER, DAVID:** (Indian) Age 75 born (About 1806) in Ontario, (Listed as a Indian Minister) a member of the Methodist Church, Margret (White/English) born in Ontario age 55. District 146, S. District, Division Number 1, Oneida, Page 62.

**SEITTIS, MITCHELL:** (Indian) Age 38, born (About 1843) in Quebec, Catholic, Mary Ann age 35, born in Quebec. District Number 146, S. District, S. Division, Number 2, Oneida, Page 35, Household 156/159.

**SILVERSMITH, CHARLES:** (Indian) Age 29, born (About 1852) in Ontario, a member of the Church of England, Mary age 19, Adam age 3, Sarah age 1. District Number 146, S. District Number 2, Oneida, Page 33, Household 145/147.

**SMITH, SERAH:** (Indian) Age 40, born (About 1841) in Ontario, a member of the Church of England, Lucy age 13, Alexander BARNES age 5, Ida BARNES age 3, Ellen HESS age 50. District Number 146, S. District, S. Division Number 2, Oneida, Page 36, District 146, S. District, S. Division, Number 2, Oneida, Household 163/169.

**SNAKE, NICHOLAS:** (Indian) Age 38, born (About 1843) in Ontario, a member of the Church of England, District Number 146, S. District, Division Number 1, Oneida, Page 70, Household 335/336.

**VAN EVERY, JOHN:** (Indian) Age 58, born (About 1823) in Ontario, a member of the Methodist Church, Moria age 31, John age 12, Marina age

8, District Number 146, S. District, Division Number 1, Oneida, Page 62, Household 298.

**WARNER, JOHN:** (Indian) Age 45, born (About 1836) in Ontario, Sarah age 36, Charlotte age 22, William age 20, Lucy age 18, Egness (A Female) age 18, Timothy age 10, Elizabeth age 8, John age 3. District Number 146, S. Division Number 2, Oneida, Page 38, Household 171/176.

**WARNER, JOHN:** (Indian) Age 64 born (About 1817) in Ontario, Margaret SCOTT (White/Irish) age 51 born in Ontario, of Irish descent. District Number 146, S. District Number 2, Oneida, Page 43, Household 195/208.

**WILLIAMS, JOSEPH:** (Indian) Age 50, born (About 1831) in Ontario, a member of the Church of England, Margaret his wife age 30, David age 7. District Number 146, S. Division, Number 2, Oneida, Page 33, Household 144/146.

| CAYUGA AND MOHAWK OF HALDIMAND COUNTY ONTARIO, CANADA IN 1881 | |
|---|---|
| **SURNAME CROSS INDEX** | **HEAD OF HOUSEHOLD** |
| **ANTHONY,** Albert | Henry DOCKSTADER |
| **BARNES,** Alexander | Serah SMITH |
| **BARNES,** Ida | Serah SMITH |
| **CRAWFORD,** Margaret | David JOHN |
| **CURLY,** Kate | Nicholas CAYUGA |
| **FISH,** James | Nicolas KECK |
| **FISH,** Jane | Nicolas KECK |
| **GARLOW,** Margret | John CURLEY |
| **HARDY,** Thomas J. | Nicolas KECK |
| **HESS,** Ellen | Serah SMITH |
| **HILL,** Hannah | David JOHN |
| **HILL,** Parting | Peter CRAWFORD |
| **HILL,** Peter | Peter CRAWFORD |
| **HUTT,** John | John McKAY |
| **HUTT,** Julia | John McKAY |
| **HUTT,** Margaret | John McKAY |
| **JOHN,** Peter | Mary MONTORE |
| **RITCHERD,** Margaret | George HOAG |
| **SCOTT,** Scott | John WARNER |

| | |
|---|---|
| **STERE,** John | Nicholas CAYUGA |
| **STERE,** Mary | Nicholas CAYUGA |
| **THOMAS,** Lucy | John HUSS |
| **THOMAS,** Susana | John HUSS |

## HASTING COUNTY, ONTARIO 1881 CENSUS ABSTACT

In 1796 the Midland District, once called the Mecklenburgh District, included Frontenac, Lennox, Addington, Prince Edward County and the southern part of Hastings County. The southern boundary was Lake Ontario. The northern boundary was the Grand River. In 1792 Kingston became the district town of the Midland District. Reference Source: "Ontario People, 1796-1803," Transcribed and Annotated by E. Keith Fitzgerald, With an Introduction and Index by Norman K. Crowder, Genealogical Publishing Company, Incorporated, Baltimore, Maryland, Copyright 1993.

This census abstract includes District 120, B-1, B-2 Tyindinaga and District 120-B, starting with Mill Point Village, including the village of Deseronto and Tyindinaga. Tyendinaga or Tyidinaga is located on the Bay of Quinte. All of the following people were listed as Native Canadians unless otherwise noted. All of the children in each household had the same surname as the head of that household unless otherwise noted. A surname was highlighted with capital letters within a family entry if that surname was different from the surname of the head of household. A question mark was placed after a name that was in doubt. This census abstract should not take the place of any tribal or goernment records. For more information write to the tribal office.

**BARDY, MARGARET:** (Indian) Age 47 born (About 1834) in Ontario, a member of the Church of England, Joseph age 20, John age 20, William age 16, Phillip age 14, Julia H. age 11, Hastings County, District Number 120, B-1, Tyindinaga, Page 28, Household 126/138.

**BARDY? OR BURDY? PETER:** (Indian) Age 26 born (About 1855) in Ontario, a member of the Church of England, Margaret age 19, Charlotte age 1. Page 63, Household 320/321, Hasings County East, District Number 129, S. District Number 5, Village of Deseronto.

**BARDY? OR BURDY? PETER:** (Indian) Age 44 born (About 1837) in Ontario, a member of the Church of England, Lydia age 31, Peter Bardy? (Indian) age 74 (Born about 1807) in Quebec, Alexander MITCHEL (Indian) age ? Hastings County, East, District 120, B-1, Tyindinaga, Page 28, Household 125/137.

**BARNHART, CHARLES:** (Indian) Age 40 born (About 1841) in Ontario, a member of the Church of England, Susan age 34, Nicolas age 16, John R. age 14, Mary A. age 12, David H. age 10, Catherine age 8, Charles age 6, Joseph age 4, Jacob age 2, Agnes age 1. Hastings County, East, District 120, B-1, Tyindinaga, Page 24/25 Household 108/120.

**BARNHART, WILLIAM:** (Indian) Age 34 born (About 1847) in Ontario, a member of the Church of England, Elizabeth age 30, Eliza Ann age 11, James age 7, Eddie age 3. Hastings County, East, District 120, B-3, Page 12/13 Household 63/63.

**BATTECE, JOHN:** (Indian) Age 51 born (About 1830) in Ontario, a member of the Church of England, Ellen age 58, Solomon age 27, John age 17, Isaac age 15, Hester CLAUSE age 43. Hastings County, East, District 120, B-1, Tyindinaga, Page 30, Household 136/148.

**BRANT (OR BENNET?) PETER B:** (Indian) Age 57 born (About 1824) in Ontario, a member of the Church of England, Margaret age 56, Hannah age 34, Florence age 10, Cary E. age 7. Hastings County, East, District Number 120, D-Millpoint Village, Page 2, Household 6.

**BRANT, ABRAM P:** (Indian) Age 43 born (About 1838) in Ontario, a member of the Church of England, Mary age 26, Adam age 21, Margret age 17, Ellen age 15, Alice C., age five months born in November. Hastings County, East, District 120, B-1, Tyindinaga, Page 12/13 Household 52/60.

**BRANT, B. JACOB:** (Indian) Age 30 born (About 1851) in Ontario, a member of the Church of England, Margaret age 26, Sarah age 4, Buryeh? (Male) age 2, Hastings County, East, District B-3, Tyindinaga, Page 32, Household 162/162.

**BRANT, BRANT:** (Indian) Age 69 born (About 1812) in Ontario, a member of the Church of England, Henry age 35, Sarah C. age 12, Isaiah age 10, Mary age 8, Henry age 6, Jerimiah age 4. Hastings County, East, District 120, B-1, Tyindinaga, Page 11, Household 48/55.

**BRANT, BRANT:** (Indian) Age 40, born (About 1841) in Ontario, a member of the Church of England, Catharine age 41, Deliah age 21, John age 15, Jacob age 10, Leidia age 8, Samuel age 6, Charlett age 3, Margaret age 2. Hastings County, East, District 120, B-3, Tyindinaga, Page 19, Household 91/91.

**BRANT, CHARLES:** (Indian) Age 31, born (About 1850) in Ontario, a member of the Church of England, Catherine age 25, Alfred age 9, James age 5, Alice age 13, Thomas REID (White/Irish) age 55 born in Quebec of Irish descent. Hastings County, East, District 120, B-3, Page 11, Household 53/53.

**BRANT, CHARLES:** (Indian) Age 25 born (About 1856) in Ontario, a member of the Church of England, Catherine age 40, Sarah age 5. Hastings County, East, District 120, B-3, Tyindinaga, Page 14, Household 68/68.

**BRANT, DAVID:** (Indian) Age 40 born (About 1841) in Ontario, a member of the Church of England, Cecelia age 50, Rebecca MERICLE age 20. Hastings County, East, District 120, B-1, Tyindinaga, Page 31, Household 141/153.

**BRANT, DAVID:** (Indian) Age 30 born (About 1851) in Ontario, a member of the Church of England, Catherine age 29, Elijah age 10, Alexander age 6, Herbert age 4, George age seven months. Hastings County, East, District 120, B-3, Tyindinaga, Page 15, Household 78/78.

**BRANT, ISAAC J:** (Indian) Age 28 born (About 1853) in Ontario, a member of the Church of England, Melissa age 28, Isaac age 8, Lazarus age 6, Abram age 4, Solomon age 2. Hastings County, East, District 120, B-1, Tyindanaga, Page 9, Household 38/44.

**BRANT, ISAAC:** (Indian) Age 50 born (About 1831) in Ontario, a member of the Church of England, Catherine age 45, Thomas age 21, Isaac age 19, Albert age 18, Margaret age 11, Elizabeth age 9. Hastings County, East, District 120, B-1, Tyindinaga, Page 24, Household 105/117.

**BRANT, JACOB B:** (Indian) Age 30 born (About 1851) in Ontario, a member of the Church of England, Margaret age 26, Sarah age 4, Burgeh? (Male) age 2. Hastings County, East, District 120, B-1, Tyindinaga, Page 32, Household 162/162.

**BRANT, JACOB O:** (Indian) Age 44 born (About 1837) in Ontario, a member of the Church of England, Margaret age 40, Catherine age 16, Eliza age 12, Georgina age 8, Hugh age 6, Elizabeth age 1. Hastings County, East, District 120, B-1, Tyindinaga, Page 18, Household 79/88.

**BRANT, JACOB:** (Indian) Age 45 born (About 1836) in Ontario, a member of the Church of England, Sussanah age 45, John A. age 21, Albert age 19, Eliza C. age 17, Francis C. age 11. Hastings County, East, District 120, B-1, Tyindanaga, Page 7, Household 28/34.

**BRANT, JAMES:** (Indian) Age 63, born (About 1818) in Ontario, a member of the Church of England, Margaret age 63. Hastings County, East, District 120, B-3, Tyindinaga, Page 15, Household 76/76.

**BRANT, JOHN S:** (Indian) Age 69 born (About 1812) in Ontario, Canada East, Margaret age 63, Benjaim Fuller (Indian) age 16. Hastings County, District 120-B, Tyindinaga, Page 24, Household 107/119.

**BRANT, JOHN:** (Indian) Age 30 born (About 1851) in Ontario, a member of the Church of England, Lydia age 25, Powlis age 7, Annie age 5, Jane age 3, Martha age 2. Hastings County, East, District 120, B-3, Tyedinaga, Page 23, Household 114/114.

**BRANT, JOHN:** (Indian) Age 28 born (About 1853) in Ontario, a member of the Church of England, Rhoda A. (White/German) age 24, born in Ontario, of German descent, Charlotte age 7 (Indian) John B. age 5 (Indian) Nelson GREEN age 18 (Indian). Hastings County, East, District 120, B-1, Tyindinaga, Page 30, Household 135/147.

**BRANT, JONAS:** (Indian) Age 37 born (About 1844) in Ontario, a member of the Church of England, Catharine age 30, Eliza age 3. Hastings County, East, District 120, B-1, Tyindanaga, Page 13, Household 56/64.

**BRANT, JOSEPH J.:** (Indian) Age 27 born (About 1854) in Ontario, Eliza age 24, Catherine age 7, Sidney (Male) age 5, Rebecca age 3, Ida age 2, Hastings County, East, District 120, B-1, Tyindinaga, Page 66, Household 308/319.

**BRANT, JOSEPH:** (Indian) Age 60 born (About 1821) in Ontario, a member of the Church of England, Mary age 45?, Mary age 17, Ceclia age 15, William age 13. Hastings County, East, District 120, B-3, Tyendinaga, Page 34, Household 170.

**BRANT, JOSEPH:** (Indian) Age 24 born (About 1857) in Ontario, a member of the Church of England, Mary A. age 17, Lydia age seven months born in August. Hastings County, East, District 120, B-1, Tyindanaga, Page 8/9, Household 34/40.

**BRANT, JOSEPH:** (Indian) Age 27 born (About 1854) in Ontario, a member of the Church of England, Elizabeth age 25, Charles age 4, William age ten months, Celine? (Female) age 2. Hastings County, East, District 120, B-3, Tyindinaga, Page 30, Household 150/150.

**BRANT, JOSHUA:** (Indian) Age 35 born (About 1846) in Ontario, a member of the Church of England, Mary age 34, Joseph age 14, Jacob age 9, Maggie age 7, Sarah age 4, Mary age nine months born in July. Hastings County, East, District 120, B-1, Tyindinaga, Page 15, Household 62/70.

**BRANT, LEWIS?** (Indian) Age 32 born (About 1849) in Ontario, a member of the Church of England, Alice age 29, Hastings County, East, District 120, Tyindinaga, Page 15, Household 74/74.

**BRANT, MICHAEL:** (Indian) Age 38 born (About 1843) in Ontario, a member of the Church of England, Catherine age 33, Susan age 16, Catherine age 14, Abram age 9, Elizabeth age 7, Charlotte age 5. Hastings County, Ontario, District 120, Tyindinaga, Page 14, Household 60/68.

**BRANT, PETER:** (Indian) Age 35 born (About 1846) in Ontario, a member of the Church of England, Deborah age 33, David age 13, Mary A. age 9, Margaret age 7, Richard age 5, Alfred age 2, Sarah KING (Indian) age 63. Hastings County, Ontario, District 120, B-3, Tyindinaga, Page 12, Household 60/60.

**BRANT? PETER B:** (Indian) Age 57, born (About 1824) in Ontario, a member of the Church of England, Margaret age 56, Hanah age 34, Florence age 10, Cary E. (A Female) age 7. Page 2, Household 6, Village of Deseronto.

**BRANT, SARAH:** (Indian) Age 67 born (About 1814) in Ontario, a member of the Church of England, Jane age 42, Brant age 40, Jane PIERCE (Indian) age 18, Sarah A., PIERCE (Indian) Age 8. Hastings County, East, District 120, B-1, Tyindinaga, Page 12, Household 49/57.

**BRANT, SETH S:** (Indian) Age 51 born (About 1830) in Ontario, a member of the Church of England, Lena age 50, David age 22, Daniel age 11, Mary age 16, Catherine age 13, Ann age 12. Hastings County, East, Number 120, B-1, Tyindinaga, Page 8, Household 33/37.

**BRANT, THOMAS J:** (Indian) Age 30 born (About 1851) in Ontario, a member of the Church of England, Mary age 25, Eliza age 6, Ann age 5, Agnes age 4, Mary age 2. Hastings County, East, Number 120, B-1, Tyindinaga, Page 27, Household 121/133.

**BRANT, WILLIAM C:** (Indian) Age 34 born (About 1847) in Ontario, a member of the Church of England, Phoebe age (White/Irish) 24 born in Ontario of Irish descent, Walter age 21, (Indian) Mary P. age 53 (Indian). Hastings County, East, Number 120, B-3, Tyindinaga, Page 14, Household 71/71.

**BRANT, WILLIAM:** (Indian) Age 41 born (About 1840) in Ontario, a member of the Church of England, Elizabeth age 37, Isaac age 21, William age 15, Celia age 11, Sophia age 9, Wellington age 6, Peter age 3, Hastings County, District Number 120, B-3, Tyindinaga, Page 14, Household 68/68.

**BRANT, WILLIAM:** (Indian) Age 40 born (About 1841) in Ontario, Maggie age 35, Mary age 16, Nelson age 14, Catharine age 10, Eliza age 7. Hastings County, East, Number 120, B-1, Tyindinaga, Page 24, Household 104/116.

**BRANT, WILLIAM:** (Indian) Age 25 born (About 1856) in Ontario, a member of the Church of England, Eliza age 4. Hastings County, East, Number 120, B-3, Tyindinaga, Page 11/12 Household 57/57.

**BRANT? (OR BENNET?) SAM?** (Indian) Age 23 born (About 1858) in Ontario, a member of the Church of England. Hastings County, East, District Number 120, S. District Number 5, Deseronto, Page 53, Household 270/2271.

**BRANT? ABRAM:** (Indian) Age 28, born (About 1853) in Ontario, a member of the Church of England, Margaret age 24, May age 5, Amos age 2, Henry age six months born in October. Page 64, Household 325/326, Hastings County, East, District Number 120, S. District Number 5, Village of Deseronto.

**BRANT? DANIEL:** (Indian) Age 46 born (About 1835) in Ontario, a member of the Church of England, Susan (White/Irish) age 48 born in Ontario of Irish descent. Page 53, Household 269/70, Hastings County, East, District Number 120, S. District 5, Village of Deseronto.

**BRANT? JOHNSON:** (Indian) Age 26, born (About 1855) in Ontario, a member of the Church of England, Ellen age 30, Lons H? or Louis H.? (A Male) age 1. Page 2, Household 7, Hastings County, East, District Number 120, D-Millpoint Village, Village of Deseronto.

**BRANT? LASURES? (OR LAZARUS?)** (Male Indian) Age 32 born (About 1849) in Ontario, Jemimah? (Female Indian) age 31 born in Ontario. Page 63, Household 319/320, Hasings East, District Number 120, S. District Number 5, Village of Deseronto.

**BROWN, FRANCIS:** (White/German) age 51 born (About 1830) in Ontario of German descent, Sarah J. BROWN (Indian) age 55, born in Ontario, Dow? CLAUSE (A Male Indian) age 26 born in Ontario, Sarah J., CLAUSE (Indian) age 18. Hastings County, East, Number 120, B-1, Tyindinaga, Page 16, Household 68/76.

**BUCK, ISAAC:** (Indian) Age 28 born (About 1853) in Ontario, a member of the Church of England, Mary age 33, Susan age 9, Lydia age 3. Hastings County, East, District 120, B-3, Tyindinaga, Page 21, Household 106/106.

**BUCK, PETER:** (Indian) Age 28 born (About 1853) in Ontario, a member of the Church of England, Sarah age 24, Susan age 8, Catharine age 6, Hastings County, East, District 120, B-3, Tyindinaga, Page 21/22 Household 107/107.

**BUCK, WILLIAM:** (Indian) Age 71 born (About 1810) in Ontario, a member of the Church of England, Susan age 47, Abraham age 21, Jane age 25, Susan age 7, Sarah age 5. Hastings County, East, District Number 120, B-3, Tyindinaga, Page 31, Household 154/154.

**BURDY, MARGARET:** (Indian) Age 47 born (About 1834) in Ontario, Canada East, Joseph age 20, John age 20, William age 16, Julia A. age 11. Hastings County, District 120, B, Tyendinaga.

**CERO ABRAM:** (Indian) Age 60 born (About 1821) in Ontario, a member of the Church of England, Christine age 60, Sarah age 19, Melissa age 8. Hastings County, East, District 120, B-1, Tyindinaga, Page 68, Household 314/326.

**CERO, ALEXANDER:** (Indian) Age 37 born (About 1844) in Ontario, a member of the Church of England, Hester age 30, William age 8, Joseph age 6, Michael age 3, Jacob age 1. Hastings County, East, District 120, B-1, Tyindinaga, Page 19, Household 82/92.

**CERO, DENNIS:** (Indian) Age 25 born (About 1856) in Canada East, a member of the Church of England, Catherine age 30, Jacob age 4, John age 2, Joseph CLAUSE age 7. Hastings County, East, District 120, B-1, Tyindinaga, Page 68, Household 315/327.

**CERO, JAMES:** (Indian) Age 46 born (About 1835) in Ontario, a member of the Church of England, Magdalene age 27, Israel age 22, Lucy 10, Isaac age 8, Peter age 6, John age 20, Sarah age 17, Sarah age 2. Hastings County, East, District 120, B-1, Tyindinaga, Page 66/67 Household 309/321.

**CERO, JAMES:** (Indian) Age 21 born (About 1860) in Ontario, a member of the Church of England, Catherine age 36, Samuel FULLER (Indian) age 21, born in Ontario. Hastings County, East, District Number 120, B-1, Tyindinaga, Page 24, Household 106/118.

**CERO, JAMES:** (Indian) Age 75 born (About 1806) in Ontario, a member of the Church of England, Christine age 64, Moses age 14, Catherine age 13, Hastings County, East, District Number 120, B-1, Page 18, Household 80/89.

**CERO, JOHN:** (Indian) Age 41 born (About 1840) in Ontario, a member of the Church of England, Maraget age 37. Hastings County, East, District Number 120, B-1, Tyindinaga, Page 10, Household 40/46.

**CERO, MARGARET:** (Indian) Age 34 born (About 1847) in Ontario, a member of the Church of England, Allen age 10. Hastings County, East, District Number 120, B-1, Tyindinaga, Page 2, Household 5/6.

**CERO, NELSON:** (Indian) Age 30 born (About 1851) in Ontario, a member of the Church of England, Lucy age 25, Hastings County, East, District Number 120, B-1, Tyindinaga, Page 18.

**CERO, WILLIAM:** (Indian) Age 31 born (About 1850) in Ontario, a member of the Church of England, Margaret age 29, Allen age 6. Hastings County, East, District 120, B-1, Tyindinaga, Page 16, Household 70/79.

**CHAUNDEAU, PETER:** (White/French) Age 49 born (About 1832) in Quebec, Canada East, Rachael (Indian) age 39 born in Ontario (All others were listed as French except Mary Hill) Julia age 23, Hattie age 20, Sarah age 19, Margaret age 17, Alexander age 16, Georgina age 12, Nelson age 9, Willit P? age 2, Mary HILL (Indian) Age 2 born in Ontario. Hastings

County East, District 120, B-1, Tyindinaga, Page 18/19 Household 81/91.

**CLAUS, MICHAEL:** (Indian) Age 39 born (About 1842) in Ontario, a member of the Church of England, Sarah J. age 32, Edith age 13, Hugh age 9, Annie age 9, Lavina (Female) age 4. Hastings County, East, District 120, B-3, Page 15, Household 75/75.

**CLAUS, WELLINGTON:** (Indian) Age 27 born (About 1854) in Ontario, a member of the Church of England, Sarah age 22, Peter age 5. Hastings County, East, District Number 120, B-1, Tyindinaga, Page 32, Household 157/157.

**CLAUSE, FRANK:** (Indian) Age 38 born (About 1843) in Ontario, a member of the Church of England, Sarah J. age 32, Christine age 14, Isaac age 12, Francis (Male) age 9, Deborah BRANT age 59, born in Ontario, Hastings County, East, District 120, B-1, Tyindinaga, Page 29/30 Household 133/145.

**CLAUSE, ISAAC:** (Indian) Age 35 born (About 1846) in Ontario a member of the Church of England, Agnes (Indian) age 28 born in Quebec, a member of the Catholic Church, John L. age 2, John DEED (Indian) age 18 born in Quebec, a Catholic. Hastings County, East, District 120, B-1, Tyindinaga, Page 32, Household 147//159.

**CLAUSE, JOHN:** (Indian) Age 39, born (About 1842) in Ontario, a member of the Church of England, Catherine age 42, Andrew age 16, Levi age 11, Arthur age 9, John age 7, Amelia age 5, Marshall age 2. Hastings County, East, District Number 120, B-3, Tyindinaga, Page 20, Household 95/95.

**CLAUSE, LAWRENCE:** (Indian) Age 31 born (About 1850) in Ontario, a member of the Church of England, Mary age 36, George W. age 13, Charles age 10, Julia A. age 8, Joseph age 6, Lucretia age 4, Essay (A Female) age 2, Leviath? (A Female) age one month born in February. Hastings County, East, District Number 120, B-1, Tyindinaga, Page 12, Household 50/58.

**CLAUSE, MARY:** (Indian) Age 50 born (About 1831) in Ontario, a member of the Church of England, Catharine age 17. Hastings County, East, District Number 120, B-1, Tyindinaga, Page 29, Household 129/141.

**CLAUSE, RACHEL:** (Indian) Age 71, born (About 1810) in Ontario, a member of the Church of England, Sarah HILL age 16. Hastings County, East, District 120, B-1, Tyindinaga, Page 11, Household 51. See the family of Peter W. Hill Household 44/50.

**CLAUSE, SAMUEL:** (Indian) Age 28 born (About 1853) in Ontario, a member of the Church of England, Ellen age 24, Thomas W. age eleven months. Hastings County, East, Number 120, B-1, Tyindinaga, Page 6, Household 25/29.

**CLAUSE, THOMAS:** (Indian) Age 65 born (About 1816) in Ontario, a member of the Church of England, Elizabeth age 60. Hastings County, East, Number 120, B-1, Tyindinaga, Page 17, Household 72/81.

**CLAUSE, WILLIAM:** (Indian) Age 33 born (About 1848) in Ontario, Margret age 32, David age 11, Mary age 8, Isaac age 6, Lydia age 4, Frederick age 2. Hastings County, East, District Number 120, B-3, Page 34, Household 169.

**COSBY? (OR COSLY?) LEWEY:** (Indian) Age 40 (About 1841) born in Quebec a member of the Church of England, Elizabeth age 26 born in Ontario, Abram age 7, Adam age 4. Page 54, Household 273/274, Hastings County, East, District Number 120, S. District Number 5, Village of Deseronto.

**CRAWFORD, JOHN:** (Indian) Age 29 born (About 1852) in Ontario, a member of the Church of England, Elizabeth age 23, Herbert age 7, Robert age 2, Scynthia age 20, Clayton age 2, Lydia M. age 17, Robert Barley? or Bailey? (White/English) age 29 born in Ontario, of English Descent. Hastings County, East, District Number 120, B-1, Tyindinaga, Page 3, Household 13/15.

**CRAWFORD, PHILLIP:** (Indian) Age 26 born (About 1855) in Ontario, a member of the Church of England, Almira age 29, Alberta age 2. Hastings County East, District Number 120, B-1, Tyindinaga, Page 3, Household 10/12.

**CULBERTSON, ARCHIBALD:** (Indian) Age 50 born (About 1831) in Ontario, a member of the Church of England, Mary E. age 40, Edward W. age 17, Jane age 14, Eliza age 10, Mary C. age 8. Hastings County, East, District Number 120, B-1, Tyindinaga, Page 10, Household 42/48.

**CULBERTSON, JNO., G:** (Indian) Age 43, born (About 1838) in Ontario, a member of the Church of England, Hanah age 41, Jno., age 17, Susan age 16, Isaac? age 13, Alex age 11, Wm age 9, Andrew age 7, Peter age 5, Jas., age 2. Page 17, Household 88, Hastings County East, District Number 120, S. District Number 5, Village of Deseronto.

**CULBERTSON, SANDY:** (Indian) Age 40, born (About 1841) in Ontario, a member of the Church of England, Sarah age 25, Ann age 1. Page 63, Household 316/317, Village of Deseronto.

**FRIZZONE, GEORGE:** (White/German) Age 51 born (About 1830) in the United States of German descent, a member of the Church of England, Matilda (Indian) born in Ontario, Louis (White/German) age 8 born in the United States of German descent. Page 17, Household 67/73, C-2, W. Hastings County, District 121.

**GREEN, ALEX?** (Indian) Age 25 born (About 1856) in Ontario, Catherine age 20, Sarah age 5, Archie age 4. Page 66, Household 330/331, Hastings East, District Number 5, Village of Deseronto.

**GREEN, ALEXANDER:** (Indian) Age 30 born (About 1851) in Ontario, Catherine age 25, Mary age 6, Arthur age 5, Margret age 2. Hastings East, District 120, B-1, Tyindinaga, Page 32, Household 159/159.

**GREEN, ALLEN:** (Indian) Age 62 born (About 1819) in Ontario, a member of the Church of England, Mary age 50, Lydia age 18, Ellen age 16, Isaac age 20, Joseph age 18, Ellen age 6. Hastings County, East, District 120, B-1, Tyindinaga, Page 22, Household 108/108.

**GREEN, ALLEN:** (Indian) Age 65 born (About 1816) in Ontario, a member of the Church of England, Lydia age 28, John age 30, Powles age 8, Ann age 6, Jane age 4, Lucy age 2, Hastings County, East, District 120, B-3, Tyindinaga, Page 22, Household 108/108.

**GREEN, HANNAH:** (Indian) Age 54 born (About 1827) in Ontario, a member of the Church of England, Joseph KERBY (Indian) age 6. Hastings County, East, District Number 120, B-1, Page 2, Household 7. See the family of Margaret Cero Household 5/6.

**GREEN, ISAAC:** (Indian) Age 55 born (About 1826) in Ontario, a member of the Church of England, Elizabeth age 31, (White/English) of English descent (The children were listed as Indians) Jonas age 4, Agnes R., age 1. Hastings County, East, District 120, B-1, Tyindinaga, Page 20, Household 87/97.

**GREEN, JESSE:** (Indian) Age 30, born (About 1851) in Ontario, a member of the Church of England, Ellen age 20, Lydia LOFT age 23. Page 63, Household 318/319, Hastings East, District Number 120, S., District Number 5, Village of Deseronto.

**GREEN, JNO:** (Indian) Age 30, born (About 1851) in Ontario, a member of the Church of England, Christeen age 25, Wm. F. age 3, W. C. (A male) age 1. Page 64, Household 324/325, Hastings East, District Number 120, S., District Number 5, Village of Deseronto.

**GREEN, JOHN D:** (Indian) Age 60 born (About 1821) in Ontario, a member of the Church of England, Agnes age 30, Dan? age 34, Isaac age 22, Joseph age 21, Washington age 2, Hastings County, District Number 120, B-3, Tyindinaga, Page 17, Household 85/85.

**GREEN, JOHN P:** (Indian) Age 30 born (About 1851) in Ontario, a member of the Church of England, Jemimah age 31, Mary age 8. Hastings County East, District 120, B-1, Tyindinaga, Page 29, Household 131/143.

**GREEN, PETER:** (Indian) Age 49 born (About 1832) in Ontario, a member of the Church of England, Catherine age 43, Maria age 56, Thomas age 20, Susan age 14, William age 13, Rosanna age 10. Hastings County, East, District Number 120, B-3, Page 17, Household 86/86.

**GREEN, SAMPSON:** (Indian) Age 40 born (About 1841) in Ontario, a member of the Church of England, Catharine age 32, Sarah A. age 13, Lewis A., age 11, Clara M. age 8, George age 4. Hastings County, East, District Number 120, B-3, page 16, Household 83/83.

**GREEN, THOMAS:** (Indian) Age 85 born (About 1796) in Ontario, a member of the Church of England, Hanah age 65, Mary age 23, Sophie? age 16. Hastings County, East, District Number 120, B-3, Tyindinaga, Page 32, Household 163/163.

**GREEN, WILLIAM:** (Indian) Age 41 born (About 1840) in Ontario, a member of the Church of England, Elizabeth age 37, Isaac age 21, William age 15, Celia age 11, Sophia age 9, Wellington age 6, Peter age 3. Hastings County, East, District Number 120, B-3, Tyindinaga, Page 14, Household 69/69.

**HILL, CATHARINE:** (Indian) Age 66 born (About 1815) in Ontario, a member of the Church of England, Elizabeth age 39, Lydia age 33, Joseph age 29, Sarah age 23, William A. age 7, John WILLIAMS (White/English) age 10, born in England of English descent. Hastings County, East, District Number 120, B-1, Tyindinaga, Page 8, Household 32/38.

**HILL, CATHERINE:** (Indian) Age 83 born (About 1798) in Ontario, a member of the Church of England. Hastings County, East, District 120, B-1, Tyindinaga, Page 16, Household 78.

**HILL, HENRY:** (Indian) Age 40 born (About 1841) in Ontario, a member of the Church of England, Mary 35, Josiah age 7, Thomas age 5. Hastings County, East, District 120, B-1, Tyindinaga, Page 16/17 Household 71/80.

**HILL, ISAAC J:** (Indian) Age 39 born (About 1842) in Ontario, a member of the Church of England, Nancy age 40, Margaret A. age 16, Percilla age 14, Emerilla age 10, Freeman age 6, Calvin W. age 4, Alexander age one month. Hastings County, East, District 120, Tyindinaga, Page 4, Household 17/19.

**HILL, JACOB:** (Indian) Age 23 born (About 1858) in Ontario, a member of the Church of England, Magdalen age 19. Hastings County, East, District 120, Tyindinaga, Page 5, Household 24.

**HILL, JOHN D:** (Indian) Age 50 born (About 1831) in Ontario, a member of the Church of England, Elizabeth age 49, William age 23, John age 19, Margaret age 16, Christine age 13, Joseph age 7, Lydia age 4, David age 2. Hastings County, East, District 120, Tyindinaga, Page 26/27, Household 118/130.

**HILL, JOHN JR? or J?** (Indian) Age 48 born (About 1833) Ontario, a member of the Church of England, Sarah age 43, Susan M. age 22, Isabell age 18, Richard age 16, Joseph age 14, Isaac age 11, John A., age 9, Robert H? age 3. Hastings County, East, District 120, B-1, Tyindinaga, Page 4, Household 16/18.

**HILL, JOHN:** (Indian) Age 21 born (About 1860) in Ontario, a member of the Church of England, Lydia age 18. Hastings County, East, District 120, Tyindinaga, Page 6, Household 21/25.

**HILL, JOSEPH W:** (Indian) Age 73 born (About 1808) in Ontario, a member of the Church of England, Hastings County, District 120-B, Tyindinaga, Page 5, Household 19/21.

**HILL, JOSEPH:** (Indian) Age 87 born (About 1794) in Ontario, a member of the Church of England, Hannah BARNHART (Indian) age 69, William BARNHART (Indian) age 51 Hastings County, East, District 120, B-1, Tyindinaga, Page 26, Household 116/128.

**HILL, LUCINDA:** (Indian) Age 40 born (About 1841) in Ontario, a member of the Church of England, Lizzie age 19, Susan age 15, James age 17, Caroline age 3. Hastings County, East, District 120, B-3, Tyindinaga, Page 13, Household 64/64.

**HILL, PETER W:** (Indian) Age 32 born (About 1849) in Ontario, a member of the Church of England, Mary age 31, Almedia F. (Female) age 7, Harry M. age 1. Hastings County, East, District 120, B-1, Tyindinaga, Page 11, Household 44/50.

**HILL, SETH W:** (Indian) Age 71 born (About 1810) in Ontario, a member of the Church of England, Catharine age 61, Hannah age 37, Josiah age 18. Hastings County, East, District 120, B-1, Tyindinaga, Page 5, Household 20/23.

**HILL, SIMON:** (Indian) Age 35, born (About 1846) in Ontario, a member of the Church of England, Jemimah age 30, Catherine age 13, Mary age 11, Ann age 9, Jane age 5, Isaac age 3, Thomas age nine months born in July. Hastings County, East, District 120, B-1, Tyindinaga, Page 15, Household 61/69.

**HILL, WILLIAM J. W:** (Indian) Age 48 born (About 1833) in Ontario, a member of the Church of England, Eve 54, Frank MARTELL (White/English) age 15 born in England of English descent, Elizabeth POWLESS (Indian) age 3 born in Ontario. Hastings County, East, District Number 120, B-1, Tyindinaga, Page 2, Household 7/9.

**HILL, WILLIAM:** (Indian) Age 57 born (About 1824) in Ontario, a member of the Church of England, Mary age 40, Solomon age 22. Hastings County, East, District Number 120, B-1, Tyindinaga, Page 16, Household 65/73.

**HOLLOWDAY, ROBERT:** (African descent) Age 27 born (About 1854) in Quebec, Ann (Indian) Age 26 born in Ontario, John Hollowday (African descent) born in Ontario, age 24. Page 66, Household 290/291, District 121, West Hastings County, Township of Sidney.

**JACK, ROBT:** (White) Age 38 born (About 1843) in Scotland, a member of the Cavalry Presbyterian Church, Elisab (Indian) age 33 born in Ontario. Page 19, Household 100, Village of Deseronto.

**JOHN, CHARLES:** (Indian) Age 42 born (About 1839) in Ontario, a member of the Church of England, Elizabeth age 33, Simon age 17, David age 15, Sarah age 9, Charles age 7. Hastings County, East, District 120, B-1, Tyindinaga, Page 29, Household 130/142.

**JOHN, JOHN:** (Indian) Age 69 born (About 1812) in Ontario, a member of the Church of England, Mary age 44, Joseph age 26. Hastings County, East, District 120, B-1, Tyindinaga, Page 16, Household 64/72.

**JOHN, PETER:** (Indian) Age 40 born (About 1841) in Ontario, a member of the Church of England, Charlotte age 20, Joseph age 2. Hastings County, East, District 120, B-1, Tyindinaga, Page 28, Household 124/136.

**JOHNSON, JOEL:** (Indian) Age 41 born (About 1840) in Ontario, a member of the Church of England, Sussanah age 31, Margaret age 12, Louise age 9, Alice age 5, Clara age 2, Susanah age two months, Hastings County, East, District 120, B-1, Tyindinaga, Page 5, Household 22.

**JOHNSON, PETER:** (Indian) Age 32 born (About 1849) in Ontario, a member of the Church of England, Margaret age 25, George age 4, Dora age 2. Hastings County East, District Number 121, S. District-C, City of Belleville, Page 21, Household 125/128.

**JOHNSON, SETH:** (Indian) Age 35 born (About 1846) in Ontario, a member of the Church of England, Margaret age 40, Hastings County, East, District Number 120, Tyindinaga, Page 23, Household 115.

**LEWEN? OR LEWIS? WILLIAM:** (Indian) Age 48 born (About 1833) in Ontario, a member of the Church of England, Deborah age 36, Simon age 19, John age 18, Juliah A. age 16, Margaret age 14, Ann age 12, Alexander age 6, Sarah age 3, William age 1. Hastings County, East, District 120, B-1, Tyindinaga, Page 15, Household 63/71.

**LEWEY, JOHNSON? (OR LEWEY JOHNSON?)** (Indian) Age 22 born (About 1859) in Ontario, a member of the Church of England, Mary age 23, Nancy BRANT? age 26 Catie BRANT age 25. Hastings County East, District Number 120, S. District Number 5, Deseronto, Page 54, Household 274/275.

**LEWEY? (OR LEURY?) JAMES:** (Indian) Age 49 born (About 1832) in Ontario, a member of the Church of England, Mary age 44, Albert age 19, Edward age 15, Burton? age 13, Godfrey age 11, Mary age 7, Lucy age 5, Julia age 1. Page 63, Household 321/322, Village of Deseronto.

**LEWEY? JOHNSON:** (Indian) Age 22 born (About 1859) in Ontario, a member of the Church of England, Mary age 23, Nancy BRANT age 26, Catie BRANT age 25. Page 54, Household 274/275, Village of Deseronto.

**LOFT, ALEX:** (Indian) Age 53 born (About 1828) in Ontario, a member of the Church of England, Ann age 43, Elisabeth age 12, Simcoe (A Male) age 10. Hastings County, East, District Number 120, S. District Number 5, Deseronto, Page 40, Household 205/206.

**LOFT, ALEXANDER:** (Indian) Age 21 born (About 1860) in Ontario, a member of the Church of England, Charlotte age 26, Ida age 16, Solomon age 36, Sarah age 34, Irene age 6, Newton age 3. Hastings County, East, District 120, B-1, Tyindinaga, Page 6, Household 30.

**LOFT, JOHN A:** (Indian) Age 34 born (About 1847) in Ontario, a member of the Church of England, Susan age 33, Clara A., age 4, Minnie A., 2, Hattie E., age eight months, Susan BISSEL? (White/French) Listed as the School mistress. Hastings County, District Number 120, Tyendinaga, Page 8, Household 30/36.

**LOFT, SETH:** (Indian) Age 47 born (About 1834) in Ontario, Catherine age 72? Christine age 27, Mary age 19, Edmund age 37, Mary age 37, Laurence age 16, Catherine age 15, Nelson age 7, Maggie age 4, Susan age 3, Edmund age nine months born in July. Hastings County, East, District 120, B-1, Tyindinaga, Page 22/23, Household 99/109.

**LOFT, JOHN A:** (Indian) Age 34 born (About 1847) in Ontario, a member of the Church of England, Susan age 33, Clara A. age 4, Minnie A. age 2, Hattie E. age eight months born in July, Susan BREAULT?

(White/French) age 24, Listed as a school mistress. Hastings County, East, District 120, B-1, Tyindinaga, Page 8, Household 30/36.

**LOFT, SOLOMON:** (Indian) Age 36 born (About 1845) in Ontario, a member of the Church of England, Sarah age 34, Irene age 6, Newton age 3. Hastings County, District Number 120, Tyindinaga, Page 7, Household 31.

**LOFT, THOMAS:** (Indian) Age 64 born (About 1817) in Ontario, a member of the Church of England. Hastings County, East, District 120, B-1, Tyindinaga, Page 20, Household 88/98.

**LORIEN? OR DORIN? PETER:** (Indian) Age 26 born (About 1855) in Ontario, a member of the Church of England, Susan age 24. Hastings County, East, District Number 120, B-1, Tyindinaga, Page 31, Household 155/155.

**LOUIS, SAMUEL:** (Indian) Age 47 born (About 1834) in Ontario, a member of the Church of England, Catherine age 43, Susan M. age 22, William P. age 21, Levi age 16, Elizabeth age 15, Norman? or Nonnon? (A Male) age 13, Chansy? (A Male) age 9, Alberta age 5, Marshal age 2. Hastings County, East, District 120, B-1, Tyindinaga, Page 9, Household 39/45.

**MARACLE, JOSEPH:** (Indian) Age 59 born (About 1822) in Ontario, a member of the Church of England, Rebecca age 54, Robert age 12, William age 17. Hastings County East, District 120, B-3, Tyindinaga, Page 14, Household 70/70.

**MARICLE, ABRAHAM:** (Indian) Age 44 born (About 1837) in Ontario, Sarah age 40, George age 20, Liddie age 16. Hastings County, Ontario, East, District 120, B-3, Tyindinaga, Page 11, Household 56/56.

**MARICLE, GEORGE:** (Indian) Age 40 born (About 1841) in Ontario, Sarah age 39, Isaac age 14, George age 10, Hannah age 16. Hastings County, Ontario, East, District 120, B-3, Tyindinaga, Page 31, Household 156/156.

**MARICLE, JAMES:** (Indian) Age 54 born (About 1827) in Ontario, a member of the Church of England, Richard age 40, Milo age 26, Elazar age 23, Joshua age 20, Emma age 18, Thomas age 16, Edward age 12, Solomon age 8, Annie age 16. Hastings County, East, District Number 120, B-3, Tyendinaga, Page 33, Household 165.

**MARICLE, JOHN C:** (Indian) Age 60 born (About 1821) in Ontario, a member of the Church of England, Amelia age 47, Sarah M., GUBBINS? or GIBBINS? (Indian) age 12. Hastings County, East, District 120, B-1, Tyindinaga, Page 7, Household 27/33.

**MARICLE, JOHN F:** (Indian) Age 39 born born (About 1842) in Ontario, a member of the Church of England, Ellen age 28, Margret age 13, Thomas age 6. Hastings County East, District 120, Number B-1, Tyindinaga, Page 1/2 Household 3/4.

**MARICLE, RACHEL:** (Indian) Age 69 born born (About 1812) in Ontario, a member of the Church of England, Lydia age 14. Hastings County, East, District 120, B-3, Tyindinaga, Page 23, Household 103/114.

**MARIKLE, SILAS:** (Indian) Age 38 born (About 1843) in Ontario, a member of the Church of England, Elizabeth age 39, Bertha A., age 9, Richard age 8, Sarah A. age 6, Albert age 5, Abraham age 2, Hastings County, District Number 121, West, S. District B, Trenton, Page 41, Household 199/211.

**MARKLE, ABRAM:** (Indian) Age 34 born (About 1847) in Ontario, a member of the Church of England, Mary age 30, Mary age 11, Eunice age 6, Abram age 2. Hastings County, East, District Number 120, S., District Number 5, Deseronto, Page 24, Household 127/128.

**MARKLE, CHAS:** (Indian) Age 46 born (About 1835) in Ontario, a member of the Church of England, Sarah age 32, Eliza age 15, Lydia age 13, Chas., age 10, Louise age 8, Richard age 6, Harriet age 2, Stsoue? (Female) age 3 months born in February. Hastings County, East, District Number 120, S., District 5, Deseronto, Page 53, Household 268/269.

**MARKLE, CORNELIUS:** (Indian) Age 50 born (About 1831) in Ontario, a member of the Church of England, Nancy age 46, Andrew age 24, Susan age 22, Margaret age 20, Catharine E. age 18, Cyrus age 16, Elisabeth age 12, Albert age 14, Lydia age 9, Ira age 7, Loretta? age 5. Page 1, Household 2. Hastings County, East, District Number 120, D-Millpoint Village, Page 1, Household 2.

**MARKLE, LUCY:** (Indian) Age 37, born (About 1844) in Ontario, a member of the Church of England, Jo (A Male) age 14, John age 12, Mary age 9, Susan? age 8, Margaret age 5, Isabelle age 1. Page 62, Household 315/316, Village of Deseronto.

**MARKLE, WILLIAM:** (Indian) Age 45 born (About 1836) in Ontario, a member of the Church of England, Margaret age 40, Mary age 16? Alex age 14, Mitchel age 12, Rachel age 8, Wm age 6, Abram age 4, Rossa? (A Female) age 2. Page 64, Household 322/323, Village of Deseronto.

**MARTIN, WILLIAM:** (Indian) Age 31 born (About 1850) in Ontario, a member of the Church of England, Eliza 39, Drucilla age 14, Nelson C. age 7. Hastings County, East, District 120, B-1, Tyindinaga, Page 26, Household 113/125.

**MARTIN?, JESSE:** (Indian) Age 56 born (About 1825) in Ontario, a member of the Church of England, Susan age 57, Ellen FINEGA? or FINYA? age 17. Page 62, Household 314/315, Village of Deseronto.

**MERACLE, ABRAHAM:** (Indian) Age 60, born (About 1821) in Ontario, a member of the Church of England, Lydia age 50, Paul JACOB ge 35. Hastings County, East, District 120, B-1, Tyindinaga, Page 32, Household 160/160.

**MERICLE, CORNELIUS:** (Indian) Age 43, born (About 1838) in Ontario, a member of the Church of England, Madalen age 42, Nancy age 15, Scynthia age 8, Alvina age 6. Hastings County, East, District 120, B-1, Tyindinaga, Page 28, Household 123/135.

**MERICLE, DANIEL:** (Indian) Age 67 born (About 1814) in Ontario, a member of the Church of England, Charlotte age 51, Daniel age 16,

Susan age 12, Nelson C. age 10, Joseph age 16. Hastings County, East, District 120, B-1, Tyindinaga, Page 27/28 Household 122/134.

**MERICLE, DAVID C:** (Indian) Age 53, born (About 1828) in Ontario, a member of the Church of England, Margaret age 41, Stephen age 23, Lucina age 16, Rebecca age 13, Mary M. age 10, Catharine age 10, Diamond (A Male) age 6, Susan age 3, Jane age 0 born in March. Hastings County, East, District 120, B-1, Tyindinaga, Page 7, Household 26/32.

**MERICLE, EDWARD:** (Indian) Age 37 born (About 1844) in Ontario, Lucy age 21, Sarah E. age 2, John W. age nine months. Hastings County, East, District 120, B-1, Page 68, Household 310//322.

**MERICLE, ELENOR:** (Indian) Age 75 born (About 1806) in Ontario, a member of the Church of England, Hastings County, East, District 120, B-1, Tyindinaga, Page 20, Household 90/100.

**MERICLE, ELLEN:** (Indian) Age 56, born (About 1825) in Ontario, a member of the Church of England, David age 12, Eliza age 18, Louise age 16, Deborah age 15, Lydia age 13. Hastings County, East, District 120, B-1, Tyindinaga, Page 21, Household 93/103.

**MERICLE, HENRY:** (Indian) Age 87? or 82? in Ontario, a member of the Church of England, Agnes age 76. East Hastings County, District 120-B, Tyendinaga, Page 27, Household 119/131.

**MERICLE, HENRY:** (Indian) Age 52 born (About 1829) in Ontario, a member of the Church of England, Hannah age 50, Susan age 23, Jacob age 22, Henry age 10, Alexander age 7. Hastings County, East, District 120, Number B-1, Tyindinaga, Page 37, Household 170/182.

**MERICLE, JACOB:** (Indian) Age 35 born (About 1846) in Ontario, a member of the Church of England, Margaret age 35, Francis age 15, Isaac age 13, Laurence 11, Regent (Female) age 9, Magdalen age 7, Richard age 5, Margaret age seven months born in September. Hastings County, East, District 120, Number B-1, Tyindinaga, Page 30, Household 138-150.

**MERICLE, JOHN C:** (Indian) Age 60 born (About 1821) in Ontario, a member of the Church of England, Amelia age 41, Sarah GUBBINS JR., (Indian) age 12. Hastings County, District 120, Tyendinaga, Page 7, Household 27/33.

**MERICLE, JOHN H:** (Indian) Age 58 born (About 1823) in Ontario, a member of the Church of England, Emma age 30, Alexander age 9, Albert age 2. Hastings County, East, District 120, Number B-1, Tyindinaga, Page 20, Household 91/101.

**MERICLE, JOHN:** (Indian) Age 27 born (About 1854) in Ontario, Canada East, Elizabeth age 22, Julia A. age 7, East Hastings County, District 120, Tyendinaga, Page 40, Household 180/192.

**MERICLE, LAURENCE:** (Indian) Age 38 born (About 1843) in Ontario, a member of the Church of England, Jemimah age 33, Catharine age 9, Margaret age 7, Elizabeth age 4, Abram age 1. Hastings County, East, 1881, District 120, Number B-1, Tyindinaga, Page 2, Household 4/5.

**MERICLE, NELSON:** (Indian) Age 26 born (About 1855) in Ontario, a member of the Church of England, Mary age 27, Mary C., age 3, Elenor A. age 1, Solomon FUNN age 6. Hastings County, East, District 120, B-1, Tyindinaga, Page 13, Household 53/61.

**MERICLE, NELSON:** (Indian) Age 26 born (About 1855) in Ontario, a member of the Church of England, Mary age 27, Mary C., age 3, Elenor A. age 1, Solomon FUNN age 6. Hastings County, East, District 120, B-1, Tyindinaga, Page 13, Household 53/61.

**MERICLE, NICODEMUS:** (Indian) Age 50 born (About 1831) in Ontario, a member of the Church of England, Mary age 48, Joseph SMART age 13. Hastings County, East, District 120, B-1, Tyindinaga, Page 34, Household 155/167.

**MERICLE, SETH:** (Indian) Age 34 born (About 1847) in Ontario, Canada East, Christine age 28, Mary age 9, Seth age 7, Sarah age 5, Eliza age 3, Elizabeth age 1. East Hastings County, District 120, Tyendinaga, Page 27, Household 120/132.

**MERICLE, WILLIAM:** (Indian) Age 25 born (About 1856) in Ontario, a member of the Church of England, Sarah age 25, Joseph E. age 2. Hastings County, East, District 120, B-3, Tyindinaga, Page 12, Household 59/59.

**MERIKLE, ELIAS:** (Indian) Age 38 born (About 1843) in Ontario, a member of the Church of England, Elizabeth age 39, Bertha A. age 9, Richard age 8, Sarah A. age 6, Albert age 5, Abraham age 2. Page 41, Household 199/211, Division No. 1, B-District, W. Hastings County, 121, Village of Trenton.

**MIRACLE, ABRAHAM:** (Indian) Age 60 born (About 1831) in Ontario, Lydia age 50, Paul JACOB age 35, Hastings County, Ontario, East, District 120, B-3, Tyindinaga, Page 32, Household 160/160.

**MIRACLE, CATHERINE:** (Indian) Age 45, born (About 1836) in Ontario, Cornelius age 28, Moses age 23, Jane age 20, Ida age 2. Hastings County, East, District 120, B-3, Tyindinaga, Page 23, Household 113/113.

**MIRACLE, CORNELIUS:** (Indian) Age 29 born (About 1852) in Ontario, Sharlot age 22, Sarah age 6, Compo? (A Male) age 4, William age 2. Hastings County, East, District Number 120, B-3, Tyindinaga, Page 23, Household 116.

**MIRACLE, DAVID A.** (Indian) Age 36 born (About 1845) in Ontario, a member of the Church of England, Ellen age 30, David age 10, Isaac age 8, Lydia age 7, John age 5, Louis age 3, Francis age 1. Hastings County, East, District 120, B-1, Page 68, Household 316/328.

**MIRACLE, JAMES:** (Indian) Age 30 born (About 1851) in Ontario, Ellenor age 32, Albert age 9, Elizabeth age 8, Mary E. age 7, Bertha age 4, Louisa age 2. Hastings County, East, District 120, B-3, Tyindinaga, Page 13, Household 67/67.

**MIRACLE, WILLIAM:** (Indian) Age 25 born (About 1856) in Ontario, Sarah age 23, Joseph E. age 2. Hastings County, East, District 120, B-3, Tyindinaga, Page 12, Household 59/59.

**MIRACLE, WILLIAM:** (Indian) Age 40 born (About 1841) in Ontario, Catherine age 40. Hastings County, East, District 120, B-3, Tyindinaga, Page 22, Household 112/112.

**MOSES, JACOB:** (Indian) Age 47 born (About 1834) in Ontario, a member of the Church of England, Sarah age 43, Sylvester age 21, Julia age 18, Sarah A. age 14, Ben age 11, Mary 8, Loretta age 5, Alace age 2. Hastings County, East, District Number 120, D-Millpoint Village, Page 1, Household 3.

**PENN, ANN:** (Indian) age 85 born (About 1796) in Ontario. Mary age 40, Joseph Moses age 17. Hastings County, East, District 120, B-3, Tyindinaga, Page 110/110, Household 110/110.

**PENN, ISAAC:** (Indian) Age 60 born (About 1821) in Ontario, Mary Ann age 50, Ann age 15, John age 12, Catherine age 9. Hastings County, East, District 120, B-3, Tyindinaga, Page 11, Household 54/54.

**PENN, ISAAC:** (Indian) Age 62 born (About 1819) in Ontario, Mary age 50, Lydia age 18, Ellen age 16, Isaac age 20, Joseph age 18, Ellen age 6. Hasting County, East, District 120, B-3, Tyindinaga, Page 22, Household 109/109.

**PENN, JOHN:** (Indian) Age 28 born (About 1853) in Ontario, Mary age 21, David age 7, William age 5, Loretta age 2. Hastings County, East, District 120, B-3, Tyindinaga, Page 15, Household 77/77.

**PENN, JOSEPH:** (Indian) Age 50 born (About 1831) in Ontario, Elizabeth age 51, John age 14. Hastings County, East, District 120, B-3, Tyindinaga, Page 22, Household 111/111.

**PENN, SAMUEL:** (Indian) Age 24 born (About 1857) in Ontario, Catherine age 22. Hastings County, East, District 120, B-3, Page 20, Household 96/96.

**PICARD, JOSEPH:** (Indian) Age 42 born (About 1839) in Quebec, a member of the Catholic Church, Eliza (Indian) age 30 born in Ontario, a member of the Church of England, Mary POWLESS (Indian) age 69 born in Ontario, Brant POWLESS age 15? or 75? born in Ontario. Hastings County, East, District Number 120, B-3, Tyindinaga, Page 31, Household 153/153.

**POWLES, ISAAC:** (Indian) Age 42 born (About 1839) in Ontario, a member of the Church of England, Joab 12, Isaac 10, Hastings County, East, District Number 120, B-3, Tyindinaga, Page 18/19, Household 90/90.

**POWLES, JACOB:** (Indian) Age 43 born (About 1839) in Ontario, a member of the Church of England, Nancy age 38, Douglas age 16, Margaret age 15, David J. age 12, George A., age 10, Robert THOMPSON (White/German) age 19 born in Ontario of German descent. Hastings County, East, District 120, B-1, Tyindinaga, Page 19, Household 83/93.

**POWLES, MARGARET:** (Indian) Age 56 born (About 1826) in Ontario, a member of the Church of England, William age 25, Frederick age 9. Hastings County, East, District Number 120, B-3, Tyindinaga, Page 19, Household 92/92.

**POWLESS, JOHN:** (Indian) Age 28 born (About 1853) in Ontario, a member of the Church of England, Margaret age 24, William age 15? Hastings County, East, District Number 120, B-1, Tyindinaga, Page 3, Household 9/11.

**SHINNEWA? JOHN:** (Indian) Age 40, born (About 1841) in Ontario, Ester age 49, John age 19, Mary age 16, James age 14, Lydia age 4. Hastings County, East, District 120, B-1, Tyindinaga, Page 13, Household 55/63.

**SMART, CHARLOTTE:** (Indian) Age 40 born (About 1841) in Ontario, a member of the Church of England, Milo age 20, Lydia age 18, William age 13, Peter age 8, Thomas age 4. Hastings County, Ontario, District 120, B-1, Page 68, Household 317/329.

**SMART, DAVID:** (Indian) Age 50 born (About 1831) in Ontario, a member of the Church of England. Hastings County, East, District 120, B-1, Tyindinaga, Page 16, Household 67/75.

**SMART, GEORGE:** (Indian) Age 22, born (About 1859) in Ontario, a member of the Church of England, Ann age 24. East Hastings County, Tyindinaga, District 120, Household 56, Page 12 See the family of Brant, Brant Household 48/55.

**SMART, GEORGE:** (Indian) Age 45 born (About 1836) in Ontario, Ann age 24. Hastings County, East, District 120, B-1, Tyindinaga, Page 12, Household 55.

**SMART, ISAAC:** (Indian) Age 24, born (About 1857) in Ontario, a member of the Church of England, Lydia M., age 19, Adeline age 3, Loretta age 1. Hastings County, East, District 120, B-1, Tyindinaga, Page 21, Household 94/104.

**SMART, MAGDALENE:** (Indian) Age 47 born (About 1834) in Ontario, John age 26, Peter age 20, Elizabeth age 12, Henry age 10, James age 8, Robert age 6. Hastings County, East, District 120, B-1, Tyindinaga, Page 16, Household 69/77.

**SMART, PETER:** (Indian) Age 48 born (About 1833) in Ontario, Catherine age 38, Mary age 14, Rachel age 13. Hastings County, East, District 120, B-1, Tyindinaga, Page 23, Household 102/113.

**SMITH, ALRA?** (White/German) Age 38 born (About 1843) in Ontario of German descent, a member of the Church of England, Ellen (Indian) Age 39 born in Ontario, a member of the Church of England, Harriet (White/German) age 11, Wm (White/German) age 8, Elisabeth POWLES (Indian) age 80. Hastings County, East, District Number 120, S., District Number 5, Deseronto, Page 54, Household 272/273.

**SMITH, DAVID:** (Indian) Age 48 born (About 1833) in Ontario, Sarah age 44, Sarah E. age 16. Hastings County, East, District 120, B-1, Tyindinaga, Page 32, Household 158/158.

**SMITH, SUSAN:** (Indian) Age 68 born (About 1813) in Ontario, a member of the Church of England, Mary age 36, Julia? or Lydia? age 14. Hastings County, Ontario, District 120, B-3, Tyindinaga, Page 30, Household 148/148.

**SNIDER, HIRUM:** (White/German) Age 55 born (About 1826) in Ontario of German descent. He was a member of the Cavalry Methodist Church, Agnes (White) age 54, Sarah (White) age 15, Sam BRANT (Indian) age 23, born in Ontario, a member of the Church of England. Page 53, Household 270/71, Village of Deseronto.

**WALKER, CHARLES E:** (Indian) Age 33 born (About 1848) in Ontario, a member of the Church of England, Ann age 30, Susan age 7, John age 6, Edmund age 3, Joseph age 2, Ellen HILL age 40. Hastings County, East, District 120, B-1, Tyindinaga, Page 30, Household 134/146.

**WILLIAM, JOHN G:** (Indian) Age 30 born (About 1851) in Ontario, a member of the Church of England, Christine age 24, Samuel age 6. Hastings County, East, District 120, B-3, Tyindinaga, Page 12, Household 62/62.

**WILLIAMS, WILLIAM B:** (Indian) Age 31 born (About 1850) in Ontario, a member of the Church of England, Mary Ann age 24, Julia age 7, Mary E., age 5, George age 3, David age eight months. Hastings County, East, District 120, B-3, Tyindinaga, Page 15, Household 73/73.

| 1881 CROSS INDEX OF HASTINGS COUNTY, ONTARIO CANADA ||
|---|---|
| **SURNAME CROSS INDEX** | **HEAD OF HOUSEHOLD** |
| **BARNHART,** Hanah | Joseph HILL |
| **BARNHART,** William | Joseph HILL |
| **BISSEL,** Susan | John A. LOFT |
| **BRANT,** Deborah | Frank CLAUSE |
| **BRANT,** Nancy | Johnson LEWEY? |
| **BRANT,** Sam | Hirum SNIDER |
| **BREAULT,** Susan | John A. LOFT |
| **CLAUSE,** Dow? | Francis BROWN |
| **CLAUSE,** Hester | John BATTECE |
| **CLAUSE,** Joseph | Dennis CERO |
| **DEED,** John | Isaac CLAUSE |
| **FINEGA? OR FINYA?,** Ellen | Jesse MARTIN |
| **FULLER,** Samuel | James CERO |
| **FUNN,** Soloman | Nelson POWLESS |

| | |
|---|---|
| **FUNN**, Solomon | Nelson MERICLE |
| **GREEN**, Nelson | John BRANT |
| **GUBBINS**, Sarah Jr. | John C. MERICLE |
| **GUBBINS**, Sarah M. | John C. MARICLE |
| **HILL**, Ellen | Charles E. WALKER |
| **HILL**, Mary | Peter CHAUNDEAU |
| **HILL**, Sarah | Rachel CLAUSE |
| **JACOB**, Paul | Abraham MERICLE |
| **KERBY**, Joseph | Hannah GREEN |
| **KING**, Sarah | Peter BRANT |
| **MERICLE**, Rebecca | David BRANT |
| **MITCHELL**, Alexander | Peter BORDY? BURDY? |
| **PIERCE**, Jane | Sarah BRANT |
| **PIERCE**, Sarah A. | Sarah BRANT |
| **POWLESS**, Brant | Joseph PICARD |
| **POWLESS**, Elizabeth | William J. W. HILL |
| **POWLESS**, Mary | Joseph PICARD |
| **REID**, Thomas | Charles BRANT |
| **THOMPSON**, Robert | Jacob POWLESS |
| **WILLIAM**, John | Catherine HILL |

## MIDDLESEX COUNTY, ONTARIO
## HISTORICAL NOTES

In 1796 the "Western District," originally called Hesse District included what is today Essex, Kent, Middlesex, Norfolk and Oxford Counties. In 1800 Norfolk, Oxford and Middlesex formed a separate District called London District. In 1827 Middlesex County included the present counties of Elgin, Oxford, Huron, Perth and Bruce. A Wesleyan Methodist mission was started among the Chippewa (Ojibway) Oneida and Muncey of Caradoc (In Middlesex County) in the 1820's. An English Church was located at Munceytown. St. Paul's English Church was at Muncey and St. John's, was at Chippewa. The Zion Church of the Oneidas was established in the late 1860's. The Oneida Methodist Mission was part of Muncey until the 1870's. The Elgin Industrial Institution was started in the late 1840's from donations collected by Peter Jones an Indian missionary in England and Scotland and from other Indians. Sources: "The Delaware and Shawnee Admitted to Cherokee Citizenship and Related Wyandotte and Moravian Delaware," By Toni Jollay Prevost, Copyright 1992, by Heritage Press, page 95. "History of the County of Middlesex," Canada, Originally published at Toronto and London by W.A. & C. L. Goodspeed in 1889, introduction by Daniel J. Brock, facsimile edition printed by Mika Studio, Belleville, Ontario, 1972. Chapter 11, "Indian residents from 1580-1888," pages 25, 26, Indian Churches and Missions Including marriage returns from Rev. Ezra Adams of the Wesleyan Church for 1834-5, Reverend Solomon Waldron, Wesleyan Methodist minister at Munceytown for part of the year 1836 and Abram Sickles, an Indian minister for 1848 to 1850.

# MIDDLESEX COUNTY, ONTARIO 1851 CENSUS ABSTRACT

This Census Abstract starts at District 4, Ojibwa (Chippewa) Indian Settlement, Township of Caradoc, page 127/128 and starts again on page 133. The 1851 Canadian Census did not provide the relationships between family members. Married couples and children with similar surnames were enumerated and grouped together. Sometimes an individual will appear within a family group with a different surname. This person may have been an adopted child, a step child or a grandparent. In this census abstract the these people were listed separately. The name of the family group or person they appeared to be living with was included after their entry. A question mark was placed after a name that was in doubt. This census abstract should not take the place of any tribal or government records. For more information write to the tribal office.

**AHNWAUJEWUN:** (Female Indian) Age 50 born (About 1801) at River Thames (Ojibwa Indian/Caradoc Reserve/Thames River) Page 141/8.

**AHZHOO:** (Male Indian) Age 23 born (About 1828) at River Thames (Caradoc Reserve/Ojibwa Settlement) Page 149/12.

**ALWAY, JAMES:** (Indian) Age 35 born (About 1816) at Amherstburgh, Mary Age 42 born in the United States, Mary age 13 born at London, Sarah age 9 born at St. Thomas, Samuel age 4 born at River Thames, Polly age 70 born (About 1781) in the United States (Ojibwa Indians/Caradoc Reserve/Thames River) Page 137/6.

**ANDERSON, JACOB:** (Indian) Age 36 born (About 1815) at River Thames (Ojibwa Indian/Caradoc Reserve/Thames River) Page 137/6.

**ANEMOMS? OR UNEMONS, JIM:** (Indian) Age 80 born (About 1771) (About 1771) at Grand River (Ojibwa Indian/Caradoc Reserve/Thames River) Page 141/8.

**ASKIN, JOHN:** (Indian) Age 49 born (About 1802) at Chatam (Caradoc Reserve/Ojibwa Settlement) Page 147/11.

**ASKIN, SOLOMON:** (Indian) Age 42 born (About 1809) at Chatham (Caradoc Reserve/Ojibwa Settlement) Page 147/11.

**BEAR, DAVID:** (Indian) Age 40 born (About 1811) at Bear Creek (Caradoc Reserve/Ojibwa Settlement) Page 147/11.

**BEAR, YOUNG:** (Indian) Age 11 (See the family of David Bear) born (About 1840) at River Thames (Caradoc Reserve/Ojibwa Settlement) Page 147/11.

**BEAVER, JOHN SR:** (Indian) Age 34 born (About 1817) at River Thames, Mary age 37 born at Amherstburgh, (Ojibwa Indian/Caradoc Reserve/Thames River) Page 133/5.

**BEAVER, JOHN:** (Indian) Age 49 born (About 1802) at London (Ontario) Ellen age 50 born (About 1801) in the United States (Ojibwa Indians/Caradoc Reserve/Thames River) Page 137/6.

**BEAVER, NELSON:** (Indian) Age 30 born (About 1821) at River Thames, Ellen age 20 born (About 1831) in the United States (Ojibwa Indians/Caradoc Reserve/Thames River) Page 143/9.

**BEAVER, PETER JR:** (Indian) Age 14 born (About 1837) at River Thames, (Ojibwa Indians/Caradoc Reserve/Thames River) Page 133/5.

**BEAVER, PETER:** (Indian) Age 44 born (About 1807) at Amherstburgh, (Ojibwa Indian/Caradoc Reserve/Thames River) Mary age 23 born at River Thames, Page 133/5.

**BEAVER, POLLY:** (Indian) Age 70 born (About 1811) at River Thames (Ojibwa Indian/Caradoc Reserve/Thames River) Page 137/5.

**BEAVER? (OR JACKSON) JACKSON:** (Indian) Age 80 born (About 1771) in the United States (Ojibwa Indian/Caradoc Reserve/Thames River) Page 139/7.

**BEESWAX, WAHBINGIE?:** (Indian) Age 55 born (About 1796) in the United States, Maria age 56 born at River Thames (Ojibwa Indians/Caradoc Reserve/Thames River) Page 137/6.

**BIRCH, JAMES:** (Indian) Age? born at River Credit, Page 143/9.

**BIRCH, JAMES:** (Indian) Age 30 born (About 1821) at River Credit (Ojibwa Indian/Caradoc Reserve/Thames River) Page 143/9.

**BOB, MARY:** (Indian) Age 25 born (About 1826) at River Thames, Page 129/2 (Munsee Indians/Ojibway Settlement).

**BRIGHAM, PETER:** (Indian) Age 25 born (About 1826) at River Thames (Ojibwa Indian/Caradoc Reserve/Thames River) Page 137/6.

**CALEB, JOHN:** (Indian) Age 35 born (About 1816) at Blenheim, Nancy age 32 born at Roundeaux (Ojibwa Indian/Caradoc Reserve/Thames River) Page 133/5.

**CAREY, GEORGE:** (Indian) Age 30 born (About 1821) at River Credit, Owanan? (Female) age 29 born at Bear Creek, Nahwangamomeqan? (Female) age 3 born at River Thames, Geo. Carey Junr., age 2 born at River Thames (Ojibwa Indians/Caradoc Reserve/Thames River) Page 141/8.

**CASE, BETSEY:** (Indian) Age 4 born (About 1847) at River Thames, (See family of Charles Halfmoon) Page 127/128 (Ojibwa Settlement).

**CASE, JOHN:** (Indian) Age 30 born (About 1821) at River Thames Page 127/128 (Ojibway Settlement)

**CASEY, JAMES:** (Indian) Age 60 born (About 1791) at River Thames, Peggy age 60 born at River Credit (Ojibwa Indians/Caradoc Reserve/Thames River) Page 137/6.

**CHICKEN, JOHN:** (Indian) Age 35 born (About 1816) at River Thames (Ojibwa Indian/Caradoc Reserve/Thames River) Page 137/6.

**CHIEF, ELIZA:** (Indian) Age 17 born (About 1834) at River Thames (Caradoc Reserve/Ojibwa Settlement) Page 147/11.

**CHIEF, JOHN:** (Indian) Age 61 born (About 1790) at River Thames, Salley age 40 born at River Sable (Ojibwa Indians/Caradoc Reserve/Thames River) Page 141/8.

**CHIEF, TALBOT:** (Indian) Age 40 born (About 1811) at River Thames (Ojibwa) Page 145/10.

**CHIEF, TOM:** (Indian) Age 40 born (About 1811) at River Thames, Shauwashqwana? age 30 born at Walpole Island (Ojibwa Indians/Caradoc Reserve/Thames River) Page 141/8.

**CHIENEKIE? THOMAS:** (Indian) Age ? born in the Untied States, Betsey age ? born at Port Credit, Page 137/6,

**CROW, SOLOMON:** (Indian) Age 24 born (About 1827) at River Thames (Ojibwa Indian/Caradoc Reserve/Thames River) Page 143/9.

**CUTCUT, MOSES:** (Munsee Indian/Ojibwa Settlement) Age 36 born (About 1815) in the United States, Catherine age 34 born in the United States, Moses age 17 born in the United States, Betsey age 70 born (About 1781) in the United States (Munsee Indian/Ojibwa Settlement) Page 133/4.

**DE CARRIE? DEL LANIE? LUIS:** (White/French) Age 23 born (About 1828) at Amherstburgh, Betsey (Indian) age 20 born at Amherstburgh (Ojibwa Indians/Caradoc Reserve/Thames River) Page 143/9.

**DELAWARE, JOHN:** (Indian) Age 32 born (About 1819) at Grand River (Munsee Indian/Ojibway Settlement) Page 131/3.

**DIXON, JOHN:** (Indian) Age 38 born (About 1813) at River Thames (Munsee Indian/Ojibway Settlement) Page 133/4.

**DOCTOR, AHM? (ABRAHAM?):** (Indian) Age 46, born (About 1805) in the United States, George age 10, (The residence of George was at Moravian Town) born at River Thames Township. Page 127/128.

**DOLSON, ISAAC:** (Indian) Age 32 born (About 1819) at Grand River Martha age 21 born at River Thames, Page 127/128 (Ojibway Settlement)

**DOLSON, ELECTA:** (Indian) Age 55 born (About 1796) at Grand River, DOLSON Joseph age 22 born at Grand River, DOLSON John age 20 born at River Thames, DOLSON Eliza age 14 born at River Thames, DOLSON Jacob age 6 born age River Thames, DOLSON Molly age 85 born at United States Page 131/3,

**DOLSON, ISAAC:** (Indian) Age 70 born (About 1781) at Grand River (Isaac Dolson resided at the Munsee Indian/Settlement) Page 131/3.

**DOLSON, JOHN:** (Indian) Age 27 born (About 1824) at Bear Creek, Maria? age 20 born at Grand River (Caradoc Reserve/Ojibwa Settlement) Page 147/11.

**DOLSON, ROBERT:** (Indian) Age 2 (See the family of Polly Logan) born (About 1849) at River Thames, Page 129/2,

**DOULAS? JOHN:** (Indian) Age 13 born (About 1838) at River Thames, Page 129/2 (Munsee Indians/Ojibway).

**DOVETALE? NANCY:** (Indian) Age 10 (See the family of James Wilcox) born (About 1841) at River Thames (Ojibwa Indian/Caradoc Reserve/Thames River) Page 141/8.

**EGG, MARTHA:** (Indian) Age 50 born (About 1801) at Walpole Island (Ojibwa Indian/Caradoc Reserve/River Thames) Page 141/8.

**FINGER, JAMES:** (Indian) Age 23 born (About 1828) at River Thames, Betsey age 16 born at River Thames, Richard age 32, born at River Thames, Wahbaughgee? (Male) age 16, born at River Credit, James Finger Age 7 born at River Credit, Nancy FINGER age 60 born (About 1791) at River St. Clair (All Ojibwa Indians/Caradoc Reserve/Thames River) Page 143/9.

**FISHER, ELIZA:** (Indian) Age 3 (See the family of Susan Waldron) born (About 1848) at River Thames (Ojibwa Indian/Caradoc Reserve/Thames River) Page 145/10.

**FISHER, THOMAS:** (Indian) Age 30 born (About 1821) at Amherstburgh, Lucinda age 25, born at River Thames (Ojibwa Indians/Caradoc Reserve/Thames River) Page 143/9.

**FOX, ELIZA:** (Indian) Age 35 born (About 1816) at River Thames (Caradoc Reserve/Ojibwa Settlement) Page 147/11.

**FOX, EMELY:** (Indian) Age 30 born (About 1821) at Bear Creek (Caradoc Reserve/Ojibwa Settlement) Page 147/11.

**FOX, JIM:** (Indian) Age 12 born (About 1839) at River Thames (Caradoc Reserve/Ojibwa Settlement) Page 149/12. See the family of Joseph Fox.

**FOX, JOSEPH:** (Indian) Age 37 born (About 1814) at River Thames (Caradoc Reserve/Ojibwa Settlement) Page 149/12.

**FRANKLIN, AMANDA:** (Indian) Age 12 born (About 1839) in the United States (Munsee Indian/Ojibway Settlement) Page 133/4.

**FRANKLIN, JOHN:** (Indian) Age 32 born (About 1819) at River Thames (Munsee Indian/Ojibway Settlement) Page 131/3.

**FRENCH, HENRY:** (Indian) Age 28 born (About 1823) at River Thames (Ojibwa Indian/Caradoc Reserve/Thames River) Page 141/8.

**FRENCH, JAMES:** (Indian) Age 22 born (About 1829) at River Thames (Ojibwa Indian/Caradoc Reserve/Thames River) Page 141/8,

**FRENCH, NANCY:** (Indian) Age 29 born (About 1822) at River Thames (Ojibwa Indian/Caradoc Reserve/Thames River) Page 141/8.

**FRENCHMAN, HENRY:** (Indian) Age 25 born (About 1826) at River Thames (Ojibwa Indian/Caradoc Reserve/River Thames) Page 135/5.

**GEORGE? KING OR GEORGE KING?** (Indian) Age 75 born (About 1776) at River Thames (Ojibwa Indian/Caradoc Reserve/Thames River) Page 143/9.

**HALFMOON, CHARLES:** (Indian) Age 36 born (About 1815) at Grand River Page 127/128 (Ojibwa Settlement).

**HALFMOON, JOHN:** (Indian) Age 21, born (About 1830) at River Thames, Page 129/2 (Munsee Indians/Ojibway Settlement)

**HALL, JOHN:** (Indian) Age 24 born (About 1827) at Amherstburgh (Ojibway Indian/Caradoc Reserve/Thames River) Page 137/6.

**HANK (HAWK?) DAVID:** (Indian) Age 23 born (About 1828) at River Thames (Munsee Indian/Ojibway Settlement) Page 131/3.

**HANK, BETSEY:** (Indian) Age 22 born (About 1829) at River Thames (Munsee Indian/Ojibway Settlement) Page 131/3.

**HANK, JAMES:** (Indian) Age ? born at Grand River, Eunice age ? born in the United States, Victoria age ? born at River Thames. Page 129/2,

**HANSTRONG? OR ARMSTRONG? GEO:** (Indian) Age? born at Bear Creek, Page 147/11.

**HAUJEWANJH?:** (Male Indian) Age 54 born (About 1797) at Bear Creek (Caradoc Reserve/Ojibwa Settlement) Page 149/12.

**HAWK, THOMAS:** (Indian) Age 32 born (About 1819) at Grand River, Phebe age 30, born at River Thames, Page 129/2 (Munsee Indians/Ojibway Settlement)

**HENRY, ISAAC JR:** (Indian) Age 35 born (About 1816) at River Thames (Ojibwa Indian/Caradoc Reserve/Thames River) Page 141/8.

**HENRY, ISAAC:** Age 44 born (About 1807) at River Credit, Mary age 48 born at Bear Creek, Charlotte age 16 born at River Thames, Jacob age 14 born at River Thames, Isaac age 9 born at River Thames, William age 6 born at River Thames, William age 4 born at River Thames, David age 2 born at River Thames (Ojibwa Indians/Caradoc Reserve/Thames River) Page 137/6.

**HENRY, JOHN:** Age 25 born (About 1826) at Blenhiem, (Ojibwa Indian/Caradoc Reserve/River Thames) Page 141/8.

**HENRY, JOHN:** Age 9 born (About 1842) at River Thames (See the family of John Riley) (Ojibwa Indian/Caradoc Reserve/Thames River) Page 145/10.

**HENRY, JOHN:** Age 19 born (About 1832) at River Thames Township, Page 127/128 (Ojibway Settlement)

**HENRY, MARY:** Age 19 born (About 1832) at River Thames, Page 127/128 (Ojibway Settlement).

**HENRY? WILSON OR HENRY WILSON?:** Age 20 born (About 1831) at River Thames (Caradoc Reserve/Ojibwa Settlement) Page 149/12.

**HILL, ABRAHAM:** Age 28, born (About 1823) in the United States (Munsee Indian/Ojibwa Settlement) Page 133/4.

**HILL, DANIEL:** Age 45 born (About 1806) in the United States (Munci Indian/Ojibway Settlement) Page 129/2.

**HILL, MARIA:** Age 5 born (About 1846) at Saugeen (See the family of Thomas Wawcosh/Ojibwa Indian/Caradoc Reserve/Thames River) Page 133/5.

**HILL, PEGGY:** Age 38 born (About 1813) in the United States (Munci Indian/Ojibway Settlement) Page 129/2.

**HOPKINS, POLLY:** Age 30 born (About 1821) at River Thames (Munsee Indian/Ojibway Settlement) Page 131/3.

**HOPKINS? JANE:** Age 20 born (About 1831) at Grand River (Munsee Indian/Ojibway Settlement) Joshua age born at Grand River, Elizabeth age born at River Thames. Page 133/4,

**HUFF, ABRAHAM:** Age 60 born (About 1791) at Grand River (Munsee Indian/Ojibway Settlement) Page 131/3.

**HUFF, CATHERINE:** Age 28 born (About 1823) at Grand River (Munsee Indian/Ojibwa Settlement) Page 133/4.

**HUFF? SARAH:** Age 36 born (About 1815) at River Thames (Munsee Indian/Ojibway Settlement) Page 133/4.

**ISAAC, POLLEY:** Age ? born at River Thames Page 137/6,

**JACK, HOLBERT:** Age 30 born (About 1821) at Bear Creek (Caradoc Reserve/Ojibwa Settlement) Page 149/12.

**JACK, NANCY:** Age 50 born (About 1831) at Amherstburgh (Ojibwa Indian/Caradoc Reserve/Thames River) Page 137/6.

**JACKSON, POLLEY:** age 40 born (About 1811) in the United States, Isaac age 11 born at River Thames (Ojibwa Indian/Caradoc Reserve/Thames River) Page 137/6.

**JACOBS, HENRY:** Age 14 born (About 1837) at River Thames (Munsee Indian/Ojibway Settlement) Page 131/3.

**JOHN, DOCTOR:** Age 46 born (About 1805) in the United States, Page 127/128 (Ojibwa Settlement)

**JOHN, JACOB:** Age 43 born (About 1808) at River Thames, Betsey age 30 born in the United States (Ojibwa Indians/Cardoc Reserve/Thames River) Page 137/6.

**JOHNSON, ALEXANDER:** Age 35 born (About 1816) at Sandwich (His residence was at Walpole Island) Polley age 23 born at River Thames (Ojibwa Indians/Caradoc Reserve/Thames River) Page 137/6.

**JOHNSON, ANN:** Age 60 born (About 1791) at River Thames, Page 127/128 (Ojibway Settlement)

**JOHNSON, JAMES:** Age 34 born (About 1817) at Bear Creek, Mrs. Johnson age 16 born at River Thames (Caradoc Reserve/Ojibwa Settlement) Page 149/12.

**JOHNSON, JAMES:** Age 1 (See the family of Alexander Johnson) born at River Thames Page 137/6.

**JONES, PETER:** (Indian) Age ? born at Grand River, Page 129/2,

**KAUZAKA? JACOB:** Age 35 born (About 1816) in the United States (Caradoc Reserve/Ojibwa Settlement) Page 147/11 and Page 149/12.

**KEEZHEGOO, MAHA?:** (Female) Age 22 born (About 1829) at River Thames (Ojibwa Indian/Caradoc Reserve/Thames River) Page 143.

**KEWA, JOHN:** Age 28 born (About 1823) at River Thames (Ojibwa Indian/Caradoc Reserve/Thames River) Page 141/8.

**KING, JOHN:** Age 8 (See the family of James Walker) born at River Thames Barbee KING age 7 (Ojibwa Indians/Caradoc Reserve/Thames River) Page 143/9.

**KIOSQUACE:** (Male Munsee/Indian Ojibwa Settlement) Age 45 born (About 1806) at Amherstburgh, Page 133/4.

**LEAVES, ISAAC:** Age 60 born (About 1791) at Grand River, Sally age 50 born (About 1801) in the United States, Joseph age 24 born in the United States, George age 2, born at River Thames. Page 127/128 (Ojibwa Settlement).

**LOGAN, DANIEL:** (Indian) Age 50 born (About 1801) at River Thames (Munci Indian/Ojibway Settlement) Page 129/2.

**LOGAN, EASE:** (Female) age 80 born (About 1771) at Grand River (Munci Indian/Ojibway Settlement) Page 129/2. Page 129/2,

**LOGAN, ELIZABETH:** Age 50 born (About 1801) at Grand River (Munci Indian/Ojibway Settlement) Page 129/2.

**LOGAN, HENRY:** Age ? born at River Thames, (All others were born at River Thames) Polly age ? William age ? Jacob age ? Hannah age ? Page 133/4.

**LOGAN, HENRY:** Age 41 born (About 1810) at River Thames (Munsee Indian/Ojibway Settlement) Page 133/4.

**LOGAN, JOSEPH:** Age 13 born (About 1838) at River Thames, Page 129/2 (Munsee Indians/Ojibway Settlement).

**LOGAN, POLLY:** Age ? born at Grand River, Page 129/2.

**LOGAN, TAYLOR:** Age 39 born (About 1812) at River Thames, Page 129/2 (Munsee Indians/Ojibway Settlement).

**LUCK, JANE:** Age 35 born (About 1816) in the United States (Munsee Indian/Ojibway Settlement) Page 133/4.

**LUKENBAUCH, MARY:** Age 50 born (About 1800) at River Thames (Munsee Indian/Ojibway Settlement) Page 131/3.

**MARGARET NICHOLAS:** age 30 born (About 1821) in the United States Page 129/2 (Munsee Indians/Ojibway Settlement).

**MASKENOOZHE, BETSY:** (female) Age 45 born (About 1806) at River Thames (Ojibwa Indian/Caradoc Reserve/Thames River) Page 143/9.

**MASKENOOZHE, JAMES:** Age 17 born (About 1834) (See the family of John Beaver Sr.) at Amherstburgh (Ojibwa Indian/Caradoc Reserve/Thames River) Page 133/5.

**MASKENOUZHE? BETSEY:** Age ? born at River Thames, Page 143/9.

**MASKINORGHA, CHICKEN:** Age 48 born (About 1803) at River Thames, Nancy age 47 born (About 1804) in the United States (Ojibwa Indians/Caradoc Reserve/River Thames) Page 141/8.

**MASKINOVZHE? JAMES:** Age 78 born (About 1773) at River Thames, Betsey age 60 born at Oxford Township (Ojibwa Indian/Caradoc Reserve/Thames River) Page 135/5.

**MASKONOOZHE, ALEXANDER:** Age 36 born (About 1815) at Dundas, Jenney age 37 born at River Thames (Ojibwa Indian/Caradoc Reserve/Thames River) Page 137/6.

**MIBNOK? SARAH:** Age 80 born (About 1771) at River Thames (Munee Indian/Ojibway Settlement) Page 131/3. (All others were born at River Thames) Sarah age ?? Mary age ?? Matilda age ?? Oshquotched? (Female) age 50 (Munsee Indian/Ojibway Settlement) Polly age 20, Uwnitchoose? (Female) age 14, Page 131/3

**MINNOW? JOSEPH:** (Munsee Indian/Ojibway Settlement) Age 70 born (About 1781) in the United States a member of the Moravian Church Page 133/4.

**MINTOUR? OR MONTOUR, WILLIAM:** Age 28 born (About 1823) at Grand River, Catherine age 24 born at River Thames, Page 129/2 (Munsee Indians/OJibway Settlement)

**MISKOKOMON, GEORGE:** Age 36 born (About 1815) at River Thames, Sarah age 23, born at River Thames (Ojibwa Indians/Caradoc Reserve/Thames River) Page 137/6.

**MISKOKOMON, JOHN:** Age 35 born (About 1816) at Walpole Island, Polly age 34 born at River Thames, Peter age 18 born at River Thames, Mary Jane age 16 born at River Thames, Elijah age 12 born at River Thames, Caroline age 10 born at River Thames, Joseph age 8 born at River Thames (Ojibwa Indians/Caradoc Reserve/Thames River) Page 135/5.

**MOSES, GEO.:** Age 21 born (About 1839) at Bear Creek (Caradoc Reserve/Ojibwa Settlement) Page 147/11.

**MOSES, GEO:** Age ? born at Bear Creek. Page 147/11, Joseph MOSES, Age 27 born at Bear Creek (Caradoc Reserve/Ojibwa Settlement) Page 147/11.

**MOSES, THOMAS:** Age 23 born (About 1828) at Bear Creek, Agakoon? (Female) age 20 born in the United States, Child age 1 born at River Thames (Caradoc Reserve/Ojibwa Settlement) Page 147/11.

**MOTTS?:** (Male) age 23 (His residence was at Kingston) born (About 1828) in the United States, John age 20 born in the United States, Rebecca age 15 born at River Thames, Elizabeth age 12 born at River Thames, Rachel age 10 born at River Thames, Christian age 7 born at River Thames, Peter age 2 born at River Thames, Page 129/2 (Munsee Indians/Ojibway Settlement).

**MUDFOVE? OR WUDFOVE? WILLIAM:** Age 22 born (About 1829) at River Thames (Munsee Indian/Ojibway Settlement) Page 131/3.

**MUDHEAD, MARY:** Age 28 born (About 1823) in the United States, William age 1 born at River Thames (Ojibwa Indians/Caradoc Reserve/Thames River) Page 143/9 and Page 145/10.

**MUNDWAY, JOHN JR:** Age 29 born (About 1822) at River Thames, Sarah age 25 born at River St. Clair, Sawgossegan age 8 born at River St. Clair, Mah-Yah-Nah-Dezid age 5 born at River St. Clair, Henry Mundway age 1, born at River St. Clair (Ojibwa Indians/Caradoc Reserve/Thames River) Page 135/5.

**MUNDWAY, JOHN:** Age 70 born (About 1781) at Grand River, Betsy age 50 born (About 1801) at Sandusky (Ohio) in the United States, Maria? age 16 born at River Thames, Agoshshee (Female) age 20 born in the United States (Ojibwa Indians/Caradoc Reserve/On the Thames River Page 135/5.

**NAIL, MARTHA:** Age 65 born (About 1814) at Bear Creek (Caradoc Reserve/Ojibwa Settlement) Page 147/11.

**NAMTY-GOOGH:** Age ? born at River Thames, Peskana-Yah age ?? born at River Thames. Page 137/6.

**NEE-GE-JEE:** (Female) Age 70 born (About 1781) at River Thames (Ojibwa Indian/Caradoc Reserve/Thames River) Page 143/9.

**NICHOLAS, GEORGE:** Age 32 born (About 1819) at Grand River (Munci Indian/Ojibway Settlement) Page 129/2.

**NICHOLAS, JOSEPH:** Age 34 born (About 1817) at Grand River, Polly age 32, Page 127/128 (Ojibway Settlement).

**NOAH, JOHN:** Age 28 born (About 1823) at River Thames (Ojibwa Indian/Caradoc Reserve/Thames River) Page 137/6.

**NOAH, POLLY:** age 58 born (About 1793) at River Thames (Ojibwa Indian/Caradoc Reserve/Thames River) Page 137/6.

**OJIBOWAQUA:** Age 20 (Female) born (About 1831) at River St. Clair, (Ojibwa Indian/Caradoc Reserve/Thames River) Page 143/9.

**OJIBWA, MARY:** Age 80 born (About 1771) in the United States (Ojibwa Indian/Caradoc Reserve/Thames River) Page 141/8.

**ONEIDA, CATHERINE:** Age 10 born (About 1841) at River Thames (Munsee Indian/Ojibway Settlement) Page 131/3.

**PAUL? (PACEL?) NANCY:** Age 50 born (About 1801) at River Thames (Ojibwa Indian/Caradoc Reserve/Thames River) Page 137/6.

**PETEE-WE-GISHEGOGNEE?:** Age ? born at River Thames, Quakauhbonoqua age ? born at River Thames. Page 137/6.

**PETERS, PETER:** Age ? born at Grand River, Page 129/2.

**PONEY OR TONEY, GEORGE:** Age 47 born (About 1804) at Grand River Page 129/2 (Munsee Indians/Ojibway Settlement).

**PO-QUAH-KO-NE-GUN?:** (Male) Age 32 born (About 1819) in the United States, Betsey age 42 born at Walpole Island, Hasmon? or Casmon? age 5 born at River Thames, Betsey age 2 born at River Thames (Ojibwa Indian/Caradoc Reserve/Thames River) Page 137/6.

**POWLIS, JOHN:** Age ? born at River Thames, Page 133/4.

**QUILL? BETSEY:** Age 50 born (About 1801) at River Thames (Ojibwa Indian/Caradoc Reserve/Thames River) Page 137/6.

**RACOON, ABAJAIH:** Age ? born at River Thames, Peter age ? Page 141/8.

**RACOON, JOHN:** Age 55 born (About 1776) at River Thames (Ojibwa Indian/Caradoc Reserve/River Thames) Page 135/5.

**RILEY, JAMES:** Age 30 born (About 1821) at River Thames (Ojibwa Indian/Caradoc Reserve/Thames River) Page 145/10.

**RILEY, JOHN:** Age 38 born (About 1813) at Amherstburgh, Betsey age 32 born at Sandwich, Nancy age 17 born at River Thames, David age 13 born at River Thames, Joseph age 10 born at River Thames (Ojibwa Indians/Caradoc Reserve/Thames River) Page 145/10.

**RILEY, TIFFINY:** Age 7 (See the family of James Riley) born at River Thames (Ojibwa Indian/Caradoc Reserve/Thames River) Page 145/10.

**SAMUEL, JOHN:** Age 6 born at River Thames (See the family of Mary Samuel) Page 127/128.

**SAMUEL, MARY:** Age 39 born (About 1812) at River Thames, Page 127/128 (Munsee Indian/Ojibway Settlement).

**SCOTHMAN? PAUL:** (Indian) Age 2 born at River Thames (See the family of Betsey Wolfe) Page 127/128 (Munsee Indian/Ojibway Settlement).

**SENECA, JOHN:** (Indian) Age 30 born (About 1821) at River Thames (Ojibwa Indian/Caradoc Reserve/Thames River) Page 145/10.

**SENECA, PETER:** (Indian) Age 32 born (About 1819) at River Thames Hannah age 30 born at River Thames, (Ojibwa Indian/Caradoc Reserve/Thames River) Page 137/6.

**SENECA, POLLY:** (Indian) Age 43 born (About 1808) at Walpole Island (Ojibwa Indian/Caradoc Reserve/Thames River) Page 145/10.

**SHAUWUNAUHORY?:** (Male Indian) Age 57 born (About 1794) at Bear Creek, Mrs. Shauwunauhory? age 36 born at Walpole Island, Nausochuhoung (Male) age 18 born at Bear Creek, Pauzmaqoud? (Male) age 13, born at River Thames, Baujanbun (Males) age 90 born at River Thames (Caradoc Reserve/Ojibwa Settlement) Page 149/12.

**SIMON, BETSEY:** (Indian) Age 20 born (About 1831) at River Thames (Ojibwa Indian/Caradoc Reserve/Thames River) Page 145/10.

**SIMON, JOHN:** (Indian) Age 23 born (About 1828) at River Thames (Ojibwa Indian/Caradoc Reserve/Thames River) Page 145/10.

**SIMON, PETER SR:** (Indian) Age 65 born (About 1786) at Long Point, Lucy age 45 born at River Thames, Peter age 25 born at River Thames (Ojibwa Indians/Caradoc Reserve/Thames River) Page 145/10.

**SKANADO, EDWARD:** (Indian) Age 27, born (About 1824) in the United States, Haneha? or Hanha? (Female) age 26, born at River Thames, Hanna age 8, born at River Thames, Abraham age 6, born at River Thames, Sampson age born at River Thames. Page 127/128 (Munsee Indians/Ojibwa Settlement).

**SMITH, ELIZA:** (Indian) Age 7 (See the family of Tahjreohejewon?) born at Round O.? Jane age 1 born at River Thames (Ojibwa Indians/Caradoc Reserve/Thames River) Page 137/6.

**SMITH, OLA?:** (Male Indian) Age 80 born (About 1771) at River Thames (Ojibwa Indian/Caradoc Reserve/Thames River) Page 143/9.

**SNAKE, CHARLES:** (Indian) Age 14 born (About 1837) at River Thames (Munsee Indian/Ojibway Settlement) Page 131/3.

**SNAKE, JAMES:** (Indian) Age 70 born (About 1781) in the United States, Fanny age 40 born at Amherstburg (Munsee Indians/Ojibway Settlement) Page 133/4.

**SNAKE, JOHN:** (Indian) Age 38, born (About 1813) at Grand River, Page 129/2 (Munsee Indians/Ojibway Settlement).

**SNAKE, REBECCA:** (Indian) Age 24 born (About 1827) at Grand River, Peter born at River Thames Page 129/2, (Munsee Indians/Ojibway Settlement).

**SNAKE, SHOEMAKER:** (Indian) Age 50 born (About 1801) in the United States, Page 127/128 (Munsee Indians/Ojibway Settlement).

**SNAKE, THOMAS:** (Indian) Age 60 born (About 1791) at Amhertsburgh (Munsee Indians/Ojibway Settlement) Lucy age ? born at River Thames, Page 131/3.

**SNAKE, WILLIAM:** (Indian) Age 2, born (About 1849) at River Thames, Page 129/2 (Munsee Indians/Ojibway Settlement). See the family of Mary Bob.

**SUNDAY, JOHN**: Age 56 born (About 1795) in the United States (A Minister) a member of the Methodist Church, Mary age 50 born at Tocut? John age 12 born at Rice Lake, Dove age 8 born at Rice Lake, James age 2 born at Rice Lake (Ojibwa Indians/Caradoc Reserve/Thames River) Page 145/10.

**TANPEOHEJEWON?**: (Indian) Age ? born at Grand River, Page 137/6.

**THOMAS, JAMES**: Age 68 born (About 1783) at Grand River Township, Peggy age 68 born in Grand River Township, James Jr. age 31 born at Dundas Township, Catherine age 8 born at Grand River Township (All others were born at Grand River) a daughter not named age 7 Sarah age 3 Angeline age 3 (Ojibwa Indians/Caradoc Reserve/Thames River) Page 133/5.

**THOMAS, JOSHUA**: Age ? born at River Thames, (See the Family of Seinekie Thomas? or Seinekie Thomas?. Page 137/6.

**THOMPSON**: Age ? born at Bear Creek, Kabake age ? , born at River Thames, Kuzabenas born at River Thames. Page 149/12.

**TIMOTHY, HENRY**: Age 12 born (About 1849) at River Thames Page 127/128 (Munsee Indians/Ojibway Settlement).

**TOM, JOSEPH**: Age 100 born (About 1751) in the United States (Munsee Indian/Ojibway Settlement) Page 133/4.

**TOM, MARY**: Age 20 born (About 1831) at Grand River (Munsee Indians/Ojibway Settlement) Page 133/4.

**TOMICO, GEO**: age 25 born (About 1826) at River Thames (Ojibwa Indian/Caradoc Reserve/Thames River) Page 141/8.

**TOMICO, JOHN**: Age 56 born (About 1795) at River Thames, Mary age 38 born in the United States, Joseph age 14 born at River Thames (Ojibwa Indians/Caradoc Reserve/Thames River) Page 137/6.

**TOMICO? RUBEN**: Age 27 born (About 1824) at River Thames, Elizabeth age 24 born at Grand River (Ojibwa Indian/Caradoc Reserve/Thames River) Page 137/6. Also Page 139/7.

**TURKEY, THOMAS**: Age 46 born (About 1805) at River Thames (Munsee Indian/Ojibway Settlement) Page 133/4.

**TURNER, MOSES**: Age 6 (See the family of Martha Egg) born at River Thames, a TURNER Sally age 6 born at River Thames (Ojibwa Indians/Caradoc Reserve/River Thames) Page 141/8.

**TURNER? EPHRAIM**: Age 35 born (About 1816) in the United States (Ojibwa Indian/Caradoc Reserve/Thames River) Page 137/6.

**WALDRON, SUSAN**: Age 61 born (About 1790) in the United States (Ojibwa Indian/Caradoc Reserve/Thames River) Page 145/10.

**WALKER, JIM**: Age 34 born (About 1817) at River Thames (Caradoc Reserve/Ojibwa Settlement) Page 149/12.

**WALKER, OLD:** Age 70 born (About 1781) at River Thames, James age 30 born at River Thames (Ojibwa Indians/Caradoc Reserve/Thames River) Page 143/9.

**WAMKEEGOOGH?:** (Male) Age 60 born (About 1791) at River Thames (Ojibwa Indian/Caradoc Reserve/Thames River) Page 139/7.

**WAMPUM, JOHN:** Age 34, born (About 1817) at the River Thames, Catherine age 27, Page 127/128, (Munsee Indians/Ojibwa Settlement).

**WAMPUN, RICH'D:** Age 16 born (About 1835) at River Thames (Munsee Indian/Ojibwa Settlement) Page 133/4.

**WAUCAUSH? JOHN J.:** Age ? born at River Thames, Anna age ? born at Sandwich (Ojibwa Indians/Caradoc Reserve/Thames River) Page 145/10.

**WAWCOSH, THOMAS:** Age 70 born (About 1781) in the United States, Nancy age 55 born at London (Ontario) James age ? born at Chatham (Ontario) William age ? born at Sandwich (Ontario) Nancy age ? born at River Thames, Wesley age ? born at River Thames (Ojibway Indians/Caradoc Reserve/Thames River) Page 133/5.

**WHITELOON, JOHN:** Age 38 born (About 1813) at Chatham, Mrs. Whiteloon age 30 born at Bear Creek, Kiesheshouy age 10 born at Grand River, Wm.? Whiteloon age 13 born at River Thames, Saugawa? age 9, born at River Thames (Caradoc Reserve/Ojibwa Settlement) Page 147/11.

**WHITELOON, JOHN:** Age 20 born (About 1831) at Walpole Island, Margaret age 30 born at River Thames (Ojibwa Indians/Caradoc Reserve/Thames River) Page 143/9.

**WHITELOON, SIMON:** Age 51 born (About 1800) at Bear Creek, Betsey age 52 born at Bear Creek, Nancy age 10 born at River Thames (Ojibwa Indians/Caradoc Reserve/Thames River) Page 143/9.

**WHITELOON, THOMAS:** Age 60 born (About 1791) in the United States, Mrs. Whiteloon age 55 born in the United States (Caradoc Reserve/Ojibwa Settlement) Page 147/11.

**WICK, MR:** Age 40 born (About 1811) in the United States, Mrs. Wick age 38 born at Amherstburgh, (Caradoc Reserve/Ojibwa Settlement) Page 149/12.

**WILCOX, JAMES:** Age 46 born (About 1805) at River Thames, Polly age 45 born at Walpole Island (Ojibwa Indians/Caradoc Reserve/Thames River) Page 141/8.

**WILLIAM, JOHN:** Age 50 born (About 1801) at Grand River (Munsee Indian/Ojibway Settlement) Page 131/3.

**WILLIAMS, JOHN:** Age 77 born (About 1774) in the United States, Polley age 80 born (About 1771) at River Thames (Ojibwa Indian/Caradoc Reserve/Thames River) Page 141/8.

**WILLIAMS, JOHN:** (Indian) Age ? born in the United States, a member of the Methodist Church, Polly age born at River Thames. Page 141/8.

**WILSON, GEORGE:** Age 4 (See the family of Mary Tom) born at Grand River (Munsee Indian/Ojibway Settlement) Page 133/4.

**WILSON, JOHN:** Age 50 born (About 1801) at River Thames, Mrs. Wilson age 56 born at Rice Lake, Kate age 21 born at River Thames, Phares age 17, born at River Thames, Child (Male) age 10, born at River Thames, Kunjwadau age 12, born at River Thames, Shauwonezanbowh? age 3 born at River Thames (Caradoc Reserve/Ojibwa Settlement) Page 149/12.

**WILSON, JOSHUA:** Age 25 born (About 1826) at River Thames (Munsee Indian/Ojibway Settlement) Page 131/3.

**WILSON, MARY:** Age 50 born (About 1801) in the United States John age 12 born in the United States (Munsee Indian/Ojibway Settlement) Page 133/4.

**WILSON, RICHARD:** Age 22 born (About 1829) at River Thames (Munsee Indian/Ojibway Settlement) Page 131/3.

**WILSON, WILLIAM:** Age 17 born (About 1834) in the United States (Munsee Indian/Ojibwa Settlement) Page 133/4.

**WOOLFE, BETSEY:** Age 28 born (About 1823) at River Thames, Page 127/128 (Ojibway Settlement).

**WOOLFE, JAMES:** Age 24 born (About 1827) at River Thames, Jane 17 age born Grand River, Hannah age 2 born at River Thames, Page 127/128 (Ojibwa Settlement).

**WOOLFE, RICHARD:** Age 98 born (About 1753) in the United States, Page 127/128 (Ojibwa Settlement).

**YAUBANS:** Age ? born at Bear Creek, Kanbuyaubenoqua? age 60, born (About 1791) in the United States. Page 147/11.

**YOUNG, TOOPAISH?:** (Female) Age 61 born (About 1790) at River Thames, Sawiocece? age 10 born at River Thames (Ojibwa Indians/Caradoc Reserve/Thames River) Page 145/10.

**YOUNG? JAMES:** Age 26 born (About 1825) in the United States, Jane age 23 born at River Thames (Ojibwa Indians/Caradoc Reserve/Thames River) Page 141/8.

**ZAUBANS?:** Age 50, (Male) born (About 1801) at Bear Creek, Konbayanbinqua age 60 (Female) born (About 1791) in the United States (Caradoc Reserve/Ojibwa Settlement) Page 147/11.

## MOUNT ELGIN INDUSTRIAL INSTITUTION 1851
### CENSUS ABSTRACT

The Mount Elgin Industrial Institution was located on the River Thames in Caradoc Township, Middlesex County, Ontario. It was founded by the Missionary Society of the Wesleyan Methodist Church in Canada in the 1840's. A note was included in this census abstract. The note stated that many of the children attending the school in 1851 were from Indian families who resided on the River Thames, New Credit River, River St. Clair and Walpole Island. Most of the children were Ojibwa (Chippewa). The following census abstract starts with District 3, Page 123. Reference Source: "History of the County of Middlesex," Canada, Originally published at Toronto and London by W. A. & C. L. Goodspeed in 1889, introduction by Daniel J. Brock, facsimile edition printed by Mika Studio, Belleville, Ontario, 1972, page 26.

**BIRD,** MARY Age 13, **BUCKWHEAT,** MARY Age 17, **BUCKWHEAT,** ROBERT Age 15, **CHEEHOOK,** ELIZA ANN Age 15, **CUTT,** JACOB Age 15, **FINGER,** MARY Age 17, **FISHER,** ADAM Age 16, **FISHER,** GEORGE Age 15, **FISHER,** JOSEPH Age 12, **FISHER,** WILLIAM Age 15, **HERKIMER,** CATHERINE Age 15, **JACKSON,** ISRAEL Age 14, **JIM,** JOHN Age 16, **JOHNSON,** JAMES Age 17, **PETEWAGAZHECK,** ELIZA Age 14, **PETEWAGAZHECK,** MARY Age 12?, **KABAAWH,** MARY ANN Age 16, **KING,** ADAM Age 13, **MC DUGAL,** ELIZABETH Age 14, **MC GEE,** ANNA Age 16, **MIKE,** JANE AMANDA Age 18, **MUSKOKOMON,** PETER Age 18, **ROWLOW?,** JOHN Age 18, **SECORD,** ALBERT Age 12, **SWALLOW,** SOLOMON Age 12, **TOWOWH,** FREDERICK Age 17, **WAWANASH,** ELIZABETH Age 21, **WAWANASH,** THOMAS Age 18, **WAWANASH,** WILLIAM Age 17, **WAWCAUCH,** JOSEPH Age 19, **WESLEY,** SOPHIA Age 14, **WILSON,** FRANCIS Age 6, **WILSON,** MARION Age 9, **WILSON,** MARGARET Age 18, **ZHEZHESHEBAY,** HENRY Age 9

## PRINCE EDWARD COUNTY, ONTARIO
## 1881 CENSUS ABSTRACT

Many Loyalists settled in Prince Edward County, Ontario. Ameliasburgh was the western most township on the Bay of Quinte in Prince Edward County. Other townships include Athol, Hallowell Marysburgh and Sophiasburg. Reference Source: "Illustrated Historical Atlas of Hastings and Prince Edward Counties," by H. Belden, Ontario, Belleville, Ontario, Mika Silk Screening 1972.

## 1881 CENSUS

All of the following people were listed as Native Canadians unless otherwise noted. All of the children in each household had the same surname as the head of that household unless otherwise noted. A surname was highlighted with capital letters within a family entry if that surname was different from the surname of the head of household. A question mark was placed after a name that was in doubt. This census abstract should not take the place of any government or tribal records. For more information write the tribal office.

**BUCK, JOSEPH:** (Indian) Age 40 born (About 1841) in Ontario, Susan age 38, Jakie (Male) age 17, Joseph age 14, Cornelius age 12, David age 7, Jane age 10. Prince Edward County, Ontario, District 119, H-2, Sophiasburgh Township, Page 9/10 Household 48.

**GREEN, ARCHIBALD:** (Indian) Age 40 born (About 1841) in Ontario, a member of the Church of England, Catharine age 22, Joseph age 2, Johanah (A Female) age five months. Prince Edward County, Athol Township, District 119, Page 18, Household 94/95.

**HILL, ISAAC:** (Indian) Age 55 born (About 1826) in Ontario, Susan? age 82 born in Ontario, Reuben age 11, Luisa age 3. Prince Edward County, Hollowell, District 119, I-1, Page 13, Household 64/64.

**MOON, SAMUEL:** (White/Irish) Age 56 born (About 1825) in Ireland, Ellen PENN (Indian) age 16 born in Ontario, N. Marysburgh Township, District 119, Page 13, Household 56/60.

**TERENE, PETER:** (Indian) Age 50 born (About 1831) in Quebec, Catholic, Margaret are 45 born in Ontario, (All others were born in Ontario) Peter JOHN age 17, Rittet? JOHN (Male) age 10, Emma JOHN age 21, Hannah JOHN age 15, Mary Jane TERENE? age 13, Caneshted? (A Female) age 9, Prince Edward County, Ontario, 1881 Census, N. Marysburgh Township, District 119, Page 5, Household 23/33.

**VANWART? WM:** (Indian) Age 28 born (About 1853) in Ontario, a member of the Methodist Church, Jane age 29, William age 10, George A., age 7, Henriett age 6, James age 4, Frank age 2. Prince Edward County, District 119, Athol Township, Page 21, Household 109/110.

## DEUX MONTAGNES, (TWO MOUNTAINS) COUNTY, QUEBEC
## 1851 CENSUS ABSTRACT
## MISSION DU LAC OU L'ANNOCIATION (OKA MOHAWK RESERVE)

A major genealogy research source for the Indians who reside on the Oka, Reserve is the Catholic Church records of "L'Annociation de la Bienheureuse Vierge Marie (Oka, Quebec)." These Records contain Indian baptisms, marriages and deaths from 1721 to 1850. The original church records have been microfilmed and made available for research by the Canada Public Archives of Canada. 1. Consult your public library interlibrary loan system. 2. Consult the Canadian Archives and the Province of Quebec Archives. 3. A microfilm copy is also available through the Church of Jesus Christ of Latter-Day Saints (Mormon) Family History Library Centers in the United States and Canada. Historical Source: "Almanac Historique des Deux-Montagnes," By Giles Boileau, St. Eustache, Quebec, Societe d' Edition et de Presse Messier et Perron 1981, 235 pages.

This Census abstract starts with District Number 6, La Mission Du Lac, Page 1. All of the people enumerated in this census abstract were Catholique (Catholic). All were listed as (Indiens) Indians unless otherwise stated. It must also be stated, that the letters in many of the following names were difficult to read. Errors may exist for some of the following names. This census abstract should not take the place of any government or tribal records. For more information write the tribal office.

**DUCHARME, DOMINIQUE:** (White/French) He was listed as the Captain of the Indian Department, age 87, French Canadian, Agathe Delorimier (White/French) French Canadian, age 63, Louise Ducharme, French Canadian, age 33, Hermine Ducharme (White/French) French Canadian age 32 (A Female) Page 1. For more information about the Ducharme family see the biographical section in this book.

| 1851 CENSUS OF DEUX MONTAGNES COUNTY, QUEBEC CANADA (TWO MOUNTAINS) | | |
|---|---|---|
| AHANONTESE, AGNES (Indian) | Age 24 | Page 21 |
| AHONSENTSIIO, CECILE (Indian) | Age 48 | Page 13 |
| AKASENJ, PAUL (Indian) | Age 43 | Page 19 |
| AMORENGER, PIERRE (Indian) | Age 25 | Page 25 |
| ANAYEHTA?, SIMON (Indian) | Age 51 | Page 9 |
| ARANHIASAKHON, PAUL (Indian) | Age 52 | Page 15 |
| ARISAKENHEN, FELIX? (Indian) | Age 22 | Page 11 |
| ARISKENHE, SCHOLASTIQUE (Indian) | Age 20 | Page 21 |
| ASANNAIEHA?, CECILE (Indian) | Age 24 | Page 9 |
| ASENNANIONT, JOSEPH (Indian) | Age 55 | Page 21 |

| | | |
|---|---|---|
| ATIENNATAK, IGNACE (Indian) | Age 51 | Page 13 |
| CHIBATIKOKSE, ELISABETH (Indian) | Age 61 | Page 13 |
| DE LANGLADE, MARIANNE (Indian) | Age 56 | Page 19 |
| DELANIERE, LOUISE (Indian) | Age 32 | Page 19 |
| HIONONSATARIHEN, GEORGE (Indian) | Age 36 | Page 9 |
| IAHAKIKABASITET?, JACQUES (Indian) | Age 43 | Page 13 |
| JKSESICH, ANGELIQUE (Indian) | Age 51 | Page 25 |
| KAHENTIAKS, M. ANNE (Indian) | Age 20 | Page 25 |
| KAHERASAKS, CECILE (Indian) | Age 70 | Page 21 |
| KAIATAHENTE, CECILE (Indian) | Age 41 | Page 9 |
| KAHIAKHON, ANGELIQUE (Indian) | Age 60 | Page 17 |
| KAIATAHESA, M. ANNE (Indian) | Age 20 | Page 9 |
| KAIATITAKHE, ELISABETH (Indian) | Age 39 | Page 15 |
| KAIATONNENS, MARIE ANNE (Indian) | Age 64 | Page 17 |
| KAIENKATATSI, MICHEL (Indian) | Age 25 | Page 11 |
| KAIENKSIRE, ETIENNE (Indian) | Age 30 | Page 11 |
| KAIENNENHTA, FELICITE (Indian) | Age 24 | Page 13 |
| KAIENNESON, MARIE (Indian) | Age 17 | Page 17 |
| KAIONHATE, SIMON (Indian) | Age 40 | Page 17 |
| KAKIKEKSE, CECILE (Indian) | Age 87 | Page 25 |
| KAKSIRAKES, MARIE (Indian) | Age 62 | Page 25 |
| KANAHERON, VERONIQUE (Indian) | Age 17 | Page 11 |
| KANAKSIOSTA, CATHERINE (Indian) | Age 32 | Page 11 |
| KANATAKONKE, GUILLAUME (Indian) | Age 34 | Page 15 |
| KANATIOKS, VERONIQUE (Indian) | Age 34 | Page 25 |
| KANATSIOHASE, NICOLAS (Indian) | Age 70 | Page 21 |
| KANEKAHES, MARIE (Indian) | Age 52 | Page 19 |
| KANENTAHASI?, M. JOSEPHTE (Indian) | Age 37 | Page 13 |
| KANENTOTON, IGNACE (Indian) | Age 59 | Page 19 |
| KANHOHISON, M. ANNA (Indian) | Age 47 | Page 13 |
| KANONKSASON, MARIE (Indian) | Age 52 | Page 25 |

| | | |
|---|---|---|
| KANONSAKANENHION, MARIE (Indian) | Age 72 | Page 15 |
| KANONTENTE, MARIE ANNE (Indian) | Age 21 | Page 11 |
| KAPEIA, VINCENT (Indian) | Age 52 | Page 19 |
| KAPEIABONOKSE, M. ANNE (Indian) | Age 24 | Page 23 |
| KARAHENTASE, GABRIEL (Indian) | Age 21 | Page 9 |
| KARAKOHARE, ALEXANDRE (Indian) | Age 47 | Page 11 |
| KARENHAHES, SUSANNE (Indian) | Age 59 | Page 9 |
| KARHATIAKS, MARIE ANNE (Indian) | Age 43 | Page 13 |
| KARONHIAKERON, PAUL (Indian) | Age 23 | Page 25 |
| KARONHIARONKSEN, JEAN BTE (Indian) | Age 34 | Page 21 |
| KASAHENTETA, LOUISE (Indian) | Age 40 | Page 17 |
| KASASENNARI, ANNA (Indian) | Age 23 | Page 9 |
| KASEIENTATSI, MARIE (Indian) | Age 60 | Page 9 |
| KASENNAIEN, LOUISE (Indian) | Age 29 | Page 9 |
| KASENNAIEN, ONASTASIE (Indian) | Age 45 | Page 21 |
| KASENNANEN, ANNA (Indian) | Age 24 | Page 11 |
| KASENNARIS, MARGUERITE (Indian) | Age 87 | Page 19 |
| KASENNARONKEN, THERESE (Indian) | Age 38 | Page 17 |
| KASENNISON, M. ANNE (Indian) | Age 28 | Page 9 |
| KASENNONSEN, MARGUERITE (Indian) | Age 45 | Page 25 |
| KATENIES, MARIE ANNE (Indian) | Age 41 | Page 13 |
| KATITSIASAKS, ANGELIQUE (Indian) | Age 20 | Page 13 |
| KATITSIASAKS, THERESE (Indian) | Age 26 | Page 15 |
| KATITSIENHASI, CECILE (Indian) | Age 18 | Page 13 |
| KATITSIENHTA, MARIE (Indian) | Age 16 | Page 9 |
| KATITSISAKS, M. ANNE (Indian) | Age 23 | Page 11 |
| KENISTINOKSE, GENEVIEVE (Indian) | Age 26 | Page 13 |
| KIJIKOKSE, CHRISTINE (Indian) | Age 39 | Page 23 |
| KIJIKOMNITO, JEAN BTE (Indian) | Age 76 | Page 23 |
| KIJUTINOKSE, MARGUERITE (Indian) | Age 21 | Page 23 |
| KIKONS, JEAN BAPTISTE: (Indian) | Age 59 | Page 23 |

|  |  |  |
|---|---|---|
| KIKONSIKSE, ANASTASIE (Indian) | Age 56 | Page 23 |
| KINTSIAKERON, JOS. (Indian) | Age 23 | Page 11 |
| KISECHKAM, MICHEL (Indian) | Age 59 | Page 23 |
| KISETEHISANOKERE, HELEINE (Indian) | Age 38 | Page 13 |
| KITCHIAPIKAN, MICHEL (Indian) | Age 35 | Page 23 |
| KOSENNI, MARIE (Indian) | Age 43 | Page 15 |
| KSASENNARONKSEN, CATH (Indian) | Age 30 | Page 21 |
| MEJAKI, BENOIT (Indian) | Age 31 | Page 23 |
| MERRY, ANTOINE (Indian) | Age 24 | Page 19 |
| MERRY, FRANCOIS (Indian) | Age 28 | Page 15 |
| MIJAKI, FRANCOIS (Indian) | Age 22 | Page 19 |
| MISAKI, JACQUES (Indian) | Age 23 | Page 25 |
| MISKOKSENIMINE, LAURENT (Indian) | Age 64 | Page 23 |
| MOMIEN, M. MADELEINE (Indian) | Age 45 | Page 19 |
| NABANOSEEHKAM, SIMON (Indian) | Age 30 | Page 23 |
| NANAMEKIJIK, MICHEL (Indian) | Age 71 | Page 25 |
| NEGOS, MARIE ANNE (Indian) | Age 56 | Page 19 |
| NIBASIKSE, MAGDELENE (Indian) | Age 33 | Page 19 |
| NIKAIAHA, LEON (Indian) | Age 47 | Page 11 |
| NIKASENNA, MARGUERITE (Indian) | Age 15 | Page 9 |
| NIOHERASA, BERNARD Iroquois Chief (Indian) | Age 57 | Page 25 |
| NIORONHIAHA, MARIE (Indian) | Age 39 | Page 11 |
| OCHKINASENS, LOUIS (Indian) | Age 53 | Page 15 |
| OHEROSKON, PIERRE (Indian) | Age 25 | Page 13 |
| OKA, PAUL (Indian) | Age 48 | Page 13 |
| OKINISASANOKERE?, SUSANNE (Indian) | Age 21 | Page 11 |
| OKITATCHISENOKSE, CECILE (Indian) | Age 24 | Page 23 |
| OMIMIKSE, LOUIS (Indian) | Age 84 | Page 23 |
| ONABANOKSE, CECILE (Indian) | Age 76 | Page 23 |
| ONAKARAKEHTE, IGNACE (Indian) | Age 81 | Page 11 |
| ONENHARISON, JEAN BTE (Indian) | Age 57 | Page 25 |

| | | |
|---|---|---|
| **ONIATARIIO, THOMAS** (Indian) | Age 45 | Page 9 |
| **ONKSETIIO, CATHERINE** (Indian) | Age 36 | Page 21 |
| **ONONKSATKASA, JOSEPH** (Indian) | Age 60 | Page 15 |
| **ONONSASENRAT, MARTIN** Iroquois Chief (Indian) | Age 42 | Page 25 |
| **ORONHIAHASE, MARIE ANNE** (Indian) | Age 60 | Page 17 |
| **ORONHIATAKON, LEON** (Indian) | Age 37 | Page 21 |
| **ORONHIOKESEN, JEAN BTE** (Indian) | Age 46 | Page 11 |
| **OSASAKSET, MICHEL** (Indian) | Age 39 | Page 19 |
| **OSISAKON, MARIE** (Indian) | Age 26 | Page 15 |
| **OTAKSATCHISENOKSE, ONASTASIE** (Indian) | ge 37 | Page 25 |
| **OTAKSETEHISANOKERE, LOUISE** (Indian) | Age 44 | Page 13 |
| **OTERONHIONENTE, ETIENNE** (Indian) | Age 47 | Page 19 |
| **OTICHKSEKIJIKOKSE, M. ANNE** (Indian) | Age 33 | Page 23 |
| **OTJIBIK, LOUIS** (Indian) | Age 24 | Page 13 |
| **OTJIK, FRANCOIS** (Indian) | Age 70 | Page 19 |
| **OTKSIROTON, JEAN, BTE** (Indian) | Age 33 | Page 15 |
| **PAKSAKONA, AMABLE** (Indian) | Age 33 | Page 19 |
| **PAPINEAU, FRANCOIS** (Indian) | Age 45 | Page 23 |
| **PEKITCHISAKAKSE, THERESE** (Indian) | Age 61 | Page 19 |
| **PIKSETAGORNOKSE, JOSEPHTE** (Indian) | Age 65 | Page 19 |
| **PIMATANOKSE, CATHERINE** (Indian) | Age 18 | Page 23 |
| **PINESIBANOKSE, ELISABETH** (Indian) | Age 32 | Page 23 |
| **PITCHASAGAME?, MARIE** (Indian) | Age 60 | Page 23 |
| **PITSESETCHISENOKERE, JOSEPHTE** (Indian) | Age 58 | Page 15 |
| **SAKAKAHE, MARIE** (Indian) | Age 25 | Page 11 |
| **SAKANOSEKAMOTEH, JEAN BTE** (Indian) | Age 24 | Page 9 |
| **SAKASAHES, XAVIER** (Indian) | Age 18 | Page 21 |
| **SAKOSIHE, THOMAS** (Indian) | Age 28 | Page 9 |
| **SANENHASI, ANASTASIE** (Indian) | Age 44 | Page 21 |
| **SASASETES, FRANCOIS** (Indian) | Age 49 | Page 25 |
| **SERACHEBLAVE?, CHARLOTTE** (Indian) | Age 51 | Page 13 |

| | | |
|---|---|---|
| SKAIENTAKHEN, ALEXIS (Indian) | Age 55 | Page 13 |
| SKANAICHA, ANNA (Indian) | Age 66 | Page 9 |
| SKANAIE, ANGELIQUE (Indian) | Age 33 | Page 21 |
| SKARISTOSANE, LAZARD (Indian) | Age 63 | Page 17 |
| SKARONHIATI, JOSEPH (Indian) | Age 31 | Page 9 |
| SKASENNIIO, MONIQUE (Indian) | Age 44 | Page 9 |
| SOHENNES, IGNACE (Indian) | Age 45 | Page 17 |
| SONAHIOSANE, FRANCOIS (Indian) | Age 25 | Page 9 |
| SONDJON, M. THERESE (Indian) | Age 24 | Page 19 |
| SONONKSISE, THOMAS (Indian) | Age 22 | Page 13 |
| SONONSENHON, THOMAS (Indian) | Age 45 | Page 21 |
| SOTERIOSKON, EUSTACHE (Indian) | Age 40 | Page 13 |
| SOTITSIOSANE, JOSEPH (Indian) | Age 45 | Page 15 |
| SOTSIENHASANE, LOUIS (Indian) | Age 49 | Page 21 |
| ST. GERMAIN, ESTHER (Indian) | Age 42 | Page 13 |
| TAIAHANHATIE, MONIQUE (Indian) | Age 36 | Page 15 |
| TAIOKERENSERE, PIERRE (Indian) | Age 45 | Page 15 |
| TANAHARISON, JOSEPH (Indian) | Age 31 | Page 21 |
| TANEKORENS, PAUL (Indian) | Age 22 | Page 11 |
| TARIHARENS, MICHEL (Indian) | Age 42 | Page 13 |
| TARONHIAKEHTON, FRANCOIS (Indian) | Age 15 | Page 9 |
| TASEIAKENRAT, JOSEPH (Indian) | Age 52 | Page 21 |
| TASENNASERE, FRS. XAVIER (Indian) | Age 29 | Page 9 |
| TASIIO, PIERRE (Indian) | Age 19 | Page 11 |
| TEHONTIOHASERE, LAURENT (Indian) | Age 51 | Page 13 |
| TEKAHOSAHKSA, ANGELIQUE (Indian) | Age 80 | Page 11 |
| TEKAIAKENTA, LOUISE (Indian) | Age 45 | Page 11 |
| TEKANATOKEN, NICOLAS (Indian) | Age 30 | Page 11 |
| TEKANENRANE, EUSTACHE (Indian) | Age 25 | Page 21 |
| TEKARAHONTI, IGNACE (Indian) | Age 62 | Page 17 |
| TEKENRANE, EUSTACHE (Indian) | Age 20 | Page 21 |

| | | |
|---|---|---|
| TEKONSAKENNION, MARTINE (Indian) | Age 42 | Page 21 |
| TEKONSENHASI, THERESE (Indian) | Age 68 | Page 15 |
| TEKOUSAKENNION, MARIE (Indian) | Age 36 | Page 9 |
| TERKERHITAHKSEN, FRANCOIS (Indian) | Age 30 | Page 9 |
| TESAHENNATE, MICHEL (Indian) | Age 37 | Page 15 |
| TESANNITOKEN, EUSTACHE (Indian) | Age 40 | Page 11 |
| TIESARAKSENTE, JOACHIM (Indian) | Age 34 | Page 11 |
| TIOHISHON, ONASTASIE (Indian) | Age 20 | Page 9 |
| TIOKENRA, JEAN BTE (Indian) | Age 24 | Page 9 |
| TIONAHASE, ANGELIQUE (Indian) | Age 70 | Page 15 |
| TIONATAKSENTE, BERNARD (Indian) | Age 25 | Page 23 |
| TIONHONTASHE, ESTHER (Indian) | Age 19 | Page 15 |
| TIORONHIATHE, ANTOINE (Indian) | Age 23 | Page 13 |
| TIOSAKATHE, JOSEPH (Indian) | Age 20 | Page 9 |
| TIOSARATHE, CHARLOTTE (Indian) | Age 31 | Page 15 |
| TIOSENNATSON, MICHEL (Indian) | Age 34 | Page 9 |
| TIOTKETSKSEN, AGNES (Indian) | Age 64 | Page 13 |
| TONSATSINE, MAGDELEINE (Indian) | Age 42 | Page 11 |
| TORONHIENHEN, LOUIS (Indian) | Age 37 | Page 13 |
| TOSENTOIASTA, ANGELIQUE (Indian) | Age 68 | Page 17 |
| TSASISON, CECILE (Indian) | Age 25 | Page 19 |
| TSIAKERIIO, CATHERINE (Indian) | Age 31 | Page 13 |
| TSINAKTIIO, MARIE (Indian) | Age 75 | Page 11 |
| WABAMIKOKSE, CATHERINE (Indian) | Age 80 | Page 23 |
| WABANIBICH, BASILE (Indian) | Age 32 | Page 19 |
| WABIKSENAKSE, ELISABETH (Indian) | Age 29 | Page 19 |
| WABISENS, FRANCOIS (Indian) | Age 34 | Page 23 |
| WAHATONTI, MARIE (Indian) | Age 17 | Page 9 |
| WAHONTIONTI, ANNA (Indian) | Age 20 | Page 9 |
| WAKESENAKSE, LOUISE (Indian) | Age 58 | Page 19 |
| WASAKARONKAHSE, M. LOUISE (Indian) | Age 66 | Page 19 |

| | | |
|---|---|---|
| **WASEBANOKSE, THERESE** (Indian) | Age 50 | Page 23 |
| **WASEIABANOKES, THERESE** (Indian) | Age 20 | Page 23 |
| **WASEMIKEK, ELISABETH** (Indian) | Age 42 | page 19 |
| **WATIORHAKSENTE, HYTH** (Indian) | Age 60 | Page 9 |
| **WISKIN, AMABLE** (Indian) | Age 54 | Page 19 |

## LA PRARIE COUNTY, QUEBEC
## HISTORICAL NOTES
### CAUGHNAWAGA RESERVE (MOHAWK)
### SAULT ST. LOUIS DISTRICT 69

In 1643 a book entitled "Les Veritables Mostifs des Messiers et Dames De la Society de Nostrea Dames de Montreal," was distributed in Paris, France. It told about the Montreal (Catholic) missionary plans to convert the Indians. One such site was at La Prairie de la Madeline settled about 1666. The Iroquois called it Kentake. Both French and Indians lived there. Among these Indians were Iroquois, Huron, Erie, Oneida, Onondaga and Mohawk. One source states that the Indians at Caughnawaga were formerly a remnant of a group of Mohawks known as the "Praying Indians," who had lived in New York. Under the French missionaries influence they removed to Canada about 1667. Sources: "Kahnawake," A Mohawk Look at Canada, by J. Beauvais. No further publication information. Henri Bechard,, S.J., "The Original Caughnawaga Indians," by S. J., Bechard, International Publishers, Montreal, Canada. 1976. "J'ai cent ans, L'eglise Saint-Francois-Xavier de Caughnawaga", by Henri Bechard S.J., ed. du Messager, Montreal, 1946,"Narrative of the Mission of Sault St. Louis," by David Blanchard. No further publication information. "Genealogy Index to Seaver's History of Franklin County," (New York) by Frederick J. Seaver, pages. 572, 573, 574, 578, 579. "Historical Sketches of Franklin County and its Several Towns," With Many Short Biographies, Frederick J. Seaver, Malone, New York, Albany, J. B. Lyon Company, Printers, 1918, Chapter 1, page 2. "Father Joseph Francois Lafitau," Customs of the American Indians compared with the Customs of Primitive Times," two volumes (2) William N. Fenton and Elizabeth L. Moore, Champlain Society, Toronto, 1974. Father Lafitau in 1712 lived among the Mohawks of the Jesuit mission at Caughnawaga."The Jesuit Relations and Allied Documents," 1610-1791 Reuben Gold Thwaites Ed., 73 Volumes. The volumes are in the original French, Latin and Italian with a page by page English translation and notes, published 1895, reprint published in New York, 1959, published in 1960 by the Microcard Foundations, Washington D.C., on microfiche. These volumes contain records of the travels of French Jesuit missionaries among the Indians of Canada and the northern and Northwestern states of what is now the United States. It includes information for the Abenaki, Algonquin, Chippewa, Huron, Montagnes, Mohawk, Ottawa and other natives groups. A major genealogy source is the "Saint-Francois-Xavier, Parishe Registers,"(Catholic) 1735-1876 La Prairie, Quebec. These church records contain Baptism, Marriage and death records for the Caughnawaga Reserve. The original records have been made available on microfilm in Canada. A researcher should consult the Canadian Archives and Province of Quebec Archives. A microfilm copy is available through the Church of Jesus Christ of Latter-Day Saints (Mormon) Family History Library Centers.

## LA PRARIE COUNTY, QUEBEC
## 1881 CENSUS ABSTRACT

All of the following people were listed as Native Canadians unless otherwise noted. All of the children in each household had the same surname as the head of that household unless otherwise noted. A surname was highlighted with capital letters within a family entry if that surname was different from the surname of the head of household. Many of the letters in the following surnames were difficult to read. Some names may be in error. A question mark was placed after a name that was in doubt. This census abstract should not take the place of any government or tribal records. If a researcher is in doubt about any of the following names they should consult the tribal office.

**ASENNASE, THOMAS:** (Indian) Age 68, born (About 1813) in Quebec, Catholic, Francoise (Female) Age 59, Francois (Male) age 29, Page 32, Household 143/191.

**BARNES, JOSEPH:** (Indian) Age 35, born (About 1846) in the United States, Louisa (Indian) age 36, born in Quebec, Charlotte age 11 (Indian) born in Quebec, Pierre HANATARIS (Indian) age 18 born in Quebec, Page 39, Household 180/234.

**BEAUVAIS, JOSEPH:** (Indian) Age 40, born (About 1841) in Quebec, Anen (Female) age 32, Page 50, Household 311.

**BEAUVAIS, LOUIS:** (Indian) Age 46, born (About 1835) in Quebec, Catholic, Marie age 41, Louis age 16, Helene age 12, Sawatis (A Male) age 2, Cecile age two months born in January, Madelene KAWENISON (Indian) age 52, Page 10, House 44/53.

**BEAUVAIS, SAKSARIE:** (Male Indian) Age 37 (Born about 1844) Marie (White/French) Age 24, Marie (Indian) age 3, Page 50, Household 310.

**BRUCE, JAMES:** (Indian) Age 33 (Born about 1848) Cecile age 28. Page 34, Household 155/203.

**CANADIEN, ANTIONE:** (Indian) Age 70, born (About 1811) in Quebec, Catholic, Marie age 66, Jacko (Male) age 22, Sawatis (A Male) age 13, Marie ORONIOKEWEN age 25, Anen (A Female) ORONIOKEWEN, age 6, Page 14, Household 67/83.

**CANADIEN, IGNACE:** (Indian) Age 32, born (About 1849) in Quebec, Catholic, Hariwatere (A Female) age 25, Hatonwa (A Male) age 6, Louis age 4, Cecile age 1. Page 14, Household 68/84.

**CANADIEN, JEAN BTE.,** (Indian) Age 38 (Born about 1843) Malvina (White/Scotch) of Scottish ancestry) Age 36, born in Quebec, John A., (Indian) age 15, Joseph (Indian) age 12, Alex (Indian) age 10, Cecile (Indian) age 8, George (Indian) age 6, Thomas (Indian) age eight months, born in August, Agathe MC COMBER (Indian) age 54 born in Quebec, Page 37, Household 171/225.

**CANADIEN, JEAN:** (Indian) Age 34, born (About 1847) in Quebec, Catholic, Marie age 28, Sisir (A Female) age 7, Ignace age 3, Page 8, Household 38/46.

**CANADIEN, LOUIS:** (Indian) Age 30 born (About 1851) in Quebec, Catholic, Marie age 26, Jean Bte., Anen (A Female) Laurent (A Male) age 2, Page 44, Household 201/264.

**CANADIEN, MICHEL:** (Indian) Age 27, born (About 1854) in Quebec, Catholic, Warisose (Female) age 24, Wari (A Female) age 3, Page 61, Household 387.

**CANADIEN, PIERRE:** (Indian) Age 42, born (About 1839) in Quebec, Catholic, Marie age 31, Marie age 31, Jean Bte., age 12, Sisir (A Female) age 7, Calastique (Female) age 4, Stevens age seven months born in August, Page 8, Household 37/45.

**CAPITAINE, PIERRE:** (Indian) Age 25, born (About 1839) in Quebec, Catholic, Marianne age 15, Page 16, Household 95.

**CHARLES? JEAN BTE.,** (Indian) Age 32, born (About 1849) in Quebec, Catholic, Clotilde (A Female) age 26, Page 29, Household 170.

**COTISERKEN? IGNACE:** (Indian) Age 40 (born about 1841) Marie age 27, Page 50, Household 235/307.

**COUTEAUKASE, MICHEL:** (Male Indian) Age 70, born (About 1811) in Quebec, Catholic, Suzanne age 60, Page 58, Household 278/360.

**CTHARAKETE? JOSEPH:** (Indian) Age 30 (Born about 1851) Suzanne age 24, born in December? Page 30, Household 177.

**CUROTTE, MICHEL:** (Indian) Age 37, born (About 1844) in Quebec, Catholic, Maria age 26, Michel age 7, Thomas age 6, Jacques age 4, Michel age 2, Joseph age six months born in March. Page 42, Household 195/256.

**DAILLEBOUT, LOUIS:** (Indian) Age 64, born (About 1817) in Quebec, Catholic, Louise age 55, Moise (A Male) age 20, Page 14, Household 65/79.

**DAILLEBOUT, MICHEL:** (Indian) Age 30 (Born about 1851) Catholic, Anne age 26, Louis age 7, Sawatis (A Male) age 3, Francois (A Male) age ten months born in June, Marie HOHS? or HOPS? (Indian) age 39, born in Quebec, Page 6, Household 32/40.

**DAILLIBOUT, FRANCOIS:** (Male Indian) Age 64, born (About 1783) in Quebec, Catholic, Joseph age 37, Emma age 22, Alex age 20, Calastique (A Female) age 13, Jacob age 12, Louisa age 10, Page 29, Household 128/169.

**DAILLIBOUT, MARIANNE:** (Indian) Age 48, born (About 1833) in Quebec, Catholic, Page 29, Household 171.

**DAILLIBOUT, SAWATIS:** (Male Indian) Age 30 born (About 1851) in Quebec, Catholic, Betsy age 27, Agathe age 9, Agnes age 5, Louis age 2, Moise (A Male) age five months born in November, Page 62, Household 391.

**DAILLIBOUT, THOMAS:** (Indian) Age 30 born (About 1851) in Quebec, Catholic, Maria age 24, Joseph age 7, Page 61, Household 299/386.

**DALAIRE? ANEN:** (Female Indian) Age 40, born (About 1841) in Quebec, Catholic, Page 46, Household 280.

**DE LORIMER, JEAN BTE:** (Indian) Age 32, born (About 1849) in Quebec, Catholic, Anen (Female) age 32, Louis age 12, Pierre age 10, Marianne age 7, Page 24, Household 103/137.

**DE LORIMER, JENNY:** (White/French) Age 29 born (About 1852) in Ontario, a widow, Rosalba (White Female) age 5 born in Quebec, (White) George age 2 born in Quebec, Page 1, Household 3/4.

**DE LORIMER, LOUISE:** (White/French) Age 64 (Born about 1817) Alexandre age (White) 38, Jean Bte., (White) age 36, Joseph (White) age 34, Louisa (White) age 27, Caroline DAVIS (White) age 28 born in Quebec, Page 5, Household 24/30.

**DELILES, IGNACE:** (Male Indian) age 77, born (About 1804) in Quebec, Catholic, Elizabeth age 72, Page 1, Household 4/5.

**DELILES, MICHEL:** (Male Indian) Age 28, born (About 1853) in Quebec, Catholic, Therese age 24, Pierre age 3, Anna age three months born in December, Page 1, Household 5/6.

**DELISLE, ANNE:** (Indian) Age 27 born (About 1854) in Quebec, Catholic, Marie age 11, Louis age 7, Pierre age 11, Page 2, Household 13.

**DELISLE, JEAN BTE.,** (Indian) Age 64, born (About 1817) in Quebec, Catholic, Marianne age 54, Alphonse age 22, Israel age 16, Cecile LA FLEUR (Indian) age 9, Page 28, Household 124/165.

**DELISLE, JOSEPH:** (Indian) Age 61 born (About 1820) in Quebec, Anasthasie (A Female) age 64, Louise TINONNAKIAEN? age 40, born in Quebec, Catholic, Page 2, Household 11/12.

**DELISLE, JOSEPH:** (Indian) Age 53, born (About 1828) in Quebec, Catholic, Anen age 48, Lazar age 24, Andre age 19, Ignace age 28, Thomas age 16, Page 7, Household 34/42.

**DIOME, JOHN:** (Indian) Age 36, born (About 1845) in Quebec, Wesleyan Methodist, Hariwatere (A Female) Age 29, John A., RICE age? (Indian) Born in the United States, Catholic, John A., Thakonwalehenthon age 6, born in Quebec, Page 33, Household 148/197.

**DIOME, JOSEPH:** (Indian) Age 23 born (About 1858) in Quebec, Catholic, age 23, Therese age 17. Page 56, Household 266/346.

**DIOME, JOSEPH:** (Indian) Age 29, born (About 1852) in Quebec, Sisir (A Female) age 20, Marie Anne age 1. Page 1, Household 6/7.

**DIOME, PIERRE:** (Indian) Age 58, born (About 1823) in Quebec, Catholic, Marie Anne 52, Jean Bte., age 26, Felix age 25, Ignace age 20, Athansase (A Male) age 13, Angelique age 16? or 10? Page 1, Household 2/3.

**DIOME? OR DIONNE? JOSEPH:** (Indian) Age 23 (Born about 1858) Theres age 17. Page 56, Household 266/346.

**DOMINIQUE, THOMAS:** (Indian) Age 34 born (About 1847) in Quebec, Catholic, Marie age 31, Marguerite age 14, Cecile age 7, Willamas age 5. Page 40, Household 182/237.

**FRASER, JOHN:** (Indian) Age 29 born (About 1852) in Quebec, Catholic, Mary age 27, John age 5, Joseph age 4, Charlotte age nine months born in July, Page 59, Household 287/371.

**HAHONTIATEKTA, LOUIS:** (Indian) Age 48 (Born about 1833) Catherine age 39, Hariwatere age 20, Hari (A Female) age 7, Agathe age 4, Francoise (Female) age 1, Page 36, Household 161/211.

**HAHONWENTIIO, CECILE:** (Indian) Age 70 born (About 1811) in Quebec, Catholic, Martin KAIOHEWKEN? age 28, Marguerite age 23, Anen (Female) age 4, Louis age 2, Marie age three months? Page 44, Household 203/206.

**HAIERI, LOUIS:** (Indian) Age 38, born (About 1843) in Quebec, Catholic, Catherine age 40, Michel age 12, Marie age 9, Warie (Female) age 5, Page 53, Household 249/325.

**HAIEWATE, PIERRE:** (Indian) Age 29, born (About 1852) in Quebec, Catholic, Louis THAWEHIATIRON age 49, Page 16, Household 73/92.

**HAIEWOTE, HATONWA:** (Male Indian) Age 30 born (About 1851) in Quebec, Catholic, Anen (Female) Age 27, Ignace age 9, Marianne age 7, Joseph age 3, Hariwatere (Female) age seven months born in September, Page 42, Household 194/255.

**HAKAWRENTHE, JOSEPH:** (Indian) Age 61, born (About 1820) in Quebec, Catholic, Elisabelle age 61, Page 30, Household 132/176.

**HAKOIRAES? IGNACE:** (Indian) Age 30 (Born about 1851) Marianne age 22, Page 58, Household 281/363.

**HAKWIRAES? PIERRE:** (Indian) Age 33 (Born about 1848) Anen (A Female) age 28, Jacques age 7, Anen (A Female) age 6, Joseph age 2, Page 65, Household 322/412.

**HAKWIRARONKEN, IGNACE:** (Indian) Age 35 (Born about 1846) Marie age 33, Sawatis age 13, Michel age 10, Joseph age 8, Marie age 3, Page 57, Household 277/259.

**HALERONIATHASE? JACQUE:** (Indian) Age 25 (Born about 1856) Agathe age 21, Page 36, Household 212.

**HANARISERE, JOSEPH:** (Male Indian) Age 60, born (About 1821) in Quebec, Marie Anne age 66, Ignace OTINEKWAS (Male) age 16, born in Quebec, Page 4, Household 22/25.

**HANATARIS, PIERRE:** (Indian) Age 18, born (About 1863) in Quebec, Catholic, Page 39, Household 181/235.

**HANATHAIEWAS, THERESE:** (Indian) Age 48 born (About 1833) in Quebec, Catholic, Page 26, Household 115/154.

**HANATHAKAIASE, THOMAS:** (Indian) Age 82 (Born about 1799) Michel age 27, Warisose (A Female) age 23, Page 25, Household 143.

**HASEMAIENTON, PIERRE:** (Indian) Age 7? Joseph SAKOKARIAS age 50, Marguerita KAKOHARIAS age 46, Elisabelle SAKOKARIAS age 15. Page 45, Household 274.

**HANATORENHA, JACQUE:** (Indian) Age 30 (Born about 1851) Anen (A Female) age 28, Page 31, Household 135/182.

**HANETHENRE, FRANCOIS:** (Indian) Age 43, born (About 1838) in Quebec, Catholic, Pierre age 14, Oliver CHAMPAIGNE (White/ French) age 30 born in Quebec, Page 44, Household 205/208.

**HANENHARONTENKWAS, JOSEPH:** (Indian) Age 34 born (About 1847) in Quebec, Catholic, Therese age 20, Hatonwa (Male) age 8, Page 60, Household 374.

**HARAKENKIATTE? THOMAS:** (Indian) Age 39 born (About 1842) in Quebec, Catholic, Monique age 37, Jean Bte. age 13, Marguerite age 11, Michel age 8. Page 50, Household 232/302.

**HARONIAHAWI, ANEN:** (Female Indian) Age 53 born (About 1828) in Quebec, Catholic, Louis HARONIAHAWI age 36, Therese THEKONWATONTI age 12, Marie WAIARONIHON age 9. Page 43, Household 196/258.

**HARONIAKENRA? PIERRE:** (Indian) Age 66 (Born about 1815) Charlot (Male) age 21, Page 58, Household 281/363.

**HARONIAWAKON, JOSEPH:** (Indian) Age 30 born (About 1851) in Quebec, Catholic, Marie age 23, Thomas age 2. Page 38, Household 173/227.

**HARONIOWANE, CHARLES:** (Male Indian) Age 57 (Born about 1824) Warianna? (Female) age 52. Page 22, Household 97/129.

**HARONTHA, LOUIS:** (Indian) Age 22 born (About 1859) in Quebec, Catholic, Marie J. age 22. Page 67, Household 333/423.

**HASAKARISON, MARTIN:** (Indian) Age 47, born (About 1834) in Quebec, Catholic, Delima (White/French) female age 46, born in Quebec, Albert age 20, Marianne age 23, Pierre age 18, John A. age 14, Joseph age 9, Marie J. age 7, Israel age 7, Jean Bte., age 3. Page 7/8, Household 35/43.

**HASEKARISERE, LOUIS:** (Indian) Age 36, Waria (Female) age 30 (Born about 1845) Anen (Female) age 7, Marie age 1, Page 50, Household 304.

**HATATON, SAWATIS:** (Male Indian) Age 27 (Born about 1854) Page 43, Household 200/269.

**HATEASERHAREN, IGNACE:** (Indian) Age 56 born (About 1825) in Quebec, Catholic, Marie age 57, Page 66, Household 326/416.

**HATEITION, IGNACE:** (Indian) Age 27 born (About 1854) in Quebec, Catholic, Therese age 25, Warie (A Female) age 2, Agathe THEKATITIHAKWA age 12, Page 51, Household 243/318.

**HATEITON, SAWATIS:** (Indian) Age 27 born (About 1854) in Quebec, Catholic, Marie age 27, Ignace age 10, Louise age 9, Anastasie age 7, Marie age 4, Page 43, Household 200/263.

**HATENHAIOTHA, JACQUES:** (Indian) Age 30, born (About 1851) in Quebec, Catholic, Therese age 25, Warisose (Female) age 4, Michel (A Male) age 1, Page 22, Household 130.

**HATEWORIATHASE? JACQUES:** (Indian) Age 25 born (About 1856) in Quebec, Catholic, Agathe age 21, Page 36, Household 212.

**HATHEWERERATON, JACQUES:** (Indian) Age 40, born (About 1841) in Quebec, Catholic, Thomas JACQUES? age 22, (Indian) Lidia Jacques (White/English) age 24, born in Ontario, Page 6, Household 34.

**HATIAHARONKWAS, FRANCIOS:** (Male Indian) Age 28 (Born about 1853) Cecile age 22, Page 31, Household 138/186.

**HATIAKTAKIE, FRANCOIS:** (Male Indian) Age 50, born (About 1831) in Quebec, Catholic, Marie age 45, Jacques age 22, Helene age 20, Marianne age 18, Waria age 16, Anen age 12, Page 13, Household 63/77.

**HATIENHAIENTON, SAWATIS:** (Male Indian) Age 36, born (About 1845) in Quebec, Catholic, Age 36, Anen (Female) age 25, Saksarie (A Male) Age 7, Pierre age 5, Wari (Female) age 2, Wateri, Koniwakeri, THKAHAWITHA (A Female) age 70, born in Quebec, Catholic, Page 52, Household 244/319.

**HATIOHAROKWAS, JOSEPH:** (Indian) Age 30 (Born about 1851) Warisose (A Female) Age 34, Page 48, Household 290.

**HATIOHAROKWAS, JOSEPH:** (Indian) Age 30 born (About 1851) in Quebec, Catholic, Warisose (A Female) age 24, Marie age 3, Agathe age 1, Page 48, Household 290.

**HATITSAK, SAWATAS:** (Male Indian) Age 50, born (About 1831) in Quebec, Catholic, Agathe age 50, Dominique age 14, Page 30, Household 130/173.

**HATOKWA, SAWATIS:** (Male Indian) Age 17 born (About 1864) in Quebec, Catholic, Page 37, Household 225.

**HAWENARAS, LAZAR:** (Indian) Age 50, born (About 1831) in Quebec, Catholic, Charlotte age 38, Laurent (A Male) age 21, Cecile age 18, Agnes age 12, Joseph age 17, Marie KARONIARORAS (A Female) age 7, Ignace HARONIAWENTE age 20, Page 22, Household 98/131.

**HAWENNAIETHA, THOMAS:** (Indian) Age 24 born (About 1857) in Quebec, Catholic, Anen (A Female) age 19, Joseph age seven months born in September, Page 17, Household 77/99.

**HAWENRATON, MICHEL:** (Indian) Age 71, born (About 1810) in Quebec, Catholic, Louise age 43, Williams age 20, Joseph age 19, Anen age 10, Page 23, Household 101/134.

**HERBERT, ANTIONE:** (Indian) Age 73, born (About 1808) in Quebec, Catholic, Page 62, Household 305/394.

**HITITSAK, SAWATIS:** (Male Indian) Age 50 born (About 1831) in Quebec, Catholic, Agathe age 50, Dominique (Male) age 14, Page 30, Household 130/173.

**HOEROSKON, ROLAND:** (Indian) Age 25, born (About 1856) in Quebec, Catholic, Warisose (A Female) age 20, Michel age 1, Page 14, Household 80.

**HOIEWAES, LAZAR:** (Indian) Age 35, born (About 1846) in Quebec, Catholic, Agathe age 28, Jean Bte., age 3, Page 54, Household 333.

**HONIHAKOTON, IGNACE:** (Indian) Age 52 born (About 1829) in Quebec, Catholic, Agathe KANOTAWAS (Female) age 37, Hatonwa HONIHAKOTON (Male) age 11, Francois HONIHAKOTON (A Male) age 16, Ignace HONIHAKOTON (A Male) age 12, Page 12, Household 57/70.

**HONONRANORON, MICHEL:** (Indian) Age 44 (Born about 1837) Cecile age 39, Thomas age 15, Pierre age 8, Page 38, Household 172/226.

**JACKO, LOUIS:** (Indian) Age 40, born (About 1841) in Quebec, Catholic, Marie age 30, Louis age 10, Sawatis age 7, Louise age 1, Sisir HATOWA (A Female Indian) age 45, Konwakeri MARTIN (A Female Indian) age 13, Page 10, Household 43/52.

**JACOB, FRANCOIS:** (A Male Indian) Age 28 born (About 1853) in Quebec, Catholic, Marie age 21, Marguerite age 3, Page 43, Household 259.

**JACOB, IGNACE:** (Indian) Age 30 born (About 1851) in Quebec, Catholic, Anen (A Female Indian) age 28, Marie age 4, Sawatis (A Male) age 1, Page 32, Household 145/193.

**JACOB, IGNACE:** (Indian) Age 44 born (About 1837) in Quebec, Catholic, Anen (A Female) age 42, Charlotte (Female) age 15, Joseph age 9, Cecile age 7. Saksarie (A Male) age 3, Michel HARONIAWENHATE age 22, Page 60, Household 291/376.

**JACOB, MICHEL:** (Indian) Age 26, born (About 1855) in Quebec, Catholic, Monique age 25, Anna age 5, Thomas age four months born in December, Page 6, Household 27/35.

**JACOB, MICHEL:** (Indian) Age 45 born (About 1836) in Quebec, Catholic, Agathe age 45, Louis age 19, Konwakeri (Female) age 14, Francois (A Male) age 12, Anen (A Female) age 8, Page 44, Household 204/207.

**JACOB, SAWATIS:** (Indian) Age 45 born (About 1836) in Quebec, Catholic, Angelique age 43, Ignace age 23, Joseph age 20, James age 18, Louise age 16, Konwakeri (A Female) age 12, Saksakrie (A Male) age 11, Peter age 9, Page 4, Household 19/22.

**JACOB, THOMAS:** (Indian) Age 23, born (About 1858) in Quebec, Catholic, Mary age 18, Page 27, Household 118/159.

**JACQUES, JEAN BTE:** (Indian) Age 48, born (About 1833) in Quebec, Catherine age 43, Louis age 16, Marie age 11, Louise age 14, John A. age 9, Anen (A Female Indian) age 2, Thomas RICE (Indian) age 26, born in Quebec, Jacques HATHEWERERATON (Indian) age 40, Page 6, Household 26/33.

**JACQUES, THOMAS:** (Indian) Age 39, born (About 1842) in Quebec, Catholic, Jean Bte., age 15, Page 39, Household 179/233.

**JACQUES, THOMAS:** (Indian) Age 29 born (About 1852) in Quebec, Catholic, Lydia (A Indian) age? born in Ontario, a member of the Church of England, Page 6, Household 34.

**JEANDRON, ANTIONE:** (White/French) age 78, born (About 1803) in Quebec, Catholic, Marie (A Indian) age 50, Page 50, Household 237/309.

**JOHNSON, BERNARD:** (Indian) Age 48, born (About 1833) in Quebec, Catholic, Felicite age 34, Page 46, Household 216/283.

**KAEROTONKWAS, FELICITE:** (Female Indian) Age 32, born (About 1849) in Quebec, Catholic, Louis SMITH, (White/English) age 7, born in Quebec. Page 19/20, Household 115.

**KAHAWAION, ANNEN:** (Female Indian) Age 25, born (About 1856) in Quebec, Agathe age one month born in March. Page 5, Household 27.

**KAHENTORETHA, CATHERINE:** (Indian) Age 56 born (About 1825) in Quebec, Catholic, Louis age 22. Page 66, Household 324/414.

**KAHERENTHA, MARIE:** (Indian) Age 39 (Born about 1842) Quebec, Catholic. Page 44, Household 202/205.

**KAHINWINETHA? CHARLOTTE:** (Indian) Age 72, born (About 1809) in Quebec, Catholic. Page 4, Household 20/23.

**KAHONWASE, PIERRE:** (Indian) Age 35 born (About 1846) in Quebec, Catholic, Marie age 35, Michel age 14, Marrianne age 7. Page 67, Household 336/426.

**KAHONWENTHA, WARIA:** (Female Indian) Age 25 born (About 1856) in Quebec, Catholic, Sose (A Male) age 3. Page 47, Household 285.

**KAIATTAKENRAL, MARIANNE:** (Indian) Age 74, born (About 1874) in Quebec, Catholic, Jean WENIENTE (A Male) age 44, Therese age 37, Alex (A Male) age 22, Mathias (A Male) age 15, Catherine age 12, Marie age 3, (All others except Marianne Kaiattakenral were listed as French?). Page 64, Household 313/402.

**KAIENTHASETHA, LOUIS:** (Indian) Age 30 born (About 1851) in Quebec, Catholic, Cecile age 26, Ignace age 9, Joseph age 4, Sawatis (A Male) age 3, Sawatis (A Male) age five months born in November. Page 53, Household 254/320.

**KAIEROSHON, KATERI:** (Female Indian) Age 60 born (About 1821) in Quebec, Catholic, Ignace age 31, Saksarie (A Male) Age 29. Page 61, Household 294/381.

**KAIONHANORON, ANDRE:** (Indian) Age 21 born (About 1860) in Quebec, Catholic, Page 65, Household 317/407.

**KAKARENRAKWAS, WARI:** (Female Indian) Age 54, born (About 1827) in Quebec, Catholic, Thomas KARONIONTIE age 55. Page 50, Household 233/303.

**KAKARENTHA, CATHERINE:** (Indian) Age 57 born (About 1824) in Quebec, Catholic, Therese age 17. Page 36, Household 217.

**KAKEWEONKWA, THERESE?:** (Female Indian) Age 57 (Born about 1824) Jacque age 22. Page 54, Household 259/337.

**KAKIATHARONE, THOMAS:** (Indian) Age 42, born (About 1839) in Quebec, Marguerite age 30, Michel age 11, Anne age 9, Joseph age 5, Pierre age 3, Sawatis QORAKUNNENTHARAKEN? (A Male) age 38, born in Quebec, Sawatis QORAKWANENTHAROKEN? (A Male) age 38, Ignace THEKANIATHARAKEN age 61, Kanathaos THEKANIATHARAKEN (A Female) age 55, born in Quebec. Page 5, Household 25/32.

**KAKWIRAES, AGNES:** (Indian) Age 48 born (About 1833) in Quebec, Catholic, Page 41, Household 190/249.

**KAKWIRISHON, CATHERINE:** (Indian) Age 48, born (About 1833) in Quebec, Catholic, David age 22. Page 54, Household 257/334.

**KANATAKLAS? THOMAS:** (Indian) Age 41 born (About 1840) in Quebec, Catholic, Catherine age 34, Jean Bte., age 11, Therese age 7, Marie age 6, Warisose (Female) age 1. Page 67, Household 331/421.

**KANATARE, CHARLOT:** (Male Indian) Age 35, born (About 1846) in Quebec, Catholic, Marie age 27, Hariwatere (Female) age 11, Suzanne (Female) age 6. Page 21, Household 91/121.

**KANATIIO, PHILIPPE:** (Indian) Age 50, born (About 1831) in Quebec, Catholic. Page 17, Household 98.

**KANATIIO, PIERRE:** (Indian) Age 44, born (About 1837) in Quebec, Catholic, Madelaine age 40, Michel age 22, Marie age 12, Louis age 1. Page 30, Household 131/174.

**KANATIOHARE, THOMAS:** (Indian) age 49, born (About 1832) in Quebec, Catholic, Marie age 46, Ignace age 19, Cecile age 16, Jean Bte. age 13, Thekanioarenkennion (A Female) age 2. Page 15, Household 72/90.

**KANATOHARE, PIERRE:** (Indian) Age 48 born (About 1833) in Quebec, Catholic, Agathe age 30? or 50? Francoise (A Female) age 13, Warisose age 11. Page 33, Household 146/194.

**KANAWENTHA, ANEN:** (Female Indian) Age 56 born (About 1825) in Quebec, Catholic, Hatonwa THEWANITHANEKON? age 25, Agnes age 20, Jarvis? age 3. Page 48, Household 225/296.

**KANENHARONTON, WATIO:** (Male Indian) Age 31 born (About 1850) in Quebec, Catholic, Marie age 24, Sawatis (A Male) age 1. Page 61, Household 298/385.

**KANENRAKE, CHARLOT:** (Indian) Age 35 born (About 1846) in Quebec, Catholic, Marie age 25? Agathe age 11, Anen (A Female) age 8, Maire age 7, Joseph age 5, Konioakeri (A Female) age 3, Sawatis (A Male) age 1. Page 39, Household 177/231.

**KANENTHAKERON, LAZAR:** (Indian) Age 25, born (About 1856) in Quebec, Catholic, Agnes age 22, Marie age 1. Page 6, Household 30/38.

**KANENTO, IGNACE:** (Indian) Age 60, born (About 1821) in Quebec, Catholic, Anastase (A Female) age 65. Page 59, Household 369.

**KANENTOTON? FRANCOIS:** (Indian) Age 31 (Born about 1850) Marie age 25, Page 43, Household 197/260.

**KANERATHAKERON, JACQUES:** (Indian) Age 32 born (About 1849) in Quebec, Catholic, Ignace age 14, Sawatis (A Male) age 10, Louise age 6. Page 43, Household 199/262.

**KANERATHENHAWI? OR KANERATHENHAIOI? CECILE:** (Indian) Age 40, born (About 1841) in Quebec, Catholic, Thomas age 20, Andre age 17, Lesime (A Male) age 12, Francois (A Male) age 9, Laurent (A Male) age 7. Page 17, Household 78/100.

**KANERATIHIO, FRANCOIS:** (Male Indian) Age 50 (Born about 1831) Anen (A Female) age 46, Louis age 18, Joseph age 14, Marie age 10, Jacques age nine months born in July. Page 13, Household 64/78.

**KANETAKTE, PIERRE:** (Indian) Age 27 born (About 1854) in Quebec, Catholic, Warisose (A Female) age 21, Anen (Female) age 5. Page 49, Household 226/296.

**KANETHA, MICHEL:** (Indian) Age 37 born (About 1844) in Quebec, Catholic, Therese age 39, Sawatis (Male) age 10, Marguerite age 5, Pinsono (Male) age 3. Page 18, Household 82/106.

**KANIOKWA, MICHEL:** (Indian) Age 36 born (About 1845) in Quebec, Catholic, Marie age 31, Cecile age 11, Warisose (Female) age 9, Louise age 1. Page 57, Household 276/358.

**KANIONTOKWAS, MARIE:** (Indian) Age 31, born (About 1850) in Quebec, Catholic, Anne age 11, Agathe age 8, Sawatis (Male) age 3. Page 12, Household 55/68.

**KANOKIAKS, CECILE:** (Indian) Age 88, born (About 1793) in Quebec, Catholic. Page 41, Household 187/246.

**KANONWAKENRA, THERESE:** (Indian) Age 59 (Born about 1822) Sawatis (Male) age 15. Page 31, Household 136/183.

**KANOTHAWAKS, CECILE:** (Indian) Age 23, born (About 1858) in Quebec, Catholic, Thomas HARAKENKIATTE age 39, Monique Harakenkiatte age 37, Jean Bte., Harakenkiatte age 13, Marguerite Harakenkiatte age 11, Michel Harakenkiatte age 8. Page 50, Household 232/302.

**KANOWATSENRE, THERESE:** (Indian) Age 31 (Born about 1850) Therese Kanawatsenre age 48? John LEFEBRE age 24, Anen LEFEBRE age 19, Joseph LEFEBRE age five months, born in November. Page 26, Household 115/154 & 155?

**KARAKONKIE, JACQUE:** (Indian) Age 36 born (About 1845) in Quebec, Catholic, Hariwatere (Female) age 23, Joseph age 8, Anen (Female) age seven months born in August. Page 42, Household 192/252.

**KARAKWATIRON, MARTIN:** (Indian) Age 41 born (About 1840) in Quebec, Catholic, Anen (Female) Age 31, Marie age 14, Sisir (Female) age 11. Page 12, Household 56/69.

**KARAKWENHAWI, ELIZABELLE:** (Indian) Age 42 (Born about 1839) Pierre age 18, Konwakeri (Female) age 16, Anen age 13, Marie age 9, Joseph age 7, Louis age 5. Page 35, Household 160/209.

**KARATHOHON, PIERRE:** (Indian) Age 37 born (About 1844) in Quebec, Catholic, Katitihawase (A Female) age 30, Kenniiakaha (A Female) age 30, Hatonwa (A Male) age 7, Saksarie (A Male) age 5, Wari (A Female) age 3, Konwakeri (A Female) age 1. Page 20, Household 87/117.

**KARATONHON, MICHEL:** (Indian) Age 23 born (About 1858) in Quebec, Catholic, Marie age 19, Konwkere (Female) age 1. Page 60, Household 380.

**KARENHAES, ANEN:** (Female Indian) Age 75, born (About 1806) in Quebec, Catholic. Page 13, Household 74.

**KARENHOTON, JACQUE:** (Indian) Age 22 born (About 1859) in Quebec, Catholic, Marie age 17. Page 56, Household 348.

**KARENISEN, MICHEL:** (Indian) Age 52 born (About 1829) in Quebec, Catholic, Agathe age 44. Page 65, Household 316/406.

**KARENTIARAKWEN, THOMAS:** (Indian) Age 47 born (About 1834) in Quebec, Catholic, Louise age 36, Francois (A Male) age 10, Marie age 7, Louis age 5, Joseph age 4 months born in February. Page 17, Household 79/102.

**KARHAIENTON, WAKIO:** (Male Indian) Age 35, born (About 1846) in Quebec, Catholic, Marie age 33, Michel (A Male) age 7, Louise age 4, Louis (A Male) age 2. Page 16, Household 75/96.

**KAROIONKIE, LOUIS:** (Indian) Age 57, born (About 1824) in Quebec, Catholic, Catherine age 50, Therese age 3, Anne HATONWA age 35. Page 12, Household 54/66.

**KARONEAKERON, LOUIS:** (Indian) Age 35 born (About 1846) in Quebec, Catholic, Cecile age 26, Wari (A Female) age 6, Ignace age ten months born in January. Page 36, Household 165/216.

**KARONEONKIE, PIERRE:** (Male Indian) Age 45 (Born about 1836) Hariwatere (A Female) age 38, Cecile age 18, Louis THARONIREN? age 5. Page 58, Household 280/362.

**KARONHIARE, MICHEL:** (Male Indian) Age 37, born (About 1844) in Quebec, Agathe age 35, Ignace age 15, Charlotte age 13, Louis age 11, Sawatis (A Male) age 9, Harenne? (A Male) age 4, Francois (A Male Indian) age 1. Page 17, Household 81/105.

**KARONIAHAWI, ANASTASIE:** (Indian) Age 67 born (About 1814) in Quebec, Therese OSOTIIO? age 55. Page 36, Household 36.

**KARONIAKERON, JOSEPH:** (Indian) Age 20 born (About 1861) in Quebec, Catholic, Marianne age 20. Page 51, Household 317.

**KARONIAKERON, MICHEL:** (Indian) Age 64 born (About 1817) in Quebec, Catholic, Hariwatere (A Female) age 50, Angelique age 19, Laurent age 18, Marianne age 15. Page 46, Household 215/281.

**KARONIARE, PIERRE:** (Male Indian) Age 38 born (About 1843) in Quebec, Catholic, Agnes age 33, Marie age 13. Page 61, Household 297/384.

**KARONIENSERE, LOUIS:** (Indian) Age 33 born (About 1848) in Quebec, Catholic, Marie age 9 born in Quebec. Page 12, Houshold 67.

**KARONIOKARE, MICHEL:** (Indian) Age 24 born (About 1857) in Quebec, Catholic, Agathe (A Female) age 19. Page 37, Household 221.

**KARONTHATI, IGNACE:** (Indian) Age 21, born (About 1860) in Quebec, Catholic, Marie age 18, Page 30, Household 133/178.

**KASAKETE, FRANCOIS:** (Male Indian) Age 82, born (About 1799) in Quebec, Catholic, Angelique age 69. Page 31, Household 139/187.

**KATERAKERAN, MICHEL:** (Indian) age 19 (Born about 1862) Page 35, Household 158?

**KATERITONTIE, DAVID:** (Indian) Age 45 (Born about 1836) Cecile Karoniathea age 88, Hariwaters SKAWENNES (Female) age 39, Sawatis KANASATIHON (Male) age 40. Agnes KANASATIHON age 6. Therese KAIANAKON, age 27, Makias KAIANAKON (Male) age eight months, born in August. Page 23, Household 100/133.

**KATHARAKENIA, FRANCOIS:** (Indian) Age 73 (Born about 1808) Warianen? (Female) Age 64, Page 36, Household 164/216.

**KATHARATIRON, JOSEPH:** (Indian) Age 38, born (About 1843) in Quebec, Catholic, Cecile age 38, Michel age 15, Jean Bte., age 11, Felicite age 7, Agathe age 2. Page 34, Household 154/202.

**KATINONKIE, PIERRE:** (Indian) Age 40, born (About 1841) in Quebec, Catholic, Suzanne age 32, Michel (Male) age 15, Marie age 5, Charlotte age one month born in February. Page 11, Household 51/60.

**KATIRAKERON, FRANCOIS:** (Male Indian) Age 32 (Born about 1849) Agathe age 30, Wari (A Female) age 1. Page 35, Household 159/208.

**KATIRANORON, MICHEL:** age 67 born (About 1814) in Quebec, Catholic, Page 36, Household 210.

**KATITENSERIIO, THOMAS:** (Indian) Age 20 born (About 1861) in Quebec, Catholic, Marie age 18. Page 17, Household 101.

**KATITIAKERO, MICHEL:** (Indian) Age 42 (Born about 1839) Marie age 39, Page 32, Louis age 18, Piere age 15, Hariwatere (A Female) age 5, Marie age 3. Page 32, Household 144/192.

**KATITIIO, JACQUES:** (Indian) Age 35, born (About 1846) in Quebec, Catholic, Therese age 22, Dominique age 4. Page 25, Household 145.

**KATTIARAKENRA, FRANCOIS:** (Indian) Age 73 born (About 1808) in Quebec, Catholic, (A Female) Warianen age 64, Joseph age 20. Page 36, Household 164/215.

**KAVANERATHAINNIE? LOUISA:** (Indian) Age 41 born (About 1840) in Quebec, Catholic, Martin age 21. Page 60, Household 288/372.

**KAWENHAIEN, CECILE:** (Indian) Age 66 born (About 1815) in Quebec, Catholic, Wari (A Female) age 29. page 37, Household 169/222.

**KAWENNAHENTE, MARIE:** (Indian) Age 50 born (About 1831) in Quebec, Catholic, Martin age 23. Page 51, Household 242/316.

**KAWENNASE, ANASTASIE:** (Female Indian) Age 57 born (About 1824) in Quebec, Catholic, Agathe THAHONTISHON age 50 born in Quebec, Ignace THAHONTISHON age 17. Page 54, Household 256/332.

**KAWENNATE, MARTINE:** (Indian) Age 63 born (About 1818) in Quebec, Catholic, Marie age 39, Joseph age 13, Catherine age 34. Page 66, Household 328/418.

**KAWENNENTHA, MARIE:** (Indian) Age 55 born (About 1826) in Quebec, Catholic, Page 60, Household 289/373.

**KAWENNIES, AGNES:** (Indian) Age 62, born (About 1819) in Quebec, Catholic. Page 3, Household 16/18.

**KAWNHANORON, ANDRE:** (Indian) Age 39? born (About 1842) in Quebec, Catholic. Page 65, Household 317/407.

**KENNEWATENRAHA, JON? OR JOS?** (Indian) Age 30, born (About 1851) in Quebec, Catholic, Marie age 27. Page 38, Household 176/230.

**KENTHOKWAKE, IGNACE:** (Indian) Age 68, born (About 1813) in Quebec, Catholic, Wariane (Female) age 59, Thomas age 20, Joseph age 17. Page 25, Household 144.

**KENTIOKWEN, LOUIS:** (Indian) Age 72, born (About 1809) in Quebec, Catholic, Louise age 50, Sose (Male) age 22, Theres (A Female) age 18. Page 20, Household 86/116.

**KENTROKOWA, LOUIS:** (Indian) Age 44, born (About 1837) in Quebec, Catholic, Therese (Female) age 39, Catharine age 22, Sisir? (A Female) age 20, Pierre age 18, Ignace age 14, born in the United States, Agathe age 11, born in the United States, Joseph age 7, born in the United States, Marie age 2, born in Quebec, Marie A. KONORONKAWAS age 70, born in Quebec, Catholic. Page 3, Household 18/21.

**KIAOHATE, IGNACE:** (Indian) Age 50, born (About 1831) in Quebec, Catholic, Marianne age 33, Anen (A Female) age 18, Marianne age 13, Louis age 7, Sawatis (A Male) age 4, Cecile age 1. Page 52, Household 247/323.

**KIOHEROTE, JOSEPH:** (Indian) Age 31 born (About 1850) in Quebec, Catholic, Charlotte age 26, Francois (Male) age 9, Marie age two months born (About ) in February. Page 46, Household 214/279.

**KIAWERON, JOSEPH:** (Indian) Age 62 born (About 1819) in Quebec, Catholic, Marguerite age 56, Jacques age 18. Page 15, Household 69/85.

**KIEROTHE, JOSEPH:** (Indian) Age 30, born (About 1851) in Quebec, Therese age 55. Page 5, Household 29.

**KIKWARONNI, TOUSSAINT:** (Male Indian) Age 35, born (About 1846) Marie age 43, Page 48, Household 222/291.

**KIOHAWISON, AGATHE:** (Indian) Age 31 born (About 1850) in Quebec, Catholic, Joseph age 14, Pierre age 12. Page 59, Household 286/370.

**KIOKEROTE, JOSEPH:** (Indian) Age 31, born (About 1850) Charlotte age 26, Page 46, Household 214/279.

**KIOKOTOKON? SAWATIS:** (Male Indian) Age 22, born (About 1859) in Quebec, Onwari (A Female) age 20, Marie age five months born in October. Page 4, Household 21/24.

**KIOKWARONNI, TOUSSAINT:** (Male Indian) Age 35 born (About 1846) in Quebec, Catholic, Marie age 43, Joseph age 19, Agathe age 15, Catheirne age 13, Lazar age 11, Cecile age 8, Anen (A Female) age 6, Haonwa (A Male) age 1. Page 48, Household 222/291.

**KIORAKOS MARIE:** (Indian) Age 48, born (About 1833) in Quebec, Catholic, Antoine GENDRON (French/White) age 79, born in Quebec. Page 5, Household 28.

**KIOTILIAKHE, FRANCOIS:** (Male Indian) Age 50, born (About 1831) in Quebec, Catholic, Catherine age 30, Marianne age 10, Pierre KIOTITITHE? age 61, born in Quebec, Marguerite KIOTITITHE? born in Quebec. Page 11/12 Household 64.

**KIVEN-KARENTIARA? THOMAS** (Indian) Age 47, born (About 1834) in Quebec, Catholic, Louise age 36, Page 17, Household 101.

**KWANEIATHAIENI, AMIE? OR ANNIE?** (Indian) Age 39 born (About 1842) in Quebec, Catholic, Louis age 11, Marie KARONIAHAWI age 60 born in Quebec. Page 39, Household 236.

**KWANONSESAKHE, CECILE:** (Indian) age 43? born (About 1838) in Quebec, Catholic, Page 62, Household 303/392.

**KWARENIIAKI, PIERRE:** (Indian) Age 46 born (About 1835) in Quebec, Catholic, Monique age 46, Ignace age 22, Wari (A Female) age 2. Page 37, Household 167/219.

**KWATONTIASE, HARIWATERE:** (Female Indian) Age 40 born (About 1841) in Quebec, Catholic, Anen (A Female) age 12, Marie age 9, Michel age 4. Page 31, Household 134/179.

**KWAWAIARONKWAS, LOUISE:** (Indian) Age 67 born (About 1814) in Quebec, Catholic, Marie age 30, Joachim age 15. Page 50, Household 290/375.

**KWAWENNESERONSOSE? ANEN:** (Female Indian) Age 67, born (About 1814) in Quebec, Catholic. Page 47, Household 221/289.

**LACHANTIERE? PIERRE:** (Indian) Age 37, born (About 1844) in Quebec, Catholic, Cecile age 34. Page 45, Household 206/269.

**LAHACHE, IGNACE:** (Indian) Age 30 born (About 1851) in Quebec, Catholic, Agathe age 22, Napoleon age 5, Marguerite age 6, Leon age 3, Francois (Male) age 1. Page 49, Household 230/300.

**LAHACHE, MARTIN:** (Indian) Age 24 born (About 1857) in Quebec, Catholic, Marie age 20, Dominique age 2. Page 62, Household 306/395.

**LAHACHE, IGNACE:** (Indian) Age 30, born (About 1851) Agathe age 22, Page 49, Household 230/300.

**LARONDE, FRANCOIS:** (Male Indian) Age 38, born (About 1843) in Quebec, Catholic, Marie (White/French) age 36, Marie age 17, (Indian) Cristina (Indian) age 15, Palmela (Female Indian) age ten months, born in June. Page 52, Household 245/320.

**LARONTE, JOSEPH:** (Indian) Age 35, born (About 1846) in Quebec, Catholic, Louise age 35, Paul age 14, Paul age 14, Marianne age 12, Sawatis OHEROSHON (Male) age 32, Louise OHEROSHON age 22. Page 47, Household 218/184.

**LATOUR, JOSEPH:** (Indian) Age 30 born (About 1851) in Quebec, Catholic, Delphine age 24, Albert age 4, Arcule? age eight months born in August. Page 36, Household 153/214.

**LE CLAIRE, FRANCOIS:** (Male Indian) Age 25, born (About 1856) in Quebec, Catholic, Hetimise (White/French) age 22, Marianne (Indian) age 2. Page 48, Household 224/293.

**LE CLAIRE, JEAN BTE.,** (Indian) Age 38 born (About 1843) in Quebec, Catholic, Henriette age 33, John age 6, Sandy (A Male) age 5, Mary age four months born in December, Ignace age 22. Page 45, Household 208/271.

**LE FEBRE, JOHN:** (Indian) Age 24 born (About 1857) in Quebec, Catholic, age 24, Anen (Female) age 19, Joseph male age five months born in November. Page 26/27, Household 155.

**LE FEBRE, LOUIS:** (Indian) Age 50, born (About 1831) in Quebec, Catholic, Agathe age 45, Thomas age 19, Sose (A Male) age 10. Page 51, Household 238/312.

**LE FEBRE, MICHEL:** (Indian) Age 28, born (About 1853) Katich age 26. Page 51, Household 239/314.

**LEFORE, MARY:** (African/American Ancestry) Age 58, born (About 1823) in the United States. Page 42, Household 257.

**MAILLOU, MOISE:** (Male Indian) Age 37, born (About 1844) in Quebec, Catholic, Cecile age 35, Marguerite age 4, Sawatis (A Male) age 18. Page 22, Household 94/126.

**MARIS, THOMAS:** (Indian) Age 42 born (About 1839) in Quebec, Catholic, Catherine age 45, John age 13, Marek (A Male) age 11. Page 63, Household 309/398.

**MARTIN, MICHEL:** (Indian) Age 38, born (About 1843) in Quebec, Catholic, Therese age 11. Page 6, Household 28/36.

**MASTOUSKI, JOHN:** (Indian) Age 62, born (About 1819) in Quebec, Catholic, Anen (A Female) age 54, Charlot (A Male) age 22, Katich? (A Female) age 20, Francoise age 15 (A Female) Page 57, Household 272/354.

**MAULEN? MARCK:** (White/Irish) Age 42 born (About 1839) in Quebec, Catholic, Monique (Indian) age 33 born in Quebec, Joseph (White) age 11, Marie (White) age 7, Michel (White) age 5, Sawatis (A male listed as white?) age 3. Page 13, Household 59/72.

**MC COMB, ALEXANDER:** (White/Scottish) Age 27, born (About 1854) Marguerite (Indian) age 18, Marie (White) age 3. Page 24, Household 140.

**MC COMBER, EDOUARD:** (White/Scottish) Age 30, born (About 1851) Agnes (Indian) Age 18, Febe (White/ Scottish) age 3. Page 49, Household 228/298.

**MC COMBER, IGNACE:** (White/Scottish) Age 71 born (About 1810) in Quebec, Catholic, Mary age 66 born in Ontario (White/Irish), James DROGHT age 26 (White/Irish ancestry) born in the United States, Helene DROGHT age 20 born in Quebec (White/Scottish ancestry) Mathew DROGHT (White) age 3 born in Quebec, Mary DROGHT (White) age 1 born in Quebec. Page 38, Household 175/229.

**MC COMBER, JEAN BTE:** (White/Scottish Ancestry) Age 30 born (About 1851) in Quebec, Catholic, Marie (Indian) age 26, Marie (White) age 8, Angelique (White) age 6, Ignace (White) age 1. Page 24, Household 105/139.

**MC COMBER, JOHN:** (White/Scottish ancestry) Age 55, born (About 1826) in Quebec, Catholic, Catherine (Indian) age 51, (All others were listed as Scottish) Constant age 20, Joseph age 18, Jacques age 14, Leon age 11. Page 24, Household 104/138.

**MICHEL, PIERRE:** (Indian) Age 40 born (About 1841) in Quebec, Catholic, Marguerite age 30, Charles age 12, Cecile age 8, Francois (Male) age 7. Page 23, Household 99/132.

**MONETTE, VITAL:** (White/French) Age 29, born (About 1852) in Quebec, Catholic, Anne (Indian) age 34, Alexandre (White) age 15, Honore age

13 (White) Meleia (White) age 11, Clementine (White) age 9, Adelard (White) age 7. Page 9, Household 41/49.

**MONIQUE, DOMINIQUE:** (Male Indian) Age 38, born (About 1843) in Quebec, Catholic, Angelique (White/Scottish ancestry) age 35, Thomas (Indian) age 10, Louis (Indian) age 7, Marie (Indian) age 4. Page 24, Household 141.

**MONIQUE, JOSEPH:** (Indian) Age 39, born (About 1842) Cecile age 27, Page 64, Household 315/404.

**MONIQUE, LOUIS:** (Indian) Age 48, born (About 1833) in Quebec, Catholic, Agathe (A Female) Age 43, Froncois (A Male) age 16, Therese KANAWATSENRI age 31? Page 26, Household 114/153.

**MONIQUE, PIERRE:** (Indian) Age 47 born (About 1834) in Quebec, Catholic, Warisose (A Female) Age 45, Dominique age 22, Anen (A Female) age 14, Konwari (A Female) age 9. Page 65, Household 323/413.

**MONIQUE, THOMAS:** (Indian) age 30, born (About 1851) in Quebec, Catholic, Agathe age 22, Joseph age 5, Margaret MONIQUE age 62. page 26, Household 109/147.

**MONTOUR, BAZIL:** (Indian) Age 45 born (About 1836) in Quebec, Catholic, Suzanne age 42, Marianne age 2. Page 59, Household 284/267.

**MONTOUR, IGNACE:** (Male Indian) Age 56, born (About 1825) in Quebec, Catholic, Marie age 39, Hatonwa age 17. Page 56, Household 271/353.

**MONTOUR, JACQUE:** (Indian) Age 35 born (About 1846) in Quebec, Catholic, Marguerite age 25. Page 51, Household 241/315.

**MONTOUR, MARTIN:** (Indian) Age 28 born (About 1853) in Quebec, Catholic, Cecile age 24, Jacques age 1. Page 56, Household 269/350.

**MONTOUR, MICHEL:** (Indian) Age 29, born (About 1852) Angelique age 24, Marianne age 6, Marie age 4, Charlot age 1. Page 51, Household 240/314.

**MOONS, MARC** (Male Indian) Age 38, born (About 1843) in Quebec, Catholic, Agathe age 37. Page 10, Household 45/54.

**MURRAY, PIERRE:** (Indian) Age 43, born (About 1838) Charlotte age 30, Joseph age 12, Therese age 5, Cecile MURRAY age 61, Louis DOUGLAS age 24, Cecile DOUGLAS age 18. Page 34, Household 156/204.

**NIAWESAHA? FRANCOIS:** (Male Indian) Age 38 born (About 1843) in Quebec, Catholic, Charlotte age 34, Anatasie KAIANERENSTHA age 23 (A Female) Francois KAIANERENSTHA (A Male) age 3. Page 56, Household 268/349.

**NICKERASA, PIERRE:** (Indian) age 25, born (About 1856) Catherine age 21. Page 13, Household 62/76.

**OHAKETE? IGNACE:** (Indian) Age 38, born (About 1843) in Quebec, Marie age 32, Thomas JACOB (Indian) age 16 born in Quebec, Agnes KANAKWINE age 72 born in Quebec. Page 2, Household 7/8.

**OLERIHONK? CHARLOT:** (Male Indian) Age 44, born (About 1837) Anen (A Female) age 41, Anen age 41, Josephine age 11, Theres age 10, Pierre age 5, Louise 7, Joseph age 11. Page 34, Household 153/201.

**ONAKARAKETE, PIERRE:** (Indian) Age 42, born (About 1839) Therese age 35, Jean Bte., age 13, Catherine age 11, Francois (A Male) age 8, Pierre age 6, Ignace age 17? Joseph age 1, Marianne age 3. Page 34, Household 152/200.

**ONAKTOKON, AGATHE:** (Indian) Age 60, born (About 1821) in Quebec, Catholic, Francoise THEHOSENNARE (A Male) age 37, Marguerite age 27, Marie age 11, Calastique (Female) 8, Michel age 3. Page 48, Household 223/292.

**ONARENKENRAT, SAWATIS:** (Male Indian) Age 22 born (About 1859) in Quebec, Catholic, Catherine age 20, Anen (A Female) age 1. Page 55, Household 345.

**ONATHAKARIAS, THOMAS:** (Indian) Age 41, born (About 1840) Marguerite age 50. Page 60, Household 293/379.

**ONENRAKETE, LOUIS:** (Indian) Age 35, born (About 1846) Anastasie (Female) Age 45, Skaweniio? (A Female) age 8. Page 32, Household 141/189.

**ONENRONTIE, THOMAS:** (Indian) Age 49, born (About 1832) Cecile age 30, Mathieu age 8, Louis age 3, Therese age 2. Page 66, Household 325/415.

**ONONSATEKA, PIERRE:** (Indian) Age 56 born (About 1825) in Quebec, Catholic, Marie age 43, Anen age 12, Cecile age 10, Marie age 4. Page 47, Household 220/287.

**ONONSAWENRATE, SAWATIS:** (Male Indian) Age 36, born (About 1845) in Quebec, Catholic, Helene age 35, Marie age 7, Cecile age Seven months? born in September. Page 49, Household 227/297.

**ONWOKONTE, LOUIS:** (Indian) Age 72, born (About 1809) in Quebec, Catholic, Anen (A Female) age 66. Page 11, Household 53/63.

**OOONTHANAWEN, PIERRE:** (Indian) Age 40, born (About 1841) Marianne age 38. Page 65, Household 318/408.

**OOROKEWENTON, SAWATIS:** (Male Indian) age 22, born (About 1859) Cecile age 19, Hariwateri (A Female) age 2, Joseph KAHENTHAKENRA age 25, Louise Manci? or Nanci? age 59, born in Quebec. Page 15, Household 70/87.

**ORIWAKETE, LOUIS:** (Indian) Age 30 born (About 1851) in Quebec, Catholic, Agnes age 24. Page 65, Household 320/410.

**ORONIOKEWEN, PIERRE:** (Indian) Age 30, born (About 1851) in Quebec, Catholic, Marie age 18. Page 26, Household 152.

**OSARAKWA, JOACHIM:** (Indian) Age 37 born (About 1844) in Quebec, Catholic, Marie age 35, Hatonwa (Male) age 2. Page 62, Household 300/388.

**OSERAKETE, JACQUE:** (Indian) Age 65, born (About 1816) in Quebec, Catholic, Elisabelle age 45, Indian. Page 9, Household 42/50.

**OTERENOKTE, LAZAR** (Indian) Age 74, born (About 1807) in Quebec, Catholic, Catherine age 72. Page 12, Household 58/71.

**OTHARAKETE, JOSEPH:** (Indian) Age 30 born (About 1851) in Quebec, Catholic, Suzane age 24, Joseph age 5, Sawatis (A Male) age 3, Hatonwa (A Male) age four months born in December. Page 30, Household 177.

**OTISERIKON, IGNACE:** (Indian) Age 40 born (About 1841) in Quebec, Catholic, Marie age 27. Page 50, Household 235/307.

**OTSITSATEKA? JEAN BTE:** (Indian) Age 33 born (About 1848) in Quebec, Catholic, Therese, age 31, Cecile age 8. Page 67, Household 335/425.

**OWISEKOWA? OR OURSEKOWA, LOUIS:** (Indian) Age 32, born (About 1849) in Quebec, Catholic, Anen (A Female) age 23. Page 15, Household 86.

**PARTUI? OR PARTIU? HOROTE:** (Female Indian) Age 54 born (About 1827) in Quebec, Catholic, Maire age 20, Pierre age 12, Warianna (A Female) age 10. Page 26, Household 110/148.

**PERRAS, ALFRED:** (White) Age 40, born (About 1841) Louise (Indian) age 38, Rosilda (White/French) age 13, Rebecca (White/French) age 11, Marie Louise (White/French) age 9, Alfred (White/French) age 7, Lucianna (White/French) age 5, Sarah (White/French) age 2. Page 9, Household 40/48.

**PHILIPPE, THOMAS:** (Indian) Age 35, born (About 1846) in Quebec, Catholic, Marguerite (Indian) age 30, Marie (Indian) age 10, Michel (Indian) age 7, Anna (Indian) age 4, Chatherine KAHETHAWAKON (Indian) age 67 born in Quebec, Louise SANSORAINTE (White/French Ancestry) age 25, born in Quebec, Medard GENDRON (White/Male with French Ancestry) age   Page 2, Household 8/9.

**PLATE? OR PLANTE? MARIE:** (Indian) Age 44, born (About 1837) Edwige (White/French Female) Age 21, Dominique (White/French Male) age 23. Page 27, Household 120/161.

**PRARCISSE? ROLAND:** (Indian) Age 51, born (About 1830) in Quebec, Catholic, marguerite age 49, Roland age 20, Marie J. age 17, Joseph age 14. Page 14, Household 86/82.

**PUCHEL, PIERRE:** (Indian) Age 40, born (About 1841) in Quebec, Catholic, Marguerite age 30, Page 23, Household 132.

**QAONTHANAWEN, PIERRE:** (Indian) Age 40 born (About 1841) in Quebec, Catholic, Marianne age 38. Page 65, Household 318/408.

**QOROKEWENTON, SAWATIS:** (Male Indian) Age 22 born (About 1859) in Quebec, Catholic, Cecile age 19, Hariwateri (A Female) age 2, Joseph KAKENTHAKENRA age 25, Louise NANCI age 59, Michel THESHOKEWEN age 13. Page 15, Household 70/87.

**RAYMENT, MARIE:** (White/French) Age 26, born (About 1855) in Quebec, Catholic, Philomaine (White/French Female) age 2, with household 224/293 (See the household of Francois LE CLAIRE?) Page 48, Household 294.

**RICE, JOHN A:** (Indian) Age 25 born (About 1859) in Quebec, Catholic, Louise age 22, Louisa age 6, Febie (A Female) age 6, William age 1. Page 58, Household 279/361.

**RICE, LOUIS:** (Indian) Age 42, Marie age 40 born (About 1839) in Quebec, Catholic, Marie age 17. Page 56, Household 352.

**RICE, THOMAS:** (Indian) Age 28 born (About 1853) in Quebec, Catholic, Marguerite age 26, Louise age 8, Charley age 6, Marianne age 3. Page 54, Household 255/331.

**RINFRET, LOUIS:** (Indian) Age 29 born (About 1852) in Quebec, Catholic, Odile (White/Female of French Ancestry) age 29, Louis (Indian) age 4, Rosina (Indian) age 7, Malvina (Indian) age 2.

**ROICE? (OR RICE?) JOSEPH:** (Indian) Age 31, born (About 1850) in Quebec, Catholic, Cecile age 25, Angelique age 5, Anne age 2. Page 11, Household 52/62.

**ROICE? OR RICE? JEAN BTE.,** (Indian) Age 36, born (About 1845) in Quebec, Catholic, Ignace age 8. Page 49, Household 229/299.

**ROLAND, NARCISSE:** (Male Indian) Age 51 born (About 1830) in Quebec, Catholic, Marguerite age 49, Roland age 20, Marie J. age 17, Joseph age 14. Page 14, Household 66/82.

**ROTSINKEN, THOMAS:** (Indian) Age 30 born (About 1851) in Quebec, Catholic, Charlotte age 29, Joseph age 13, Laurent age 11, Alexandre age 9, Marie age 7, Sawatis (A Male) age 5, Page 58, Household 282/365.

**ROUCH, JOSEPH:** (Indian) Age 29 born (About 1852) in Quebec, Catholic, Anen (A Female) age 23. Page 53, Household 253/329.

**SAHAHAWITHA, JEAN:** (Male Indian) Age 44 (Born about 1837) Anen (Female) age 42, Sawatis (A Male) Age 24, Page 52, Household 246/321.

**SAKAHAHETELHA, THOMAS:** (Indian) Age 72 born (About 1809) in Quebec, Catholic, Louise KONWAIAKI (A Female) age 47, Ignace KONWAIAKI age 30, Laurent KONWAIAKI (A Male) age 22. Page 65, Household 319/409.

**SAKAHAWITHA, JEAN:** (Indian) Age 44 born (About 1837) in Quebec, Catholic, Anen (Female) age 42, Sawatis (A Male) age 24, Joseph age 13, Louis age 9. Page 52, Household 246/321.

**SAKAHESE, CHARLOT:** (Male Indian) Age 36 born (About 1845) in Quebec, Catholic, Warisose (Female) Age 43, John age 21, Therese age 13, Louise age 11. Page 55, Household 262/341.

**SAKARAIATHAKWA, MARTIN:** (Indian) Age 60, Catholic, born (About 1821) in Quebec, Marguerite age 50, Marie Sose age 20, Francoise (A Female) age 14, Louise KAIAONWARITHA age 77, born in Quebec, Page 6, Household 29/37.

**SAKOKARIAS, JOSEPH:** (Indian) Age 50 born (About 1831) in Quebec, Catholic, Marguerite age 46, Elisabelle age 15. Page 45, Household 274.

**SAKOWAES, PIERRE:** (Indian) Age 30, born (About 1851) in Quebec, a Catholic, Marie Ann age 27, Joseph age 10, Katis (A Female) age 4, Louis (A Male) age five months born in October. Page 4, Household 23/26.

**SANARIATAIER, MARIE:** (Indian) Age 29 (Born about 1852) Page 65, Household 321/411.

**SANSORAINTE, LOUISE:** (Indian) Age 25, born in Quebec, Catholic, Nicdard? Gendron (A Male) age 19, born in Quebec. Page 2, Household 8/9.

**SATEKARENKES? MATHIAS:** (Indian) Age 43 born (About 1838) in Quebec, Catholic, Marianne age 35, Agathe age 14, Louis age 13, Saksarie age 11, Agathe age 6. Page 66, Household 327/417.

**SAWATAS, JACOB:** (Indian) Age 45, born (About 1836) in Quebec, Catholic, Angelique age 43, Page 3, Household 19/22.

**SHAIAKOKATSTON, THOMAS:** (Indian) Age 37 born (About 1844) in Quebec, Catholic, Marie age 33, Pierre age 15, Louis age 7, Saksarie (A Male) age 3, Sawatis (A Male) age 1. Page 61, Household 296/383.

**SHAIONESAKESEN? PIERRE:** (Indian) Age 54, born (About 1827) in Quebec, Catholic, Marie age 40, Waria (A Female) age 19, Anen (A Female) age 12, Marie age 10. Page 47, Household 219/286.

**SHAIONSATONTI, ANGELIQUE:** (Indian) Age 45, born (About 1836) in Quebec, Catholic. Page 50, Household 305.

**SHAIOWISAKEREN? SOSE:** (Male Indian) Age 46 born (About 1835) in Quebec, Catholic, Cecile age 42, Pierre HASEMAIENTON age 7. Page 45, Household 210/213.

**SHAKAHONTETHA, IGNACE:** (Indian) Age 26 born (About 1855) in Quebec, Catholic, Charlotte age 23, Joseph age 4, Jean Bte., age 2, Page 47, Household 288.

**SHAKAHONTINETHA, MICHEL:** (Indian) Age 30 born (About 1851) in Quebec, Catholic, Marie age 26, Ignace age 6, Pierre age 2. Page 60, Household 378.

**SHAKAWENTELHA, SAKSARIE:** (Male Indian) Age 28 (Born about 1853) Anen (A Female) age 20, Page 63, Household 308/397.

**SHAKAWENTETHA, JACQUES:** (Indian) Age 68 born (About 1813) in Quebec, Catholic, Suzanne age 56, Anastasie (Female) age 27, Agnes age 19, Warie (A Female) age 16. Page 41, Household 191/251.

**SHAKAWENTETHA, SAKSARIE:** (Male Indian) Age 28 born (About 1853) in Quebec, Catholic, Anen age 26. Page 63, Household 308/397.

**SHAKEKAREIENES? MICHEL:** (Male Indian) Age 37 born (About 1844) in Quebec, Catholic, Marie age 33, Anen (A Female) age 11, Marianne age 6. Page 40, Household 185/242.

**SHAKOIANISAKAS, JOSEPH:** (Indian) Age 30 born in Quebec, Catholic, Therese age 23. Page 16, Household 91.

**SHAKOREWATHA, PIERRE:** (Indian) Age 40, born in Quebec, Catholic, Warisose (A Female) age 35, Joseph age 19, Regis age 12, Jacque age 3, Angelique age five months born in October. Page 62, Household 304/393.

**SHAKOTEN, IGNACE:** (Male Indian) Age 40, born in Quebec, Catholic, Marianne age 30. Page 12, Household 65.

**SHAKOWITE? SAWATIS:** (Male Indian) Age 30 born in Quebec, Catholic, Anen (A Female) age 22, Sawatis (Male) Age 4, Warie age 2. Page 32, Household 142/190.

**SHALEKARONICS? OR SHATEKARONIES? RENE:** (Male Indian) Age 60, born in Quebec, Catholic, Antoinette age 58. Page 18, Household 107.

**SHARONIHA, SAWATIS:** (Male Indian) Age 23, born in Quebec, Catholic, Agnes age 18. Page 23, Household 135.

**SHARONKWASKON, THOMAS:** (Indian) Age 59? or 39? born in Quebec, Catholic, Angelique age 35, Page 39, Household 178/233.

**SHATEKAIENTON, LOUIS:** (Indian) Age 48, Page 50, Household 236/308.

**SHATEKARONIES, RENE:** (Indian) Age 60 born in Quebec, Catholic, Antoinette age 58. Page 18, Household 107.

**SHATIENTON, MICHEL:** (Male Indian) Age 50 born in Quebec, Catholic, Marie age 39, Ignace age 4. Page 13, Household 61/75?.

**SHAWENNAKAREN, MICHEL:** (Male Indian) Age 55, born in Quebec, Catholic, Anen (A Female) age 19. Page 17, Household 104.

**SHAWENNAKARON, MICHEL:** (Male Indian) Age 35 born in Quebec, Catholic, Anen (A Female) age 19. Page 18, Household 104.

**SHAWENTHANEN, FRANCOIS:** (Male Indian) Age 60, Cecile age 42, Hatonwa (A Male) Age 21, Saksarie (A Male) age 17. Page 55, Household 363/342.

**SHAWENTIOWANE, THOMAS:** (Indian) Age 20, born in Quebec, Catholic, Angelique age 17. Page 26, Household 112/150.

**SHENRANONIATON, PIERRE:** (Indian) Age 40, Agathe age 36, Jean Bte., age 31. Page 33, Household 150/198.

**SHOHENRISE, PIERRE:** (Indian) Age 28, born in Quebec, Catholic, Cecile age 16, Ignace THAKENIATE age 30. Page 54, Household 338.

**SHOIONIWESE, FRANCOIS:** (Male Indian) Age 36, Marie 9, Cecile age 8, Ignace RAIONTHAKERON age 20. Page 40, Household 239.

**SHONIATHARONANE, LOUIS:** (Indian) Age 50, born in Quebec, Catholic, Elisabelle age 42, Thanekerewas (A Male) age 10, Hanarishon (A Male) age 8, Thiawenion age 5, Jacque age 1, Thomas HIHANNTEASA? age 78, Theres HIHANNTEASA? age 51. Page 19, Household 84/112.

**SHORAKOWANE, JOSEPH:** (Indian) Age 24, born in Quebec, Catholic, Marie age 24, Marianne age 3, Martha age 1. Page 54, Household 335.

**SHOREWANE? LOUIS:** (Indian) Age 57 born in Quebec, Catholic, Marie age 27, Elisabelle age 17, Charlotte age 15, Pierre age 11, Michel age 7. Page 63, Household 310/399.

**SHORIWAIENTON, LOUIS:** (Indian) Age 44, Louise (A Female) age 42, Anen (A Female) age 14, Cecile KAKENTHAKWAS age 4. Page 38, Household 174/228.

**SHORONKWASKON, THOMAS:** (Indian) Age 39 born in Quebec, Catholic, Angelique age 35, Pierre age 18, Sawatis (A Male) age 16, Agathe age 13, Anen age 4. Page 39, Household 178/232.

**SHORONWESE? FRANCOIS:** (Indian) Age 36 born in Quebec, Catholic, Marie age 9, Cecile age 8. Page 40, Household 239.

**SHOSHAWETSE, PIERRE:** (Indian) Age 25 born in Quebec, Catholic, Maria age 20, Joseph age 1. Page 45, Household 276.

**SHOTERAKWEN, LAZAR:** (Indian) Age 23 born in Quebec, Catholic, Wari (A Female) age 18. Page 41, Household 250.

**SHOTIOWANE, LOUIS:** (Indian) Age 44, born in Quebec, Catholic, Wari (A Female) age 39, Louise age 12, Cecile age 10. Page 41, Household 189/248.

**SHOTOKWEN, JOSEPH:** (Indian) Age 49 born in Quebec, Catholic, Agathe age 42, Michel age 20, Sawatis (A Male) age 15, Marianne age 8, Francois age 5, Louis age 2. Page 43, Household 198/261.

**SKAHONTHARIAKON, SAKRARIE?** (Male Indian) Age 30 born in Quebec, Catholic, Marie age 26, Pierre age 8, Joseph age 6, Rosina age 4, Anen (A Female) age three months born in January, Pierre THEWASKWENTON age 79 born in Quebec, Charlotte THEWASKWENTON age 70 born in Quebec. Page 46, Household 213/278.

**SKAIENTHAKEN, JACQUE:** (Indian) Age 60, born in Quebec, Catholic, Marie Age 76, born in Quebec, Catholic. Page 40, Household 186/243.

**SKAIONHATI, SOSE:** (Indian) Age 43, born in Quebec, Catholic, Charlotte age 41, Jacques MAILLOUX (Indian) age 45, born in Quebec, Catholic. Page 7 Household 31/39.

**SKAKAHONTINETHA, MICHEL:** (Indian) Age 30, Marie age 26, Page 60, Household 292/377.

**SKAKORENNAKETE, SAKSAKRIE:** (Male Indian) Age 25 born in Quebec, Catholic, Marie age 20, Pierre age 1. Page 10, Household 46/55.

**SKAKOTIN, IGNACE:** (Male Indian) Age 40, born in Quebec, Catholic, Marianne age 30 born in Quebec. Page 12, Household 65.

**SKANENROTI, LOUIS:** (Indian) Age 56 born in Quebec, Catholic, Warianne (A Female) age 52, Mathias (Male) age 16. Page 40, Household 184/240.

**SKANONTON, IGNACE:** (Indian) Age 31 born in Quebec, Catholic, Agathe age 27, Kasennison (A Female) age 4, Angelique age 2. Page 18, Household 108.

**SKAWENNIIE, CATHERINE:** (Indian) Age 24? Wari (Female) 14, Pierre SAKOKENNI age 83, Wari (A Female) Age 83. Page 42, Household 193/253.

**SKAWENNIIO, CATHERINE:** (Indian) Age 44 born in Quebec, Catholic, Wari (Female) age 14, Pierre SAKOKINNI age 83 born in Quebec, Wari SAKOKINNI (A Female) age 83 born in Quebec, Page 42, Household 193/253.

**SOKETOWANE, PIERRE:** (Indian) Age 49, born in Quebec, Catholic, Agathe age 44. page 66, Household 329/419.

**SPAHONTHARIAKON, SAKSARIE?** (Male Indian) Age 30, Marie (White/Scottish) age 26, (All other listed as Indians) Pierre age 8, Joseph age 6, Rosina age 4, Anen (Female) Age three months, born in January, Pierre THEWASKWENTON age 79, Charlotte Thewaskwenton age 70? Page 46, Household 213/278.

**STACEY, PIERRE:** (Indian) Age 38, born in Quebec, Catholic, Marie age 34. Page 3, Household 19.

**STACY, JEAN BTE.,** (Indian) Age 29, Rosina age 23, Jean Bte. age 4, Alex age 2. Page 35, Household 158/206.

**STACY, JOSEPH:** (Indian) Age 34, born in Quebec, Virginie (French/White) age 29, born in Quebec, Marie age 11 (Indian) Joseph age 7 (Indian) Jean Bte. JACOB (Indian) age 84 born in Quebec, Marie JACOB (White/ French Ancestry) age 64 born in Quebec. Page 8/9, Household 39/47.

**STUMP, WILLIAM:** (White/German Ancestry) Age 40 Born in the United States, Agathe (Indian) age 28 born in Quebec (All others were listed as of German origins born in Quebec) Marie J. age 11, Therese age 10, Louise age 12. Page 68, Household 337/427.

**THAHATIE, JACQUE:** (Indian) Age 47 born in Quebec, Catholic, Anen (A Female) Age 38. Page 45, Household 211/275.

**THAHENTETHA? MOISE:** (Male Indian) Age 43 born in Quebec, Catholic, Cecile age 46, Hatonwa age 12, Sawatis (A Male) age 10. Page 63, Household 307/396.

**THAHONSETE, PIERRE:** (Indian) Age 32, born in Quebec, Catholic, Katich (A Female) age 27, Ignace age 11, Marie age 8, Marguerite age 2. Page 25, Household 108/146.

**THAHONTHAKETE, JOSEPH:** (Indian) Age 59 born in Quebec, Catholic, Madelaine age 40. Page 20, Household 88/118.

**THAIAWENSERE, HATONWA:** (Male Indian) Age 35, born in Quebec, Catholic, Cecile age 32, Thomas age 4, Sawatis (Male) age six months born in September. Page 22, Household 96/128.

**THAIEHONSOTE, IGNACE:** (Indian) Age 50, Therese age 21, page 41, Household 245.

**THAIEKWARIEKI, PIERRE:** (Indian) Age 39 born in Quebec, Catholic, Waria (A Female) age 29, Francois (A Male) age 10, Marie age five months, Marguerite age 4, Sawatis (A Male) HATOKWA. Page 37, Household 224.

**THAIETIARONSERE, JOSEPH:** (Indian) Age 30 born in Quebec, Catholic, Marianne age 25, Pierre age 4, Anen (A Female) age six months born in November. Page 53, Household 252/328.

**THAIOAONIOTE, JOSEPH:** (Indian) Age 61 born in Quebec, Catholic, Warisose (A Female) age 56. Page 40, Household 183/238.

**THAIORAKARON, JOSEPH:** (Indian) Age 45, born in Quebec, Catholic, Marie age 16, Pierre age 14, Louis age 10, Anen (A Female) age 7, Madelaine age 4, Marianne age 2, Ignace THAWAKON age 75, Marie THAWAKON age 64. Page 18, Household 110.

**THAIORAKARON, LOUIS:** (Indian) Age 67, born in Quebec, Catholic Marie age 58, Lazar (A Male) age 18. Charles THIONIATI age 22, born in Quebec, Catholic, Agathe THIONIATI age 20. Page 3, Household 15/17.

**THAIORONIOTE, LOUIS:** (Indian) Age 69 born in Quebec, Catholic, Marie age 49, Maria age 13. Page 55, Household 265/344.

**THAIORONIOTE, MICHEL:** (Indian) Age 38 born in Quebec, Catholic, Warisose (A Female) age 31, Sabsarie age 11, Sawatis (A Male) age 4. Page 27, Household 117/158.

**THAKAHONWATHE, LOUIS:** (Indian) Age 51, born (About 1830) in Quebec, Catholic, Louise age 48, Page 33, Household 149/197.

**THAKENIATE, IGNACE:** (Indian) Age 35, born (About 1846) in Quebec, Catholic, Sawatis (A Male) THEKARATENSERE age 28, Angelique THEKARATENSERE age 17. Page 55, Household 260/339.

**THAKENIATHE, IGNACE:** (Indian) Age 35, born (About 1846) in Quebec, Catholic, Marie age 32. Page 31, Household 138/185.

**THAKERITONKIE, THOMAS:** (Indian) Age 54, born (About 1827) in Quebec, Catholic, Marianne age 50, Marie age 26, Sawatas (A Male) age 24, Marie age 15. Page 13, Household 60/73.

**THAKOWENNAHAWS? LOUIS:** (Indian) Age 32 born (About 1849) in Quebec, Catholic, Elisabelle age 31, Francois (A Male) age 4. Page 39, Household 181/235.

**THANEKORENS, JACQUES:** (Indian) Age 35, born (About 1846) in Quebec, Marie age 25, Sawatis (A Male) age 5. Page 3, Household 14/16.

**THANENHENRISON, THOMAS:** (Indian) Age 29 born (About 1852) in Quebec, Catholic, Cecile age 31, Konwakeri (A Female) age 5, Louis age 3, Ignace age 1. Page 66, Household 329/419.

**THANENRISHON, IGNACE:** (Indian) Age 25 (Born about 1856) Angelique age 20, Pierre age 3, Sawatis (A Male) age 1. Page 11, Household 61.

**THANIENNOKEN? PIERRE:** (Indian) Age 46 born in Quebec, Catholic, Jean Bte., age 20, Marguerite age 13. Page 67, Household 332/422.

**THANONSAKATHA, JOSEPH:** (Indian) Age 49, Therese age 45, Ignace age 16, Jacques age 8, Michel age 2. Page 59, Household 285/368.

**THARETHANE, THOMAS:** (Indian) Age 49 (Born about 1832) Therese age 41. Page 60, Household 292/377.

**THARONIAKETEN? FRANCOIS:** (Male Indian) Age 45, born (About 1836) in Quebec, Catholic, Hariwatere (A Female) Age 38, Alexandre age 19. Page 31, Household 137/184.

**THARONIORENS? LOUIS:** (Indian) Age 36 born (About 1845) in Quebec, Catholic, Agathe age 27, Warcose (A Female) age 10, Wari age 7, Elisabelle age 5, Thomas age 2, Agnes age two months born in February, Thomas HONATHAKAIASE age 82. Page 25, Household 106/142.

**THARONKATHA, PIERRE:** (Indian) Age 41, born (About 1840) in Quebec, Catholic, Anne age 38, Pierre age 13, Agnes age 2, Anen (A Female) age one month born in March, Marie THEKAENTONTIE age 67, born in Quebec, Catholic. Page 6, Household 33/41.

**THASENNONKIE, LAURENT:** (Male Indian) Age 49, born (About 1832) in Quebec, Catholic, Monique age 43. Page 27, Household 157.

**THASONTERHA, IGNACE:** (Male Indian) Age 51, born (About 1830) in Quebec, Wesleyan Methodist, (All others were listed as Catholic) Mathieu age 24, Angelique age 20, Jean Bte., age 17, Pierre age 13, Joseph HANONTIENES? age 31, born in Quebec, Wesleyan Methodist. Page 67, Household 334/424.

**THAWAKON, SAWATIS:** (Male Indian) Age 35, born (About 1846) in Quebec, Louise age 22. Page 19, Household 111.

**THAWEHALIRON? J,. BTE:** (Indian) Age 42, born (About 1839) in Quebec, Catholic, Warisose (Female) age 40, Marie age 14, (Listed of German Origins?) Page 68, Household 338/428.

**THAWEKIATIRON, LOUIS:** (Indian) Age 49 born (About 1832) in Quebec, Catholic, Page 16, Household 93.

**THAWENNAKE, SAWATIS:** (Indian) Age 25 born (About 1856) in Quebec, Catholic, Louise age 21, Pierre age 1. Page 42, Household 254.

**THAWENNAKE, SAWATIS:** (Male Indian) Age 20? Louise age 21, page 42, Household 254.

**THAWENRATHE, CALASTIQUE:** (Listed as a White Female of German Ancestry?) Age 46 born (About 1835) in Quebec, Joseph (Indian) age 25, Napoleon (Indian) age 17, Qrall? (A Male Indian) 11. Page 55, Household 364/343.

**THAWRONIOTE, MICHEL:** (Indian) Age 38 (Born about 1843) Warisose (A Female) age 31, Page 27, Household 117/159.

**THEIONERATOKEN, SAWATIS:** (Male Indian) Age 36 born (About 1845) in Quebec, Catholic, Sophie (White/French) of French ancestry age 36, born in Quebec, Marie (Indian) age 11, Celina (Indian) age 7, Louisa (Indian) age 5, Napoleon (Indian) age 2, Sophie KINFRET or RINFRET? (Indian) age 66 born in Quebec. Page 63, Household 311/400.

**THEKAHONWAEN? ABRAHAM:** (Indian) Age 34 born (About 1847) in Quebec, Catholic, Marie age 24, Anen (A Female) age 6, Hatonwa (A Male) age 4. Page 54, Household 258/336.

**THEKAHONWOTHE, LOUIS:** (Indian) Age 51 born in Quebec, Catholic, Louise age 48, Pierre age 26, Charles age 11, Joseph age 7, Marianne age 13. Page 33, Household 149/197.

**THEKAKWATHA, ANASTASIE:** (Female Indian) Age 30 (Born about 1851) Page 30, Household 175.

**THEKAKWATHA, ONASTASIE:** (Female Indian) Age 30 born (About 1851) in Quebec, Catholic, Page 30, Household 175.

**THEKALITIANEKO, PIERRE:** (Indian) Age 26 (Born about 1855) Charlotte age 21, Page 31, Household 180.

**THEKANAKENSERAKENE? SAWATIS:** (Male Indian) Age 31 (Born about 1850) Therese age 21, Marguerite age six months, Louis THAWENNATIENTON age 47, Michel KATIRAKERON, Page 35, Household 157/205.

**THEKANENNOWIHEN, HATONWA:** (Male Indian) Age 31, born (About 1850) in Quebec, Catholic, Anen (A Female) age 27, Marie age 9, Lazar (A Male) age 7, Ignace age 31, Jacques age two months born in February. Page 37, Household 168/220.

**THEKANERERSKEN, IGNACE:** (Indian) Age 61, born (About 1820) in Quebec, Anna (Indian) age 53, Michael Hine (White) born in Ireland, Catholic, Page 2, Household 9/10.

**THEKANIATAREKWEN, CHARLOT:** (Male Indian) Age 52 born (About 1829) in Quebec, Catholic, Marianne age 48, Louis age 22, Ignace KANERATHAWENTHA (Male) age 10, Anen WAKIATIIOSTHA (A Female) age 76 born in Quebec. Page 56, Household 270/351.

**THEKANIVARENKENNION?** (Female Indian) Age 2? born (About 1879) in Quebec, Catholic, Joseph SHAKOIANSAKAS age 30, born in Quebec, Therese SHAKOIANSAKAS age 23. Page 16, Household 91?

**THEKANNOTHAWON? HATONWA:** (Indian) Age 29 (Born about 1852) Cecile age 28, Page 32, Household 140.

**THEKANONNOWIHEN, HATONWA:** (Male Indian) Age 31 born (About 1850) in Quebec, Catholic, Anen age 27, Marie age 9, Lazar age 7, Ignace age 5, Jacques age two months born in February. Page 37, Household 168/220.

**THEKANONSOKON Or THEKANONSOKERE, JACQUES:** (Indian) Age 22 born (About 1859) in Quebec, Catholic, Marguerite age 19, Anen age five months. Page 31, Household 181.

**THEKANONWENSERE, LOUIS:** (Indian) Age 33 (Born about 1848) Waria (A Female) age 27, Wari (A Female) age 2, David PHILLIPPE (Indian) age 34 born in Quebec. Page 33, Household 147/195.

**THEKARATENSERE, SAWATIS:** (Indian) Age 28 born (About 1853) in Quebec, Catholic, Angelique age 19. Page 55, Household 260/339.

**THEKARATHANEKEN, HYANCINTHE:** (Male Indian) Age 33 born (About 1848) in Quebec, a member of the Methodist Church, Suzanne age 29, Catholic, Thaietiaronsere (A Male) age 2. Page 18, Household 109.

**THEKARENOTE, THOMAS:** (Indian) Age 51 (Born about 1830) Catherine age 42, Agathe age 14, Anen (A Female) age 10. Page 56, Household 267/347.

**THEKARENTENSERE, LAZAR:** (Indian) Age 24 born (About 1857) in Quebec, Catholic, Angelique age 21. Page 50, Household 234/306.

**THEKARIHONTIE, LOUIS:** (Indian) Age 30, born (About 1851) in Quebec, Catholic, Warisose (A Female) age 20, Kanatishon age 5, Joseph age 3, Cecile age seven months born in August. Page 17, Household 80/103.

**THEKARIWAKEN, PIERRE:** (Indian) Age 36 born (About 1845) in Quebec, Catholic, Ignace age 7, Marie age 4. Page 55, Household 261/340.

**THEKATITENSERE, MARTIN:** (Indian) Age 48 born (About 1833) in Quebec, Catholic, Marianne age 42, Charlot age 18, Agathe age 15, Laurent age 8. Page 62, Household 301/387.

**THEKATITIAKWAS, CATHARINE:** (Indian) Age 36, born (About 1845) in Quebec, Catholic, Anen (A Female) age 14, Hatonwa (A Male) age 6, Wari (A Female) age 3. Page 26, Household 111/149.

**THEKONATHONHEN? IGNACE:** (Male) age 26 born (About 1855) in Quebec, Catholic, Marianne age 21. Page 41, Household 244.

**THENIAKIE, JOSEPH:** (Indian) Age 68 born (About 1813) in Quebec, Catholic, Marie age 60. Page 53, Household 251/327.

**THEOHATHEKWEN, FRANCOIS:** (Male Indian) Age 24 (Born about 1857) Katick age 19. Page 19, Household 113.

**THERONIOTEN, PIERRE:** (Male Indian) Age 40, born (About 1841) in Quebec, Catholic, Warisose (A Female) age 39, Marguerite age 18, Thomas age 12, Jules (A Male) age 8, Pierre age 6, Louisa age nine months born in June. Page 16, Household 76/97.

**THESHOKWEN, ANASTASI:** (Female Indian) Age 35, born (About 1846) in Quebec, Catholic. Page 15, Household 88.

**THESOHWEN, MOISE:** (Male Indian) Age 29, born (About 1852) in Quebec, Catholic, Odile (White/French) age 24 born in Quebec, Marianne (Indian) age 8, Joseph (Indian) age 5, Louis (Indian) age 2. Page 40, Household 241.

**THETIAIENNI? LOUIS:** (Indian) Age 42 (Born about 1839) Angelique age 40, Francois (A Male) age 20, Antoine age 18, Marianne age 14, Marie age 4. Page 41, Household 188/247.

**THEWANIKASE, THOMAS:** (Indian) Age 51, born (About 1830) in Quebec, Catholic, Catherine age 45, Betsey age 16. Page 27, Household 116/156.

**THEWATERONIAKWAS, CECILE:** (Indian) Age 59 born (About 1822) in Quebec, Catholic, Sawatis (A Male) age 38, Hariwatere KAWENAHENTE? (A Female) age 77. Page 46, Household 217/283.

**THEWATHERONWARAKOTHA, IGNACE:** (Indian) Age 70, born (About 1811) in Quebec, Kanarthasi (A Female) age 65, born in Quebec, John A. THEWATHERONWARAKOTHA age 9, born in the United States, Catholic. Page 3, Household 17/20.

**THEWENASHON? SAWATIS:** (Male Indian) Age 70, Michel SHARENESE (A Male) Age 31, Hariwatere (A Female) age 26, Hatonwas (Male) age 8, Therese age 5, Saksarie? (A Male) age 2, Jacque (A Male) born in April. Page 64, Household 314/403.

**THIOHATHEKWEN, FRANCOIS:** (Male Indian) Age 24 born (About 1857) in Quebec, Catholic, Katich (A Female) age 19. Page 19, Household 113.

**THIORONWASERE, JACQUES:** (Indian) Age 27 born (About 1854) in Quebec, Catholic, Konwakere (A Female) KWAHENTENSE age 45 born in Quebec, Cecile (A Female) KWAHENTENSE age 19, Sawatis (A Male) KWAHENTENSE age 17. Page 45, Household 207/269.

**THEKALITENSERE, MARTIN:** (Indian) Age 48 (Born about 1833) Marianne age 42, Page 62, Household 301/389.

**THIOWIRATI, JACQUE:** (Indian) Age 49, born (About 1832) in Quebec, Catholic, Marie age 45, Louise age 24, Saksakrie (A Male) age 22. Page 8, Household 36/44.

**THIRES, FRANCOIS:** (Indian) Age 37, born (About 1844) in Quebec, Catholic, Marianne age 34, Charlotte. Page 33, Household 151/199.

**THITIALEKHA? MICHEL:** (Indian) Age 24, born in Quebec, Catholic, Page 62, Household 390/302.

**THKANNOTHAIRON? HATONWA:** (Male Indian) Age 29, born (About 1852) in Quebec, Catholic, Cecile age 18, Charles age 5, Hariwatere (A Female) age 4, Sawatis (A Male) age 1. Page 32, Household 140/188.

**THOHARAKENR, MICHEL:** (Indian) Age 75, born (About 1806) in Quebec, Catholic, Marie age 57, Michel age 30, Francis (A Male) age 15, Anen (A Female) age 12. Page 19, Household 85/114.

**THOMAS, MICHEL:** (Indian) Age 25 born (About 1856) in Quebec, Catholic, Josephine (White/French) age 15, Thomas LA FORCE (Indian) age 24, Marie J. LA FORCE (Indian) age 19, both born in Quebec. Page 9, Household 51.

**THOWNIAHEN? OR THORONIAKEN? JOSEPH:** (Indian) Age 47 born (About 1824) in Quebec, Catholic, Martine (A Female) age 45, Agathe age 12, Francois (A Male) age 6. Page 16, Household 74/94.

**TIAKAHAWI, CATHERINE:** (Indian) Age 70 born (About 1811) in Quebec, Catholic. Page 37, Household 166/218.

**TIAKOHAWI, CATHERINE:** (Indian) Age 30 born (About 1851) in Quebec, Catholic, Joseph age 11. Page 53, Household 253/326.

**TIANATIIOHA, KONWAKERI:** (Female Indian) Age 37, born (About 1844) Therese age 13, Louise 10, Warisose (A Female) age 6, Pierre WISHON age 30, Cecile KANOTHAWAKS age 23. Page 49, Household 231/301.

**TIIOATONE? MICHEL:** (Indian) Age 47 born (About 1834) in Quebec, Catholic, Marie age 43, Louise age 6, Agathe age 2, Marie LARONDE (Indian) age 5. Page 53, Household 248/324.

**TIOHAIEN, HARIWATERE:** (Female Indian) Age 46 (Born about 1835) Michel age 16. Page 46, Household 212/277.

**TIOHERISEN? PIERRE:** (Indian) Age 30 (Born about 1851) Philomine age 26. Page 52, Household 322.

**TLAKOWENNAHAWE? LOUIS:** (Indian) Age 32, born (About 1849) in Quebec, Catholic, Page 39, Household 180/233.

**TLARONIORINS? LAZAR:** (Male Indian) Age 36, born (About 1845) in Quebec, Catholic, Agathe age 27, born in February. Page 25, Household 106/142.

**VIAU, JEAN BTE:** (White/French) Age 65, born (About 1816) in Quebec (The Following people were listed as white) Melie age 60, Theodule (A Male) age 24, Osiasse? (A Male) age 19, Delphice? (A Male) age 17 Louis RINFRET (Indian) age 29, born in Quebec, Odile RINFRET (White/French Female) age 29, Louis Rinfret (Indian) age 4, Rosina Rinfret (Indian) Age 7, Malvina Rinfret (Indian) Age 2. Page 20, Household 90/128.

**VIGNEAU, OLIVER:** (White/French) Age 33, born (About 1848) in Quebec, Catholic, Caroline (Indian) age 33 (All others were listed as French) Oliver age 12, Delia age 10, Rosaline age 6, Albina age 3, Louisa born in June. Page 59, Household 283/366.

**VINCENT, JACQUEARI:** (Male Indian) Age 60 born (About 1821) Sipryn? (Male) age 28. Page 35, Household 207.

**WAIEWAS, AERVIS:** (Male Indian) Age 40, born (About 1841) in Quebec, Catholic, Agathe (A Female) age 34. Page 26, Household 113/151.

**WILLIAMS, JOSEPH:** (Indian) Age 34, born (About 1847) in Quebec, Catholic, Anen age 29, Cecile age 11, Thomas CUROTTE (Indian) age 40. Page 27, Household 121/162.

**WINGO, SAWATIS:** (Indian) Age 40, born in Quebec, Catholic. Page 37, Household 170/223.

**WRIGHT, THOMAS H:** (White/English) Age 40, born in England, Therese (Indian) age 38 born in Quebec. Page 61, Household 295/282.

## HUNTINGDON OR HUNTINGTON, COUNTY QUEBEC
## HISTORICAL NOTES (ST. REGIS MOHAWK)

From 1760 the western part of what is now Huntingdon County, Quebec was regarded by the Canadian government as an Indian reserve. In 1795 a Catholic Church was erected. A few members of the tribe lived on Cornwall Island. Reference Sources: "The History of The County of Huntingdon and The Seigniories of Chateaugay and Beauharnois," by Robert Sellar, Huntingdon, Quebec, The Canadian Gleaner, 1888, pages 169-174, Chapter 18, page 542. "Map of the Provinces of New York, New Jersey and part of Pennsylvania and the Province of Quebec 1777." Pennsylvania Archives, Third Series, Volume 1-10, app. 21 (Claude Joseph Sauthier). A major genealogy source for the Indians that reside in the area of Huntingdon County, Quebec is "The Church Records of Saint-Francois-Regis (Catholic) Parishe Registers," 1762-1876, Huntingdon County, Quebec, Canada in English, French and Latin. The original records have been made available on microfilm in Canada. Consult the Canadian Archives and the Province of Quebec Archives. A copy is available through interlibrary loan at the Church of Jesus Christ of Latter-Day Saints (Mormon) Family History Centers. Reference Source: "Parish Registers of Baptisms, Marriages and Deaths of St. Regis, from 1784," Roman Catholic Mission (Early Jesuit) south-side of the St. Lawrence River, by: Dunc (Darby) Mc Donald & Transcribed from French to English by Anne Mc Donell, Heisler of Chicago, Brockville, Ontario, D. Mc Donald, 1989, 117 pages.

## HUNTINGDON OR HUNTINGTON, COUNTY QUEBEC 1881 CENSUS ABSTRACT
## DUNDEE TOWNSHIP DISTRICT NUMBER 72

All of the following people were listed as Native Canadians unless otherwise noted. All of the children in each household had the same surname as the head of that household unless otherwise noted. A surname was highlighted with capital letters within a family entry if that surname was different from the surname of the head of household. Many of the letters in the following surnames were difficult to read. Some names may be in error. If a researcher is in doubt about any of the following names they should consult the tribal office.

**ADAMS, JOHN:** (Indian) Age 36, born (About 1845) in Quebec, a Catholic, Sarah age 30, born in the United States, Peter age 7 born in Quebec, Maggie age 5 born in Quebec, Paul age 2 born in Quebec, Household 181/181, Page 44.

**ALICK, FRANCIS:** (Indian) Age 32, born (About 1849) Allice age 23, Nancy age 13, John age 9, Louis age 7, Alexis age 4, Elizabeth age 1. Page 50, Household 226/226.

**ALLICK, CECIL:** (Indian) Age 35, born (About 1846) in Quebec, Catholic, Nancy age 16, Pierre age 12, Hannah age 9, Maryann age 7, Cecil age 1. Page 57, Household 255/255.

**ANANUTA? (OR ANONHUTA?) MITCHELL:** (Indian) Age 60, born (About 1821) in Quebec, Catholic, Catharine age 40, Mitchell age 18, Joseph age 12, Sake (Male) age 7, Louis Anonhuta (female) age 4. Page 56, Household 254/254.

**ANGUS, JOHN:** (Indian) Age 55, born (About 1826) in Quebec, listed as the Chief. Margaret age 57. Household 182/182/ Page 44.

**ANSWARYA, MOYSE:** (Male Indian) Age 47, born (About 1835) in Quebec, Susan age 43, Margaret age 15, Cemon? age 13, Peter age 8, Thomas age 6, Louis age 3. Page 44, Household 187/187.

**ARNAWAYS, JOHN:** (Male Indian) Age 22, born (About 1859) in Quebec, Harriette age 18, a female with no name age 6 months, born in November. Page 44, Household 188/188.

**ARAKANKIAK, JOHN:** (Indian) Age 38 born (About 1843) in Quebec, a member of the Catholic Church, Marie Joseph age 31, Sawatis? (male) age 15, Cecil age 12, Pierre age 9, Margaret age 7, Jacob age 4. Page 58, Household 262.

**ARNAWAYA, THOS:** (Indian) Age 40, born (About 1841) in Quebec, Catholic, Elizabeth 38, David age 11, Anna age 9, Celia age 9, Margaret age 6, Mary Ann age 4. Page 43, Household 182/183.

**ARREWASIAWA?** (Female Indian) Age 44, born (About 1837) in Quebec, a member of the Catholic Church, Cecelia age 28, Mitchell age 31, Catharine Age 80, Loran age 16, Sawatas (Male) age 13, Mary Joseph age 3 months born in January. Page 48, Household 210/210.

**ARNAWAYA, LORAN:** (Male Indian) Age 24 born (About 1857) in Quebec, a member of the Catholic Church, Mary age 16, Mary BUCKSHOTT age 8, Louis age 5, Sarah age 2. Page 44, Household 185/185.

**BOOTSE, OR BOOTS? CHARLES:** (Indian) Age 65, born (About 1816) in Quebec, Catholic, Theresa age 50. Page 57, Household 257/25.

**BROKEN-LEG, LOUIS:** (Indian) Age 54, born (About 1827) in Quebec, Catholic, Loretia? age 60, Kiendese age 15 (female) Kakator age 14 (Male), Cate age 5, Ignace (Male) age 7. Page 59, Household 260/260.

**BUCKSHOTT, MARGARET:** (Indian) Age 43, born (About 1838) in Quebec, Catholic, Alexander age 22, Mitchell age 14, Mary age 11. Page 43, Household 190/190.

**CHARRON? (Or CHAREON?) MARTIN:** (Indian) Age 30, born (About 1851) in Quebec, a member of the Catholic Church, Agnes age 26, Mary age 12, Sarah age 7 born in Ontario, Angus age 4 born in Ontario. Page 42, Household 179/179.

**COOK, JOSEPH:** (Indian) Age 50, born (About 1831) in Quebec, Catholic, Hannah age 50, Guessy? (Male) age 20. Page 60, Household 269/269.

**COOKE, JOSEPH:** (Indian) Age 50 born (About 1831) in Quebec, a member of the Catholic Church, Theresa age 44, Ontra (Male) age 20. Page 48, Household 212/212.

**COOKE, THOMAS:** (Indian) Age 50, born (About 1831) in Quebec, Catholic, Theresa age 44, Ontra (Male) age 20, Sawatas age 17 (Male) Mary Joseph age 12, Karisata? (Female) age 10, Dominique age 8 (Male). Page 48, Household 212/212.

**CURLEY, LOUIS:** (Indian) Age 40, born (About 1841) in Quebec, Sake (Male) age 20, Nancy age 16, Mary Ann age 11, Hannah age 6. Page 57, Household 258/258.

**DAYE, THOMAS:** (Indian) Age 40, born (About 1841) in Quebec, Catholic, Nancy age 30, Mary Ann age 14, Loron LA FRANCE age 21, Margaret Daye age 10, all born in Quebec all Catholic. Page 53, Household 235/235.

**FOOTE, PETER:** (Indian) Age 36, born (About 1845) in Quebec, a member of the Catholic Church, Mary Ann age 42, Keriseteri? age 5. Page 60, Household 270/270.

**FOX, JOHN:** (Indian) Age 30, born (About 1851) in Quebec, a member of the Catholic Church, Margaret age 22, Angus age 3, Paul age 2. Page 43, Household 184/184.

**FRIDAY, JOHN:** (Indian) Age 33, born (About 1848) in Quebec, Catholic, Mary age 15. Page 45, Household 196/196.

**GARROW, IGNACE:** (Indian) age 37, born (About 1844) in Quebec, Catholic, Catharine Garrow age 22, Hanah age nine months, born in July, Page 50, Household 220/200.

**GEORGE, THOMAS:** (Indian) Age 74, born (About 1807) in Quebec, Catholic, Louis WHYTE age 30, Charlotte WHYTE age 24. Page 53, Household 237/237.

**GORREAN, JOHN:** (Indian) Age 25 born (About 1856) in Quebec, a member of the Catholic Church, Christy age 18. Page 48, Household 210/210.

**IGNACE, LOUISE:** (Indian) Age 40, born (About 1841) Mary Ann age 60, Catherine age 29, Charlie age 36, Louise age 16, Rolland CHARRON age 21, Mary Ann RAFT age 50, Mary RAFT age 16, Dominique RAFT (Male) age 12. Page 51, Household 229/228.

**ISAAC, JOHN OR KARISTATES:** (Indian) Age 54, born (About 1827) in Quebec, Louis age 40, Celia age 20, Ononoka (Female) age 18, Nancy age 3, Kariseta (Female) age 14. Page 47, Household 206/206.

**ISAAC, JOHN:** (Indian) Age 36, born (About 1845) in Quebec, Catholic, Celia age 40. Page 45/46, Household 199/199.

**JACK? OR JOCK?, FRANCOIS:** (Indian) Age 30, born (About 1851) in Quebec, a member of the Catholic Church, Nancy age 25, Loran (Male) age 11, Thomas age 8, Henry age 4, Margret age 5, Luakche? or Luwkaie? (Female age 1). Page 42, Household 177/177.

**JACOB, BIG? PETER:** (Indian) age 59, born (About 1822) in Quebec, Margaret age 70, Mitchell age 21. Page 50, Household 222/222.

**JACOB, CECIL:** Indian, female, age 70, born (About 1811) in Quebec, a Catholic, Page 50, Household 219.

**JACOBS, ALEXANDER:** (Indian) Age 29, born (About 1852) in Quebec, a member of the Catholic Church, Cecelia age 37, Margaret age 9, Mary age 7, Louis age 5. Page 45, Household 195/195.

**JOCQUE? JENNY?:** (Indian) Age 55, born (About 1826) in Quebec, a Catholic. Joseph age 20, Marie age 23. Household 176/176. Page 42.

**JOHN, LOTT:** (Indian) Age 46, born (About 1835) in Quebec, Marie Joseph age 47, Louis age 26, Nancy age 17, Catherine age 7, Jerma? age 1, Joab Sake John age 15, Paul age 13, Regise? (Male) 11, Thomas age 5. Page 58, Household 261/261.

**JOSEPH, JOCQUE?:** (Indian) age 75, born (About 1806) in Quebec, Jacque JACOB age 30, Anna JACOB age 20, Page 50, Household 225/225.

**KARISTATIE? JOHN ISAAC:** (Indian) Age 54 born (About 1827) in Quebec, a member of the Church of England, Louise age 40, Celia M. age 20, Ononoka (Female) age 18, Nancy age 3, Kariseta (Female) Age 14. Page 47, Household 206/206.

**KARALETA? LOUIS:** (Indian) Age 39, born (About 1842) in Quebec, a member of the Catholic Church, Sarah age 38, Sawatas? (Male) age 8, Sock? or Srcke? (Male) age 7, Agnes age 3. Page 60, Household 268/268.

**KARESTATIE, FRANK? (OR PAUL?):** (Indian) Age 94, born (About 1787) in Quebec, a member of the Church of England, Mary 81 (Irish?) Mary 45, Mary MOORE (Indian) age 16, Susan KARISTATIES age 40, Kariseta? (Female) age 14. Page 60, Household 272/272.

**KWAWENNESERON, SOSE? OR ANEN:** (Indian) This person was listed as both male and female? age 67 born (About 1814) in Quebec, Catholic, Page 47, Household 221/289.

**LA FRANCE, JACOB:** (Indian) Age 40 born (About 1841) in Quebec, a member of the Catholic Church, Karaseta? (Female) age 23.

**LORAN, ARNAWAGANA?:** (A Male Indian) Age 24 born (About 1857) in Quebec, Mary age 16, Mary BUCKSHOTT age 8, Louis BUCKSHOTT age 5, Sarah BUCKSHOTT age 2. All were Catholic. Page 43, Household 185/185.

**LORAN? OR COOKE?, TERESA:** Indian, age 39, born (About 1842) in Quebec, Sarah age 19, Loran age 8, Pierre age 5, Page 50, Household 221, 221.

**LOZOIRE, PETER:** (Indian) Age 29, born (About 1852) in Quebec, a member of the Catholic Church, Nancy age 21. Page 45, Household 194/194.

**MARCOUX, FRANCOIS:** (Indian) Age 75, born (About 1806) in Quebec, a Catholic, Abraham age 57, Francis LONGQUIL? (A male Indian) age 75, born in N.W.L. ? or North West Territory?, Catholic, Victoire MANSOR age 52, (Female/Indian) born in Quebec. Page 42, Household 175/175.

**MC DONALD, ALEXR:** (Indian) Age 28, born (About 1853) in Quebec, a member of the Catholic Church, Louisa age 5. Page 45, Household 191/191.

**MITCHELL, FRANCIS:** (Indian) Age 41, born (About 1840) in Quebec, Catholic, Cecil age 37, Jacob age 20, Sarcksalia (Male) age 16, Loran (Male) age 4, Thomas age seven months, born in September, Oneke? (Female) age 13, Margaret? 10. Page 54/55, Household 246/246.

**MITCHELL, FRIDAY:** (Indian) Age 38, born (About 1843) in Quebec, a member of the Church of England, Annas (female) age 30, Theresa age 10, Celia age 8, Louis age 14, Anna age 2. Page 44, Household 189/189.

**MITCHELL, GEORGE:** (Indian) Age 21, born (About 1860) in Quebec, a member of the Catholic Church, Sarah age 18, Jacob age 2. Page 43, Household 180/180.

**MITCHELL, ISAAC:** (Indian) Age 30, born (About 1851) in Quebec, a member of the Catholic Church, Mary age 20, Peter age 8. Page 42, Household 178/178.

**MITCHELL, JACOB M:** (Indian) Age 40, born (About 1841) in Quebec, a member of the Catholic Church, Charlotte age 38, Margaret age 10, Anna (Female) age 8, Louis age 6, Agnes age 4, Mary age 3. Page 60, Household 267/267.

**MITCHELL, SOLOMON:** (Indian) Age 43, born (About 1838) in Quebec, a member on the Catholic Church, Nancy age 39, Mary age 27, Charlie age

18, Louis age 16, Sarah age 11, John age 3. Page 46, Household 200/200.

**MITCHELL, THOMAS:** (Indian) Age 60 born (About 1821) in Quebec, a member of the Catholic Church, Cecilia age 25, Lewis age 11, Mary Ann age 9, Jacob age 7, Rosina? age 5, Nancy age 2. Page 59, Household 263/263.

**MUSKETOES, JOHN:** (Indian) Age 40, born (About 1841) Mary age 30, Nancy age 9, Oneike age 7, Margaret age 5, Louse age 30, Mitchell age nine months, born in July, Page 54, Household 240/240.

**MUSKOLAS, THOMAS:** (Indian) Age 32, born (About 1849) in Quebec, Catholic, Mary Ann age 25, Sawata age 11, Rota RAFFIE? OR RAFT? age 80 (Indian) born in Quebec, Catholic. Page 48, Household 213/213.

**OAKE, MARY CHARLOTTE:** (Indian) Age 60, born (About 1821) Hannah WHITE (Indian) age 28, Mitchell age 11, Antre (Male) age 9, Karisseta WHITE (female) age 4. Page 50, Household 224.

**ONEIKE:** (Female Indian) Age 84, born (About 1798) in Quebec, Catholic, John PETERS age 50 (All other listed as Peters) Margaret age 50, Oneike (Female) age 23, Mary age 21, Sawatas (Male) 18, Tresa (female) age 7. Page 54, Household 240/240.

**PAPINEAU, JOHN:** (Indian) Age 28, born (About 1853) in Quebec, a member of the Catholic Church, Mary age 25, Pierre age 5, Hannah age 3, Sawatas age one month born in April. Page 48, Household 211/211.

**PARK? JOSEPH:** (Indian) Age 50 born (About 1831) in Quebec, a member of the Catholic Church, Hannah age 50, Guessey? or Gressey? (Male) age 25. Page 60, Household 269/269.

**PAUL, JOE FRANCIS:** (Indian) Age 31, born (About 1850) in Quebec, a Catholic, Christy (A female Indian) age 21, born in the United States. Addie age 4, born in the United States, Annie age 2, born in the United States, Jacob Francis age 12, born in Quebec. Page 44, Household 186/186.

**PHILIPS, JOE:** (Indian) Age 40 born (About 1841) in Quebec, a member of the Catholic Church, Mary age 30, Margaret age 14, Christy age four months born in December, Antie? (Male) age 5.

**PIKE, LORAN:** (Indian) Age 45, born (About 1836) in Quebec, Louisa age 41, Mary age 26, Nancy age 17, Agnes age 14, Mary Ann age 11, Lucretia age 7, Louis age 4. Page 56, Household 250/250.

**PIQUE, LOUIS:** (Indian) Age 70, born (About 1811) in Quebec, a member of the Catholic Church, Annie (female) age 70, born in Quebec, Nancy age 20. Page 45, Household 192/192.

**RANARO, FRANCIS:** (Male Indian) Age 60, born (About 1821) in Quebec, Teressa (Female) age 50, Household 250/250/ Page 56.

**SABATTOS, THOMAS:** (Indian) Age 35, born (About 1846) in Quebec, a member of the Catholic Church, Cate age 23, Helen age 4, Mary age 1. Page 46, Household 201/201.

**SARAGUASKA, JOHN:** (Indian) Age 60, born (About 1821) Nancy age 57, Louis age 19, all born in Quebec, all Catholic. Page 53, Household 238/238.

**SAWATAS, ARAKANKIAK?** (Indian) Age 65, born (About 1816) in Quebec, Catholic, Margaret age 50, Peter age 24, Ignace age 20, Mitchell age 17, Thomas age 14, Sacke age 11, Antre age 8, Mary Joseph ARAKANKIAK age 4, Walter age 20, all born in Quebec, all Catholic. Page 53, Household 236/236.

**SAWATAS, LOUIS:** (Indian) Age 28, born (About 1853) Hanah age 22, Regis age 3, Ignace age 1, Page 51, Household 227/227.

**SAWATAS, THOMAS:** (Indian) Age 36 born (About 1845) in Quebec, a member of the Church of England, Catharine age 23, Helen age 5, May age 1. Page 47, Household 207/207.

**SAWYER, JOSEPH:** (Indian) Age 30, born (About 1851) in the United States, a Methodist. Page 41, Household 174/174.

**SHARROW? (Or CHARRON?) GEORGE:** (Indian) Age 60, born (About 1821) in Quebec, Catholic, Mary age 45, Alexander (Male) age 26, David age 22, John age 15, Sarah age 12, Frank age 7, Joseph age 5. Page 57, Household 256/356.

**SHEEPE, JOSEPH:** (Indian) Age 44, born (About 1837) in Quebec, Mary age 40, Mitchell age 8, Paul age 5. Page 53, Household 239/239.

**SKIN, JOHN:** (Indian) Age 16 born (About 1865) in Quebec, Waterie (Female) age 45, Jacob age 24, Mary age 22, Mary Ann age 10, Nancy age 17, Helen seven months born in July. Page 59, Household 264/264.

**SKIN, PAUL:** (Indian) Age 38, born (About 1843) in Quebec, Onique age 38, Peter age 10, Nancy age 12, Mary age 8, Louis age 6. Page 51, Household 228/228.

**SKINE (OR SKIN?) PETER:** (Indian) Age 72, born (About 1809) in Quebec, a member of the Catholic Church, Olive age 66, born in Quebec. Page 46, Household 203/203.

**SMOKE, ANNIS:** (Female Indian) Age 67, born (About 1814) in the United States, a Catholic, Wood LOUIS? or Louis WOOD? (Indian) born in Quebec. All of the following have Wood LOUIS? same surname. Catharine age 37, Joseph age 5, Mary age seven months, born in October. Page 45, Household 197/197.

**SOLOMON, FRANCIS:** (Indian) Age 30, born (About 1851) in Quebec, Catholic, Charlotte age 26, John age 7, Loran age 5, Kiatota (female) age 2. Page 56, Household 252/252.

**SOLOMON, LORAN:** (Indian) age 68, born (About 1813) in Quebec, Catharine age 76, Teressa RAFT age 64, Louis Raft age 23, Elizabeth Raft age 24, Page 50, Household 223/223.

**SOLOMON, MITCHELL:** (Indian) Age 61, born (About 1820) in Quebec, a member of the Catholic Church, Anna age 60, Thomas OAKE age 20, Mary Ann OAKE age 27. Page 47, Household 204/204.

**STOGNA, LOUIS:** (Indian) Age 65, born (About 1816) in Quebec, a member of the Catholic Church, Noah? or Roah? (Male) Stogna age 17, Louis BACKE? age 25, Catherine BACKE age 23, Abraham BACKE age 6, Louise BACKE age 4, Christy BACKE age 2. Page 45, Household 198/198.

**STREET, LOUIS:** (Indian) Age 39, born (About 1842) in Quebec, a member of the Catholic Church, Sara age 24. Page 45, Household 193/193.

**SUCKSILIA, MITCHELL:** (Indian) Age 23, born (About 1858) in Quebec, Catholic, Cecil age 18, Margaret age 1. Page 54, Household 243/243.

**SUGAR-BUSH, PETER:** (Indian) Age 47 born (About 1834) in Quebec, a member of the Catholic Church, Teresa age 47, Nancy age 17, Susan age 14, Pierre age 12, Joseph age 10, Mary age 8, All born in Quebec, all Catholic, Page 59, Household 265/265.

**THOMPSON, ALEX'R:** (Indian) Age 60, born (About 1821) in Quebec, Catholic, Arcout (Female) age 35, Sawata (Male) Age 16, Louis age 23, Mary (Female) age 20, David SAWATAS age 20. Page 54, Household 243/243.

**THOMPSON, JOSEPH:** (Indian) Age 38, born (About 1843) in Quebec, Catholic, Nancy age 34, Agnes age 14, Alexander age 10, Caratoxon age 7, Sataka Hereha (Female) age 4. Page 54, Household 245/245.

**WOOD, JOSEPH:** (Indian) Age 38, born (About 1843) in the United States, a member of the Catholic Church, Mary age 32, Margaret age 12, Wauinaqua? (A female) age 10, Marie Josey age 8, Hannah age 6, Liera? Tiers? (A Male) age 4, Mary Ann age six months, born in October. Page 47, Household 205/205.

**WOODMAN, THOMAS:** (Indian) Age 37 born (About 1844) at Onedia, Ontario, a member of the Methodist Church, Louise age 33, born in Quebec, Sarah age 2 born in Quebec, Nancy age 1 born in Quebec. Page 46, Household 202/202.

www.ingramcontent.com/pod-product-compliance
Ingram Content Group UK Ltd.
Pitfield, Milton Keynes, MK11 3LW, UK
UKHW051301180426
11947UKWH00020B/1830